COOKING AT COOKTIQUE

COOKING AT

Over 200 International Food

COOKTIQUE

Classics from a Teaching Kitchen

Silvia Lehrer

ILLUSTRATIONS BY MONA MARK

DOUBLEDAY & COMPANY, INC.
GARDEN CITY, NEW YORK
1984

To my mom—who inspired me to cook.
To my dad—who taught me the meaning of taste.

DESIGN BY M FRANKLIN-PLYMPTON

"Giuliano Bugialli's Frittata of Green Tomatoes", Copyright © 1977 by Giuliano Bugialli. Reprinted by permission of *Times Books*/The New York Times Book Co., Inc. from *The Fine Art of Italian Cooking*.

Library of Congress Cataloging in Publication Data
Lehrer, Silvia.
    Cooking at Cooktique.
    Includes index.
    1. Cookery, American. 2. Cookery, European.
I. Title.
TX715.L475 1985   641.5
ISBN 0-385-18168-X
Library of Congress Catalog Card Number 83-20691

CONTENTS

HOW TO USE THIS BOOK

Whenever the name of a recipe is capitalized, the recipe is included elsewhere in the book; consult Index for page numbers.

Whenever a method or technique is marked with an asterisk,* how-to information is described in full detail elsewhere in the book; see Glossary of Techniques and Kitchen Inventory.

Acknowledgments

Writing a cookbook is all about putting together sound and practical ideas that one longs to share. The years of research and study, of testing, tasting and typing, of fun and laughter, of agonizing and concern have been realized in the pages that follow. So many have contributed in so many ways. I would like to give everlasting thanks to:

Pat Greenfield—there is something special about "first experiences." She took my hand in hers from the initial "knife lesson" to the balance and organization of "cooking for company," some twenty-odd years ago.

Lynne Rogers—I always think of her as my star pupil. She shared her innate ability to work with food and tremendous talent for entertaining.

Edward Holland—formerly of Holland Beef, for his generous gift of time and invaluable advice.

Claire Held—who was always there to offer sage advice and unfailing support. And finally,

Barbara Soyster—who orchestrated and defined my flow of words, and who, whenever I had doubts (and I had many), kept me believing in what I was doing.

I add with pleasure my sincere thanks to Karen Van Westering, my editor, for her quiet blend of professionalism and humor as she patiently guided me into doing my best, and to Anne Sweeney, Karen's editorial assistant. Also to Mona Mark for her skillful line-art interpretations of techniques and recipes. I gratefully acknowledge and thank those wonderful professionals whose teachings have allowed me to develop and grow and innovate—to become a professional in my adored field: Mme. Grace Chu, Marcella Hazan, Lydie Marshall, Giuliano Bugialli, Jacques Pepin, Paula Wolfert, Maida Heatter, John Clancy, Elizabeth Andoh, and Martha Stewart in order of their appearance in my career.

I am further indebted to Simone (Simca) Beck, that great lady of cuisine, whose sense of food is timeless.

S.L.

INTRODUCTION

It seems to me I've always cooked. Perhaps it seems so because cooking and eating good, wholesome food, interestingly and well prepared, was an accepted way of life as I was growing up. My love of and interest in food, I realize now, was a wonderful gift from my mother.

I found using food as a means of communication was a natural enjoyment. As I studied, traveled, tasted, and learned more about food, I found it added a creative dimension to my life. Wanting to share was the challenge that led me to a career as a cooking teacher. As my skills and respect for food matured, I taught others: beginner cooks, experienced cooks, and natural cooks. But in each case, as with this book, I sought to teach a respect for classic foods—some in modern dress and some completely revised into new ideas. The results have been better food—not just its taste, but nutritionally as well.

I started teaching cooking in the early seventies and later opened Cooktique, a cooking school, culinary cookware, and gift shop in Tenafly, New Jersey, which provided the setting for a major cooking experience. I continued to teach my own classes, as well as work side by side with eminent guest teachers who augment a regular cooking school staff.

As director of the school, I felt the need to be part of and interact with the cooking public. I was inspired. I observed. I talked. I listened and simply heard what they wanted to know. Not just about the latest model food processor or how a pan will work for a particular recipe—but the way they wanted to eat—and cook! The shop, as well as the classroom, was a source of inspiration. The impetus for developing new material was constant. The desire to share was unceasing.

The recipes in this book were created to make your mouth curious. They are intended to suggest a new dimension for your cooking endeavors—now, in the eighties, and beyond—not just for the special events in your life, but on a day-to-day basis. I have tried to encourage you to make your next dinner at home a special family dinner—for after all, who deserves the best? But of course, I also offer you a total plan for entertaining.

I have reflected on my interest in foods and written joyously, yet seriously. I have attempted to open new food vistas for the reader and to tempt you into the unfamiliar—to challenge yet support you with clear, precise, logical, step-by-step instructions. But basic to all the natural or learned skills, I am convinced that if people only recognize that they don't have to be the Gourmet Chef on the block and simply relax and enjoy the naturalness of cooking, the end results will be more pleasurable for all. Good food need not be extravagant, rich, or highly flavored. The finished dish will please even the connoisseur's palate when it reflects your caring—in your use of the freshest quality ingredients—in your articulate blending of flavors—and in your natural regard for food.

Take the time to build on these food philosophies. They will provide a foundation for years of pleasure and perhaps you will adapt and develop your own.

And from philosophy one's thoughts flow naturally enough toward "the recipe." Think of it as a guideline: *doing* provides the skills; *imagination* provides the fun; *creativity* provides the satisfaction; and *development of the techniques,* the so-called "secrets of the trade," all will work together to make cooking for you the enjoyment it is for me.

When I plan a class, I try to incorporate within the lesson various types of techniques so that students may learn in one session: how to use a knife properly; how to deglaze a pan; how to fold a mixture; how to know by looking and touching when a vegetable, meat, or fish is done; to read through a recipe before starting, so the proper utensils will be at hand; and how to substitute ingredients. The pages of this book contain that same approach and information. While I understand you aren't going to cook all day, every day, I believe you will find the more you cook, the more you will learn about food and the freer you will become to improvise, be relaxed and achieve that simple, well-orchestrated meal—well-balanced and attractively presented.

1

SOUP, SOUP, SOUP

Soup is like a good friend—always dependable. For me, soups evoke memories of conviviality. I readily recall my childhood and its abundance of comforting soups and their wondrous smells!

When you are stymied for a fresh, interesting beginning, middle, or end to an otherwise pedestrian meal . . . think soup! Soups can be made from just about anything. Their versatility allows them to be served at any time and in any season, and imaginative combinations allow you to create refreshing fruit, hearty peasant, and delicate cream soups that can be hot or cold, simple or elegant.

Soup can simplify a menu. In summer, a cold creamy vegetable soup is perfect to take the edge off appetites—follow it with a light fresh seafood salad and a bowl of cherries or grapes. In winter, a hot hearty soup is a meal in itself, served with a loaf of bread and a bottle of wine. Most kitchens already have on hand the simple utensils necessary for making soup. A large, heavy-bottomed pot of any material with a tight-fitting lid will do. For me, a flavorful homemade stock is a rich, nutritive beginning to a tasty soup. However, if you don't have stock, start with water or the liquid obtained from cooking vegetables. Too many American cooks throw away that precious bit of liquid. As the final step when blanching or boiling vegetables, continue cooking down the stock until it has been reduced enough to be flavorful. Strain the juices, store in a covered jar, refrigerate or freeze. This base can be used for vegetable soups, of course, but can also be added to any soup, adding nutrients and flavor as well.

Another use for that vegetable water is as a homemade health drink: Reduce 3–4 quarts of water used for blanching vegetables to about 1½ quarts. Add 1 cup tomato juice. Season with a variety of finely chopped fresh herbs. Refrigerate and enjoy this ''pick-me-up'' bonus.

One of the wonderful things about soups is the opportunity they provide to be creative with seasonings. Herbs and spices are an important addition, but add them with caution. Use salt in moderation and a fresh grinding of pepper.

The flavor of most soups benefits from a few hours to an overnight stay in the refrigerator; many also freeze well. Since preparation time can be anything from a quick whirl in the blender or food processor to a long, slow simmer, soups are practical to serve as a first course, freeing you to mingle with your guests. A few extra moments of cooking will not hurt the simmering soup.

The serving of soups provides an opportunity to be creative, too. Soups are wonderful ladled from the pot or an elegant tureen directly at the table. In a rustic setting, big crockery bowls provide a country touch. However, let the soup itself determine your selection of an appropriate dish. A colorful chilled fruit soup can be charmingly served from wide-mouthed champagne glasses or in individual glass bowls. A variety of snipped herbs or chopped vegetables as garnishes will add an interesting touch and will provide visual appeal as well as flavor and texture. Fresh croutons are a satisfying and popular garnish.

STOCK . . . IN THE BEGINNING

Everyone enjoys flavorful food. Yet more than ever we are being urged to use less salt and sugar in our diets. So, where will the taste come from? It will come from seasonings. Stock is an all-important basic ingredient in the collective world of seasonings.

Simply stated, stock is the liquor or broth prepared by cooking beef, chicken, or fish with vegetables and seasonings in water and is used as a foundation in soup, stews, and sauces. There are white and brown stocks, fish stocks, glazes, and classic variations of each. Recipes for specific stocks and demi-glace (glaze) are given later in this chapter. For now, I'm concerned with getting you in front of the kitchen stove and simply making stock.

People are too often intimidated by the very idea of making a stock. And no wonder! Detailed methods of stock preparations taking many hours and even days to cook can be found in almost every cookbook from Escoffier down to the present. But stock is not complicated to make and it isn't necessary to prepare gallons at a time.

When you bring a chicken home from the market, what do you do with the packet of giblets tucked into its cavity? Throw it away? I've seen many students nod affirmatively to this question. Whenever I teach a class, I urge my students to look upon bones and trimmings as culinary gold. Simply freeze the bones and giblets for later use or put them into a pot and cover with water. It is that simple to get a stock going. Chances are if you peek into the crisper of your refrigerator, you are likely to find one or two carrots, a rib or more of celery, some parsley leaves, and perhaps even some green of leek or dill. Any or all may be gathered up, tied in a bundle with herbs and added to your cooking water to prepare a basic stock. When you have some leftover uncooked carrots, celery, parsley, leeks, etc., wash, trim, chop, and freeze them. They will be available to toss into a stock whenever you are ready to make one. You are not only being economical but saving time as well.

Having brought home the chickens for dinner and while I'm cooking, I prefer to throw the giblets and trimmings into a three- or four-quart saucepan and make a small amount of stock rather than take the time to package them for the freezer. I just have to be around and let the timer do the rest. Chicken stock should cook for a minimum of three hours, while veal and beef stock should cook for up to six hours to realize their full flavor potential. As with all stock making, the stockpot, cover ajar, should maintain a lazy surface bubble at all times. Then cool, uncover, and strain through a chinois or fine sieve. Refrigerate for several hours, skim off and discard congealed fat, and the stock is ready to use. It's that easy.

At least once in every class, someone asks me about canned broths and bouillon cubes. At the risk of sounding pedantic, I think bouillon cubes have no place in the kitchen. Canned broths can be useful at times. However, I find making my own stock rewarding and worth the time. I have the satisfaction of knowing I have used the best ingredients available. It's important to me to get the most flavor from my food, and the gelatinous richness of a homemade stock is a good basic way to help me achieve this. Since I can eliminate salt and fat completely by preparing my own stock, I stay in full control of my cooking, which is not true with commercially prepared broths.

To store your stock in the freezer, divide the defatted liquid into quantities suitable for 4–6-cup soup recipes, or 1–1½-cup sauce recipes, and place in freezer containers. Or fill an ice cube tray with stock and freeze. When frozen, turn the individual cubes into a plastic bag and tie securely. Since many recipes call for one cup of stock, or even a few tablespoons, as is often the case with Chinese cooking, these preportioned amounts are a great convenience.

Occasionally, a demi-glace is called for in a recipe. This highly reduced concentration of stock helps to strengthen the flavor and texture of a sauce or a stew and is used in a myriad of other culinary preparations. For instance, one-half cup added to some shallots and vinegar will give you enough sauce for two chickens in the charred and succulent Poulet au Bresse Grillé. In the words of my friend and colleague, Jacques Pépin, ''You can become a three-star chef in mere minutes by using a tablespoon or two of this concentrated stock to deglaze the drippings in a pan.''

For a quick demi-glace, simply braise some vegetables in butter, add some seasonings and stock, and reduce the mixture to one cup. Strain and refrigerate. It will keep for months. If a bit of mold should appear on the surface of the demi-glace, just skim it off with a small spoon and discard. The demi-glace is perfectly all right to use. You may also freeze it, but then you don't have the convenience of taking a spoonful or two when you are cooking a small amount of food.

A fish stock is used less often than other stocks. It can be made easily by cooking fish heads and bones for a relatively short time—twenty-five to thirty minutes. Most times, however, it can be the side product of cooking the fish itself, for example, with any poached fish preparation. (See Poached Bass with Tomato Vinaigrette or Mayonnaise Verte.) It can also be reduced to intensify its flavor and then used to heighten the taste of other sauces, for such dishes as Salmon in Chive Cream Sauce.

Armed with the knowledge that stock is worth trying and a willingness to spend a little time in the kitchen getting one started, you will find a whole new world of recipes opening to you.

BASIC CHICKEN STOCK

Was at the butcher today. He was boning eight whole chicken breasts for a customer. I asked what he was planning to do with the bones. ''I'll sell them,'' he said. ''How much are they?'' I asked. ''Thirty-three cents a pound,'' he replied. There were about two pounds of bones. Undoubtedly a premium price was paid for the boned breasts. My sixty-six-cent bargain along with some giblets, aromatic herbs and vegetables (from freezer and fridge), yielded about 6½ cups of stock.

2 pounds chicken bones
1 pound giblets
1 carrot, scrubbed
1 celery rib, rinsed
Green of leek or scallion
2–3 sprigs parsley or dill

1 bay leaf
1 onion studded with 2
    whole cloves
5–6 whole black
    peppercorns

1. Place chicken bones and giblets in a 5½-quart saucepan and fill with fresh cold water to cover. Bring to a boil over moderately high heat, then adjust heat to a brisk simmer. With a fine mesh skimmer, remove scum that rises to surface. Add ½ cup or so of water, bring back to a boil, and skim again. When surface is free of scum, tie carrot, celery, leek or scallion greens, parsley, and bay leaf with kitchen string into a neat bundle. Drop into and immerse in simmering liquid. Cook, with cover ajar, for about 3 hours. Check the stock from time to time to be sure that a lazy surface bubble is maintained.

2. Place a chinois* or a cheesecloth-lined strainer over a mixing bowl. Strain stock into bowl and proceed as in Classic Chicken and Veal Stock—steps 3, 4, and 5.

COURT BOUILLON

A broth made in advance and used to prepare many fish recipes. A quick version can be made by bringing 3 cups of water to a boil for 15 minutes with a carrot, celery, onion, bay leaf, peppercorns and wedge of lemon.

2 quarts water	1 large bay leaf, crushed
2 tablespoons white wine vinegar	1 tablespoon fresh thyme leaves *or* 1 teaspoon dried
1 cup dry white wine	
1 large onion, peeled and sliced	1 tablespoon fresh tarragon leaves *or* 1 teaspoon dried
2 carrots, scrubbed and sliced	6 sprigs Italian flat-leaf parsley
2 celery ribs, rinsed, trimmed, and sliced	2 teaspoons coarse (kosher) salt
10 peppercorns	

Combine all ingredients in a large saucepan or fish poacher. Bring mixture to a boil over high heat, adjust heat, and simmer 20–30 minutes. Use as directed in poached fish recipes. If necessary, add more water to immerse fish for poaching.

I never prepare a court bouillon in advance of actually poaching the fish, since I consider it part of the total do-ahead preparation. It would be nonsense to take up room in the refrigerator or freezer for seasoned water, which is all that a court bouillon is.

CLASSIC CHICKEN AND VEAL STOCK

The stockpot brimming with rich beef bones, veal bones or poultry, the fresh vegetables and fragrant herbs to season is a welcoming scent in any kitchen. Here is a practical do-ahead guide for preparing basic stocks.

3–4 pounds breast of veal or veal bones and trimmings

1 3–4-pound boiling chicken, cut into eighths *or* 3–4 pounds chicken backs, necks, and giblets

10–12 quarts cold water

1 large unpeeled onion, pierced with 2 whole cloves

10 whole black peppercorns

2 medium-sized leeks (tough bruised leaves removed), cut lengthwise into quarters and washed thoroughly between remaining layers to remove dirt and sand

2 carrots, scrubbed clean

2 large celery ribs with leaves, scrubbed clean

Bouquet Garni

2 bay leaves

3–4 sprigs Italian flat-leaf parsley

3 fresh thyme sprigs *or* 1 teaspoon dried thyme

Have on Hand

12–16-quart stockpot

Fine mesh skimmer

Kitchen string

Chinois* or large strainer lined with cheesecloth

Yield 6–8 quarts

1. Place veal breast, bone side down, or veal bones in bottom of stockpot and brown over moderate heat until lightly glazed, turning breast or bones occasionally with tongs. Add chicken parts to veal, then pour on water, which should cover meat by 2–3 inches. Bring liquid to the edge of a boil over moderately high heat; then, with a fine mesh skimmer, skim off and discard the scum that rises to the surface. Add ½ cup cold water to stop the cooking and slowly bring the liquid back to the edge of a boil again. Repeat the process of adding water and bringing to a boil two or three additional times until liquid is free of scum. Reduce heat and simmer uncovered without stirring about 30

minutes. Do not allow water to boil at any time during cooking or stock will be cloudy.

2. In the meantime, prepare vegetables and bouquet garni. Trim, scrub, or wash leeks, carrots, and celery; then, with kitchen string, tie into a bundle with bay leaves, parsley, and thyme. Add to the simmering liquid with the clove-pierced onion and peppercorns. (If dried thyme is used, add at this time.) Push all ingredients into liquid to be sure everything is submerged. If necessary, skim liquid again, but never stir the contents or otherwise disturb them in any way. From time to time it may be necessary to adjust heat so that the tiniest suggestion of a simmer is maintained at all times. With cover ajar, simmer stock 5½–6 hours.

3. With a slotted spoon, lift out and discard the heavy bones, then place a chinois, or a large strainer lined with a double thickness of moistened cheesecloth, over a deep bowl. Strain stock into bowl. Remove debris from sieve between pourings to allow the clear liquid to pass through. Let stock cool to room temperature, then refrigerate overnight.

4. After a thorough chilling the surface of the stock will be covered with a layer of solidified fat. Remove stock from refrigerator, then with a large kitchen spoon, carefully remove and discard the fat. Stock will keep 3–4 days in refrigerator.

5. Since many recipes call for 1 cup stock for a stew or a sauce and soup recipes call for 4 cups stock or more, I suggest that you freeze the stock. With a ladle, divide stock into quantities of 1 cup or more and portion into freezer-going containers. For smaller quantities, you can also freeze stock in an ice cube tray. Each individual cube is approximately ¼ cup.

To Prepare Ahead
Follow steps 1 through 5 up to three or four months ahead and freeze. Or refrigerate and use within three to four days.

BEEF STOCK

2 tablespoons oil
4 pounds beef short ribs or
   shin bones, cracked
   into 2-inch pieces
3 carrots, scrubbed and cut
   into thirds
3 ribs celery with leaves,
   trimmed and cut into
   thirds
2 medium-sized leeks (tough
   bruised leaves
   removed), cut
   lengthwise into quarters
   and washed thoroughly
   between remaining
   layers to remove dirt
   and sand, cut into 1-
   inch lengths
3 parsnips, scrubbed and cut
   into thirds
6–8 quarts cold water

1 large onion, unpeeled and
   pierced with 2 whole
   cloves
6 peppercorns
1 clove garlic, unpeeled,
   mashed with broad side
   of chef's knife

Bouquet Garni
1 bay leaf
3–4 sprigs Italian flat-leaf
   parsley
3 fresh thyme sprigs *or* 1
   teaspoon dried

Have on Hand
10–12-quart stockpot
Fine mesh skimmer
Kitchen string
Chinois* or large strainer
   lined with cheesecloth

Yield 3 quarts

1. In the bottom of the stockpot, heat oil and sauté beef bones in batches; turn to brown evenly and be careful not to burn them. As they are done, transfer the glazed bones to a deep bowl or platter. This careful procedure can take up to 30 minutes.

2. Add vegetables to drippings in stockpot and sauté over moderate heat for several minutes until tender, stirring occasionally with a wooden spatula. Return beef bones and accumulated drippings to stockpot. Add water, which should cover meat by 2–3 inches, and bring to the edge of a boil. Stir to deglaze drippings in bottom of pot. Bring liquid to the edge of a boil over moderately high heat, then with a fine mesh skimmer, skim off and discard scum that rises to surface. Add ½ cup cold water to stop the cooking and slowly bring liquid back to the edge of a boil again. Repeat process of adding water and bringing to a boil 2 or 3 additional times until the liquid is free of scum.

3. Prepare a bouquet garni with bay leaf, parsley, and thyme sprigs,

and tie with kitchen string into a small bundle. Add to simmering liquid with clove-pierced onion, peppercorns, and garlic. (If dried thyme is used, add at this time.) Push all of the ingredients into liquid to be sure everything is submerged. With cover ajar, simmer 5½–6 hours and follow straining, cooling, storing, and do-ahead procedures described above for Classic Chicken and Veal Stock.

BASIC DUCK STOCK

Reserved duck carcass and
    wings
1 tablespoon vegetable oil
Giblets
2 carrots, trimmed, scraped,
    and coarsely chopped
2 celery ribs, trimmed and
    coarsely chopped
1 medium onion, peeled and
    coarsely chopped
2 cloves garlic, peeled and
    coarsely chopped

2 teaspoons tomato paste
½ cup white wine
2 cups Basic Chicken Stock
    or water (enough to
    cover bones)
3–4 sprigs parsley
2 fresh sprigs thyme *or* ½
    teaspoon dried thyme
1 bay leaf, crushed

Yield 3 cups

Preheat oven to 400 degrees.

1. Brown bones and wings in a roasting pan in preheated oven for 1 hour, turning once.

2. Choose a saucepan that can later accommodate the bones; heat oil and add giblets, carrots, celery, and onion. Cook over moderate heat until giblets are lightly browned and vegetables are slightly tender. Reduce heat to a simmer and add the garlic. Cook a few seconds, then add tomato paste and stir to mix. Put in all the bones and pour on wine and stock to barely cover them. Bring mixture to a boil, then reduce heat to a simmer. Add remaining ingredients and cook with cover ajar over moderate heat, maintaining a lazy surface bubble, skimming surface as necessary for about 1 hour. Strain through a chinois* or a fine strainer, pushing the vegetable pulp through with a wooden spoon. Set aside to cool slightly, then refrigerate or freeze in a suitable container.

Use as directed in recipe of your choice.

FISH STOCK (FUMET)

3 pounds fish heads, bones, and trimmings from fresh, firm-fleshed white fish such as sole, flounder, bass, red snapper. Do not use oily or dark-fleshed fish such as mackerel or bluefish.

Shells from shrimp, crab, or lobster, if available

2 quarts cold water

3 ripe tomatoes, coarsely chopped

1 carrot, scrubbed and cut into thirds

1 onion, peeled and quartered

2 cloves garlic, peeled and left whole

1 bay leaf

6 peppercorns

½ teaspoon coarse (kosher) salt

3 sprigs Italian flat-leaf parsley

Have on Hand

5–6-quart enamel-over-iron or stainless steel saucepan or flame-proof casserole

Fine mesh skimmer

Cheesecloth-lined strainer

Yield 1½ quarts

1. Wash fish trimmings under cold running water.

2. Combine all ingredients in a large saucepan and cover with 2 quarts cold water. Bring liquid to the edge of a boil over moderate heat; then, with a fine mesh skimmer, skim off and discard scum that rises to surface. Simmer uncovered, maintaining a lazy surface bubble at times and cook about 25–30 minutes. Any prolonged cooking will produce a bitter flavor.

3. Line a strainer with two thicknesses of moistened cheesecloth and anchor over a bowl. Strain fish stock by gently pressing out juices with back of a large kitchen spoon and bring to room temperature.

4. With a ladle, divide stock into quantities of 1 cup or more and portion into freezer-going containers. Use in recipes as needed.

To Prepare Ahead
Follow steps 1 through 4 and freeze up to three months. Or refrigerate and use within two to three days.

MOCK DEMI-GLACE

A demi-glace is based on a reduction of water with aromatic vegetables and browned meat bones. This short-cut version is made creditable by the use of homemade stock in the ingredient list. A canned broth will simply not have the gelatinous quality to give the essence its depth of flavor and texture.

2 tablespoons butter
1 carrot, chopped
1 small onion, chopped
1–2 tomatoes, chopped
1 rib celery, chopped
1 teaspoon tomato paste

2 parsley sprigs
¼ teaspoon thyme
1 bay leaf, crushed
4 cups Classic Chicken and
    Veal Stock

Yields 1 cup (some recipes will require no more than 1–2 tablespoons)

1. Melt butter in a large heavy saucepan. Add carrot, onion, and celery, and sauté a few minutes over low heat, stirring occasionally. When vegetables are tender but not colored, add tomatoes and tomato paste. Add remaining ingredients including stock and bring to the edge of a boil. Reduce heat to a brisk simmer and cook about 1 hour. Surface scum should be skimmed from time to time and discarded.

2. As stock begins to reduce, brush down glaze that adheres to sides of pot with a pastry or feather brush dipped in water. When stock has reduced more than halfway, transfer all the ingredients to a smaller saucepan. Add a little water to larger pan and wash down any particles of glaze sticking to it with the wet brush. Add this small amount of liquid to vegetables and stock in smaller saucepan. Continue to reduce stock until you have about 1 cup concentrated liquid. Strain into a small container. Cover and refrigerate or freeze. Some recipes will require no more than one or two tablespoons. To make a sauce, add to deglazed pan drippings and continue according to recipe.

To Prepare Ahead
This can be made ahead and frozen indefinitely. You can refrigerate it for several months. If some surface mold should appear, scrape off and discard.

HUNGARIAN GOULASH SOUP

3 tablespoons vegetable oil
2 pounds medium onions,
   peeled and thinly sliced
3½ pounds lean chuck,
   trimmed well and cut
   into ½-inch cubes
2–3 cloves garlic, finely
   chopped
3 tablespoons red wine
   vinegar
2 tablespoons imported
   sweet Hungarian
   paprika
1½ teaspoons coarse
   (kosher) salt
Freshly ground pepper
1 teaspoon tomato paste
1 tablespoon fresh snipped
   rosemary leaves *or* 1
   teaspoon dried

1½ tablespoons finely
   chopped Italian flat-leaf
   parsley
½ pound sweet Italian
   sausage, thinly sliced
5–6 cups Beef Stock or
   broth
2 pounds boiling potatoes,
   peeled and cut into tiny
   dice
½ pound fresh mushrooms,
   quickly rinsed,
   trimmed, and quartered
1 tablespoon capers
French Croutons (optional)

Serves 8–10

1. In a heavy 5–6 quart enamel-over-iron or stainless steel saucepan heat oil, add onions, and sauté until translucent, being careful not to brown. With wooden spatula, move onions to side of pan, add meat, and sauté over moderately high heat until lightly brown on all sides. Add garlic and vinegar and cook just until vinegar evaporates. Add paprika, salt, pepper, tomato paste, rosemary, parsley, and sausages, and stir to mix. Stir in stock, then simmer with cover ajar 45–50 minutes.

2. Add potatoes, mushrooms, and capers and gently stir to mix. Cover and cook 15–20 minutes longer or until meat and potatoes are tender. Serve piping hot in heated soup bowls or present in a heated soup tureen. Serve with French croutons if desired.

To Prepare Ahead
Follow step 1 up to two days ahead. The flavor of the soup is infinitely better when it stands for at least one or two days. Refrigerate covered. Bring to room temperature and complete step 2 before serving.

HERBED SQUASH BISQUE

3 tablespoons unsalted butter
1 butternut squash (2–2½
    pounds) cut in half,
    peeled, seeded, and cut
    into 1-inch pieces
2 tart green apples (Granny
    Smith or greenings)
    peeled, cored, and cut
    into 1-inch pieces
1 large onion, thinly sliced
1½-inch piece fresh ginger,
    peeled and finely
    chopped
¾ teaspoon fresh rosemary
    leaves *or* ¼ teaspoon
    dried

1 teaspoon fresh marjoram
    leaves *or* ¼ teaspoon
    dried
¾ teaspoon fresh thyme
    leaves *or* ¼ teaspoon
    dried
4½–5 cups Classic Chicken
    and Veal Stock
¾ teaspoon coarse (kosher)
    salt
Freshly ground pepper
½ cup Crème Fraîche or
    heavy cream
2–3 tablespoons dry sherry
Julienne of fresh ginger for
    garnish (optional)

Serves 8

1. Melt butter in a large saucepan. Put in squash, apple pieces, onion, and ginger. Season with herbs, cover, and cook slowly over low heat, stirring occasionally, 5–7 minutes to sweat vegetables. Pour on stock; season with salt and pepper and simmer over moderate heat 20–25 minutes.

2. Ladle soup and vegetables in batches into workbowl of food processor fitted with steel knife or into blender, and purée until very smooth. Transfer to a clean bowl as you process each batch. When all the soup is puréed, return to a rinsed saucepan and bring just to the edge of a boil. Add the crème fraîche or heavy cream and stir to mix. Taste to adjust the seasoning if necessary. Can be made ahead to this point.

3. Just before serving, bring the soup to the edge of a boil and add sherry. Stir to mix. Ladle into warm soup bowls, garnish with julienne of ginger if desired, and serve hot.

To Prepare Ahead
Follow steps 1 and 2 up to two days ahead and refrigerate in suitable container or freeze. Bring to room temperature and transfer to a saucepan. Add sherry and complete step 3 just before serving.

POTAGE CRÈME D'OR

It was my pleasure to learn about this soup when I first studied many years ago at the Cordon Bleu in London. It is a magnificent soup with a lovely golden-orange color and the surprise flavor of curry and orange juice.

1 pound fresh carrots with greens on
3 tablespoons unsalted butter
1 medium onion, thinly sliced
3½–4 cups Classic Chicken and Veal Stock
1 cup orange juice made from frozen juice concentrate, using half the water indicated to dilute

1 cup Crème Fraîche or heavy cream
1–2 teaspoons curry powder
¼ teaspoon freshly grated nutmeg
1 teaspoon coarse (kosher) salt
Freshly ground pepper
1 tablespoon finely chopped parsley for garnish

Serves 6–8

1. Remove carrot tops, scrub carrots with a vegetable brush or peel if necessary, and cut into ¼-inch slices.

2. Melt butter in a large heavy saucepan. Add onions and carrots and stir to coat. Cover and cook slowly over low heat, stirring occasionally, 5–7 minutes, to sweat vegetables without allowing them to brown. Pour on the stock or broth. Bring to a boil, then simmer until carrots are tender, about 20–25 minutes. Allow to cool several minutes.

3. Ladle soup and vegetables in batches into workbowl of food processor fitted with steel knife or into blender, and purée until very smooth. Transfer to a clean bowl as you process each batch. When all the soup is puréed, return to a rinsed saucepan and bring to the edge of a boil. Add orange juice, crème fraîche or heavy cream, season with curry, nutmeg, salt, and pepper, and stir to mix. Taste to adjust seasonings if necessary. Can be made ahead to this point.

4. Just before serving, heat through and ladle into warm soup bowls. Garnish with a sprinkle of finely chopped parsley and serve hot.

To Prepare Ahead

Follow steps 1 through 3 up to two days ahead and refrigerate covered in suitable container or freeze. Bring to room temperature and complete step 4 just before serving.

Note: This soup is equally delicious served cold.

AVGOLEMONO

This classic Greek lemon soup has the surprise taste of mint.

4 cups Basic Chicken Stock
　　or broth
⅓ cup uncooked converted
　　rice
1 rib celery, trimmed,
　　rinsed, and sliced thin
1 large boneless, skinless
　　chicken breast, cut into
　　small dice
½–¾ teaspoon coarse
　　(kosher) salt

Freshly ground pepper
2 eggs
6–7 tablespoons fresh lemon
　　juice
2 teaspoons fresh-snipped
　　mint leaves *or* ½
　　teaspoon dried
　　(optional)

Serves 4–6

1. In a saucepan bring stock or broth to a boil. Add rice and celery and cook, covered, over moderate heat 6–8 minutes. Add diced chicken and cook 8–10 minutes longer. Season with salt and pepper and taste to be sure rice is tender.

2. In a mixing bowl, whisk eggs until frothy. Add lemon juice and stir to mix. Add a ladleful or two of the hot soup to egg mixture and stir to mix. In a slow, steady stream, return egg mixture to saucepan, whisking soup constantly over low heat. Continue to whisk soup and heat just to the edge of a boil. Do not allow soup to boil or it may curdle. Serve hot in warm soup bowls with a touch of mint sprinkled over the top.

To Prepare Ahead
Follow step 1 up to one hour ahead. Complete step 2 before serving.

SERIOUSLY . . . A DUCK SOUP

January 5, 1982, I had an outstanding vegetable soup at the American Hotel in Sag Harbor, a quaint waterfront village on Long Island. Their stock was made from wild duck bones and produced a very rich broth. My version is simply a basic duck stock (the clue to its success) transformed into something magical with the abundant variety of vegetables.

5–6 cups Basic Duck Stock
5–6 large leaves Swiss chard, washed, trimmed, and thinly sliced
2 cups thinly sliced cabbage
4 whole fresh mushrooms, quickly rinsed, trimmed, and thinly sliced
1 large leek, trimmed, thoroughly rinsed clean and thinly sliced— white and light green part only
2 carrots, trimmed, scraped, and cut into ½-inch dice
1 small zucchini, cut into ½-inch dice

1 small white turnip, peeled and cut into ½-inch dice
3 cloves garlic, finely chopped
2–3 tomatoes, peeled, seeded, and coarsely chopped, *or* ½ cup canned whole tomatoes, drained and chopped
2 teaspoons coarse (kosher) salt
Freshly ground pepper
1 tablespoon fresh rosemary leaves *or* 1 teaspoon dried
2 boiling potatoes, peeled and cut into ½-inch dice

Serves 8–10

1. Pour stock into a 5½-quart saucepan and add prepared vegetables, except potatoes, in the order they are given. Bring liquid to the edge of a boil, then adjust heat to a simmer and stir to mix. Cook with cover ajar 1½ hours to blend flavors. Can be prepared ahead to this point.

2. Add potatoes to vegetables and stock and continue to simmer for additional 30 minutes until potatoes are tender. Taste to adjust seasoning if necessary and serve hot.

To Prepare Ahead

Follow step 1 up to one day ahead and refrigerate, covered, or up to one month ahead and freeze in suitable container. Bring to room temperature or defrost and complete step 2 just before serving.

Note: Food Processor Directions Using a food processor will speed up the vegetable preparation. Start with your slicing blade to prepare Swiss chard, cabbage, mushrooms, and leek, emptying workbowl after each vegetable is sliced; remove slicing blade and insert steel knife to coarsely dice, then finely chop remaining vegetables.

GINGER SOUP WITH GREENS

This Chinese-style soup is remarkably simple to do. Just simmer your homemade stock with lots of fresh ginger, add partially cooked greens and serve.

1 large bunch fresh greens,
    such as Swiss chard,
    escarole, or mustard
    greens
8 cups Classic Chicken and
    Veal Stock

3½–4 tablespoons thinly
    sliced julienne of
    ginger
1 teaspoon coarse (kosher)
    salt
Freshly ground pepper

Serves 8

1. Trim and thoroughly wash greens, discarding any bruised portions of leaves.

2. In several quarts of boiling water, partially cook greens 3–4 minutes until tender. If using Swiss chard, pull leaves from stems and cook separately until stems are tender. Drain greens immediately and fan* to cool or quickly rinse under a spray of cool water. Spread on clean dry kitchen towel to absorb excess moisture. If leaves are very large, cut them into halves or thirds.

3. Combine stock and ginger in a clean dry saucepan, bring to the edge of a boil, then allow to simmer 15–20 minutes. Season with salt and pepper, add greens, and cook for 2 minutes longer. Serve hot.

To Prepare Ahead
Follow steps 1 and 2 early in the day. Complete step 3 just before serving.

CARIBBEAN PEACH SOUP

A cooling and peachy soup as explained to me by a chef from Little Dix in Virgin Gorda, British West Indies. Since it was winter, I questioned the source of the peaches and was told they were "tinned." Here is my version using ripe, firm, and flavorful fresh peaches.

2 pounds ripe, firm peaches

Sugar Syrup
Enough water to cover
    peaches
⅔ cup sugar

½ cup heavy cream
½ cup apple juice
½ cup light rum
Dash allspice
Fresh mint leaves and sliced
    strawberries for garnish

Serves 6–8

1. Rinse peaches and set aside.

2. Place about 6 cups water in a saucepan with sugar and bring to a boil. Reduce heat and simmer liquid briskly 15–18 minutes. With a slotted spoon, gently lower peaches into sugar syrup and simmer 1 minute. Transfer peaches to a side dish and, when slightly cool, remove skin; then halve and stone the peaches. Cut into chunks and set aside.

3. In the meantime, reduce poaching liquid to about 1 cup until syrup has thickened slightly. Be careful not to let the syrup caramelize; you should be able to pour it easily. Set aside.

4. Place peach chunks in the workbowl of food processor fitted with steel knife or a blender and purée. Add remaining ingredients except mint and strawberries and process until the mixture is a smooth purée, about 1–2 minutes. Add cooled sugar syrup and process just to mix. Transfer to a suitable container and chill until ready to serve. Garnish with fresh sprigs of mint and sliced strawberries just before serving, if desired.

To Prepare Ahead
Follow steps 1 through 4 up to two days ahead. Refrigerate, covered, until ready to serve.

CHILLED STRAWBERRY-RHUBARB SOUP

Sometimes fruit soups are so sweet that the only place they have in a meal is at the very end. This refreshing fruit soup is kept minimally sweet and works as a colorful beginning to a summer meal.

1½ pounds rhubarb
2 pints strawberries (reserve
   ½ pint for garnish—do
   not hull)
2 cups water

½ cup sugar
⅓ cup red port wine
1 cup Crème Fraîche or sour
   cream (optional)

Serves 10–12

1. Wash rhubarb; cut off and discard leaves and bruised ends and pull off strings. Cut into 1-inch pieces. Wash and hull 1½ pints of the strawberries. Drain on paper towels to absorb excess moisture.

2. In a large saucepan, combine rhubarb, 2 cups water, and sugar. Bring mixture to a boil over high heat, then simmer, covered, about 10 minutes. Pour rhubarb mixture through a strainer over a bowl pushing down hard with the back of a wooden spoon to extract as much liquid as possible. Discard pulp.

3. Combine 1 cup rhubarb liquid and strawberries in a food processor or blender and process until mixture is puréed. Return to remaining rhubarb liquid. Add port wine and stir to mix. Can be made ahead to this point.

4. *Strawberry Garnish:* With a small paring knife, cut reserved strawberries into slices starting opposite the stem end, but not through to the stem. With thumb and index finger, gently spread slices to fan the strawberries. Set aside.

5. When ready to serve, ladle soup into wineglasses or mugs or pour into a tureen. Add dollops of crème fraîche or sour cream to individual servings, topping with a strawberry fan, or float strawberries in the tureen. Serve chilled.

To Prepare Ahead
Follow steps 1 through 3 up to several days ahead. Refrigerate covered. Follow step 4 up to several hours ahead. Complete step 5 before serving.

A TUSCAN BEAN SOUP

This hearty soup is typical of Tuscany and is a meal in itself.

8 ounces dried cannellini
  beans
¼ pound thinly sliced
  prosciutto
6 tablespoons olive oil
2 large cloves garlic, finely
  chopped
1 large red onion, peeled
  and coarsely chopped
1 large celery rib, coarsely
  chopped
2 carrots, scraped and
  coarsely chopped
¼ cup finely chopped Italian
  flat-leaf parsley
2 tablespoons fresh basil
  leaves, chopped, *or*
  ½ teaspoon dried
½ small head savoy
  cabbage, rinsed, cored,
  and thinly sliced
1¼ pounds kale, leaves
  removed from stems
  and soaked in several
  changes of lukewarm
  water to remove sand
  (or spinach, if kale is
  not available)

1 large or 2 small boiling
  potatoes, peeled, and
  cut in ½-inch dice
1 (1 pound) can whole
  tomatoes and their
  liquid
4–5 cups Beef Stock or
  broth
1 teaspoon coarse (kosher)
  salt
Freshly ground pepper
12–16 slices crusty French
  or Italian bread, oven-
  toasted
Imported extra virgin olive
  oil
6–8 tablespoons freshly
  grated Parmesan cheese

Have on Hand
Food mill

Serves 8–10

1. Soak beans overnight in cold water. The next day drain beans and put them into a large saucepan with 2 quarts water and prosciutto slices. Bring the liquid to a boil and skim off and discard scum that rises to the surface. Simmer beans so that a lazy surface bubble is maintained at all times. If beans absorb too much water, add a little more to keep them

covered. Cook with cover ajar about 1 hour. When beans are just tender, remove from heat and drain into a sieve-lined bowl. Transfer bean liquid to a smaller saucepan and reduce by half. Lift out whole slices of prosciutto from beans, cut into shreds and set prosciutto and beans aside separately.

2. While bean liquid is reducing, heat oil in same large saucepan that beans cooked in. Be sure to wipe pan dry before adding oil. When oil is hot, add garlic, onion, celery, and carrots. Cook covered and simmer 10–12 minutes to sweat vegetables. Add parsley, basil, and reserved prosciutto, and stir to mix. Add the prepared cabbage, kale, potatoes, tomatoes, stock or broth, and reduced bean liquid to mixture in saucepan. With a wooden spoon, break up tomatoes against the side of the pan and gently immerse the vegetables below the liquid. Cover and simmer for 15 minutes. Do not stir.

3. Put half the drained beans through a food mill or strainer and purée. Add bean purée with whole beans to vegetables in stockpot. Stir to mix very gently, being careful not to break beans, and cook at a gentle simmer 45 minutes to 1 hour longer, until beans are tender but not falling apart. Add salt and pepper. Taste to adjust seasoning if necessary.

Preheat oven to 375 degrees.

4. Toast bread slices on a cookie sheet until they just color lightly. (I like to rub the warm slices with a crushed clove of garlic for added flavor. This is an option.)

5. Place one to two slices of toasted bread in warm soup bowls. Ladle the soup and vegetables into each bowl; then drizzle over a trace of olive oil and sprinkle with freshly grated cheese. Serve immediately.

To Prepare Ahead

Follow steps 1 through 3 up to two days ahead. Refrigerate covered in a suitable container. Follow step 4 early in the day and place toast slices aside until needed. Bring soup to room temperature and warm to heat through for about 15 minutes and complete step 5 just before serving.

Note: Food Processor Directions If using a processor, place garlic in workbowl fitted with steel knife and process with several on/off turns until finely chopped. Remove and set aside. Add onion, carrots, celery, and potatoes, one at a time. Chop coarsely until small dice with several on/off turns and set aside. Replace steel knife with slicing blade. Cut cabbage to fit feed tube, slice with light pressure, and set aside.

A THICK AND MEATY PEA SOUP

1 package (1 pound) green
    split peas
1 pound Italian sweet link
    sausage
3–4 short ribs of beef
3 fresh carrots with greens
    on, scraped or peeled if
    necessary and thinly
    sliced
1 rib celery, rinsed and
    thinly sliced
1 large onion, thinly sliced
2 quarts water

2 parsley sprigs
1 bay leaf
2 sprigs fresh thyme *or*
    ½ teaspoon dried
2 cloves garlic, peeled and
    finely chopped
2 teaspoons coarse (kosher)
    salt
Freshly ground pepper
½ teaspoon freshly grated
    nutmeg
Shredded carrots for garnish

Serves 8–10

1. Rinse and sort peas in a strainer under cold running water and set aside.

2. Brown sausage over moderate heat in the bottom of a heavy 6-quart stockpot. Remove sausage and drain on paper towels. Brown short ribs well on both sides in sausage drippings. Place carrots, celery, onion, and meats in pot with 2 quarts cold water to cover. Prepare a bouquet garni by tying parsley sprigs and bay leaf with string; then add to the liquid. Bring to a boil, skimming the surface well of the scum that rises. Repeat procedure 2–3 times until liquid is clear.

3. Continue cooking over moderate heat at a brisk simmer and slowly add split peas so that the bubbling does not stop. Add thyme, garlic, salt, pepper, and nutmeg and stir to mix. Taste to adjust seasoning if necessary. Cover and cook over low heat for about 2 hours. Remove short ribs and sausages and set aside. Remove bouquet garni and discard. Allow soup to cool slightly.

4. Ladle the soup and vegetables in batches into workbowl of food processor fitted with steel knife or into blender and purée until very smooth. Transfer to a clean bowl as you process each batch. Return to a rinsed saucepan when all the soup is puréed.

5. Cut sausages into 1-inch lengths; remove meat from short rib bones and cut away as much fat as possible. Discard fat and bones. Add meats to the soup and heat through for 15–20 minutes before serving.

6. Ladle into warm large soup bowls and garnish with shredded

carrots. Serve with Herb Casserole Bread and Endive and Grapefruit Salad and a crisp red wine.

To Prepare Ahead
Follow step 1 up to two days before. Follow steps 2 through 5 up to one day ahead and refrigerate, covered, in a suitable container. Bring to room temperature and complete step 6.

Note: If you refrigerate soup, it may later be necessary to thin it a little with additional water or stock.

PEAR AND LEEK SOUP

4 leeks, about 1 inch thick, white and light green part only
3 tablespoons unsalted butter
1 boiling potato, peeled and cut into small dice
4 cups Classic Chicken and Veal Stock
4 ripe pears (red or green Bartletts or Anjou)

1 cup Crème Fraîche or heavy cream
1 teaspoon coarse (kosher) salt
Freshly ground pepper
Dash of paprika
2 tablespoons snipped chives for garnish

Serves 6–8

1. Trim off the root end of each leek and discard. Trim off the bruised leaves of the upper green part and discard. Split the leeks in half lengthwise through the root end. Hold each half intact in the palm of your hand and rinse thoroughly between the leaves with cold running water to remove all trace of sand. Thinly slice and set aside.

2. Melt butter in a large heavy saucepan and, when foam subsides, add leeks and stir to coat. Cover and let simmer over low heat 3–4 minutes. Add potatoes, pour on stock and simmer 25–30 minutes. Allow to cool.

3. In the meantime, peel and core pears, making certain to remove all pits. Cut up coarsely and put into workbowl of food processor fitted with steel knife or blender and purée. Use a rubber spatula to scrape sides as necessary and process until smooth.

4. Strain soup into a sieve-lined bowl and add the leek and potato

with a ladleful of soup to pears in workbowl of processor or blender. Process or blend to a smooth purée, scraping down sides of bowl as necessary. Return purée to reserved liquid in bowl and stir to mix with a wire whisk.

5. Pour contents of bowl into rinsed saucepan and add crème fraîche or cream. Place over moderate heat, season with salt and pepper, and bring to the edge of a boil. Add a dash or two of paprika, stir to mix, and taste to adjust seasoning if necesssary. Can be made ahead to this point.

6. Just before serving, bring the soup to the edge of a boil; stir to mix. Ladle into warm soup bowls and serve hot, garnished with snipped chives.

To Prepare Ahead
Follow steps 1 through 5 up to two days ahead and refrigerate in suitable container or freeze. Bring to room temperature and transfer to a saucepan and complete step 6 just before serving.

2

IN AND OUT OF THE SALAD BOWL

A salad is a dish for all seasons. It can consist simply of plain greens and a basic vinaigrette; a combination vegetable or fruit salad; or even a meat or fish salad. A salad composed of meat or fish with eggs and cheese can be a complete and balanced meal. Many Americans will have a salad regularly as an introduction to their dinner. It is a way to extend the meal, and affords nutritive value at the same time.

The French and Italians generally offer a salad after the main course. The vinegar or lemon juice in the dressing will "cleanse" the palate, so they say. This does make sense. However, there are times when I prefer to do a salad presentation at the introduction to a meal—salads such as my Poached Leeks Vinaigrette or the Radicchio, Leek, and Chèvre Salad. (Radicchio, an Italian import which resembles cabbage, is really lettuce with crisp red-and-white leaves.)

Nouvelle cuisine, a term which has unfortunately been prone to distorted meanings, has helped raise salads to new heights as well as introduce new food combinations that fit a more contemporary life-style. The emphasis is on lightness and less pretension in basic dishes. Salads, ever important for their nutritional values, have become an even more significant part of the menu. We often hear ourselves saying, "I would like to have something light—a salad perhaps?" The increasing availability of fresh ingredients at supermarkets has made it easier to find an abundance of splendid greens and other produce to prepare a well-dressed salad. Innovative young chefs have taught us a way to salads beyond our wildest imaginations. Sliced duck foie gras, wild mushrooms, lobster or scallop medallions on warm greens, or the colorful radicchio and stir-fry julienned peppers in a blaze of color are examples of recent culinary innovations. Such inventiveness has led us to discover and use light, fruity oils, grainy mustards, and the enormous variety of vinegars now readily available. Keep a *batterie de cuisine* of these condiments in your cupboard. Mix and match them to make your own taste discoveries. Do not merely confine them to your daily "tossed greens." They are, in short, a gastronomic entertainment.

I think of my oils, vinegars, mustards, herbs, and spices as accessories in my pantry. Having them on hand affords me the luxury of seasoning and flavoring foods in a variety of ways. Shall I use the balsamic vinegar on these greens or will a lighter red wine vinegar be right? Will tarragon or rosemary do it for the chicken tonight? It's almost like completing a wardrobe. Accessorize then, and experience a very practical way of making all foods, not just salads, more savory, stimulating, and zesty.

One cautionary word on preparing a simple salad with plain greens: a rule of thumb is never to add the dressing until just before you toss and serve or the delicate lettuce will go limp. I always advise my students to wash their salad greens, dry them thoroughly, then wrap them in paper toweling and store until ready to use. A salad spinner is indispensable and will save the cost of the paper towels you would ordinarily need to hand-dry the greens. Drying greens properly cannot be stressed enough. They should be bone dry in order to "hold" the fine dressing you have prepared for them.

Oils: Serious cooks have become as choosy about their oils as they are about fine wines. There are dozens of quality olive oils on the market today especially in specialty food and kitchen shops. This was not always so.

However, the demand created by cooking teachers and other serious food people has led to large-scale importing of extra virgin olive oils, a cold-pressed oil made almost entirely by hand from the first pressing of the highest-quality olives. Use such oils for cold vegetable salads and for cold sauces, like pesto or an uncooked tomato sauce, and, of course, for pasta, both hot and cold. I value the light, milder and fruity tastes of a quality French olive oil, also extra virgin, for delicate salads, such as Bibb lettuce and endive or Salade de Champignons, and for fish dishes or in combination with corn oil for your mayonnaise.

These first-pressed olive oils are costly and I would not recommend them for your everyday cooking. However, there are olive oils available on the supermarket shelves that are perfectly suitable for cooking; you'll find they are not as flavorful when used in a salad dressing.

I keep several oils on hand, using them for different purposes. The full complement includes a good-quality corn oil used in combination with butter for sautéing, or alone for both pan and deep frying; and a mild but rich-flavored peanut oil from France that has a smoking point just slightly lower than that of corn oil. An oil that has grown in popularity in recent years is walnut oil from the Périgord and Grenoble regions of France. Its pronounced walnut flavor makes salads absolutely come alive.

Another oil that has a definite place in my kitchen is sesame oil, extracted from the seeds of the sesame plant. Its rich, nutty flavor lends itself perfectly to Chinese and Indian food.

All oils should be stored in a cool, dark place; warmth increases the process of deterioration and oils will become rancid. A rancid oil will smell and taste acrid and stale. If you open a recently purchased container of oil and it has an "off" flavor, return it to the store at once. I try to buy oils in sizes that will be used within several weeks. Since I do not use walnut and sesame oils frequently, I keep them in the refrigerator, which is safe for oils kept longer than two weeks. People disagree on whether or not oil should be refrigerated. Some say it loses no flavor at all but just becomes cloudy. Even if there is a slight loss of flavor when chilled, it is far better than having an oil go rancid.

Vinegars: I urge you to look beyond the mundane commercial vinegars and explore the wide varieties of flavor offered. The spectrum of vinegars is downright glamorous, from the delicate sweetness of raspberry vinegar to the gutsy, full-bodied, aged-in-a-barrel red wine balsamic vinegar from Italy. They'll add a newness and excitement to many of your recipes. One can dress freshly poached asparagus with a blueberry vinegar; deglaze pan drippings with a raspberry or red wine vinegar; add sherry vinegar to a sauce reduction; or tickle a vegetable salad with homemade herb vinegars. The possibilities are endless.

Vinegars can be sharp, rich, or fruity, but they do have one thing in common: they are all acidic and will gnaw at or corrode most metals, i.e., aluminum, iron, copper, etc. So, when you use vinegars in a marinade for pickling, etc., be sure to mix them in glass, enamel, or earthenware containers.

It's fun to keep an assortment of the popular fruit vinegars on hand, as well as the more staple wine and herb vinegars, to lend variety to your dressings and marinades. One of the great joys of an herb garden is the ready supply of fresh herbs for flavoring vinegars.

A simple way to make a tarragon vinegar is to work with the following proportions: Combine about 75 percent of a basic white vinegar easily found on supermarket shelves with approximately 25 percent of a dry white table wine—even leftovers will do. Sprigs of fresh tarragon and white and black peppercorns are added in a covered jar or earthenware crock and left to mellow for a minimum of three months. It gets better with age. Bottle it in the summer and it's ready for your holiday gift giving.

Like oils, it is best to buy vinegars in small quantities, as they do produce a sediment and will sometimes mold. Sediment can be strained out; a moldy vinegar, however, should be discarded.

Mustards: These too come in a variety of flavors—sweet to tart, mild to hot, sharp, pure, and vibrant. This popular condiment, second only to black pepper, has been known and appreciated since biblical times as a flavoring, as a digestive stimulant and as a warming application to the body. (Are you too young to remember mustard plasters?)

Basically, the uniqueness of mustards lies in the blend of seasoning and spices added to the mustard seeds. There are only two varieties of mustard plants: one yielding black or brown seeds which are more flavorful and pungent and are mostly used for prepared and dry mustard; and white and yellow seeds, which are used in pickling and salad dressings.

Some of the best mustards are from Dijon in Burgundy. They're made from milling the choicest seeds and mixing them with white wine, vinegar, spices, and the juice of green grapes (verjuice). Imported Dijon mustards can cost up to six times as much as a popular domestic brand. Sometimes their packaging and the word "import" make them appealing to give as gifts alone or with other specialty food items. Grainy mustards, such as those from Provence, actually contain whole, ground, or partially ground seeds. They are superb for coating meats, chicken and fish and lend textural interest when added to dressings, sauces, and marinades. Their tastes range from rich, sharp, and spicy to hot. A new dimension in flavoring can be achieved when exploring the world of mustards.

While you can have fun working with the different varieties of mustard, you should be aware that flavored mustards are now being produced which sometimes combine unlikely ingredients. Some work well, like herb mustards; others seem to me an affectation of color and taste, rearing their ugly heads as olive and anchovy, peanut, and even lemon and lime mustards. New in this category, too, are peppercorn mustards. Generally speaking, when commercially prepared, they are not very exciting. Though they are fairly expensive, a good mustard base is not always used. A satisfying project would be to create your own by combining green or black peppercorns with a good-quality Dijon. Herbs or honey would also make fine additions and result in substantial savings as well.

Mustards vary from region to region. Some food experts have written (and I agree) that mustard has a special affinity for certain regional foods. Add a grain mustard to a mixture of shallots, tarragon vinegar, and a light, fruity olive oil and marinate a leg of lamb for roasting or grilling as in my Gigot St. Tropez, or add honey to a Dijon mixture and coat chickens for Poulet au Bresse Grillé. Düsseldorf, a hot German mustard, goes well with smoked pork products.

The familiar American-produced Grey Poupon brand is based on an old French recipe from Dijon. In France, in 1777, a certain Mr. Grey with a secret recipe for making a wine-based mustard got together with a Mr. Poupon, who had the money to back him. Thus the Grey Poupon Company was formed, with rights being sold to produce and sell Grey Poupon in this country. It can be found in most supermarkets and is affordable. It is a perfectly fine mustard to use alone or in combination with other mustards for your vinaigrettes, marinades, or mayonnaise.

The traditional favorite of small children and sports fans is a mild yellow mustard usually atop a hot dog. It contains fillers of sugar, flour, mustard oil, and turmeric, which gives it its strong yellow color.

Mustard, English style, comes in a dry (powdered) form and is mixed with cold, not hot, water half an hour before use to bring out its fullest flavor. It is the ideal condiment for roast beef, ham, and sausage and is relatively hot, like Jamaican or Chinese mustards. Do not prepare for use hours or days ahead, as the flavor changes once moisture is added.

Although there is almost an infinite range of mustards with subtle variations of flavor and texture, a workable collection for a home kitchen could consist of a good Dijon, grainy mustard, the powdered English, and a good delicatessen mustard. Mustards give flavor to so many dishes there is hardly a time that most recipes, with the exception of dessert, would not benefit by a judicious addition.

Mayonnaise: If you own either a food processor or a blender, there is no reason not to make your own mayonnaise. This useful sauce combines well with many cold foods for salads and is also used as a sauce for poached fish and chicken.

When making a mayonnaise, it is important to have all the ingredients at room temperature, about 65–70 degrees, or the sauce can easily curdle. If your oil is kept in a cool, dark cupboard as wine is, measure out the required amount and let stand in a warm place in your kitchen. Use only the freshest eggs and fine-quality oil and vinegar for a light, creamy, and flavorful mayonnaise. If a thicker consistency is preferred, use two egg yolks. If the mayonnaise should curdle, it can be brought back to smoothness by whisking it a little at a time into a clean bowl containing either 1 tablespoon of hot water, vinegar, or another egg yolk. The addition of a Dijon mustard will not only flavor your homemade mayonnaise, but aid in the emulsion of egg and oil.

Herbs and Spices: The recent emphasis reducing sodium in our diets has spurred an even greater interest in cooking with herbs and spices. Herbs bring out the flavor of other ingredients when knowledgeably used—for instance, burnet leaves with cucumber, chives with onion, parsley with root vegetables.

Experiment with herb combinations or simply with a new herb to create new taste sensations. Rosemary, with its distinctive, sweetish taste, is excellent when used to flavor veal, lamb, and pork dishes; soups and stews. Tarragon, a delicate, fresh-flavored herb, is well known for its use in tarragon vinegar. Roast chicken, egg, and tomato dishes also benefit from it. Bay leaves are a strong herb and should be used sparingly. Bury a small leaf in your pilaf next time you prepare one. It lends a certain excitement—but be sure to remove it before serving. Bouquet garni, frequently mentioned in French cooking, usually consists of parsley, thyme, and bay leaf and is used to flavor a soup or a stew. Fines herbes—a combination of parsley, chervil, tarragon, and sometimes chives—is a favorite seasoner on meat, fish, poultry, cheese, and egg dishes.

Fresh herbs are unquestionably superior to dry; however, if it is more convenient, better to use the dry than none at all. Remember that some herbs are absolutely useless dried, like parsley, sage, chervil—or basil for a fresh pesto sauce. Parsley is available fresh all year long; powdered sage is too strong and dominates other flavors; dried chervil is tasteless and, therefore, a waste of money; dried basil will not work in a pesto sauce. Fresh chervil, sage, and basil leaves will simply have to be among summer's great pleasures. Also, to have the best flavor from dry herbs buy the best quality and remember that shelf life is limited. People will buy a bottle of herbs and use it for years; after six months herbs are nothing but dried grass.

Cooking at its most pleasurable is a wonderfully sensual experience and for a culinary "high," very few things can compare to the heady aroma and flavor of fresh herbs. I think it is one of the reasons that people who love to cook frequently love to garden as well—even if it is only a tiny patch by the back door or a few pots in a sunny window. Show me a gardener who wouldn't brag about his sun-warmed tomatoes, the purple smoothness of eggplant, or the verdant beauty of green peppers. And, oh, the joy of a fresh sprig of tarragon added to a dressing or a marinade. Edge your garden with a luxurious growth of both wild and lemon thyme. Thyme is such a pretty herb to grow.

When planning an herb garden, choose the herbs you most frequently use in cooking. American preferences today seem to run toward basil, thyme, French tarragon, rosemary, Italian parsley, dill, mint, savory, and oregano—or its more delicate relative, marjoram. I personally sing the virtues of what rosemary will do for a veal roast or even a pilaf, or thyme for a stew or the rich full fragrance of fresh basil for summer salads and sauces.

When you use fresh herbs frequently you will be able to judge approximately the number of sprigs needed for a recipe. Fresh herbs are chopped fine or snipped with kitchen shears before adding to food. I strip the leaves from the stems of parsley, basil, tarragon, or mint leaves and chop them on a wooden board. However, I snip chives with small kitchen scissors, as a knife is likely to mash them. To measure fresh chopped herbs, press the minced leaves gently into the measuring spoon; don't pack.

If you want to dry fresh herbs to preserve them, do not wait for the growing season to end, as you want to retain as much of the fresh flavor as possible. Process quickly before these qualities disappear, by washing and drying the leaves of herbs (examples: basil, mint, sage) or branches of leaves (examples: thyme, tarragon, and rosemary). Lay them out on a cheesecloth-lined clean window screen or cheesecloth tacked to a frame. Place the frame in a well-ventilated dark, cool room and let them dry thoroughly, then crumble, push through a sieve to strain bits and pieces of stem and branch, and store in airtight bottles.

In general, use herbs with a light hand and sprinkle judiciously, as you would salt and pepper. When flavoring foods with dry herbs, use about a third less than fresh herbs. For instance—depending on the herb—use ½ to 1 teaspoon dry to 1 tablespoon minced fresh. Bear all this in mind, particularly when using some of the stronger-flavored herbs like thyme, oregano, marjoram, mint, dill, and savory.

Spices, historically, have been highly prized commodities used as precious offerings. Herbs and spices have also been revered for their medicinal values. Many cultures, particularly in the Orient, continue to put their faith in spices for medicinal purposes as well as for preserving and flavoring foods.

While it is convenient to purchase spices ground to a powder, whole spices, ground as needed, are far more aromatic. Just the aroma of such flavorings can make life more pleasurable for someone on a restricted diet. Grind small amounts of whole spices in a small electric coffee grinder kept only for this purpose. Properly stored in airtight containers, they will keep fresh for up to three months. A pepper mill is absolutely essential for whole peppercorns and will also grind out many of your seeds.

Spices should blend harmoniously and not overwhelm. One of the charms of fine Japanese, Chinese, and Indian cooking is the subtlety of taste which is achieved by a careful blending of spices. In some instances, however, the flavor of a particular herb or spice is meant to be accentuated, as in the Chicken and Broccoli Salad with Tarragon Cream Vinaigrette.

Some people seem to assume all spices are hot, but that is not so. Cinnamon and paprika are spices, yet are sweet; ginger is spicy-sweet; cayenne is hot.

As with herbs, there are good marriages in food using spices. Paprika, a rich source of Vitamin C, is splendid with roasts; a touch of ginger works magic in a warm apple pie or in my Herb Squash Bisque; and nutmeg has great affinity for homemade pumpkin breads, custards, and milk dishes. One could go on ad infinitum.

You can bring a whole world of cooking to your fingertips by reaching for your herbs and spices. A good working selection will be more than rewarding whenever you use them.

Salt: As you expand your creative use of herbs and spices, you will find yourself using salt less and less often as a way of making food more tasty. However, it has its place, and my choice, in that case is to use coarse kosher salt, for several reasons.

First of all it is pure, and does not have the additives and chemicals that make pouring salt pour as easily as it does. Kosher salt is lighter than pouring salt—it weighs half as much. I know this may sound strange because of its coarse texture, but it is so. A number of years ago, whenever I read a recipe that called for salt, it was suggested that one use twice as much as kosher salt as regular because it weighed half as much. Tuned in as we are these days to being careful of our salt intake, I find that I use coarse kosher salt in lesser quantities, thereby using much less than suggested. I find the taste of kosher salt is far superior to that of pouring salt. Do your own taste test and you will find a more natural taste with the kosher salt and a somewhat burning aftertaste on the rear of the tongue when the pouring salt is tasted.

I keep my kosher salt in a small, wide-mouth pottery bowl with a cover. When I am cooking, I pick up the salt with my fingertips. I think you will find it feels good in your hand and you will have more control as you lightly sprinkle your foods. You will also be amazed to discover how much less salt you are using than is specifically called for in teaspoon or half-teaspoon measures. Remember, you are in charge whenever you cook, and this is just another way to keep control. The wide choice of flavorings and condiments available today has made it easier to cook tasty dishes—made tastier with simple embellishing touches. For pure everyday fun, experiment and interchange ideas and condiments with friends to create some interesting new taste sensations—and remember, tasting is only half the fun.

ENDIVE, WATERCRESS, AND BEET SALAD

2 cups canned julienne-cut
    beets, drained
1 tablespoon sugar
¼ cup white wine vinegar
½ pound endive
Watercress, washed and
    spin-dried, heavy stems
    removed
1 hard-cooked egg, sieved
    (optional)

Vinaigrette
2 cloves garlic, finely
    chopped

2 shallots, finely chopped
¾ teaspoon coarse (kosher)
    salt
Freshly ground pepper
1 teaspoon sugar
2 teaspoons Dijon mustard
1 teaspoon water
3 tablespoons tarragon
    vinegar
6 tablespoons light, fruity
    olive oil

Serves 6–8

1. Place beets in a bowl and pour on sugar and vinegar. Toss gently to mix, and marinate at least 1 hour.

2. Separate endive leaves and wash thoroughly. Place on a clean kitchen towel to drain. Set aside.

3. *Prepare Vinaigrette:* Place chopped garlic and shallots in a mixing bowl or chop finely in workbowl of food processor fitted with steel blade. If using processor, process with several on/off pulses, scraping down the sides with a rubber spatula as necessary. Add salt, pepper, sugar, mustard, water, and vinegar, and stir or process to mix. Gradually add oil in a thin stream into the bowl or through feed tube of processor and stir vigorously or process until mixture is thoroughly blended. Taste to adjust seasoning if necessary.

4. Arrange endive leaves in a circle with points out toward the edge of a bowl or platter. Drain beets from marinade and toss with half the prepared dressing. Spoon beets into the center of the serving bowl or platter forming a mound. Place a ring of watercress at the base of the endive leaves encircling the beets and top with sieved hard-cooked egg if desired. Serve remaining dressing in a sauceboat or small pitcher.

To Prepare Ahead
Follow steps 1 through 3 up to one day ahead. Refrigerate marinated beets, endive, and watercress separately in suitable containers. Prepare vinaigrette and refrigerate covered. Complete step 4 up to one hour ahead. Cover lightly with plastic wrap and refrigerate until ready to serve.

ASPARAGUS IN CAPER VINAIGRETTE

2 pounds fresh asparagus
Coarse (kosher) salt
2 whole red pimentos cut
    into ½-inch wide strips
Additional tablespoon capers
    for garnish

Freshly ground pepper
2 tablespoons sherry vinegar
    or tarragon vinegar
1 teaspoon lemon juice
¼ cup capers, drained
⅓ cup light, fruity olive oil

Caper Vinaigrette
2–3 teaspoons Dijon mustard
½ teaspoon coarse (kosher)
    salt

Have on Hand
Heavy skillet with cover
Rectangular or round serving
    dish

Serves 6–8

1. When ready to cook asparagus, hold each one in your hands and snap off the white, woody part of the stalk where it naturally bends. Discard end portion. With the tip of a paring knife, trim away the triangular scales along the stalk, leaving the tender scales at the head. Rinse clean under a spray of cold water.

2. In a heavy skillet with cover, arrange heavier stalks close together in center of skillet, graduating thinner asparagus to either side of the pan. Pour over ½ inch water to barely cover asparagus. Sprinkle lightly with salt and bring to a boil. Adjust heat and cook with cover ajar over moderate heat 5 minutes, maintaining a lazy surface bubble. The asparagus will take 4–6 minutes to cook, depending on the thickness of the stalks. If thinner spears cook more quickly, remove as they are done. Drain all asparagus and fan* quickly or cool under a spray of cold water. Spread on a clean kitchen towel to pat dry and absorb any excess moisture.

3. *Caper Vinaigrette:* In a mixing bowl or workbowl of food processor fitted with steel knife, combine mustard, salt, pepper, vinegar, lemon juice, and capers and stir or process to mix. Gradually add oil in thin stream into the bowl or through feed tube and mix or process until mixture is thoroughly blended. Taste to adjust seasoning if necessary. Can be made ahead to this point.

4. *To Serve:* Arrange on a round or rectangular serving dish so cut ends of asparagus meet in the center of dish with tips facing outer edges. Place strips of pimento over cut ends in center and top pimento with

additional capers. Spoon dressing over spears, leaving the tips exposed. Serve at room temperature.

To Prepare Ahead
Follow steps 1 through 3 up to one day ahead. Cover asparagus with plastic wrap and store dressing in screw-top jar and refrigerate. Bring to room temperature and complete step 4.

MELON FANS WITH PROSCIUTTO AND GREEN PEPPERCORNS

1 ripe cantaloupe, cut into 8 even-sized wedges
6–8 thin, moist slices imported prosciutto

2–3 teaspoons green peppercorns packed in brine (not vinegar)

Serves 6–8

1. With a sharp paring knife cut away and discard skin from melon wedges. Working with one wedge at a time, cut into 3–4 lengthwise slices. As you cut each wedge, arrange by spreading slices like a fan on 6–8 plates.

2. Lift prosciutto slices one at a time and gently drop like a handkerchief at the point where the melon slices join. Sprinkle a few green peppercorns into the crevices between prosciutto slices. Continue until all are done. Chill until ready to serve.

To Prepare Ahead
Follow steps 1 and 2 up to several hours ahead. Refrigerate, covered with a light tent of plastic wrap until ready to serve.

Note: When melons are not in season, substitute ripe Anjou pears. Peel and core pears, cut into thin slices, and sprinkle with lemon juice to prevent discoloration. Proceed as above.

GREEN BEAN, CHÈVRE, AND PIGNOLI NUT SALAD

½ pound firm, crisp green
    beans with gracefully
    curved tails
¼ pound aged domestic
    chèvre
¼ cup pignoli nuts, lightly
    toasted

2 teaspoons Dijon mustard
1 tablespoon raspberry
    vinegar
3 tablespoons light, fruity
    olive oil
Freshly ground pepper

Vinaigrette
1 large finely chopped
    shallot

Serves 6

Note: When working with whole green beans in a recipe, I never top and tail them. I simply line them up several at a time with stem ends meeting and cut through the stem ends to discard. Leave the tails on— they really are quite pretty.

1. Wash green beans and remove stem ends. Bring 2 quarts water to a boil, add salt, then put in beans. Cover and cook in briskly simmering water 2–3 minutes. Drain in a colander and fan to cool or quickly refresh under a spray of cold running water. Transfer to a clean kitchen towel and pat dry to absorb excess moisture. Place the beans in mixing bowl and set aside.

2. *Prepare Vinaigrette:* Place shallot in a mixing bowl, add the mustard and vinegar, and stir to mix. Whisk in the oil in a thin, steady stream until mixture is thoroughly blended. Add a bit of pepper, then taste to adjust seasoning if necessary.

3. Pour the vinaigrette over the beans and toss to mix. Transfer green beans to a salad bowl. Crumble the chèvre into bite-size pieces and scatter over the beans. Top with a sprinkle of toasted pignoli nuts and it's ready to serve.

To Prepare Ahead
Follow step 1 up to several hours ahead. Refrigerate, covered with plastic wrap. Complete steps 2 and 3 before serving.

PEPPERS AND ZUCCHINI

I developed several antipasto recipes for an Italian dinner party class. Two recipes follow. For a third, Cannellini and Shrimp, see index. These three recipes work beautifully together and as antipasti will serve 10–12.

3 red bell peppers
3 firm zucchini, about 1¼–
   1½ pounds
2 tablespoons vegetable oil
1 tablespoon capers

Vinaigrette
2 cloves garlic, finely
   chopped

Coarse (kosher) salt
Freshly ground pepper
2 teaspoons Dijon mustard
1 tablespoon balsamic wine
   vinegar
5–6 tablespoons imported
   Italian olive oil

Serves 6–8

Preheat broiler.

1. Place peppers on a foil-lined cookie sheet and broil about three inches from source of heat until the skin blisters and blackens. Move peppers around as necessary to char evenly on all sides, about 15 minutes. Transfer peppers to a brown paper bag, close tightly and let stand a minute or two to capture the steam. Remove peppers while still warm and peel over a bowl to catch juices. Strain juices for vinaigrette and set aside. Remove heavy stems and seeds from peppers, then cut into ½-inch-wide strips and set aside.

2. Scrub zucchini clean, trim off and discard ends, and slice ¼ inch thick. Spread on work surface or cookie sheet and sprinkle lightly with salt. Let stand 20 minutes or so to exude juices. Rinse in a colander and spread on a clean kitchen towel to absorb excess liquid.

3. In a skillet, heat vegetable oil, add zucchini slices, and sauté until lightly golden on both sides. Do not overcook. Drain on paper towels.

4. *Vinaigrette:* Place chopped garlic in a mixing bowl or chop finely with several on/off pulses in workbowl of food processor fitted with steel knife. Add salt, pepper, mustard, vinegar, and reserved juices, and stir or process to mix. Gradually add oil in a thin stream into the bowl or through feed tube and mix or process until mixture is thoroughly blended. Taste to adjust seasoning.

5. Add 2–3 tablespoons vinaigrette to pepper strips in mixing bowl and toss gently to mix. Remove the most perfect pepper strips and

arrange them neatly in a spurlike pattern on a round serving plate, preferably white. Combine zucchini slices with remaining peppers and vinaigrette and toss gently to mix. Mound mixture in the center of your dish, covering the ends of the pepper strips. Sprinkle some additional capers on top and serve at room temperature.

To Prepare Ahead
Follow steps 1 through 5 up to one day ahead. Refrigerate, covered with plastic wrap. Bring to room temperature and serve.

CHICKEN AND BROCCOLI SALAD WITH TARRAGON CREAM VINAIGRETTE

Court Bouillon
1 carrot, scraped and
    trimmed
1 celery rib, trimmed
2–3 sprigs of Italian flat-leaf
    parsley
1 small onion
5–6 peppercorns
½ teaspoon coarse (kosher)
    salt
3 whole chicken breasts,
    halved
1 bunch broccoli, trimmed,
    cut into "little trees"
    and blanched*

Tarragon Cream Vinaigrette
1 clove garlic, finely
    chopped
1 whole egg
1 egg yolk (at room
    temperature)

3 tablespoons Dijon mustard
1 tablespoon imported red
    wine vinegar
2 tablespoons tarragon wine
    vinegar
2 tablespoons fresh tarragon
    leaves *or* 2 teaspoons
    dried
½ teaspoon coarse (kosher)
    salt
Freshly ground pepper
½ cup light fruity olive oil
½ cup vegetable oil
2 teaspoons snipped chives
    or scallions
1–2 tablespoons Crème
    Fraîche or heavy cream
1–2 tablespoons coarsely
    chopped toasted
    hazelnuts for garnish

Serves 6–8
1. Prepare a court bouillon to poach chicken breasts. Place carrot, celery, parsley, onion, and peppercorns in 4-quart saucepan with about

2½ quarts of water. Bring to a boil over high heat, add salt, then reduce heat and simmer 15 minutes. Put in chicken breasts and poach gently for about 12 minutes. Turn off heat and allow chicken breasts to sit in liquid 1 or 2 minutes more. Remove with slotted spoon and allow to cool. Remove skin, fat, and bones from chicken breasts and cut into 1-inch chunks.

2. *Tarragon Cream Vinaigrette:* Place chopped garlic in mixing bowl or chop finely with several on/off pulses in workbowl of food processor fitted with steel knife. Add egg and egg yolk, mustard, vinegar, tarragon wine vinegar, tarragon, salt, and pepper, and stir or process to mix. Combine oils in a glass measure with a pouring spout and gradually add in a thin stream into the bowl or through feed tube of processor and mix or process until mixture is thoroughly blended. Mixture will thicken slightly. Add crème fraîche and chives and stir or process to mix. Taste to adjust seasoning if necessary.

3. In a large mixing bowl combine chicken and blanched broccoli. Add enough dressing to coat and toss very gently. Taste to adjust seasoning for salt, pepper, and herbs if necessary. Any leftover dressing can be stored in a screw-top jar and refrigerated.

4. Before serving, transfer the salad to a large glass serving bowl, being careful to have an even distribution of the chicken and broccoli. Perky pieces of broccoli should peek through creamy chunks of chicken. Garnish with a sprinkle of chopped hazelnuts. A tall glass trifle bowl is well suited to the presentation of this dish.

To Prepare Ahead
Follow steps 1 through 3 up to one day ahead. Refrigerate, covered in a suitable container. Complete step 4 just before serving.

Hint: After you trim the chicken, return the bones to the court bouillon and simmer, cover ajar, for one hour. Strain and use for stock. Can be refrigerated two to three days, or frozen in a suitable container.

ENDIVE AND GRAPEFRUIT SALAD WITH MUSTARD VINAIGRETTE

Arlene Battifarano is a multitalented cooking teacher at Cooktique and has offered this perfect wintertime salad as an accompaniment to lighten a heavy meal.

½–¾ pounds endive
2 grapefruit, sectioned (pink, if available)
2 teaspoons finely chopped fresh chives, or Italian flat-leaf parsley if chives are unavailable

Mustard Vinaigrette
1 clove garlic, finely chopped
½ teaspoon dry mustard
1 teaspoon Dijon mustard
1 hard-cooked-egg yolk, sieved

½ teaspoon fresh lemon juice
2 tablespoons tarragon vinegar
½ teaspoon coarse (kosher) salt
Freshly ground pepper
⅛ teaspoon sugar
2 tablespoons light, fruity olive oil
4 tablespoons vegetable oil
¼ cup light cream

Serves 6–8

1. Separate the leaves of endive and wash thoroughly by soaking in a bowl of cold water. Drain in a colander and pat dry with paper towels or a clean kitchen towel.

2. With a thin, sharp paring knife, remove the skin and pith of the grapefruit so that no white remains. Carefully cut down between the membranes and lift out the sections, keeping them whole.

3. *Mustard Vinaigrette:* Place chopped garlic in a mixing bowl or chop finely with several on/off pulses in workbowl of food processor fitted with steel knife. Add mustards, egg yolk, lemon juice, vinegar, and seasonings, and stir or process to mix. Combine oils in a glass measure with a pouring spout and gradually add in a thin stream into the bowl or through feed tube and mix or process until mixture is thoroughly blended. Add the cream and stir to mix. Taste to adjust seasonings. Can be made ahead to this point.

4. *To Serve:* Choose a shallow attractive glass salad bowl or a round serving platter. Arrange the endive one by one standing or resting close together around the sides of the serving piece. Place grapefruit sections

in a mound in the center of the dish. Spoon some of the dressing over the grapefruit sections and sprinkle with chives. Remaining dressing can be passed at the table, served in a small pitcher.

To Prepare Ahead
Follow steps 1 through 3 up to one day ahead. Refrigerate separately in suitable containers. Complete step 4 up to one hour before serving.

POACHED LEEKS VINAIGRETTE

Leeks are not just for stockpots.

8 leeks about 1 inch thick
2 tablespoons unsalted butter
Salt and freshly ground
     white pepper

Dressing
2 cloves garlic, finely
     chopped
¼ cup Dijon mustard
¼ teaspoon coarse (kosher)
     salt
Freshly ground pepper

⅓ cup imported red wine
     vinegar
⅔ cup light, fruity olive oil
Sliced radishes and parsley
     sprigs for garnish

Have on Hand
12-inch skillet or Dutch
     sauté pan
Cake rack

Serves 8

1. Trim off root end of each leek. Remove any outer soft bruised layers of leek and discard. Cut off and discard tough green leaves (good for stockpot) at top of the still tender light green portion just above white. Insert a paring knife into center and lift it right up through top. Then, holding top together cut down to split the leek in two. To clean: fan leek halves one at a time under cold running water until all the sand is removed, then reform layers. Place in a 12-inch skillet or sauté pan and add enough water to barely cover them.

2. Place thin slices of butter on water's surface. Season with a sprinkling of salt and white pepper. Bring to a boil over high heat, then reduce heat and simmer 10–12 minutes or until tender. Do not overcook. If leeks are not of equal size, remove them as they are done. Keep halves intact and drain on a cake rack over paper towels to cool.

3. *Dressing:* Place chopped garlic in mixing bowl or chop finely with several on/off pulses in workbowl of food processor fitted with steel knife. Add mustard, salt, pepper, and vinegar, and stir or process to mix. Gradually add oil in a thin stream into the bowl or through feed tube and whisk or process to mix until mixture is thoroughly blended. Taste to adjust seasoning if necessary.

4. Place two halves of leek side by side, cut side down, on a salad plate. Spoon some sauce over the center of the vegetable, letting it fall onto the plate. Garnish with radish slices and parsley sprigs. Arrange remaining plates with leeks and garnish. Serve at room temperature.

To Prepare Ahead
Follow steps 1 through 3 up to one day ahead. Refrigerate leeks and dressing separately. Complete step 4 just before serving.

MEDITERRANEAN EGGPLANT CAVIAR

One of my mother's frequent surprises. This is a rustic appetizer and deserves a simple setting. Pile in an attractive pottery dish or crock and serve with thin slices of toasted French bread.

1 large or 2 medium
    eggplants
2 medium-large red peppers
    (or green if red is not
    available)
1 red onion, finely chopped
2–3 cloves garlic, finely
    chopped
2 tablespoons balsamic
    vinegar
4–5 tablespoons vegetable
    oil

½ teaspoon coarse (kosher)
    salt
Freshly ground pepper to
    taste
2 tablespoons finely chopped
    Italian flat-leaf parsley
Sprigs of curly parsley for
    garnish
French Croutons or crisp
    crackers

Serves 10–12

Preheat broiler.
1. Slice eggplant and peppers in half lengthwise. Prick eggplant skin with a fork and place both vegetables cut side down on a foil-lined cookie sheet.

2. Broil 4–5 inches from the source of heat. Peppers will cook in 6–7 minutes or until skin bubbles and chars. Transfer to brown paper bag. Close tightly and let stand a minute or two to capture the steam before peeling. Eggplant will take 5–7 minutes longer. Remove as they are done.

3. Remove skin from peppers and eggplant while still warm, as they will peel more easily. Clean pepper halves of all seeds and trim vegetable well. With a chef's knife, cut pepper halves into strips then into small dice. Set aside. Spoon eggplant pulp into a mixing bowl and mash with a fork until chunky.

4. In the meantime, soak chopped onion in a bowl of cold water for 15 minutes. Drain well and transfer to a clean kitchen towel. Wrap ends of towel around onion and squeeze out as much excess moisture as possible.

5. Add onion and red pepper to eggplant and stir to mix. Season with garlic, vinegar, oil, salt, pepper, and Italian parsley, and toss. Taste to adjust seasoning if necessary. Spoon into a serving dish and mound neatly. Just before ready to serve, garnish with a ring of curly parsley and several additional sprigs centered on top of the eggplant mixture. Serve with French croutons or crisp crackers.

To Prepare Ahead
Follow steps 1 through 5 up to several days ahead. Refrigerate, covered, in suitable container. Bring to room temperature, transfer to serving bowl, and garnish before serving.

MUSHROOMS AND CELERY ITALIAN STYLE

½ pound fresh mushrooms
1 tablespoon lemon juice
2 ribs celery, tender inner
   ribs
½ pound mozzarella cheese

Vinaigrette
1 clove garlic, finely
   chopped
½ teaspoon coarse (kosher)
   salt

2 tablespoons finely chopped
   Italian flat-leaf parsley
Dash or two Tabasco sauce
2 tablespoons fresh lemon
   juice
3 tablespoons imported
   Italian olive oil

Watercress for garnish

Serves 8–10

1. Cut and discard woody stem ends from the mushrooms, then rinse quickly in a colander under a spray of cool water. Pour boiling water over the mushrooms, then transfer to a clean kitchen towel and pat dry to absorb excess moisture. Slice mushrooms into thin, even slices, then stack and cut into julienne strips. Sprinkle lemon juice over the mushrooms to prevent discoloration and toss lightly. Set aside.

2. Rinse celery clean; trim off and discard bottom edge and branched tops. With vegetable peeler, remove and discard strings. Cut ribs into 2-inch lengths, then stack and cut into julienne strips. Add to mushrooms.

3. Slice mozzarella about ⅛ inch thick or as thin as possible. Stack several slices at a time, cut into julienne strips, and add to mushrooms and celery in a mixing bowl.

4. *Vinaigrette:* Place chopped garlic in a mixing bowl or chop finely with several on/off pulses in workbowl of food processor fitted with steel knife. Add salt, parsley, Tabasco, and lemon juice, and stir or process to mix. Gradually add oil in a thin stream into the bowl or through feed tube and mix or process until mixture is thoroughly blended. Taste to adjust seasoning. Vinaigrette should have a piquant flavor.

5. Add dressing to ingredients in mixing bowl and toss to mix. Transfer to a serving dish and mound neatly. Garnish with a ring of crisp watercress.

To Prepare Ahead
Follow steps 1 through 5 up to two days ahead. Cover with plastic wrap and refrigerate. Garnish with watercress just before serving.

MELON SALAD VINAIGRETTE

An unusual but colorful combination with the fresh taste of summer.

1 melon (cantaloupe or
    honeydew)
1 cucumber, rinsed and very
    thinly sliced
1 pound cherry tomatoes,
    peeled
Coarse (kosher) salt

Herb Vinaigrette
1½ teaspoons finely chopped
    Italian flat-leaf parsley
2 tablespoons chopped fresh
    mint leaves
1½ teaspoons snipped chives
1½ teaspoons fresh thyme
    leaves *or* ½ teaspoon
    dried

½ teaspoon coarse (kosher)
    salt
Freshly ground pepper
1 teaspoon Dijon mustard
½ teaspoon Worcestershire
    sauce
2 tablespoons white wine
    vinegar
⅓ cup light, fruity olive oil

Have on Hand
Melon-ball scoop

Serves 6–8

1. Halve melon; remove and discard seeds. With melon scoop make melon balls. Transfer to a strainer over a bowl and set aside to drain.

2. Spread cucumber slices in a single layer on a large dinner plate (you may need two). Sprinkle lightly with salt. Cover with another plate and refrigerate weighted down with something heavy from your refrigerator. Let stand at least one hour so cucumbers will exude juices. Rinse and drain cucumbers in a colander, then transfer to a clean kitchen towel to absorb excess moisture and set aside.

3. Plunge cherry tomatoes into a saucepan of boiling water 8–10 seconds, working with a few at a time. Watch timing carefully so tomatoes do not soften and lose their shape. Remove with slotted spoon and slip off skins with the tip of a paring knife.

4. Combine melon balls, cucumber slices, and cherry tomatoes in a mixing bowl. If you leave it standing for several hours or overnight, be sure to drain off and discard accumulated liquid from bowl. It is important that ingredients be as dry as possible, or they will water down vinaigrette.

5. *Herb Vinaigrette:* In a mixing bowl or in workbowl of food processor fitted with steel knife, combine all ingredients except oil and stir or process to mix. Gradually add oil in a thin stream into the bowl

or through feed tube and mix or process until mixture is thoroughly blended. Taste to adjust seasoning. Can be made ahead to this point.

6. Shortly before serving, combine vinaigrette with fruits and toss lightly to mix. Transfer to an attractive serving bowl.

To Prepare Ahead
Follow steps 1 through 5 up to one day ahead. Refrigerate the combined melon, tomatoes, and cucumbers in a covered container and refrigerate vinaigrette separately in a screw-top jar. Complete step 6 up to one hour before serving.

FRENCH POTATO SALAD

An inspiration from Simone Beck—not your ordinary potato salad. The crisp greens afloat above the creamy potato slices give the dish a light and airy feeling and an eye-appealing charm. I leave the skins on the potatoes because they hold together and taste better in their jackets, and further enhance the appearance of the dish.

Vinaigrette
2 tablespoons Dijon mustard
2 tablespoons red wine
      vinegar
1 tablespoon tarragon
      vinegar
2–3 tablespoons fresh
      tarragon leaves *or* 1
      teaspoon dried
2 teaspoons snipped fresh
      chives (optional)
2 teaspoons fresh chervil
      leaves (optional)
¾ teaspoon coarse (kosher)
      salt
Freshly ground pepper
¼ cup light, fruity olive oil
¼ cup vegetable oil
1–2 tablespoons Crème
      Fraîche
2 tablespoons cold milk

Salad
2½ pounds new red potatoes
Coarse (kosher) salt
2–3 tablespoons thinly sliced
      white and light green
      of scallions
1 large clove garlic, finely
      chopped
4–5 tablespoons dry white
      wine

To Finish
1 bunch chicory
⅓ cup niçoise olives
1½ tablespoons red wine
      vinegar
3–4 tablespoons light, fruity
      olive oil

Serves 8–10

1. In a mixing bowl or in workbowl of food processor, combine mustard, vinegar, water, and seasonings. Whisk or process to mix. Combine oils in a glass measure with a pouring spout. Gradually add oil in a thin stream into the bowl or through food tube of processor and mix or process until mixture is thoroughly blended. Add crème fraîche and finally the cold milk, which will bind the mixture. Process to mix. Mixture will thicken like a mayonnaise. Taste to adjust seasoning if necessary.

2. Scrub potatoes in their jackets and place in plenty of salted boiling water to cover. Cook, covered for 15 to 20 minutes, or until tender but not falling apart when pierced with a knife. Drain in a colander, and while still warm cut into ½-inch slices. Place in mixing bowl and sprinkle over the white wine. With hands, mix carefully to coat with the wine. Allow potatoes to marinate for about an hour at room temperature to absorb the liquid. Turn occasionally.

3. Add vinaigrette, scallions, and garlic to sliced potatoes, and toss gently to coat. Cover and chill until ready to serve.

4. *To Serve:* Wash greens well and spin dry. Place potato salad in a clear salad bowl. Top with a layer of crisp greens (do not toss through potatoes). Scatter olives on the greens, then sprinkle lightly with additional vinegar and oil.

To Prepare Ahead
Follow steps 1 through 3 up to two days ahead. Refrigerate, covered in a suitable container. Greens can be washed and stored separately in refrigerator up to one day ahead. Complete step 4 just before serving.

ROASTED PEPPERS VINAIGRETTE WITH FRENCH CROUTONS

2 red bell peppers
2 green bell peppers
2 yellow bell peppers

Vinaigrette
1 large clove garlic, finely
    chopped
1 teaspoon Dijon mustard
2 teaspoons fresh basil
    leaves *or* ½ teaspoon
    dried
¼ teaspoon coarse (kosher)
    salt

Freshly ground pepper
1 tablespoon imported red
    wine vinegar
3 tablespoons light, fruity
    olive oil

French Croutons

Clumps of curly parsley and
    tiny black niçoise
    olives, for garnish

Serves 6–8

Preheat broiler.

1. Place peppers on a foil-lined cookie sheet and broil about three inches from source of heat until skins blister and blacken. Move peppers around as necessary, to char evenly on all sides, about 15 minutes. Transfer peppers to a brown paper bag, close tightly, and let stand a minute or two to capture the steam. Remove peppers while still warm and peel them over a bowl to catch the juices. Strain juices for vinaigrette and set aside. Remove heavy stems and seeds from peppers, then cut into thin julienne strips. Set aside.

2. *Vinaigrette:* Place chopped garlic in a mixing bowl or chop finely with several on/off pulses in workbowl of food processor fitted with steel knife. Add mustard, basil, salt, pepper, vinegar, and reserved juices, and stir or process to mix. Gradually add oil in a thin stream into the bowl or through feed tube and mix or process until mixture is thoroughly blended. Taste to adjust seasoning.

3. Pour dressing over peppers and toss gently to mix. Refrigerate and marinate, covered, for several hours or overnight.

4. Spread a small amount of pepper mixture on the French croutons and arrange on a platter. Garnish with little clumps of parsley and niçoise olives in the spaces between the croutons.

To Prepare Ahead
Follow steps 1 through 3 up to one day ahead. Refrigerate, covered in

suitable container. Keep croutons crisp and fresh in a cookie tin or wrapped in a clean towel in breadbox. Complete step 4 before serving.

MARINATED BRUSSELS SPROUTS

A sprightly hors d'oeuvre with thanks to Bonnie Barnes, friend and cooking teacher, who served it to me some years ago.

1 container fresh Brussels
    sprouts in season
Coarse (kosher) salt for
    cooking water
3–4 shallots, finely chopped
1 large clove garlic, finely
    chopped
2 teaspoons fresh tarragon
    leaves *or* ½ teaspoon
    dried

1 teaspoon coarse (kosher)
    salt
Freshly ground pepper
½ cup tarragon vinegar
¼ cup vegetable oil
1½ teaspoons Dijon mustard

Serves 6–8

1. Thoroughly rinse Brussels sprouts, trim off stem ends and loose leaves. Cut a shallow cross in the stem end and soak in salted water for about 15 minutes.

2. Drain Brussels sprouts and cook in boiling salted water to cover 15–18 minutes or until tender. Drain and refresh, fan or rinse quickly under a spray of cold water. Transfer to a clean kitchen towel and pat dry. Let cool completely and set aside.

3. Combine shallots, garlic, tarragon, salt, pepper, vinegar, and oil in a noncorrosive saucepan. Stir to mix and bring to the edge of a boil. Reduce heat and with cover ajar gently simmer the mixture for 10 minutes. Remove from heat, stir in mustard, and allow to cool.

4. Place Brussels sprouts in a glass or ceramic mixing bowl, pour on marinade, and gently fold in to coat sprouts. Can be made up to several weeks ahead. Refrigerate covered and serve at room temperature.

To Prepare Ahead
Follow steps 1 through 4 up to two weeks ahead. Refrigerate, covered, and serve at room temperature.

PINEAPPLE JELLY SALAD

2 cups canned pineapple
  juice
½ cup orange juice (fresh or
  frozen concentrate)
½ cup dry white wine
1 tablespoon white wine
  vinegar
6 tablespoons cold water
2 envelopes unflavored
  gelatin
1 can (1 pound, 4 ounces)
  pineapple cubes or
  crushed pineapple,
  drained

Dressing
6 ounces cream cheese,
  softened
½ cup light cream
¼ teaspoon coarse (kosher)
  salt
Freshly ground pepper

1 bunch watercress for
  garnish

Serves 8–10

1. In a mixing bowl, combine pineapple juice, orange juice, white wine, and vinegar. Set aside.

2. Place 6 tablespoons cold water in a small saucepan and sprinkle on the gelatin. Let stand 3–5 minutes until gelatin has absorbed the liquid. Do not stir. Dissolve gelatin by shaking saucepan slowly over low heat until it becomes a clear liquid and granules can no longer be seen. Pour immediately into combined juices and stir vigorously to mix well.

3. Drain pineapple cubes or crushed pineapple. (Discard or reserve liquid for other purpose.) Add pineapple pieces to the liquid-gelatin mixture and pour into a 1½-quart mold or individual aspic molds. Refrigerate overnight or several hours until set.

4. *Dressing:* Rest a wire strainer over a mixing bowl and with tips of fingers, push cream cheese through strainer as well as possible, scraping off the underside into the bowl with a rubber spatula. Beat cream into the cream cheese a little at a time with a wire whisk. Add salt and pepper and taste to adjust seasoning if necessary. Pour dressing into a small pitcher or pretty glass dish for serving.

5. *To Unmold:* Run an ordinary kitchen knife carefully around the inside of the mold, then dip mold into a bowl of warm water for no more than 5–10 seconds. Remove to test if gelatin has loosened from mold by giving it a quick shake. You can feel if gelatin is ready to unmold. It may need to be returned to the warm water for a second or

two. Place serving platter or individual dishes on top and invert to unmold. Garnish with watercress. Pass the dressing to spoon out over individual servings.

To Prepare Ahead
Follow steps 1 through 4 up to two days ahead. Cover mold with plastic wrap and place dressing in a covered container and refrigerate. Complete step 5 up to several hours before serving and refrigerate until ready to serve.

RADICCHIO, LEEK, AND CHÈVRE SALAD

2 heads radicchio or red-
   tipped leaf lettuce
1 leek, trimmed, white part
   only
½ pound aged domestic
   chèvre

1–2 shallots, finely chopped
3–3½ tablespoons imported
   raspberry vinegar
½ cup walnut oil

Serves 8

1. Gently unfurl leaves from the tight heads of radicchio one by one. Rinse and place in a salad spinner in batches. Transfer to a large glass or pottery salad bowl and set aside.

2. Cut white part of leek in half lengthwise. Place in a bowl of cold water and let soak 10–15 minutes, keeping halves intact. When they are thoroughly cleaned, remove from water and place on cutting board, flat side down. With a sharp knife, carefully cut lengthwise into very thin julienne strips. Set aside.

3. Cut chèvre into slices about ¼ inch thick and set aside.

4. *To Prepare Dressing:* Place shallots in a mixing bowl. Add vinegar and stir to mix. Gradually whisk in oil in a slow, steady stream until mixture is smooth. Toss radicchio leaves with dressing to coat evenly.

5. *To Serve:* Divide radicchio leaves equally on 8 salad plates. Arrange julienne leek strips over the center of the radicchio and top with a slice of chèvre. Plates can be arranged up to ½ hour before serving.

To Prepare Ahead
Follow steps 1 through 3 up to several hours ahead. Refrigerate ingredients separately. Dressing can be prepared up to several hours ahead and left standing at room temperature. Complete steps 4 and 5 before serving.

SALADE MESCLUN

Remembering . . . one wonderful week spent in St. Tropez several years ago. It seems wherever I went for luncheon or supper, this glorious salad was being served. Mesclun comes from the niçois word mecla, *meaning "to mix." This is a strong, bitter, invigorating salad made from mixing dandelion, arugula, parsley, watercress, endive, etc. It is special when topped with poached eggs as a main luncheon or supper dish.*

1 medium head chicory, or dandelion when available washed, spin-dried, and broken into pieces

1 bunch arugula, washed, spin-dried, and root ends trimmed off

1 bunch watercress, washed, spin-dried, and trimmed, heavy stems removed

½ pound endive, rinsed, patted dry, and sliced into ½-inch rounds

1¼ pounds salt pork

Day-old narrow French bread or firm white bread to be cut into chapons (a rectangular crouton)

Vinaigrette

3 large cloves garlic, finely chopped

1 teaspoon coarse (kosher) salt

Freshly ground pepper

3–4 teaspoons Dijon mustard

4 tablespoons imported red wine vinegar

Enough light, fruity olive oil that combined with rendered grease from salt pork will equal about ¾ cup

Serves 12–14 as a side salad or about 8 for a luncheon or supper dish

1. Prepare greens according to individual instructions and set aside. As you finish working with each type of greens, wrap in paper towels and slip into plastic bag. Refrigerate until ready to serve.

2. Cut rind off salt pork, slice into strips, then cut into ½-inch dice. Sauté in skillet until all fat is rendered. With slotted spoon, remove crisped salt pork and drain on paper towels. Strain and reserve rendered grease for use in salad dressing. Yields about ⅓–½ cup. Set aside.

3. To make chapons with French bread, cut bread into ½-inch slices, then into rectangles. If white bread is used, remove and discard crusts. Cut each slice into four equal strips. Place enough oil in a skillet to come about 1½ inches up the sides to deep-fry chapons. Cook the strips quickly in hot fat until golden brown on both sides, working with several at a time. Remove with slotted spoon and drain on paper towels to dry. Set aside.

4. *Vinaigrette:* Place chopped garlic in a mixing bowl or chop finely with several on/off pulses in workbowl of food processor fitted with steel knife. Add salt, pepper, mustard, and vinegar, and stir or process to mix. Gradually add combined oil and bacon grease in a thin stream into the bowl or through feed tube and mix or process until mixture is thoroughly blended. Taste to adjust seasoning. Dressing should have a garlicky and mustard flavor.

5. Just before serving, combine greens, crisped salt pork and chapons, pour over vinaigrette, and toss with abandon to mix very well.

To Prepare Ahead

Follow steps 1 through 4 up to one day ahead. Refrigerate greens as specified. Refrigerate salt port in suitable covered container. Wrap croutons in a clean kitchen towel and store in breadbox or food storage bag. Refrigerate vinaigrette in a screw-top jar. *Note:* Vinaigrette will solidify because of the rendered grease. Bring to room temperature and stir to mix very well before adding to the salad. Salt pork should also be brought to room temperature and stirred with a fork to separate before adding to the salad.

SALADE DE CHAMPIGNONS

A quick and delicious salad to satisfy without fattening. Buy firm, blemish-free mushrooms for maximum flavor.

¾ pound fresh mushrooms
2 tablespoons fresh lemon
   juice

Dressing
2–3 shallots, finely chopped
1 egg yolk
2 teaspoons Dijon mustard
½ teaspoon coarse (kosher)
   salt

Freshly ground pepper
¼ teaspoon sugar
1½ tablespoons white wine
   vinegar
⅓ cup light, fruity olive oil

Watercress, washed and
   spin-dried, for garnish
   (optional)

Serves 4–6

1. Cut and discard woody stem ends from mushrooms, then rinse them quickly in a colander under cold running water. Transfer to a clean kitchen towel and gently pat dry. Slice mushrooms about ⅛ inch thick and place in a mixing bowl. Sprinkle, then toss, with lemon juice to prevent discoloration and set aside.

2. Place chopped shallots in the mixing bowl or chop finely in workbowl of food processor fitted with steel knife. Add egg yolk, mustard, salt, pepper, sugar, and wine vinegar. Whisk or process to mix. Gradually add oil in a thin stream into the bowl or through feed tube of processor and whisk or process to mix until mixture is thoroughly blended.

3. Pour dressing over mushrooms and toss gently to coat thoroughly. Taste to adjust seasonings if necessary. Arrange crisp watercress on a serving plate and mound mushrooms on watercress. Serve at room temperature. I frequently serve the mushrooms as an appetizer on a cocktail buffet along with smoked salmon slices, wedges of hard-cooked eggs, and radish roses.

To Prepare Ahead
Follow steps 1 through 3 up to several hours ahead. Cover loosely with plastic wrap and refrigerate. Bring to room temperature before serving.

BASIC FRENCH DRESSING

In cooking class I always advise my students that a basic French dressing consists of nothing more than vinegar, oil, and some seasoning mixed in—usually just salt and pepper. It can be further enhanced by the addition of Dijon mustard and some finely chopped garlic or shallots. This dressing has absolutely no relation to the gloppy pink mess that comes pouring out of a bottle. It's quick and easy to make. Just be sure to use a good wine vinegar and a first-class oil. The ratio of oil to vinegar is generally three parts oil to one part vinegar.

1 teaspoon finely chopped
    garlic or shallots
2 teaspoons Dijon mustard
Dash coarse (kosher) salt
Freshly ground pepper

1 tablespoon imported red
    wine vinegar
3 tablespoons light, fruity
    olive oil

1. In a mixing bowl combine the garlic or shallots with mustard, salt, pepper, and vinegar, and with a fork or a whisk stir to mix. Gradually whisk in oil in a slow, steady stream until mixture is thoroughly blended. Taste to adjust seasoning if necessary.

To Prepare Ahead
If necessary, prepare dressing up to several hours ahead. Dressing can be kept at room temperature in a covered jar until just before serving on crisp young greens.

CRÈME FRAÎCHE AND ITS DELICIOUS VERSATILITY

Crème fraîche is a thick, silky, matured double cream. My love for crème fraîche intensifies each time I use it and I am continuously amazed at its great versatility. I have found that it is a wonderful substitute for heavy cream in the sauce for Fettuccine alla Panna, and a tablespoon or two is a superb way to enrich a classic sauce. When it is poured on summer berries or poached winter fruits, its tangy flavor satisfies so much more than the heavy sweetness of plain whipped cream. It can also add delightfully unexpected smoothness to the taste and texture of a vinaigrette or classic mousseline.

In fact, crème fraîche can be used in almost any way that cream is used in a recipe. It whips beautifully and has a shelf life of up to three weeks when refrigerated. When making crème fraîche, it is best to use pasteurized cream, since ultra-pasteurized will take longer to thicken and will not produce the acidity so necessary to the product. Constant reminders to the dairy manager at your food market that you prefer pasteurized cream to ultra-pasteurized may encourage him to stock it. In addition, do not use low-fat buttermilk, since proper fat content is essential to ingredient reactions.

In order to achieve the same nutty flavor and pouring consistency of the French version of our heavy whipping cream, we must allow heavy cream combined with either buttermilk or sour cream to ferment and thicken naturally as it matures. Crème fraîche is ideal to cook with, as it will not curdle or separate.

To Make Crème Fraîche: Combine 2 cups heavy cream with 3 tablespoons active-culture buttermilk (I prefer this to sour cream) in a saucepan and stir until the mixture is smoothly blended; then heat to lukewarm (65–80 degrees). Be careful not to overheat, or mixture will break down. Warming the liquids together acts as a starter, which causes the mixture to clot and aids the process of fermentation. Pour into a wide-mouth screw-top jar and cover. Let stand, unrefrigerated, 24–36 hours, until surface has thickened. Remove cover and stir mixture with a wooden spoon. Then store in the refrigerator until ready to use. This simple formula makes a good facsimile of French crème fraîche.

A recent introduction into the gourmet market is a cultured-food cooker called Solait. It can be used to make a more remarkably flavored crème fraîche, as well as to prepare yogurt and diet and cooking cheeses. Included are full instructions for preparing cultured foods, a thick insulating plastic shell into which the large screw-top jar fits for incubation, and a thermometer. For now I will just concentrate on crème fraîche. The directions on the instruction sheet suggest that you add 2 tablespoons cultured buttermilk to 4 cups heavy cream and mix well. I use 3 cups heavy cream and 5 tablespoons buttermilk. Place heavy cream in sauce pan, clip thermometer to side of pan, and heat to lukewarm (80 degrees). It is essential that you do not overheat the cream. Remove from heat, unclip thermometer, and stir in 5 tablespoons buttermilk. Pour liquid into screw-top jar provided and place it in Solait cooker. Let it sit undisturbed 18–24 hours. Uncover screw-top jar, stir contents with a wooden spoon, cover, and refrigerate. The results a day or two later are exceptional.

MAYONNAISE

Don't think of this as a recipe. After you have prepared it once or twice and realize how simple it is to prepare and how high the quality of its taste and texture, it will become a habit. You'll never go back to the commercial variety again.

1 whole egg
1 egg yolk
½–¾ teaspoon coarse
    (kosher) salt
Freshly ground pepper
1 teaspoon Dijon mustard

1 teaspoon fresh lemon juice
½ cup vegetable oil
½ cup imported light, fruity
    olive oil
2 teaspoons imported red
    wine vinegar

Yield 1½ cups

Note: Have all ingredients at room temperature.

1. In workbowl of food processor fitted with steel knife or blender, combine whole egg, egg yolk, salt, pepper, mustard, and lemon juice, and process or blend about 10 seconds.

2. Pour oil into a liquid measure. With machine running, start adding oil from a tablespoon at first, dribbling it in drop by drop through feed tube of processor or into blender. After you have added 3–4 tablespoons of oil, add remaining oil by pouring it in, in a slow, steady stream until the emulsion of the eggs and oil is complete and the mayonnaise has thickened.

3. Remove cover from processor or blender, add wine vinegar, replace cover, and process or blend just until vinegar is blended. Turn off machine, and when blade has completely stopped turning, taste mayonnaise to adjust the seasoning if necessary. Transfer sauce to a screw-top jar, cleaning out the bowl as well as possible with a rubber spatula. If some of the thickened mayonnaise is sticking tenaciously to the blade and the bottom of the bowl, run the machine briefly. This will clean the blade for easy removal, then scoop out the remaining mayonnaise from bottom of bowl with rubber spatula. Refrigerate, covered, up to 10 days in cool weather or a week in warm weather.

To Prepare Ahead
Follow steps 1 through 3 up to ten days ahead. Cover and refrigerate.

SCALLION FLOWERS

1 or 2 bunches scallions

1. Remove any bruised and soft outer leaves from scallions and discard. Cut away and discard darker green ends of scallions just above the white and pale green portion.

2. Hold root end in one hand and with the sharp side of a paring knife facing upward, insert the knife into the white of the scallion above the root and cut through the light green top. The layered leaves will spread a bit. Now give the scallion a half turn and repeat procedure so that you have made four slits away from the root end. Repeat with remaining scallions. I frequently leave the root ends on—they're kind of fun.

3. Half fill a mixing bowl with water and several ice cubes. Drop bulbs into the bowl as you prepare them. In a little while scallions will open and flower at cut end.

To Prepare Ahead
Follow steps 1 through 3 up to one day ahead. Refrigerate in bowl of ice water covered with plastic wrap. Drain and pat dry before using.

TOMATO ROSE

A tomato rose is created by cutting a continuous spiral of skin from around the tomato, starting with a cap from the base of the tomato. The length of peel is rolled up to sit in the cap base, opening to form a rose garnish.

1 large, firm red tomato

1. Hold tomato in one hand, core end into palm. With sharp paring knife, slit into the skin at base of tomato and cut a caplike circle. As you cut around, to create a cap, come away from the point where you began and continue to cut in a spiral for as long as you can go with your knife. If knife slips off, breaking skin before you are done, cut another strip from where the first one ended and continue to peel until you get as much spiral from the tomato as possible. Paring knife will cut approximate ½-inch-wide strips.

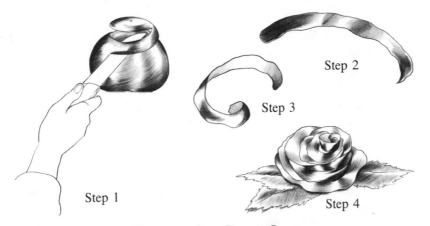

How to make a Tomato Rose

2. Stand cap of tomato on a flat surface and curl the attached end around and around to form the outer leaf of the rose. Roll up the second spiral tightly as though you were rolling a length of tape measure and fit it into the center of base. If a third spiral has been cut, roll tightly and tuck into very center of base.

3. Do not cut tomato rose more than several hours ahead, or it will dry out. If necessary, slip into a plastic bag and refrigerate until ready to use.

SKORDALIA

I will never forget the first time I tasted Frankie Hazan's skordalia. It was a warm, clear, sunny day many summers ago and my parents were having a barbecue. Frankie, a distant relative, arrived with a jar of skordalia—a thick, smooth, garlicky sauce. I marveled at the taste of the steak, tinged with this pungent, creamy sauce. Perhaps it was then that I decided to carve out a career in food. Skordalia, incidentally, is extremely well suited to almost any grilled meat—and even some fish dishes.

1 10-ounce loaf Italian bread
6–8 medium garlic cloves,
    finely chopped
1½ teaspoons coarse
    (kosher) salt

Freshly ground pepper
1 egg
3–4 tablespoons fresh lemon
    juice
½ cup vegetable oil

Yield 2 cups

1. Cut bread into 3 or 4 sections with a serrated bread knife and carefully remove crusts. (Crusts can be toasted in a moderate oven, then processed into bread crumbs.) Tear the soft white bread into small pieces, yielding about 4 cups, and place in a mixing bowl. Pour over enough cold water to moisten, then tip the bowl into the sink and pour off excess water. Press down gently on the bread to extract more liquid and pour liquid out. Allow bread to remain moist; be sure, however, to pour off as much water as possible. Set aside.

2. Place chopped garlic in a mixing bowl or chop finely in workbowl of food processor fitted with steel knife. (There is quite a bit of garlic to chop. If using a food processor, scrape down sides of workbowl with a rubber spatula as necessary to mince garlic fine.) Add bread, then salt, pepper, egg, and lemon juice. Stir or process to mix. Add oil to bowl in a slow, steady stream or through feed tube of processor and mix or process until thick and smooth. Pour into a serving bowl and serve with grilled meats.

To Prepare Ahead
Follow steps 1 and 2 up to one week ahead. Refrigerate, covered in a suitable container, until ready to use.

3

VEGETABLES
ARE
BEAUTIFUL

Americans are rediscovering vegetables. Lessons in buying, preparing, and serving vegetables are perhaps the most popular ones in my cooking school.

There is definitely a new awareness of less familiar vegetables, and imaginative cooks are finding wondrous new ways to handle old favorites. How gratifying it is to know that we no longer need be subjected to "peas and carrots." Today the range of vegetables available to us both in season and out provides us with delicious tastes and interesting textures along with the added benefits of nutritious, low-calorie food.

Selecting vegetables is mostly visual and tactile. Be choosy at the marketplace and trust your senses, selecting vegetables as close to their natural state as possible. If vegetables look, feel, and smell good, they are probably fresh. It's best to shop in markets where high turnover helps assure freshness. In addition, let your choice of vegetables be decided by the season. Not only will you have the best to choose from, but purchases will be more economical.

Artichokes: Compact, heavy whole artichokes with tight green leaves make an appealing first course when served with a vinaigrette sauce or a flowerlike addition to a blanched Crudité Basket. They are pretty to look at and it's fun to pick off the leaves for dipping. They are easier to prepare for cooking if left whole than if you take time to prepare hearts and bottoms.

When ready to cook, use a sharp stainless paring knife to cut off the stem end evenly so artichoke can stand, leaving about a ½-inch stub. Starting at the open leaves near the base, remove and discard any bruised tough leaves. With scissors, cut off the tips of each leaf, spiraling the vegetable. Near the top of the artichoke, the leaves cling very tightly. Lay the vegetable on its side and with a knife make a sharp, straight cut about 1 inch from the top. Rub the exposed cut surfaces with the cut side of a lemon or dip into acidulated water (lemon juice and water) to prevent discoloration.

Place artichokes side by side in a deep saucepan just large enough to hold them in one layer. Pour in enough water to come about ⅔ of the way up the sides. Drizzle in 1 tablespoon vegetable oil and about 2 tablespoons lemon juice, dropping in the squeezed lemon half or halves as well. Bring to a boil over high heat, uncovered, adjust heat, then cook at a brisk simmer 35–50 minutes (according to size) until tender. Be careful not to overcook or artichokes will be soggy. Test for doneness by pulling off a leaf. If it releases easily, artichoke is cooked. With a slotted spoon, remove artichokes and turn upside down on a rack over a dish to drain. When cool, serve whole.

If using as artichoke bottoms, pull off outer leaves from uncooked artichokes until only center cones of tender, yellow-tipped leaves remain. Scoop out fuzzy heavy chokes and hard-tipped purple leaves with a spoon, then trim around the base until it is smooth and rounded, rubbing cut edges with cut side of lemon. A helpful hint: Use a serrated grapefruit spoon for removing chokes.

Asparagus: I adore it! Great joy springs up inside of me when I see them at the market. I don't like to do very much with them, since I enjoy them in their natural state. This allows their true delicate flavor to be enjoyed.

Choose asparagus that have compact, closed tips, making sure there is as much rich green color as possible along the length of the stalk. Ideally, try to match the thickness of the stalks as well. If the spears are ridged and flabby, they are old and shouldn't be purchased. Although an abundance of asparagus on your greengrocer shelves is a sure sign of spring, asparagus can be purchased at premium prices at other times of the year. Nothing, however, can match the first tender stalks of the season for flavor and texture.

Thick asparagus, rather than thin, are preferred by asparagus growers. They can be just as tender as small ones, yet have time to develop better flavor. The real secret of good asparagus lies in its freshness, not in its size.

Take asparagus home from the market and submerge in a tall pitcher or jar partly filled with water to cover the woody stems, then refrigerate. Use within a day or so of purchase for maximum flavor. When ready to cook, hold each one in your hands and snap off the white part at the bottom of the stalk where it naturally bends. Discard the end portion. With the tip of a knife, trim away the triangular scales along the spear, leaving the tender ones that form the head. Rinse clean under a spray of cool water and proceed as directed in recipe.

Broccoli: Should have compact buds that are tightly closed with a good green color and a pale purplish hue. When briefly blanched for a

Crudité Basket or Fresh Vegetable Salad, its color sets a deep green and it will also be more digestible.

Very often broccoli flowerets are called for in recipes. Cut heavy base from broccoli at the point it begins to branch out and set it aside. Remove and discard tiny leaves. If flowerets are very large, you can cut each one in half vertically. Sometimes I refer to these as "little trees." When I know the broccoli is especially fresh, I trim away the coarse outer covering of the heavy stalks and slice them into strips for eating raw out of hand. They have a delicious flavor reminiscent of anise. And they are popular in Chinese cooking for stir frying.

Cabbage and Kale: Happily, sturdy cabbage and kale are making a comeback. Their nutritive values are high and calories reasonably low. Cabbages are available the year round in many different market types.

When buying, look for the domestic green cabbage that is solid with compact round heads; the crinkly-leafed loose-head savoy is used frequently in Mediterranean recipes; red cabbage is fun to use as a container for dips on a vegetable platter and is also frequently used in the German-style sweet and sour cabbage. Chinese cabbage also comes in different varieties, bok choy being perhaps one of the most popular with Americans.

Kale is an important member of the cabbage family but does not form a head. The loose leaves with frilly edges have deep green color with a bluish tinge. It is an extremely healthful vegetable, high in fiber content. I love its robust flavor in Tuscan Bean Soup.

Carrots: Fortunately, carrots are available year round. Of course, they are preferable when purchased with their greens still attached. They are fresher, will taste sweeter, and will probably not need anything more than a good scrubbing with a vegetable brush and the root end trimmed and discarded. If they are topped and prepackaged in plastic bags, chances are you will have to peel them with a vegetable parer. In any event, choose them even-sized, firm, smooth, and well shaped, with a good orange color. Stored unwashed in the refrigerator, they will keep a week or so. You will be well rewarded for choosing carefully, as in one of my favorite carrot recipes that seems to work well with any dinner—the simply prepared Carrots With Raspberry Vinegar.

Cauliflower: The snowy white compact heads of cauliflower are one of my favorite foods. I sometimes hunger for the full, sweet taste of cauliflower just steamed whole and drizzled with melted unsalted butter and fine bread crumbs. This aristocratic vegetable peaks with the first chill of early fall, but quality unblemished heads are available through midspring.

To prepare cauliflower for cooking, remove and discard pale green leaves and cut off heavy stem. For use in its most popular form, it's easiest to pull flowerets away from the bottom first.

Celery: It has got to be one of the most familiar ingredients in a cook's larder. Be sure to look for crisp stalks with fresh leaves. Celery has the advantage of being available all year, is inexpensive, flavorful, and can be eaten raw or cooked.

Corn: Sweet corn, or maize, as the Indians originally called it, is an important American crop. Corn is a rich source of carbohydrates and, therefore, a high-energy food. This delicate vegetable is irresistible when just picked from the stalk, husked, and cooked immediately. Once the corn is picked, its sugar starts to turn to starch and the ear begins to lose its sweet flavor. It is available in the market throughout the year shipped from different regions of the country; however, it is best to eat corn from your local farms in peak season, July through September.

Select ears that have fresh, tightly closed green husks with a brown silk. The white or yellow kernels should be of medium size, plump, milky, and slightly resistant to pressure. Very small kernels indicate immature corn that lacks flavor. Avoid dried-out husks and decay from worm damage. Examine an ear of corn by pulling back the husk and looking at the kernels. Store husked corn wrapped in damp paper towels in crisper drawer of your refrigerator.

Cook as soon after purchase as possible. Husk fresh corn and remove the silk. If silk clings, try using a vegetable brush to remove it. Plunge corn into rapidly boiling lightly salted water and cook 1–2 minutes. Drain and serve immediately with melted butter.

Cucumbers: It may be impossible to find unwaxed cucumbers, but no amount of cosmetic treatment can hide the limpness and indentations that signal a vegetable past its prime. Look for bright green, firm, narrow, well-shaped cucumbers. They are best in the summer months. Cucumbers are not just for salads: see Julienne of Parsleyed Cucumbers.

Eggplant: When I select an eggplant, I enjoy holding it to feel its sleek, shiny, smooth skin and at the same time examine it for bruises, dents, or signs of decay. Aubergine, the rich, dark purple color of eggplant, has been adopted as a color description used in the fashion and home decorating industries. Aubergine is the French word for eggplant.

Refrigerate eggplant and use as soon as possible. The skin can be peeled or not, depending on the vegetable and its use. It works well with tomatoes in sauces; it is popularly used in Eggplant Caviar; when sliced, breaded and fried, it can be eaten as is or used as a base for other recipes. I love to marinate and grill the tender baby eggplants in late summer as part of my Marinated Vegetables on the Grill.

Green Beans: Choose firm, thin, clear green beans with gracefully curved tails. Line them up several at a time with other stem ends meeting. Cut through the stem ends and discard. Do not remove the tails. Think about it—they are really rather pretty. Blanch for a Crudité Basket or precook for Green Bean, Chèvre, and Pignoli Nut Salad.

Mushrooms: Perfectly white mushrooms have been bleached and treated, then smothered by cellophane wrapping. Look for mushrooms in their natural state with caps closed around the stem and some remnants of the earth they were grown in still clinging to them. Their color should be creamy, not brown.

We are told not to wash mushrooms. However, I find it a nuisance to clean the individual mushroom caps by wiping them with a damp towel. It is perfectly fine to rinse them quickly in a colander under a spray of cool water. Gently reach under the mushrooms as the water runs over them, lifting quickly to expose the bottom layers to the spray. This will take only a few seconds. Then transfer mushrooms to a clean kitchen towel to pat dry and absorb excess moisture. Do not clean mushrooms until just before you are ready to use them. When storing mushrooms, refrigerate in a brown paper bag, not in plastic, which retains moisture.

Onions: Basic to cooking, onions add much flavor and are used around the world. Select onions that are well shaped, firm, and dry, with crackly skin free of blemishes. Avoid soft onions with spongy, wet, or decayed areas around their neck and those that have sprouted.

Varieties of onions include: Bermuda, Spanish, sweet red Italian, scallions, leeks, shallots, and garlic—and the very useful yellow all-purpose onion. They can be used whole—large ones to stuff and bake; medium onions for roasting and poaching; and small ones to glaze. Use them to flavor other ingredients; sauté, braise, or stew them; or add fresh to salads.

To peel onions, cut in half lengthwise, then peel. If you are leaving them whole, slice off root and neck ends and peel. If you are going to chop, slice, or grate onions, it is a good idea to place them in the freezer for about 10 minutes to prevent your eyes from tearing. But don't forget they're in the freezer or they will become waterlogged. When using them fresh in salads (sweet red Italian best), trim, peel, and slice thin, then soak in ice water 15–20 minutes. Drain and dry, and they will emerge sweet and crisp.

SCALLIONS are young green onions pulled while the tops are still green and sold in bunches. Their popularity has increased, since their flavor lends lightness to cooking and their texture, shape, and color are used in many ways for presentation. Use them as Scallion Flowers, diced as a garnish, or leave whole, resting on a food, such as a fillet of sole or a whole chicken breast to brighten its appearance.

SHALLOTS are available in the marketplace in all different sizes, from tiny to rather large and are often in clusters. Choose rounded shallots that are dry and firm. When my students have a shallot in clusters, they will ask if I consider that one shallot. My answer is a qualified "no." "Look at the size," I suggest, "and determine whether it is two or maybe even three shallots." A guideline might be: one finely chopped shallot equals about one teaspoonful. Shallots, like garlic, should be kept in a well-ventilated place. If you do not use them frequently, store in a tightly covered jar in the refrigerator.

GARLIC—I wouldn't be without it! The most pungent of the onion family, its heavily clustered cloves form a bulb which should be firm and plump, with clean dry skins.

I finely chop garlic for many food preparations and am frequently asked why I don't use a garlic press. A garlic clove mashed in a press creates a concentrate far stronger than garlic that is chopped, minced, or sliced. Also, there is almost never a reason to use garlic powder and garlic salt, since fresh garlic is easily obtained and is available all through the year. One can use a great number of garlic cloves whole and unpeeled and produce a subtle flavor, as evidenced by the Veal Chops with Twenty Cloves of Garlic.

To peel garlic, place a clove squarely in front of you and close to the front edge of your cutting board. Stand sideways—that is, perpendicular to the board—and firmly grip the handle of your chef's knife. Position the broad end of the blade directly over the garlic clove. Your hand gripping the handle is in front of and free of the board completely. Now rest the tip of the knife blade on the board, bring the broad side of the knife over the clove, and lightly press down on it with your other hand. The skin will split open under the weight of the knife, making it easy for you to peel.

Most recipes will call for garlic to be finely chopped. With the tip of your knife make several horizontal and vertical slits away from core end, then slice carefully through cuts to make small dice (discard core end). Now speed up the process by "rocking" the knife blade with a rolling motion over the garlic as swiftly as you can. Be very cautious when cooking finely chopped garlic. Added to hot oil, it can burn on contact, in which case it must be discarded. I will add finely chopped garlic or

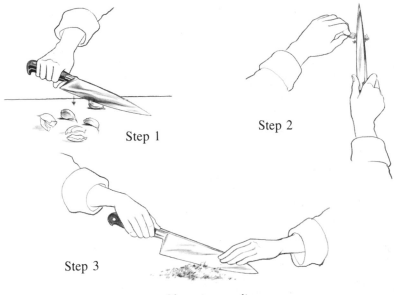

Step 1

Step 2

Step 3

Chopping garlic

shallots to the pan immediately after I start to heat some oil or butter and then cook it for just a few seconds without allowing it to color.

I have always kept garlic in a small open basket hanging from a hook on the side of my kitchen window. Buy in small quantities and do not refrigerate.

LEEKS are often used in making stock. For this purpose I use only the washed green of leek tied in a bundle. When the stock has been cooking for an hour or two, I tie the clean white part of the leeks into a separate bundle, drop them into the simmering stock, and poach them for five minutes or so until tender. They are luscious warm, served as is, or cold in Poached Leeks Vinaigrette. They make a distinctive Crustless Quiche, as well as a wonderfully crisp julienne topping on a green salad (Radicchio, Leek, and Chèvre Salad). This giant scallion look-alike has a mild onion flavor. Look for green tops with medium-sized necks; the whites should be at least 2–3 inches from the root.

Since leeks are almost always very sandy, after discarding bruised outer leaves and root ends, cut the leek crosswise at the top of the still tender light green portion from just above the whites. With a knife, split leeks lengthwise and spread them under a spray of running water. In addition to this, I like to soak the halves, intact, in a bowl of fresh, clean water for 15 minutes to assure the removal of all sand.

Peas: Fresh shelled sweet garden peas are a special treat. When I see them on a produce stand, I will pick up a good handful—enough perhaps for two people and it *is* a special treat. Or I will use the same amount as a food stretcher in a pasta or rice dish, such as Insalata de Riso. Frankly, the idea of shelling mounds of the garden pea discourages me from preparing it as a separate vegetable for a number of people.

Peas are intermittently available through the year and not all that frequently. The majority of the pea crop is preserved and fresh peas are hard to come by. Tiny frozen peas are perhaps the one exception I make in my vegetable purchases. The frozen variety works perfectly well with any dish where I would use the fresh. Some brands will feature tiny, tender frozen peas and this is my choice. To cook them, drop still frozen peas into about ½ inch boiling salted water. Cover and cook very quickly, 2–3 minutes, shaking pan over heat until just tender.

When choosing fresh peas, buy fresh-looking, bright green, and well-filled pea pods.

Snow Peas: A variety of the sweet pea, the snow pea has a soft edible pod and is eaten whole. Choose snow peas that are firm and bright green, avoiding those blemished with brown spots. Stylized oriental presentations are a mark of nouvelle cuisine, and the snow pea, a popular ingredient in oriental cooking, has found what seems like a permanent home. It is a vegetable—it is edible—and it is a garnish.

Peppers: Range from sweet to intensely hot. There are sweet bell peppers and Italian frying peppers in red, green, and yellow. There are a hundred or more varieties of the very hot pepper all referred to as chile pepper. Most popular in this country are: green chiles (chile verde), poblano, jalepeño, and serrano. The listing ranges from mildly hot to very hot and are available fresh, dried, and powdered.

The varieties most often used are the sweet bell and Italian frying peppers, although the hotter peppers are gaining in popularity. I love to prepare my Marinated Italian Yellow and Red Peppers recipe and look forward to the time when I see the abundance of the colorful vegetable on produce stands.

Choose well-formed peppers that are shiny and firm and free of bruises. To trim bell peppers, lay a pepper on its side and, with a sharp knife, slice off the top. Reach in to pull out and discard the cluster of seeds, then rinse out any excess seeds. Leave whole or slice into julienne or dice. Or slice into rings as in the Crudité Basket. You can push out the stem from the top slice and use the ring surrounding it. For Italian frying peppers, remove seeds as above and cut in half lengthwise.

Spinach: I prefer to buy loose spinach with a fresh dark green color. Leaves should look perky and not wilted. If you must buy spinach in plastic bags, be certain the leaves are not bruised and slimy and do not have heavy, fibrous stems. Pick over spinach and remove any blemished leaves and heavy stems. Wash in several changes of lukewarm water to clean the leaves of dirt and sand before cooking. Avoid cooking in aluminum or iron, both of which leave a metallic aftertaste to this vegetable.

Squash: ACORN SQUASH is a dark, dull green, and wide-ribbed vegetable usually shaped like an acorn. It has a hard, smooth shell and an orange, pumpkinlike flesh with a large seeded cavity. Its ease of preparation makes it a popular vegetable. Simply cut it in half, seed it, then season with a bit of sweet butter and brown sugar baked in the cavity and it will be absolutely delicious.

BUTTERNUT SQUASH has a thin, smooth, hard shell with a light creamy-tan skin. Buy only those that are long-necked and slightly bulbous at the base. The neck has solid yellow flesh, whereas the base is mostly cavity filled with seeds. Use it to bake, stuff, or boil; or as in one of my favorite soups, Herbed Squash Bisque.

SUMMER SQUASH is delicate in flavor and delicious when simply sautéed in butter with a little fresh dill. Its tender yellow skin need not be removed.

ZUCCHINI is enjoying great popularity these days and may be served in any number of ways. Since it is a relatively sandy vegetable, it needs to be scrubbed well. Look for small and narrow zucchini with smooth, unblemished soft skin. In general, the skin is edible and never peeled from the vegetable. This favorite of home gardeners is available all year round but peaks in summer. When growing your own, you have the added pleasure of the blossoms, which are so prized in Italian cooking for batter-frying.

Swiss Chard: Leafy Swiss chard can be used interchangeably with spinach but has a more delicate flavor. Leaves should be separated from the stalks; stalks and leaves are cooked separately. Both are delicious, very high in nutrients, and very low in calories. This is best in summer when local supplies are available. Look for moist, thick white stalks with tender crisp leaves.

Tomatoes: Those ripened on the vine are plump, bright red, and have a rich aroma—quite different from the hothouse imitations wrapped in cellophane. Only during the summer months can most of us buy tomatoes that even approximate the ideal state of this prized fruit. In winter months, I use only canned tomatoes packed in their natural juices.

A technique frequently called for in recipes using peeled and seeded tomatoes is: Bring 2–3 cups water to a boil in a saucepan. Plunge tomatoes into the boiling water 20–30 seconds, depending on their size. Remove with slotted spoon and fan* to cool, or cool briefly under cold running water. With the tip of a knife, remove skin, which will slip off easily. Cut in half crosswise, hold in palm of your hand, and squeeze gently to remove and discard seeds. If you want to save the juice (for soups, stews, and sauces), squeeze tomatoes over a strainer straddling a bowl, pushing the pulp and liquid through. Discard seeds left in strainer.

New Vegetables: Some new vegetables on the scene are fiddleheads, Sunchokes, spaghetti squash, jicama, and nopales (cactus leaves). Check with your greengrocer for availability and enjoy a new adventure in eating.

FIDDLEHEADS are coiled young fronds of ostrich ferns. They may not be found in the average market, or even in a specialty market, but an adventurous, food-loving friend, Lynne Rogers, managed to find and cook this delicate, tender, wild vegetable for dinner one night. The fiddleheads were steamed until tender, then served with a drizzle of melted butter. Their curved shape and intense green color were so spectacular on the dinner plate I will never forget them.

JICAMA is a brown tuber with a turniplike shape. It is crisp and juicy and delicious served raw as an appetizer. When cooked, it has the texture of water chestnuts. A favorite quick way with jicama is to slice it into ¼-inch-thick rounds, then dip it into a small dish of extra virgin olive oil, then into another dish of coarse (kosher) salt.

NOPALES *(Cactus Leaves)*, a new vegetable from South of the Border, has come our way via California. Its thorny, prickly leaf requires a gloved hand when you prepare it for cooking. The reward is in the eating. You will be surprised at its succulent flavor and interesting texture.

SPAGHETTI SQUASH, when cooked, will separate into spaghettilike strands with the texture of firm cooked spaghetti. It looks like a smaller version of a yellow watermelon and has a textured skin.

To prepare, cut squash in half lengthwise and remove seeds. Place cut side down in a pot with two inches of water. Cover and bring water to a boil, adjust heat, and cook about 20 minutes or until slightly tender. Remove squash halves and scoop out insides by running a fork through to pull out the strands into a mixing bowl. I like to simply add some sweet butter and a bit of salt and pepper and serve. For a variation, reserve empty shell, combine some grated cheese, a little tomato sauce, some seasonings such as basil, garlic, salt, and pepper, stir to mix with cooked spaghetti squash, and spoon back into the empty shell. Sprinkle on additional grated cheese. Place on a baking sheet and bake in a preheated 350-degree oven 20 minutes until cheese is bubbly. This will add a new dimension to your vegetable repertoire. (Thanks to Frieda of California for product information.)

SUNCHOKES (JERUSALEM ARTICHOKES) are a vegetable native to North America. Although Sunchokes are also called Jerusalem artichokes, they have nothing to do with either Jerusalem or the artichoke. This is the knobby underground tuber of the sunflower and may be eaten raw, or cooked, as in my Jerusalem Artichoke Sauté. Choose Sunchokes, usually available in plastic bags at the market, without pink discoloration. Skin should be free of mold and firm. Refrigerate in plastic bag or store in dry place.

Eating vegetables is good for the psyche. It brings us closer to nature and gives us a chance to enjoy something that's good for us. There's no need to spend large sums of money on overpriced "health foods" when the best source of fiber, vitamins, and minerals is available in your supermarket produce department.

JULIENNE OF CARROT BUNDLES WITH SCALLION TIES

This is an adaptation of chef Michel Fitouchi's inspired creation.

1–2 bunches fresh carrots   ¼ cup melted butter
Coarse (kosher) salt   Freshly ground pepper
1 bunch scallions

Serves 6–8

1. Peel carrots with a vegetable peeler, then trim and discard ends. With a chef's knife cut each carrot in half lengthwise, then cut each half through the center so that the lengths are 2–3 inches long. Place one piece of carrot at a time flat side down on a cutting board and cut into julienne strips ¼ inch wide.

2. Bring 2–3 quarts water to a boil, stir in 2 teaspoons salt, and add the carrots. Cook about 2 minutes until slightly tender but firm. Drain in a colander and fan* or rinse quickly to cool. Transfer to a clean kitchen towel and pat dry to absorb excess moisture. Set aside.

3. To make scallion ties, use green part only. Discard wilted or bruised greens. Cut off the white root end and use for other purpose.

4. Blanch scallion greens in boiling water 10–20 seconds. Drain and cool. Place scallion greens in a single layer on cutting board. Working with one at a time, hold on to one end and, with a paring knife held at a 45-degree angle, gently ease the blade across the green to extrude the moisture.

5. Divide carrot julienne into little bundles, 8–10 sticks each. Spread a scallion green on work area to its full length. Place "bundle" of carrots in center of scallion, lift up the two ends and tie a double knot over the carrots to secure them. Repeat with remaining carrots and scallions. Can be made ahead to this point.

6. Before serving, brush carrot bundles with melted butter and sprinkle lightly with salt and pepper. Arrange them in a steamer over simmering water for just a few minutes to warm through. Serve immediately.

To Prepare Ahead
Follow steps 1 through 5 up to one day ahead. Refrigerate, covered, in a suitable container. Bring to room temperature and complete step 6 before serving.

BROCCOLI-DUXELLE LOAF

This tasty, mushroom-accented broccoli purée is a family favorite at Thanksgiving dinner and can be done completely ahead.

2 bunches broccoli (3–3½
   pounds)
¾ pound mushrooms
2 tablespoons unsalted butter
4–5 shallots, finely diced
1 teaspoon coarse (kosher)
   salt
Freshly ground pepper
2 eggs
2 egg yolks

½ cup bread crumbs
½ cup heavy cream
¼ teaspoon freshly ground
   nutmeg

Have on Hand
1½-quart loaf pan, well
   buttered
Bain-marie*

Serves 10–12

Preheat oven to 375 degrees.

1. Remove heavy stalks and leaves from broccoli, cut flowerets into "little trees," and rinse clean. Steam broccoli over simmering water, covered, about 15 minutes, until tender. Drain in a colander under a spray of cold water to stop cooking; then transfer to a clean kitchen towel and pat dry. Reserve 6–7 flowerets for garnish and set aside.

2. Trim woody ends of mushroom stems and discard; then rinse mushrooms quickly in a colander under a light spray of cool water or wipe clean with a dampened paper towel and pat dry. Chop finely with a chef's knife or chop in a workbowl of food processor fitted with steel knife. (The processor is a miracle worker and especially when it comes to duxelle. Pulse the machine several times, stopping to redistribute the mushrooms with a rubber spatula as necessary. They'll be done perfectly in seconds.)

3. Melt butter in a skillet and when foam subsides add shallots and sauté quickly until tender. Add mushrooms and sauté over moderately high heat 2–3 minutes until moisture has evaporated. Season with salt and pepper.

4. Purée broccoli in a food processor fitted with steel knife or in batches in a blender. Add eggs and egg yolks and process or blend to mix. Add duxelle, bread crumbs, cream, and nutmeg. Process or blend to mix, then taste to adjust seasoning if necessary.

5. Transfer the mixture to a well-buttered loaf pan and cover mixture with a strip of buttered wax paper. Set the mold in pan containing enough hot water to reach ⅔ up the sides (bain-marie). Place in oven and bake 45–50 minutes or until a cake tester or knife inserted in the center comes out clean. Let stand in mold for minimum of 10 minutes before unmolding if serving immediately. However, it can be done ahead to this point.

6. To unmold, insert a knife between the cooked loaf and inside of pan and release the sides. Invert a warmed serving platter over the mold, grasp the mold and the platter with both hands and quickly invert to release the vegetable loaf. Garnish base of platter with reserved broccoli flowerets and serve at once.

To Prepare Ahead

Follow steps 1 through 5 up to one day ahead, cover, and refrigerate. Complete step 6 up to two hours ahead. Let stand at room temperature and just before serving reheat in a 350-degree oven covered with a strip of buttered parchment or wax paper 15–20 minutes. Then garnish.

CAULIFLOWER MOUSSE TIMBALES

This is a light vegetable mousse without the heaviness of a Béchamel base and is my version of a delicate but spectacular timbale as served to us at Roger Verge's Moulin de Mougins.

1 head cauliflower (about 1¾ pounds), fresh and snow white
1 tablespoon coarse (kosher) salt for cooking water
2 tablespoons unsalted butter
3 whole eggs
1 egg yolk
1 teaspoon coarse (kosher) salt
½ teaspoon freshly ground white pepper
½ cup Crème Fraîche or heavy cream

¼ teaspoon freshly grated nutmeg
⅔ cup grated Gruyère cheese
Watercress for garnish

Have on Hand
10–12 baba au rhum timbales, well buttered, *or* 8–10 custard molds, well buttered
Bain-marie*
Food mill or strainer

Serves 10–12

1. Wash cauliflower, trim off the leaves and heavy base, and discard. Break into flowerets and cook in salted boiling water to cover about 12–14 minutes until tender but firm. Drain in a colander, fan*, or run under a spray of cold water to stop the cooking. Pat dry in a clean kitchen towel.

2. Melt the butter in a skillet and, when foam subsides, add cauliflower and sauté over moderate heat 2–3 minutes to evaporate the moisture. Push through a food mill or with the back of a wooden spoon through a strainer into a bowl, puréeing all cauliflower. Do not purée in a processor or texture will be too watery. In the event mixture is a little watery, drain in a sieve for several minutes before continuing.

3. In a mixing bowl, whisk whole eggs and egg yolk until combined. Add purée and remaining ingredients. Stir gently to mix, then taste to adjust seasoning if necessary.
Preheat oven to 375 degrees.

4. Spoon mousse into well-buttered timbales, fill about ¾ full, and place in baking pan. Place a buttered length of parchment or wax paper across tops of molds large enough to cover, to prevent tops of mixture from drying. Pour enough hot water to come about ⅔ of the way up

sides of molds and bake in preheated oven 35–40 minutes, or until a cake tester or a knife inserted in the center of the custard comes out clean. Remove from oven and allow molds to sit at least 5 minutes before unmolding.

5. *To Unmold:* Run an ordinary kitchen knife between the mousse and the inside of the mold. Tip over onto a warm serving platter and garnish with watercress. Serve hot. Or use as an edible decoration around a roast.

To Prepare Ahead
Follow steps 1 through 3 early in the day. Follow step 4 up to one hour ahead, and complete step 5 just before serving.

ESCAROLE SAUTÉ

Escarole, a variety of endive, is used mostly as a salad green. The simple preparation that follows is an ideal vegetable accompaniment to sautéed or grilled meat or fish. Be sure to cook in plenty of boiling salted water to cover. If exposed to air, the greens will discolor and turn an unappetizing brown.

1 large head escarole
Coarse (kosher) salt
1½ tablespoons imported
    extra virgin olive oil
2 cloves garlic, finely
    chopped

½ teaspoon coarse (kosher)
    salt
Freshly ground pepper

Serves 6–8

1. Separate escarole leaves and wash as you would lettuce leaves (no need to spin-dry, however).

2. Bring 3–4 quarts water to a boil. Dissolve 1 tablespoon salt in the water and add escarole all at once, immersing greens in water with a wooden spoon. Cover pan and immediately bring water back to a boil. With cover ajar, simmer escarole 3–4 minutes until just tender. Drain in a colander and fan* to cool or refresh under a spray of cool running water to stop the cooking. Transfer to a clean kitchen towel to absorb excess moisture. Set aside. Can be done ahead to this point.

3. In a 12-inch skillet, heat oil with chopped garlic, being careful not to brown the garlic. Add the escarole and with a large wooden spoon

stir to coat in the garlic-oil, then cook briefly just to heat vegetable through. Sprinkle lightly with salt and pepper to taste, toss again, and serve immediately.

To Prepare Ahead
Follow steps 1 and 2 up to several hours ahead and set aside. Complete step 3 just before serving.

CARROTS WITH RASPBERRY VINEGAR

This is a delightful recipe and with the addition of the raspberry vinegar it's a surprise taste.

1 bunch fresh carrots, trimmed, scrubbed, or peeled if necessary	1 teaspoon brown or raw sugar
2 tablespoons unsalted butter	1 tablespoon raspberry vinegar
½ teaspoon coarse (kosher) salt	Snipped chives for garnish (optional)

Serves 4–6

1. To roll-cut carrots: With a chef's knife, make a first diagonal cut through the end of the carrot. Give the carrot a quarter turn to make the next diagonal cut. Continue to make quarter turns to roll and cut until all the carrots are done.

2. Melt butter in a heavy 2½-quart saucepan. Put in carrots and toss to coat. Add salt and sugar and stir to mix. Cook, covered, over very low heat 20–25 minutes. Shake the pan every so often to be sure the contents are not sticking. Remember, there isn't any water in the pan. The carrots are cooking in butter and their own juices. If necessary, remove cover and stir to redistribute carrots.

3. When carrots are just tender, add vinegar and stir to mix. Let cook 1 minute longer and serve immediately. Top with snipped chives for garnish if desired.

To Prepare Ahead
Follow steps 1 and 2 up to one hour ahead. Set aside, covered, to stay warm. Complete step 3 just before serving.

CAULIFLOWER WITH MUSTARD MAYONNAISE

1 large cauliflower, fresh
   and snow white
1½ cups Mayonnaise—your
   own, of course
1 teaspoon Dijon mustard
1 teaspoon finely chopped
   shallots
¼ teaspoon coarse (kosher)
   salt

Freshly ground pepper
2–3 tablespoons heavy or
   light cream
Dash cayenne
1 large carrot, scraped and
   shredded
Few sprigs curly parsley for
   garnish

Serves 6–8

1. Wash cauliflower, trim off the leaves, and leave whole. If necessary, use a sharp knife to cut into the core at the base of the cauliflower so that it can sit comfortably on the center post of a steamer rack. Try not to let cauliflower break up into flowerets. If a few pieces fall from the bottom of the cauliflower as you trim it, they may be steamed together with the head and reassembled.

2. Steam over briskly simmering water in a tightly closed pan 8–10 minutes until tender but firm. Drain and pat dry with paper towels. Transfer to a serving dish.

3. In a mixing bowl, combine mayonnaise with mustard, shallots, salt, pepper, cream, and cayenne. Stir to mix. Taste to adjust seasoning if necessary.

4. Shred carrot on large holes of hand grater or grate in a food processor fitted with shredding blade. If using processor, cut carrot in lengths to fit the feed tube horizontally. Process with full pressure to obtain large shreds. Fold approximately ⅔ of shredded carrot into prepared mayonnaise. Set aside remaining shredded carrot for garnish.

5. Spoon dressing in a crisscross design over top of the cooked cauliflower, allowing sauce to fall to the rim of the plate. Sprinkle top with remaining carrot shreds and dash of cayenne. Garnish with sprigs of curly parsley.

To Prepare Ahead
Follow steps 1 through 4 up to one day ahead and refrigerate, covered, in suitable containers. Complete step 5 before serving. Serve at room temperature.

CRUDITÉ BASKET

Our one-day Vegetable Class at Cooktique has become the single most sought-after program. The most important feature of the class is our Crudité Basket. It didn't matter at what time of the year the class was given, as we would only include the freshest and finest produce in a particular season. The ingredient list might seem extensive, but I merely want to suggest the variety that one can use in the Crudité Basket at a given time. While crudité is a French word meaning raw vegetables, I prefer to blanch certain vegetables, since they taste better, produce a more brilliant color, will look fresher if held overnight, and are more digestible. In the words of Simone (Simca) Beck, "We are not rabbits."

Note: This is a completely do-ahead preparation and may be organized up to 1 day before your party. This recipe is a fine lesson plan. If you cook your way through it, there will hardly be a vegetable you couldn't handle.

Uncooked

1 medium-size well-rounded red cabbage

Cucumber, peeled, cut in half lengthwise, seeded, and sliced into ¼-inch half-moons

Fennel, trimmed, root and stem ends discarded; cut into vertical sticks, any bruised outer leaves cut away

Jicama, peeled and cut into thin slices

1–2 leeks, left whole—to be used for decoration only—(see Garnishes)

Red and green peppers, cored, trimmed, and sliced approximately ¼ inch thick

2 bunches large, firm radishes, scrubbed and left whole

2 bunches scallions, left whole; any bruised outer leaves and tips removed and discarded (see Scallion Flowers)

Cherry tomatoes, washed and left whole

White turnips, pared and sliced

1 large or 2 medium zucchini, scrubbed, sliced into rounds or sticks

Cooked/Blanched

Artichokes (see Artichoke Vinaigrette for preparation)

Asparagus in season, tender younger spears, left whole (see Index for cleaning and trimming)

1 head broccoli, heavy stalks
and leaves removed,
cut into flowerets
1 bunch even-size carrots
with greens on, cut
into even-size sticks
1 head cauliflower, cut into
flowerets
½ pound green beans,
whole, stacked and cut
at stem end only
½ pound small mushrooms,
wiped clean and rubbed
with cut side of lemon

½ pound pea pods, whole
2 tablespoons coarse
(kosher) salt for
cooking water

Have on Hand
Strainer-skimmer or slotted
spoon
Fan*
10–12-inch shallow round or
oval basket

Serves 25–30

1. *Crudité Dip Container:* Red cabbage is used raw and as a container for dip. Pull off and set aside bruised outer leaves for use as basket liner. Cut base evenly so that cabbage is level. Slice about 1½ inches from top of cabbage and discard. With a sharp paring knife, hollow out a portion of the cabbage to creat a container for dip.

2. *Uncooked Vegetables:* Prepare raw vegetables ahead according to ingredient list and store individually and securely wrapped in plastic bags.

3. *Cooked Vegetable:* Artichoke is completely cooked according to above reference.

4. *Blanched Vegetables:* Try to cut each group to an approximately even size. To blanch, bring 3–4 quarts salted water to a boil in a 5-quart saucepan. Cook vegetables, one at a time, according to the time schedule on page 400. Remember—the timetable is a guide and relates to the thickness and heaviness of your vegetables or the way you cut them. Put the vegetables in water, reduce heat, and maintain a surface bubble at all times. Cook each vegetable until crisp-tender. Remove vegetables from cooking water with a strainer-skimmer and transfer to colander to drain. Cool quickly to tepid with a fan or under a spray of cold water. Immediately transfer one layer deep to a clean kitchen towel to absorb excess moisture. The action from the time the vegetables are removed from the water on their way to the kitchen towel must be very swift, as the vegetables continue to cook in their own heat.

5. *To Arrange Crudité Basket:* Line basket with excess red cabbage

leaves and center red cabbage container. I try to arrange the basket according to the variety of vegetables I have before me and I prefer to clump them together. For instance, I take all the green broccoli and arrange it together and then all of the white cauliflower. Place the artichoke near the cauliflower, close to the rim of the basket for easier access. I will stand up groups of asparagus, pea pods, scallions, zucchini, carrot sticks, and pepper strips so that they are holding each other up, again keeping an eye to color and texture as I place them. Whole mushrooms, cherry tomatoes, and radishes can be inserted into open areas of the arrangement. Any remaining vegetables can be placed in individual groupings wherever your eye will take them according to their shape and color. Remember, arrange your vegetables as though you were an artist with a paint brush and palette, letting your eye mix the colors.

    6. Fill cabbage container with Crudité Dip just before serving.

To Prepare Ahead
Follow steps 1 through 4 up to one day ahead. I prefer to cut any raw vegetables the same day of the party to keep them from drying out. Follow step 5 up to 1–3 hours before and refrigerate if room is available, covered with a tent of plastic wrap. Complete step 6 just before serving.

CRUDITÉ DIP

1 large clove garlic, finely
    chopped
2–3 scallions, trimmed
    clean, white and light
    green part only, finely
    chopped
1 tablespoon finely chopped
    fresh chives (optional)
1 tablespoon finely chopped
    Italian flat-leaf parsley
1¼ cups Mayonnaise,
    preferably homemade

¼–⅓ cup sour cream
1 teaspoon anchovy paste
2 tablespoons tarragon
    vinegar
1 teaspoon fresh lemon juice
Coarse (kosher) salt and
    freshly ground pepper,
    to taste (may be
    necessary only if using
    commercial
    mayonnaise)

Yields 1½ cups

1. In a mixing bowl, combine all ingredients and stir to mix. Taste to adjust seasoning if necessary. Transfer to a serving bowl, cover with plastic wrap, and refrigerate until ready to use.

Note: For suggested use, see Crudité Basket.

To Prepare Ahead

Follow step 1 up to three days ahead. Refrigerate in suitable container.

Note: A food processor or blender may also be used to incorporate ingredients quickly and evenly.

PURÉE OF PARSNIPS AND CARROTS

4 medium parsnips (about 1 pound), trimmed and scraped

4 medium carrots (about ½ pound), trimmed and scraped

1 tablespoon coarse (kosher) salt

Freshly ground pepper

¼ Crème Fraîche or heavy cream

¼ teaspoon freshly grated nutmeg

Serves 4–5

1. Cut parsnips in half, then cut each piece in half lengthwise. Put into a saucepan.

2. Cut carrots into thirds and add to pan with parsnips. Add water to cover, with salt and several grinds of pepper. Bring to a boil. Reduce heat, cover, and simmer about 5 minutes until tender. Do not overcook.

3. Drain thoroughly and refresh under a spray of cool water or fan*. Pat dry in a clean kitchen towel. Cut into 1-inch chunks and pass through a food mill directly into a saucepan, or purée in blender or food processor and transfer to a saucepan.

4. Add crème fraîche or heavy cream with nutmeg and stir to mix. Cook, stirring, over moderate heat until piping hot. Taste to adjust seasoning if necessary. Serve immediately.

To Prepare Ahead

Follow steps 1 through 3 up to several hours ahead. Let stand, covered, at room temperature. Complete step 4 just before serving.

TIMBALE OF LETTUCE CHIFFONADE

This delicate custard is simple to make, but the idea of lettuce as a cooked vegetable will surprise many.

2 large heads (about 1
    pound) Boston lettuce
    (fresh, crisp, and
    without brown spots)
4 tablespoons clarified
    butter*
3 whole eggs
1 egg yolk
⅓ cup Crème Fraîche or
    heavy cream
½ teaspoon coarse (kosher)
    salt

Freshly ground pepper
⅛ teaspoon freshly grated
    nutmeg
1 tablespoon snipped chives
    for garnish

Have on Hand
8–10 baba au rhum
    timbales, well buttered,
    or 6–8 custard molds,
    well buttered
Bain-marie*

Serves 8–10

Preheat oven to 350 degrees.

1. Remove any bruised leaves from the lettuce and discard. Wash remaining whole leaves in a colander and spin-dry. Stack several leaves at a time and slice crosswise into ¼-inch ribbons (a chiffonade).

2. In a heavy skillet or saucepan, heat butter over moderate heat until lightly browned. When foamy, add the lettuce strips, and cook, stirring occasionally, about 3 minutes. Transfer to a fine sieve and press lightly to remove excess moisture.

3. Put into workbowl of food processor fitted with steel knife or a blender and purée until smooth. Add whole eggs and egg yolk one at a time and process with quick on/off turns or blend until thoroughly mixed. Add crème fraîche or heavy cream and seasonings and process or blend briefly just to mix. Taste to adjust seasonings if necessary.

4. Fill each buttered mold with about 3 tablespoons of the mixture, tap each one lightly on a pot holder or folded towel to remove air pockets, and arrange in a shallow baking pan. Pour enough hot water into the pan to come about ⅔ up sides of molds. (Be very careful not to splatter water into the mixture.) Bake in preheated oven 20–25 minutes, or until custard is firm but springy to the touch and a knife inserted in the center comes out clean. Remove from oven and allow molds to sit for at least 5 minutes before unmolding them.

5. *To Unmold:* Run an ordinary kitchen knife between the custard and the inside of the mold and invert onto a warm serving dish or use to garnish a meat or fish course. Sprinkle with chives and serve warm.

To Prepare Ahead
Follow steps 1 through 4 early in the day. Remove from oven and let stand. Return to a 350-degree oven in the water bath and warm through 10–15 minutes just before serving. Complete step 5.

SAUTÉ OF JERUSALEM ARTICHOKES

This delightful vegetable, also known by its brand name, Sunchokes, has a crisp texture and sweet nutty flavor. Try them the next time you see them in the market.

1 pound Jerusalem
    artichokes (Sunchokes)
2 tablespoons unsalted butter
2–3 shallots, finely chopped
¼ teaspoon turmeric

¼ teaspoon coarse (kosher)
    salt
Freshly ground pepper
⅓ cup white wine vinegar

Serves 6–8

Note: Choose Sunchokes (usually available in plastic bags at the market) free of pink discoloration; skin should be firm and free of mold.

1. Scrub Sunchokes with a vegetable brush, then soak in bowl of water to get rid of excess dirt. It is not necessary to peel Sunchokes. Place in saucepan of clean water to cover. Cover pan and bring to a boil. Adjust heat to medium and simmer briskly with the cover ajar about 30 minutes. Drain and pat dry with a clean kitchen towel. Cut into ¼-inch slices.

2. In a skillet, melt butter and, when foam subsides, sauté the shallots briefly until tender. Add the sliced Sunchokes, season with turmeric, salt, and pepper, and cook over moderate heat, shaking pan back and forth gently to coat evenly with the butter. Add vinegar, continuing to shake pan gently back and forth until vinegar evaporates. Taste to adjust seasoning if necessary and serve immediately.

To Prepare Ahead
Follow step 1 up to several hours ahead. Complete step 2 just before serving.

SAVORY STUFFED MUSHROOMS

These herb-flavored stuffed mushroom caps make an ideal pickup hors d'oeuvre or can be used as an edible garnish with a roast.

24 medium even-sized snow-white mushrooms
7 tablespoons unsalted butter
2 cloves garlic, finely chopped
2 tablespoons finely chopped Italian flat-leaf parsley
½–¾ cup Basic Chicken Stock or broth
3 tablespoons dry sherry

½ teaspoon coarse (kosher) salt
Freshly ground pepper
3–4 tablespoons lemon juice
1 tablespoon chopped fresh tarragon leaves *or* 1 teaspoon dried
1–1¼ cups dry Bread Crumbs

Serves 8–10

Note: Fresh mushroom caps should be white without any blemishes or dark spots, their caps closed tightly so that the gills beneath are not visible. Prepackaged, washed mushrooms should be avoided, as they have little flavor.

1. To clean mushrooms, wipe with dampened cloth or rinse quickly under a spray of cool running water, drain, and dry in a clean kitchen towel. Remove stems completely and set caps aside. Cut off and discard the woody end of the stems and finely chop the remaining portion.

2. Melt 3 tablespoons butter in a large skillet, place mushrooms cap side down in the hot foamy butter, and sauté quickly over moderately high heat until lightly browned. With slotted spoon transfer to a side dish and turn over to drain.

3. Melt remaining butter in skillet, add garlic, and sauté quickly without browning. Add parsley, and stir to mix. Pour on stock and sherry and stir with a wooden spoon to deglaze pan juices, then reduce liquid by a third. Season with salt, pepper, lemon juice, and tarragon, and stir to mix. Add chopped mushroom stems and cook stirring over moderate heat 3–4 minutes. Stir in enough bread crumbs to bind the mixture. Remove from heat.

4. Fill each mushroom cap with about one tablespoon of the mixture, mounding neatly. Transfer them to a lightly buttered baking dish or buttered oven-going serving dish. Can be done ahead to this point.

5. Just before serving, bake in a 350-degree oven for 15 minutes and serve immediately.

To Prepare Ahead
Follow steps 1 through 4 up to one day ahead. Cover baking dish with plastic wrap and refrigerate. Bring to room temperature before completing step 5.

FENNEL RINGS

This anise-flavored plant makes an aromatic and delicious appetizer from October through April.

1 firm, crisp fennel bulb   *Have on Hand*
   (finocchio)   2 custard cups or ramekins
¼ cup coarse (kosher) salt   Cocktail napkins
⅓ cup light, fruity olive oil

Serves 4–6

1. Refrigerate fennel with tall outer branches and feathery tops until ready to use to insure freshness. Remove tops at bulb level, then remove and discard tough outer stalks. Cut off and discard hard base. Wash and drain. Cut horizontally with the grain into ¼-inch slices.

2. Arrange slices overlapping on a serving dish. Do not be concerned if some of the rings (formed from slicing) separate. Just arrange neatly alongside the slices.

3. Put salt and olive oil in 2 separate ramekins. Place next to the serving dish containing fennel rings and flank with cocktail napkins. Instruct your guests to pick up a ring of fennel, then, holding it, dip first into the oil, allowing excess to drip back into the ramekin, then dip into the salt. Watch with delight as they smile with pleasure at this new taste experience.

To Prepare Ahead
Follow steps 1 and 2 up to several hours ahead. Refrigerate, covered with plastic wrap. Complete step 3 before serving.

ZUCCHINI-TOMATO GRATIN

Don't overlook this familiar combination of vegetables—as a gratin it is special!

1 pound zucchini, scrubbed, sliced about ¼ inch thick
Coarse (kosher) salt
¼ cup olive oil
2 small onions, thinly sliced
2 green peppers, finely diced
2 cloves garlic, finely chopped
4–6 ripe tomatoes, peeled, seeded, and coarsely chopped *or* 1 can (1 pound, 16 ounces) whole tomatoes, drained, seeded, and coarsely chopped

½–¾ teaspoon salt
Freshly ground pepper
2 teaspoons fresh thyme leaves *or* ½ teaspoon dried
2 teaspoons fresh basil leaves, coarsely chopped, *or* ½ teaspoon dried
½ cup freshly grated Parmesan cheese

Have on Hand
Oven-going serving dish

Serves 6–8

1. Spread zucchini slices in one layer on a cookie sheet and salt lightly. Let stand 20–30 minutes, to exude juices. Place in a colander and rinse off salt. Transfer to a clean kitchen towel and pat dry.

2. Heat oil in a 12-inch skillet and sauté zucchini in batches over moderate heat until lightly browned on both sides. Remove with slotted spoon as they are done to drain on paper toweling. Add a little more oil to the skillet, if necessary, and sauté onions and green peppers until slightly tender, being careful not to brown them. Add garlic and cook just a few seconds longer. Stir in tomatoes, salt, pepper, thyme, and basil. Simmer, stirring occasionally, for about 10 minutes. Taste to adjust seasoning if necessary.

3. Arrange zucchini slices in the bottom of a lightly greased gratin serving dish. Distribute tomato mixture evenly over slices. Can be done ahead to this point.
Preheat oven to 350 degrees.

4. Sprinkle zucchini slices with Parmesan cheese and bake in oven 25–30 minutes until hot and bubbly. Serve immediately.

To Prepare Ahead
Follow steps 1 through 3 up to one day ahead. Refrigerate, covered with plastic wrap. Bring to room temperature before completing step 4.

JULIENNE OF PARSLEYED CUCUMBER

Most people would not think of cooking cucumbers, but unless you're growing them yourself or buying them farm-grown, they are not very palatable. When cooked, they become something uncommonly delicious.

2 firm cucumbers
1 teaspoon coarse (kosher)
    salt
3 tablespoons unsalted butter
Freshly ground pepper

3 tablespoons finely chopped
    Italian flat-leaf parsley
Grated rind of 1 whole
    lemon

Serves 4–6

1. Peel, then halve cucumbers lengthwise. With a teaspoon, scrape out seeds and discard. Place cucumber halves flat side down on a work surface and with a chef's knife or long slicing knife cut lengthwise into thin julienne strips to resemble spaghetti

2. Spread in a colander, sprinkle lightly with ½ teaspoon salt and let stand 15–20 minutes. In the meantime, bring 2–3 quarts salted water to a boil. Drop in cucumber julienne and blanch 1–2 minutes until crisp-tender. Drain immediately and refresh under a spray of cool water to stop the cooking. Transfer to a clean kitchen towel and gently pat as dry as possible.

3. Just before serving, melt butter in a 9- or 10-inch skillet. Put in the cucumber julienne, season with remaining ½ teaspoon salt, several grinds of fresh pepper, and sauté quickly over moderately high heat 1 or 2 minutes. Sprinkle on parsley and lemon rind and stir gently to mix. Serve at once.

To Prepare Ahead
Follow steps 1 and 2 up to two hours ahead. Complete step 3 just before serving.

RATATOUILLE AUX OEUFS

This is almost a classic recipe for ratatouille but has the Tunisian special touch of baking the eggs on top of the vegetables. For ease of preparation, all of the vegetables can be prepared in the processor (see Note below).

½ pound mushrooms
3 tablespoons vegetable oil
2 red onions, thinly sliced
2–3 cloves garlic, finely
  chopped
2–3 green peppers, thinly
  sliced
2–3 red peppers (green if red
  is not available), thinly
  sliced
2 zucchini, thinly sliced
2 pounds tomatoes, peeled,
  seeded, and shredded

1 teaspoon coarse (kosher)
  salt
Freshly ground pepper
2 teaspoons chopped fresh
  basil leaves *or* ¾
  teaspoon dried
2 teaspoons fresh thyme
  leaves *or* ¾ teaspoon
  dried
¼ teaspoon coriander
1 bay leaf
8–10 medium-size eggs

Serves 8–10

1. Place mushrooms in a colander in the sink and run a spray of cold water over them, lifting mushrooms with both hands under the spray to quickly rid them of their dirt. Place all the mushrooms in a clean kitchen towel and gently pat them dry. Trim the stem ends of mushrooms and discard. Quarter mushrooms and set aside.

2. In a heavy skillet with a cover, heat oil, add onions, toss to coat, and sauté 2 minutes until tender. Add garlic and cook 1 minute longer. Add peppers and zucchini and sauté for 5 minutes, stirring to mix with onions and garlic. Add tomatoes, mushrooms, and seasonings; stir to mix; then cover and simmer over very low heat for 30 minutes. Taste to adjust seasonings if necessary.

3. With slotted spoon, transfer cooked vegetables into a lightly greased shallow baking dish. Reduce liquid remaining in skillet in half by cooking over moderately high heat, remove bay leaf, and pour over vegetables. *Preheat oven to 350 degrees.*

4. With the back of a spoon, make 8–10 depressions in the surface of the vegetables spaced about 1 inch apart. Break an egg into each depression and bake in preheated oven about 15 minutes to heat through and· set the eggs. Serve on a brunch buffet with Torta de Salmon and Tyropita.

To Prepare Ahead

Follow steps 1 through 3 up to one day ahead. Cover with plastic wrap and refrigerate. Bring to room temperature and complete step 4 just before serving.

Note: Food Processor Directions If using a processor, place garlic in workbowl fitted with steel knife and process with several on/off turns until finely chopped. Remove and set aside. Replace steel knife with slicing blade and prepare mushrooms, peppers, zucchini, and onions to fit feed tube of processor. Stack each vegetable separately in feed tube and slice with light pressure. Transfer from bowl as they are done. Set aside.

BUFFET TOMATOES MIMOSA

A beautiful and delicious accompaniment to any roast or on a buffet.

8 medium ripe tomatoes
Salt and pepper for tomatoes
Vegetable oil for brushing
2 tablespoons coarse
    (kosher) salt for
    cooking water
½ pound fresh broccoli,
    washed and trimmed
½ pound green beans,
    washed and trimmed
5 tablespoons unsalted
    butter, softened
2 shallots, finely chopped

¼ cup heavy cream
½ teaspoon coarse (kosher)
    salt
¼ teaspoon freshly ground
    pepper
¼ teaspoon nutmeg
2 hard-cooked eggs
Watercress for garnish

Have on Hand
Strainer-skimmer or slotted
    spoon

Serves 8

Preheat oven to 350 degrees.

1. Slice off core end of tomato and discard. With a teaspoon, scoop out about ⅓ of tomato flesh and seeds. Place tomatoes on a cookie sheet, cut side up, and sprinkle insides lightly with salt and pepper and brush skin lightly with vegetable oil. Bake about 5 minutes. Invert tomatoes on paper towels to drain.

2. In the meantime, bring 2–3 quarts of salted water to a boil. Add

broccoli, and cook, covered, 7–8 minutes until tender. Remove with strainer-skimmer or slotted spoon to a colander and refresh under a spray of cool water to stop cooking. Transfer to a clean kitchen towel to absorb moisture. Repeat cooking procedure with green beans, using the same water.

3. Melt 1 tablespoon of the butter in a skillet and, when foam subsides, sauté shallots until tender. Add vegetables and sauté over moderately high heat 1–2 minutes to dry them as well as possible, being careful not to brown vegetables.

4. Vegetables can be puréed in a food mill, blender, or food processor fitted with a steel knife. Purée until either a smooth or a slightly coarse texture is achieved, whichever you prefer. Whisk or blend in remaining softened butter, cream, and seasonings, and mix until all ingredients are thoroughly combined. Can be done ahead to this point.

5. For mimosa egg garnish, with the back of a wooden spoon or with fingertips, push hard-cooked eggs through a sieve and set aside.

6. Spoon equal amounts of purée into tomato cavities, mounding them nicely. Transfer stuffed tomatoes to a lightly buttered baking dish and bake in preheated oven 10–15 minutes or until hot. Arrange on a platter lined with a bed of watercress and sprinkle tops with mimosa egg garnish.

To Prepare Ahead
Follow steps 1 through 4 up to one day ahead. Store tomatoes and vegetable purée separately in refrigerator in covered containers. Preheat oven to 350 degrees and complete steps 5 and 6 just before serving.

Note: A purée of peas may be substituted for the above green vegetables.

MARINATED ITALIAN YELLOW AND RED PEPPERS WITH BABY CARROTS AND ONIONS

I recently visited a quaint hillside restaurant in Assisi where every dish was worth copious note-taking. A wonderful beginning to our meal was a vegetable antipasto that included yellow peppers. In early fall, look for Italian peppers in varying shades of yellow to red to green in your marketplace. I was fortunate to find a few distinctly yellow ones mingling among the red. Today, yellow peppers from Holland, although expensive, are more readily available.

1¼ pounds yellow and red Italian frying peppers (or use all red if yellow is not available)

1 package (12 ounces) fresh baby carrots *or* 1 bunch fresh carrots with greens on

2¼ cups dry white wine

¾ cup white vinegar

1–2 bay leaves, crushed

1 large onion, peeled and thinly sliced

Imported Italian extra virgin olive oil

½ teaspoon coarse (kosher) salt

Freshly ground pepper

Stuffed green olives, slices of prosciutto, and sticks of Italian salami for garnish

Serves 10–12

1. Cut off and discard stem ends of peppers. Cut in half lengthwise and remove seeds and membrane. Rinse, then dry peppers in a clean kitchen towel. Trim, peel, and rinse carrots. Baby carrots look very pretty in this dish; however, if they are not available, use large carrots, trimmed, peeled, and rinsed, then cut into 1-inch pieces. Set aside.

2. Place peppers and carrots in a saucepan. Pour on white wine and white vinegar to barely cover. Add bay leaves and bring to a boil. Reduce heat and simmer briskly with cover ajar 20–25 minutes. Stir occasionally to distribute vegetables. Peppers will cook more quickly than carrots. When peppers are quite tender but not falling apart, transfer them with a slotted spoon to an earthenware or glass shallow baking dish. Add onions to saucepan with carrots and cook, uncovered, 5–10 minutes longer until carrots are tender.

3. Add contents of saucepan to peppers. Allow vegetable mixture to marinate 30 minutes or until at room temperature. Drain in a colander, discarding the marinade (most of which will have evaporated). Pour over

just enough olive oil to coat the vegetables lightly. Season with salt and pepper and stir vegetables gently to mix. They are best when allowed to marinate in the light dressing of oil for 2–3 days. Arrange attractively on a platter with stuffed green olives and cornucopias of prosciutto wrapped around sticks of Italian salami.

Suggestion: In Italy, these were also served with Italian garlic bread toast.

To Prepare Ahead
Follow steps 1 through 3 up to one week ahead. Refrigerate covered with plastic wrap. Bring to room temperature before serving.

MARINATED VEGETABLES ON THE GRILL

6–8 whole large snow-white mushrooms, rinsed or wiped clean, patted dry, and trimmed, woody stems discarded

2 red onions, peeled and sliced into 1-inch rounds

3–4 unpeeled baby eggplants, about ¼ pound each, rinsed and cut in half lengthwise; *or* 6–8 1-inch slices from a large unpeeled eggplant

6–8 whole plum tomatoes, rinsed

4–6 Italian frying peppers *or* 2–3 red or green bell peppers

Marinade
3 cloves garlic, finely chopped

1 tablespoon white wine or tarragon vinegar

2 tablespoons lemon juice

1 tablespoon finely chopped Italian flat-leaf parsley

2½ teaspoons fresh rosemary leaves *or* ¾ teaspoon dried

½ teaspoon coarse (kosher) salt

Freshly ground pepper

¾ cup light, fruity olive oil *or* ½ vegetable oil and ½ olive oil

Have on Hand
Hinged broiling rack or metal skewers

Serves 6–8

1. Trim and cut vegetables as directed and set aside. For peppers cut a ¼-inch slice off top. Remove seeds and membrane. Cut Italian peppers in half lengthwise and bell peppers into 3–4 sections.

2. *To Prepare Marinade:* Place garlic in a mixing bowl or whole cloves of garlic in workbowl of food processor fitted with steel blade. Add vinegar, lemon juice, parsley, rosemary, salt, and pepper, and whisk or process to mix. Add oil in a slow steady stream into mixing bowl or through feed tube of processor and whisk or process until mixture is homogenous. Set aside.

3. Place vegetables in a nonmetallic baking pan and pour over marinade. Allow to marinate 3–4 hours or overnight, turning once or twice to coat. As an added precaution marinate the onion slices separately, one layer deep to prevent them from separating into rings.

4. Lift vegetables from marinade, arrange closely in individual groupings in a hinged broiling rack, and close rack securely, or spear one kind of vegetable to each skewer. Place rack or skewers on a foil-lined cookie sheet and let stand at room temperature until ready to cook.

5. Preheat your grill and place the hinged broiling rack or skewers about 3 inches from ashen hot coals. Grill 8–10 minutes on one side, turn rack or skewers and grill 6–8 minutes on other side. Brush with marinade several times during the cooking. Timing is approximate and should be done to your taste and according to how hot your coals are. Return rack or skewers to foil-lined pan and serve immediately. Eat while crisp and warm.

To Prepare Ahead
Follow steps 1 through 3 up to one day ahead. Follow step 4 up to two hours ahead. Complete step 5 before serving.

FRESH VEGETABLE SALAD WITH CRÈME FRAÎCHE VINAIGRETTE

This is an all-inclusive vegetable and salad and will feed a crowd at a buffet or any large gathering. I love to include it in a summertime barbecue menu.

1 head broccoli, heavy stalks and leaves removed, reserving stalks. Cut broccoli into flowerets; pare stalks and slice at an angle

1–2 narrow, firm zucchini, scrubbed clean, ends discarded and sliced at an angle into 1-inch slices

10–12 spears asparagus in season, tender and young; spears cut at an angle into thirds

½ pound green beans. Stack and cut at stem end only, leaving tail on. Cut in half at an angle

½ pound snow-pea pods. Rinse and cut a tiny "V" from both ends of each pod

½ pound fresh mushrooms, wiped clean, and rubbed with cut side of lemon

½ pint firm ripe cherry tomatoes, rinsed clean

1 bunch fresh radishes with 1 inch of greens on

Vinaigrette

1 tablespoon finely chopped shallots

3 tablespoons thinly sliced scallions (white and light green part only)

1 tablespoon Dijon mustard

1 tablespoon fresh lemon juice

1–2 tablespoons Crème Fraîche or heavy cream

1 tablespoon red wine vinegar

1 teaspoon coarse (kosher) salt

Freshly ground pepper

½ cup peanut or vegetable oil

Serves 10–12

1. Blanch* all vegetables, except mushrooms, tomatoes, and radishes. Carefully dry each vegetable after blanching by blotting well on clean dry kitchen towels. Combine vegetables in a large bowl, and if doing ahead, cover with plastic wrap and refrigerate. It is best to blanch

mushrooms on the same day of serving; wrapped in plastic they will become mushy.

2. *Prepare Vinaigrette:* Place chopped shallots in a mixing bowl. Add scallions, mustard, lemon juice, crème fraîche or heavy cream, vinegar, salt, and pepper, and whisk or process to mix. Gradually add oil in a slow steady stream into the bowl or through feed tube and mix or process until mixture is thoroughly blended. Taste to adjust seasoning. If made ahead, store in screw-top jar and refrigerate.

3. Several hours before serving, prepare the mushrooms by simply placing them in a colander and pouring boiling water over them. Transfer to a clean dry kitchen towel and pat dry. Cut into ½-inch slices and set aside.

4. Up to one hour or so before serving, remove prepared vegetables from refrigerator, add the prepared mushrooms, and pour on the dressing. Toss gently until vegetables are well coated with vinaigrette. Transfer to a large salad bowl. Rinse and halve cherry tomatoes and carefully mix them through salad, keeping some of their bright red color in view. Scrub and dry radishes, then arrange them over the top of the vegetables. Check the salad for distribution of color and texture before serving.

To Prepare Ahead
Follow steps 1 and 2 up to one day ahead. Follow step 3 early in the day. Complete step 4 up to an hour or so before serving.

BASIC TOMATO SAUCE

Over the years, whenever I received a recipe from my mother that called for tomato sauce, I assumed she referred to a popular brand of canned sauce. During my research for this book, I scheduled a work day with her at my home. She brought her "canned sauce." It was in a jar and one that she prepared from scratch and apparently always had on hand. How did it elude me? I guess I've been away from home too long.

3 pounds ripe (preferably
    plum) tomatoes
1 tablespoon vegetable oil
3 large cloves garlic, peeled
    and finely chopped
3 large or 2 medium
    shallots, peeled and
    finely chopped
1 teaspoon coarse (kosher)
    salt

Freshly ground pepper
2 teaspoons fresh thyme
    leaves *or* ½ teaspoon
    dried
2 teaspoons coarsely
    chopped fresh basil
    leaves *or* ½ teaspoon
    dried

Yields 3½–4 cups

1. Plunge several tomatoes at a time into a kettle of boiling water for about 30 seconds. Remove with slotted spoon and cool under cold running water briefly. Skin will slip off easily at the point of a knife. Cut tomatoes in half crosswise, hold in palm of hand, and squeeze gently to remove and discard seeds. Slice into narrow shreds and set aside.

2. In 3–4-quart saucepan, heat oil with garlic for just a few seconds. Add shallots, and sauté until translucent, being careful not to brown. Add prepared tomatoes, season with salt, pepper, and herbs, and stir to mix. Let simmer over moderately low heat with cover ajar about 30 minutes. Remove cover, raise heat a bit, and cook at a brisk simmer an additional 25–30 minutes until some of the liquid has evaporated and sauce has thickened slightly. Let cool, then transfer to a screw-top jar and refrigerate. Use as directed in recipes.

To Prepare Ahead
Follow steps 1 and 2 up to three weeks ahead. Store covered in refrigerator. Or transfer to freezer-going containers and freeze for up to six months.

4

A SELECTION OF FISH

Many people are just venturing into the world of fish after many years of being enthralled with a largely meat diet. Nutrition-conscious consumers, supported by today's emphasis on health and physical fitness, have had a considerable impact on seafood consumption. In addition, increased travel and exposure to properly and interestingly prepared fish dishes have given fish an added boost.

Fish: One of the things that truly surprises many cooks is the incredible versatility of fish. Fish is nutritious, and is simple and quick to prepare. It makes very good sense to cook it more often at home. But you want to be absolutely certain that you are buying it fresh. Carefully choose a market where you have confidence that the fish is the very freshest available. When fresh, fish does not smell fishy, which is the concern of so many home cooks.

When buying whole fresh- or saltwater fish, look for bright red gills, not sticky or discolored. Scales should glisten with a lustrous sheen and adhere tightly to all parts of the fish. Eyes on a fresh fish are generally clear, but they can cloud over from resting on a bed of ice. Sunken or bloodied eyes are unacceptable.

No self-respecting European would buy fish *sans* head. This is the best way to tell just how fresh the fish is. Because it's easier and convenient, we tend to buy fillets of fish. I urge you whenever possible to select a whole fish of top quality and have it filleted. You will be getting more for your money in terms of flavor and wholesomeness. When the fish is suitable (white, firm flesh fish, such as bass, snapper, whiting, etc.) use the bones and heads for preparing a small amount of Fish Stock—a wonderful convenience when preparing Salmon in Chive-Cream Sauce.

When I buy fresh fish I prefer to cook it the day of purchase for maximum enjoyment. Once home, rewrap the fish loosely. If you must keep it for a day, put it into a glass or ceramic dish (a rectangular Pyrex lasagna baking dish is perfect) lined with a layer of ice cubes and place the loosely wrapped fish over the ice. Store in the coldest section of your refrigerator. (Never store any kind of fish or shellfish in a sealed plastic bag.)

Many fish cooking instructions will tell you that when fish flakes easily with a fork it is done. In my opinion, when fish flakes easily with a fork it is already overcooked and dry. Overcooking is the most common mistake people make with fish. The Canadian method of cooking fish has been adopted by many professionals and is a dependable barometer: Place the fish on its side and stand a ruler perpendicular to it at the thickest point just before the gills. Allow approximately ten minutes of cooking time per inch. The moment the flesh becomes opaque it is done. Pieces of cooked fish should slide away from each other rather than flake with a fork. This timing applies no matter which cooking method you use. Naturally, when you are baking stuffed whole fish, timing will be increased according to your recipe. When poaching a whole fish, use the ten-minutes-per-inch method as a guide and, when ready, insert a regular match from a soft-cover matchbook into the thickest part of the fish near the gills. If there is some resistance, the match will bend, meaning the fish is not thoroughly cooked. If the match moves smoothly through the flesh to the bone, the fish is done.

Most cooking techniques can be used successfully with fish—poaching, broiling, grilling, pan frying and sautéing, deep frying and baking. Firm-fleshed, white-textured fish lends itself to many or all of these procedures. Characteristically oily fish such as bluefish and mackerel, are more suitable for baking or grilling. Cook bluefish with acidic foods such as tomatoes and lemon—to cut the oiliness. Mackerel, of course, is perfect for pickling.

The following is a general idea of some types of fish and suitable cooking procedures:

FRESHWATER

Most freshwater fish is not chosen but caught. One of the pleasures of life for many people is pan-frying their freshly caught trout by the side of the stream.

	Deep Frying	Poaching	Broiling/ Grilling	Baking	Pan Frying/ Sautéing	Compound Mixtures
Bass			x	x	x	
Brook trout			x	x	x	
Carp				x		x
Catfish	x			x	x	
Perch				x	x	

SALTWATER

	Deep Frying	Poaching	Broiling/ Grilling	Baking	Pan Frying/ Sautéing	Compound Mixtures (for use in fish terrines or mousses)
Bluefish			x	x		
Grouper			x	x		
Haddock	x			x		x
Halibut		x	x	x		x
Mackerel			x	x		
Red snapper		x	x	x		
Salmon		x	x	x		
Scrod		x	x	x	x	
Sea Trout			x		x	
Sole or flounder fillets	x		x		x	x
Striped bass		x	x			
Swordfish			x	x		
Tilefish			x	x		x

Shrimp: Most people are unaware when they are buying "fresh shrimp," that it has already been frozen at the source (with occasional exception), thawed at the fish dealer, then packed in ice in the fishmarket's showcase. Shrimp are referred to as raw or "green"—a misleading term, since their color can range from pale pink or red to translucent with a greenish-white tinge. Their color is related to diet and habitat and not freshness.

Jumbo and large shrimp are generally more expensive, and somewhat less sweet than medium or small shrimp but are easier to prepare, since there is less shelling to do. Once shrimp has been shelled, cooked or uncooked, remove the intestinal vein which runs along the outer back curve. Make a shallow incision with the tip of a sharp knife or a toothpick, then rinse in a colander under cold running water and pat dry in a clean kitchen towel. It is not necessary to remove the long thin vein just under the curve of the body and just inside the shell.

Shrimp are also sold shelled, deveined, and frozen in bags. They are more expensive this way and some I have tasted have an iodine smell and flavor.

Shrimp cooked with their shells on will retain more flavor and are ideal when served cold with fresh mayonnaise and peeled as eaten—or marinated, then skewered and grilled over ashen hot coals.

Mussels, Clams, and Oysters: Popular are mussels, clams, and oysters whose shells should be well scrubbed in several changes of water. To clean these shellfish, put two mixing bowls in the kitchen sink; then put the shellfish in one bowl and cover with cold water.

For clams, hold one in each hand and scrub the shells against each other right in the water before transferring them to the empty clean second bowl. When all the clams are in the second bowl, cover them with fresh cold water. Empty the first bowl of the sandy water and rinse clean. Repeat scrubbing and transferring the clams as above three or four times. The job is done when the final water is free of sand.

The task of cleaning mussels and oysters is essentially the same as that of clams, except that I prefer to scrub each one individually with a strong wire brush. The barnacles and beards of mussels must be removed before scrubbing by scraping and tugging with a strong knife. Then scrub carefully several times, transferring shellfish to a clean bowl each time, as was done with clams. When you handle shellfish, it is important to keep them alive up to the point of cleaning and preparing.

Scallops: Creamy, tender, sweet scallops are one of my favorite seafoods. While the entire scallop with its delicate roe is edible, only the muscle of the scallop is consumed in this country. Because of the way scallops leap through water to avoid capture, they cannot hold their shells closed. Consequently, in captivity they quickly lose body moisture and die. Commercial fishermen shuck the scallop muscle while on board their boats and place them on ice to insure freshness. Tiny bay scallops come from tidal inlets and bays, such as Peconic Bay off Long Island, and are not as widely distributed as the larger sea scallop. Bay scallops are available in late summer through winter in the Northeast. Sea scallops, on the other hand, are available for most of the year.

Look for scallops that are pearly and translucent. A heavily opaque-white look could be the result of their having been soaked in a brine to increase their weight. Be sure to dry scallops in a clean kitchen towel before cooking them. Then cook quickly and briefly or they will lose moisture and flavor. Correctly prepared, they will retain a sweet, nutlike flavor with the fragrance of the sea.

Other Seafood Delicacies: Having a good fish dealer close at hand is a true blessing, especially when you are buying lobsters, which have become a luxury. Remember, you are looking for lobsters that flap their tails and wave their claws and look alive.

Fresh hard-shell crabs should also be moving around in a lively fashion. Fresh soft-shell crabs are a great delicacy; they may appear dormant but should be firm and odorless and move when touched.

Squid is growing in popularity on American tables and, although seasonal, is available in markets from about the last two weeks in March throughout the summer, when it becomes abundant. As with all seafoods, the fish dealer *is* your best friend when he markets fresh fish that has been properly cared for. This insured freshness can then be translated by you into a delicious dish for all to enjoy.

GRILLED FILLET OF SOLE WITH CRÈME FRAÎCHE

4 even-sized fillets of sole or flounder	½ teaspoon coarse (kosher) salt
2 tablespoons fresh lemon juice	Freshly ground pepper
1½ tablespoons finely chopped Italian flat-leaf parsley	½ cup Crème Fraîche
	Dash cayenne
	Lemon slices for garnish

Preheat broiler to highest setting for 15 minutes.

1. Rinse fillets in a little acidulated water (water sprinkled with 1 teaspoon lemon juice). Drain and pat dry with paper towels. Sprinkle with remaining lemon juice and let stand 15 minutes while broiler is preheating.

2. Remove grid from broiler pan. Line pan with foil, shiny side down, and put on the fish fillets in a single layer. Sprinkle evenly with parsley, salt, and pepper. Spoon about 3 tablespoons crème fraîche over each fillet, then color with a dash of cayenne.

3. Adjust your rack to about 4 inches from source of heat. Slide pan containing fillets into the broiler. The surface of the fish should be about 3 inches from source of heat. Broil 4–5 minutes until nicely glazed. (It is not necessary to turn broiled fish.) Use a wide spatula to transfer fillets to warmed plates and serve immediately accompanied by lemon slices.

To Prepare Ahead
Follow steps 1 and 2 up to several hours ahead. Refrigerate lightly covered with a tent of plastic wrap. Bring to room temperature 1 hour before serving and preheat broiler for 15 minutes before broiling fillets.

TERRINE OF FISH AND SPINACH WITH MOUSSELINE SAUCE

With the advent of the food processor, the fish mousse, more than any other dish, has been made accessible to the home cook. It has helped produce the properly light texture so necessary to this classic preparation. Serve it as an elegant luncheon main dish or a most impressive first course.

1 pound loose fresh spinach, fibrous stems and blemished leaves removed
1 tablespoon unsalted butter
2 shallots, finely chopped
¾ teaspoon coarse (kosher) salt
Freshly ground pepper
⅛ teaspoon nutmeg
2 tablespoons chopped Italian flat-leaf parsley
1¼ pound fish fillets (flounder, fillet of sole, snapper, etc.)
3 whole eggs
1 egg white
5 ounces cream cheese

5 tablespoons Crème Fraîche or heavy cream
2 tablespoons dry vermouth *or* ¼ cup dry white wine
½ teaspoon coarse (kosher) salt
Freshly ground pepper
5–6 drops Tabasco sauce
Tomato Rose and watercress for garnish
Mousseline Sauce (recipe follows)

Have on Hand
5-cup loaf pan, well buttered
Bain-marie*

Serves 8–10

To Prepare Loaf Pan: Place pan on sheet of wax paper and with the tip of a paring knife trace and cut an outline around the bottom of the pan. Insert rectangular piece of wax paper firmly in the bottom of the loaf pan and butter paper and sides of pan very well.

Preheat oven to 375 degrees.

1. Wash spinach in several changes of lukewarm water to clean the leaves of dirt and sand. Transfer spinach to a heavy saucepan with about 1 inch of water. Cover tightly and cook 3–4 minutes, stirring occasionally, until tender. Drain and refresh by fanning* and briefly running under cold water to set the color and stop the cooking. With your hands, squeeze spinach to remove moisture, then place in a clean kitchen towel and squeeze very dry. Place on a wooden board and chop coarsely.

2. In the meantime, melt butter in a skillet and, when foam subsides,

add shallots and sauté quickly over moderate heat until tender but not brown. Add spinach, salt, pepper, and nutmeg, stir to mix, and sauté just until butter is absorbed. Add parsley, stir into mixture, and remove from heat. Set aside.

3. *To Prepare Fish Mousse:* Place fish fillets on work counter. Cut away reed-thin lines that run lengthwise down the center of fillets and discard. Cut into 1-inch pieces and place in workbowl of food processor fitted with steel knife or in batches in a blender and purée. Add eggs and egg white and process or blend to mix. Then add cream cheese, crème fraîche or heavy cream, wine, and seasonings, and process or blend to thoroughly mix ingredients.

4. Spoon half fish mousse into prepared mold and level with rubber spatula. Place spinach mixture over mousse in an even layer. Spoon remaining fish mixture over spinach and smooth top. Give mold several sharp taps on a flat surface to settle mixture. Cover securely with foil.

5. Place in baking pan, then pour in enough hot water to come at least ⅔ of the way up the sides of the loaf pan (bain-marie). Bake in preheated oven 20–25 minutes or until a knife inserted in center comes out clean. Be careful not to overcook or mousse will be dry and rubbery. When touched with fingertips, the baked mousse should spring back slightly.

6. *To Unmold:* Insert ordinary kitchen knife between pan and mousse to loosen the sides. If serving warm, invert heated platter over top of pan and unmold. Remove and discard wax paper. Surround mousse with crisp watercress leaves and garnish the top with a tomato rose if desired. Serve with mousseline sauce.

To Prepare Ahead
If serving warm, follow steps 1 through 4 up to one day ahead. Refrigerate covered with foil. Bring to room temperature before completing steps 5 and 6.

If serving cold, follow steps 1 through 6 up to one day ahead; refrigerate, covered, and garnish just before serving.

MOUSSELINE SAUCE

For Terrine of Fish and Spinach with Mousseline Sauce or over other poached-fish dishes. Basically, this is a mayonnaise with cream instead of a vinegar seasoning.

2 egg yolks
1 teaspoon Dijon mustard
1 tablespoon dry vermouth
    or 2 tablespoons dry
    white wine
¼ teaspoon coarse (kosher)
    salt
Freshly ground pepper

1½ tablespoons fresh lemon
    juice
¾ cup vegetable oil
⅓ cup Crème Fraîche, or
    heavy cream, whipped
2 teaspoons snipped chives
    or finely chopped
    parsley

Yields 1½ cups

Place yolks, mustard, vermouth, salt, pepper, lemon juice in workbowl of food processor fitted with steel knife or in blender. Process or blend for a few seconds to mix. With machine running, gradually add oil in a slow steady stream through the feed tube of processor or into blender. Remove cover and add crème fraîche or whipped cream and fresh chives or parsley and process with 1 or 2 quick on/off pulses or blend to mix.

To Prepare Ahead
Can be completely prepared up to two days ahead and refrigerated in a suitable container. Bring to room temperature before serving.

CEVICHE AT THE OYSTER FACTORY

The old Oyster Factory is a restaurant on the north fork of Long Island.
The combined scallops and oysters make a new and appealing ceviche.

1 pound sea scallops
½ pound shucked oysters
½ cup fresh lime juice
¼ cup orange juice
      concentrate, diluted
      half strength
½ cup thinly sliced
      scallions, white and
      light green part only
2 cloves garlic, peeled and
      finely chopped
¾ teaspoon coarse (kosher)
      salt
Freshly ground pepper
Grated rind of 1 whole
      lemon

1 fresh hot chili pepper,
      seeds removed and
      finely chopped

Garnish
Boston or red-tipped lettuce
      leaves
Avocado slices
Fresh lemon juice
1 red pepper, seeds removed
      and finely diced (green
      pepper if red
      unavailable)

Serves 8–10

1. Rinse scallops, remove and discard sinew, then cut crosswise into 3 or 4 slices. Pat dry in a clean kitchen towel and put into a nonmetallic bowl along with oysters. Add lime juice, orange juice, scallions, garlic, salt, pepper, and lemon rind. Cover and let mixture marinate overnight.

2. Store chili pepper separately in a suitable container and chill.

3. Next day, drain scallop-and-oyster mixture of excess liquid. Add chili pepper and stir to mix. Taste to adjust seasoning if necessary.

4. *To Serve:* Wash and spin-dry lettuce leaves. Arrange 2 or 3 leaves to one side of 8 or 10 salad plates and fan avocado slices opposite, but touching, lettuce. Sprinkle avocado slices with lemon juice to avoid discoloration. Mound ceviche in center of avocado-lettuce arrangement. Top with sprinkling of diced red pepper. Serve at room temperature.

To Prepare Ahead
Follow steps 1 and 2 up to one day ahead. Store in refrigerator, covered. Store lettuce leaves in refrigerator wrapped in clean kitchen towel, then complete steps 3 and 4 up to 1 hour before serving.

Notes: When using hot peppers, remember there are several varieties of strength. Use cautiously depending on your taste.

Do not cut avocado until just before serving.

BOURRIDE WITH AÏOLI SAUCE

Bourride, a cousin of the famed bouillabaisse, is a glorious fish stew, creamy from its distinctive addition of Aïoli Sauce and made only with firm white-flesh fish.

3 pounds white-flesh fish
  fillets—bass, cod,
  halibut, or other
  nonoily fish
3 tablespoons olive oil
1 large onion, peeled and
  finely chopped
1 carrot, scrubbed, trimmed,
  and sliced
1 large leek, white part
  only, trimmed,
  thoroughly rinsed, and
  sliced
3 tomatoes, coarsely
  chopped
2 quarts Fish Stock
1 cup dry white wine
2 teaspoons fresh tarragon
  leaves *or* ½ teaspoon
  dried
1 teaspoon fresh thyme
  leaves *or* ¼ teaspoon
  dried

2 cloves garlic, finely
  chopped
2 2-inch strips fresh or dried
  orange peel
⅛–¼ teaspoon powdered
  saffron to taste
1 bay leaf
1 recipe Aïoli Sauce (recipe
  follows)
8–10 French Croutons

Have on Hand
6- or 7-quart flameproof
  enamel-over-iron
  casserole or 5–6-quart
  heavy stainless steel
  saucepan
Strainer-skimmer

Serves 8–10

1. Place fish fillets on work counter. Cut away reed-thin bony lines that run lengthwise down center of fillets and discard. Cut into 2-inch chunks and set aside.

2. Heat oil in flameproof casserole/saucepan. Add onion, carrot, and leek, and toss to coat in oil. Cover and cook over moderately low heat to sweat the vegetables 6–8 minutes or until tender but not brown. Add tomatoes and stir to mix and simmer for a minute or two. Add fish stock, white wine, herbs, garlic, orange peel, saffron, and bay leaf. Bring to a boil and simmer 15–20 minutes. Taste for salt and pepper and adjust seasoning as necessary. Remove bay leaf.

3. Ladle broth in batches and purée in a food processor fitted with steel knife or in a blender, then strain into a bowl. Return to rinsed-out casserole/saucepan.

4. Bring liquid back to a boil, reduce heat to a simmer, maintaining a lazy surface bubble, and add fish. Cook, uncovered, 3–4 minutes. With a strainer-skimmer or slotted spoon, transfer fish to warm platter when it is done.

5. Put half of aïoli sauce in a mixing bowl, place the rest in a serving dish or sauceboat, and set aside. Gradually pour a cupful of the hot broth into the aïoli in the mixing bowl while whisking vigorously. Return this mixture to the hot broth in casserole/saucepan and whisk continuously for a minute or two until soup is thick enough to coat a spoon. Do not allow it to boil or soup will separate.

6. *To Serve:* Place 1 or 2 prepared croutons in warm, wide soup bowls and moisten with a ladleful of the hot, creamy broth. Arrange chunks of fish over the bread and top with a dollop of aïoli sauce, or pass sauce at table. Serve at once.

To Prepare Ahead
Follow steps 1 through 3 early in the day or several hours ahead. Let stand at room temperature. Complete steps 4 through 6 just before serving.

AÏOLI SAUCE
A Garlic Mayonnaise

There is a traditional French recipe known as "Le Grand Aïoli" which is completely prepared ahead and served at room temperature for special holiday meals. However, it is most frequently identified with Bourride, a French fish stew.

3–4 cloves garlic, finely
   chopped
1 cup cubed Italian or
   French bread
3 tablespoons red wine
   vinegar
1 tablespoon Dijon mustard
¼ teaspoon coarse (kosher)
   salt

Dash cayenne
2 egg yolks, room
   temperature
⅔–¾ cup light olive oil or
   combination of olive
   and vegetable oil

Yield 1½ cups

Place chopped garlic in a mixing bowl or chop finely in workbowl of food processor fitted with steel knife. Add cubes of bread and sprinkle with wine vinegar to moisten. Add mustard, salt, and cayenne. Stir or process to mix. Add egg yolks one at a time and stir vigorously or process to mix. Gradually add oil in a slow, steady stream into bowl or through feed tube of processor until mixture is thick enough to hold its shape in a spoon. Transfer to a screw-top jar or other suitable container and refrigerate for up to 2 weeks.

LET'S GRILL A FISH

Cooking a fish over coals is a very delicate procedure, but correctly done it can produce a dish that is extremely moist and flavorful. So oil your hinged double-sided oval fish grill and "Let's Grill a Fish."

5–6-pound striped bass or
    red snapper, head and
    tail on, cleaned, gills
    and scales removed
Coarse (kosher) salt
Freshly ground pepper
3 tablespoons unsalted
    butter, melted
2 teaspoons fresh rosemary
    leaves *or* ½ teaspoon
    dried
1 bay leaf, crushed

Herb Dressing
2 cloves garlic, finely
    chopped
3 tablespoons finely chopped
    Italian flat-leaf parsley
2 teaspoons fresh oregano
    leaves *or* ¾ teaspoon
    dried

1 teaspoon dried fennel
3–4 tablespoons fresh lemon
    juice
1 tablespoon anisette
⅓ cup imported light olive
    oil

Lemon Butter Sauce
    (optional)
10 tablespoons unsalted
    butter at room
    temperature
2–3 tablespoons fresh lemon
    juice
Coarse (kosher) salt
Dash cayenne pepper

Have on Hand
Hinged fish-shaped grill

Serves 6–8

1. Rinse fish quickly in a basin of salted water, then dry very well in several layers of paper toweling. Lightly salt and pepper inside of fish. Add rosemary and bay leaf to butter. Brush this mixture all over the inside of fish.

2. *To Prepare Herb Dressing:* Put garlic and parsley together in a mixing bowl. Add oregano, fennel, lemon juice, and anisette, and stir to mix. Gradually whisk in olive oil until mixture is thoroughly blended.

3. With a sharp paring knife, cut 2–3 diagonal incisions through the skin of the fish on both sides. Coat fish liberally with the herb mixture, then lightly salt and pepper both sides. Can be done several hours ahead to this point.

4. Oil a hinged fish grill and lay fish on its side. Secure grill closed. Mound a deep bed of coals in your barbecue and burn them down until they show a film of gray ash. Place fish about 3 inches from source of heat and cook about 15 minutes on each side, turning grill every 5 minutes over the coals. Fish is done when flesh is opaque, which can be seen through the slanted incisions, and when skin is crisp. Be careful not to overcook.

5. *To Prepare Lemon Butter Sauce* (optional): Cooking on an outdoor grill often involves a partnership. This optional sauce is a lilting addition to the grilled fish but requires another pair of hands. The technique for preparing it is that of a Beurre Blanc, which is a classic butter sauce.

Cut 8 tablespoons of the butter into a mixing bowl and whip until light and fluffy. Set aside. Melt remaining 2 tablespoons butter in a heavy saucepan. Over very low heat, whisk in whipped butter a little at a time so that it does not break down and becomes a thoroughly blended creamy mixture. It may be necessary to adjust heat so that butter does not get too hot and liquefy. Remove from heat and whisk in lemon juice and a sprinkle of salt and pepper. Should be prepared just before serving to assure its proper consistency and timed with the cooking of the fish.

6. *To Serve:* Transfer fish to a heated platter and spoon on lemon butter sauce, if desired. Since this is a favorite summertime outdoor barbecue, it is timely to surround the fish with a kaleidoscope of seasonal vegetables. I like to serve it with Marinated Vegetables on the Grill.

To Prepare Ahead
Follow steps 1 through 3 up to one day ahead. Refrigerate covered with a tent of plastic wrap. Bring to room temperature and complete steps 4 through 6 before serving.

STEAMED RED SNAPPER WITH
GINGER HOLLANDAISE

I was so taken with the idea of doing a ginger-spiked hollandaise for broiled or steamed fish that the sauce recipe was responsible for the following procedure. Orientals know more about steaming whole fish than most, so I borrowed this technique from my good friend Dee Wang, cooking teacher and author. The results were spectacular.

2 red snappers, 1–1¼
    pounds each, gutted,
    gills removed, and
    scaled, head and tail on
3–4 scallions, rinsed,
    trimmed, and thinly
    sliced, white and light
    green part only
½-inch piece fresh ginger,
    peeled and cut into fine
    julienne strips
¼ cup Basic Chicken Stock
    or broth

Ginger Hollandaise Sauce
    (recipe follows)

Have on Hand
Round porcelain quiche or
    any round pottery or
    porcelain baking dish
    that will fit into your
    wok
Wok with cover and rack

Serves 3–4

1. Pour about 6 cups water in bottom of wok, place over moderately high heat, and bring to a boil. Put porcelain dish next to wok. Dip fish into boiling water, lift out immediately with the aid of tongs, and transfer to waiting dish. This procedure rinses fish and removes any fishy odor. Repeat with second fish.

2. Scatter scallions and ginger over fish and pour chicken stock or broth around it. Pour off water in wok, leaving about 1½ inches in the bottom. Insert rack into wok and place the heatproof porcelain dish on it. Cover, bring the water underneath back to a boil, adjust heat to keep water at a brisk simmer and steam for about 12–15 minutes.

3. Remove heatproof dish from wok and place on work counter. To serve one portion, roll back the skin with a fork and knife and lift steamed fish from over the backbone onto a heated plate. Lift and discard bone and serve remaining fish portions in the same manner. Spoon Ginger Hollandaise Sauce over fish and serve immediately.

To Prepare Ahead
Follow step 1 up to one hour ahead. Complete steps 2 and 3 just before
serving.

GINGER HOLLANDAISE SAUCE
Made in the Food Processor

*Steamed, broiled, or poached snapper, bass, or sole fillets become something
quite extraordinary when served with this simply prepared, classic, ginger-
spiked sauce.*

2 teaspoons finely chopped
    fresh ginger
3 egg yolks
2 teaspoons fresh lemon
    juice

¼ teaspoon coarse (kosher)
    salt
Dash of cayenne pepper
1 stick (8 tablespoons)
    unsalted butter

Yield 1 cup sauce

1. Remove and discard peel from about a 1-inch knob of ginger root.
Cut into thin slices, stack, and cut into thin strips. Now cut in the
opposite direction to achieve tiny dice. Measure approximately 2 teaspoons chopped ginger and place in workbowl of food processor fitted
with steel knife or blender and process with several on-off pulses or
blend to chop ginger as finely as possible.

2. Add egg yolks, lemon juice, salt, and cayenne to workbowl or
blender and process a few seconds to mix ingredients. Set aside.

3. In a small saucepan, melt butter to a rapid boil. With machine
running, pour hot bubbling butter through feed tube of processor or into
blender in a slow, steady stream. When all the butter is incorporated,
turn off machine. If not using immediately, transfer to the top of a
double boiler over, not in, simmering water or to a small heavy saucepan
on a flame tamer over gentle heat, and keep warm, whisking occasionally.
Spoon over servings of steamed, broiled, or poached fish.

To Prepare Ahead
Follow steps 1 through 3 up to thirty minutes before serving.
Note: It is important for the butter to be hot and bubbly when added
to the food processor or blender, otherwise your hollandaise will be thin
and soupy.

SALMON IN CHIVE-CREAM SAUCE

The setting was Roger Verge's Moulin de Mougins in the South of France in 1977. We were a party of six, and I opted, along with another guest, for the salmon specialty of the day. We were, indeed, the two luckiest people at the table.

2 pounds center cut of
    salmon
2 tablespoons finely chopped
    shallots
¾ cup dry white wine
⅔ cup reduced Fish Stock
⅔ cup Crème Fraîche
½ cup heavy cream
1 egg yolk
½ teaspoon coarse (kosher)
    salt
Freshly ground pepper

1 tablespoon fresh lemon
    juice
3 tablespoons unsalted butter
3 tablespoons freshly
    snipped chives

Have on Hand
2 2-quart rectangular Pyrex
    baking dishes
Parchment paper
Sharp slicing knife
Batticarne* (meat pounder)

Serves 6

Preheat oven to 350 degrees.

1. Have your fish dealer do the following procedures for you: Cut a 2-pound piece of salmon, preferably from the center. Fillet the fish off the bone in 1 thick piece and repeat procedure with other side. Then, skin side down, slide a sharp knife between the skin and the salmon to remove and discard skin. You should be able to do the rest yourself: Cut each solid piece of salmon horizontally into 3 slices. Place salmon on a cutting board and with a sharp knife cut against the grain, making 3 long thin equal pieces. Repeat with remaining salmon side to yield 6 slices.

2. Place each slice, one at a time, between sheets of wax paper and, with a batticarne dipped into a bowl of water, pound gently until thin— about as thick as veal scallopine.

3. Line 2 baking dishes with parchment paper, extending it beyond the rim of each dish at both ends to act as handles later. Place 3 salmon fillets next to each other one layer deep over the parchment. Cover with another layer of parchment. Repeat with second baking dish and set aside.

4. *To Prepare Sauce:* In a heavy saucepan, combine shallots and wine. Cook over moderately high heat until reduced by half. Add fish

stock and simmer about 5 minutes. Strain liquid through a fine sieve, pushing shallots with the back of a wooden spoon to extract their juices. Discard shallots.

5. Return liquid to saucepan; add crème fraîche and heavy cream. Simmer about 5 minutes.

6. In a small bowl combine egg yolk with a few tablespoons of the warm liquid and stir to mix. Gradually whisk this mixture into the saucepan. Add salt, pepper, lemon juice and stir to mix. Taste to adjust seasonings if necessary. Swirl in butter 1 tablespoon at a time to flavor and thicken sauce slightly. Add chives; stir through and keep warm. Do not allow to boil. Cover surface of sauce with a disk of buttered wax paper to prevent a skin from forming. Can be made ahead to this point.

7. Place salmon in preheated oven and bake 1½–2 minutes. This is not a timing error—*I mean minutes*. Remove parchment paper and with a large metal spatula transfer fish to warm dinner plates. Spoon equal portions of sauce over salmon and sprinkle with snipped chives for garnish. Serve immediately. This was a nouvelle cuisine presentation at the height of its popularity.

To Prepare Ahead
Follow steps 1 through 3 up to one day ahead. Refrigerate, covered. Follow steps 4 through 6 up to an hour or so ahead. Keep warm in a bain-marie.* Complete step 7 just before serving.

SCALLOP PENNIES WITH GINGER SAUCE

½ pound sea scallops
5 ounces snow peas
4–5 large fresh snow-white
    mushrooms
Half a lemon
Watercress, washed and
    dried

2 tablespoons Dijon mustard
2 teaspoons hoisin sauce
2 teaspoons red wine vinegar
1 teaspoon light soy sauce
Dash cayenne
2 tablespoons sesame oil
2 tablespoons peanut oil

Dressing
2 tablespoons finely chopped
    ginger

Serves 6

1. Place scallops in a steam basket or strainer over simmering water and cook, covered, 3–4 minutes. Remove from heat and allow to cool. When cool, slice into thin rounds and set aside.

2. Blanch snow peas in boiling water to cover 1 minute. Drain and refresh under cold running water. Pat dry with a clean kitchen towel. Stack 2–3 pods on cutting board, then cut a small V shape from both ends. Continue until all are done. Set aside.

3. Rinse mushrooms quickly under a spray of cold running water. Gently pat dry in a clean kitchen towel. Rub caps with cut side of lemon to retain whiteness. Trim off and discard woody stem ends.

4. Put chopped ginger in a mixing bowl or chop finely in workbowl of food processor fitted with metal blade. Add mustard, hoisin, wine vinegar, soy sauce, and cayenne to bowl, and whisk or process to mix. Add oils in a thin stream, whisking by hand or processing through feed tube of machine until thoroughly blended.

5. When ready to serve, place 3 tablespoons sauce inside rim on each of 6 medium-sized dessert plates. Center 6–8 scallop slices in a ring within the sauce. Overlap several mushroom slices to one side and along the rim of the plate. Arrange 3–4 snow peas in a single layer on the opposite rim of the plate. Fill open spaces on rim with a few sprigs of watercress. Serve as a first course.

To Prepare Ahead
Follow steps 1 through 4 up to one day ahead. Refrigerate vegetables and sauce separately in suitable containers. Complete step 5 before serving.

BAKED RED SNAPPER FROM SALONIKA

Salonika is a seaport town in northern Greece where a large Sephardic Jewish community once dwelled. This recipe comes from a friend now living in Paris and is a hand-me-down from her family in Salonika. It is simple to execute—all the ingredients are layered in an oven-going serving pan and, in a sense, marinates in the combination of oil, garlic, parsley, and tomatoes. Since this dish benefits from a do-ahead preparation, instructions for preheating come after step 3. Bake just before serving and plan to cook lots of fluffy white rice to absorb the resulting flavorful juices.

2 red snappers, 1¼–1½ pounds each, filleted with skin on

3–4 tablespoons imported olive oil

2–3 ripe tomatoes, thinly sliced

Persillade (a culinary term for chopped parsley mixed with varying amounts of chopped garlic)

⅓ cup firmly packed Italian flat-leaf parsley, washed, spin-dried, and finely chopped

2–3 large cloves garlic, peeled and finely chopped

1 teaspoon coarse (kosher) salt

Freshly ground pepper

⅛ teaspoon cayenne

1–2 lemons, sliced very thin

Have on Hand

2-quart Pyrex, porcelain, or enamel baking pan

Heavy-duty aluminum foil

Serves 6

1. Rinse fish fillets in salted water and dry well with paper toweling.

2. Drizzle 2 tablespoons oil in bottom of a 2-quart baking dish. Arrange half of cut tomatoes in the dish. Combine chopped parsley and garlic and sprinkle ⅓ of this mixture over tomatoes and place the 2 fillets skin side down over persillade.

3. Drizzle a tablespoon or so of olive oil over exposed surface of the fish and season with a light sprinkling of salt, pepper, and additional ⅓ of persillade. Place remaining fillets skin side up over fish fillets underneath. Drizzle remaining oil over fish. Season again with a touch of salt, pepper, remaining persillade, and a healthy dash or two of cayenne. Scatter remaining tomatoes and lemon slices over fish. Cover

baking pan securely with aluminum foil. Can be done ahead to this point.

Preheat oven to 350 degrees.

4. Place in preheated oven and bake 30–35 minutes or until skin loses its sheen, fish is opaque, and flesh is still moist and not dry. Serve with hot buttered rice.

To Prepare Ahead

Follow steps 1 through 3 up to one day ahead. Refrigerate, covered. Bring to room temperature and complete step 4 just before serving.

SALMON EN PAPILLOTE

En papillote means encased in parchment. Here, the fish is enveloped in parchment paper with vegetables and when the paper is sealed, the combination bakes in its own juices. It is an intriguing way to present a fish and helps to insure its moistness.

3 tablespoons unsalted butter
1 medium onion, peeled and finely chopped
3 shallots, peeled and finely chopped
1 pound carrots, scrubbed clean or peeled and thinly sliced
½ pound fresh mushrooms, quickly rinsed clean, dried, and thinly sliced
3 ripe tomatoes, peeled, seeded, and sliced into shreds
1½ teaspoon coarse (kosher) salt
Freshly ground pepper

2 teaspoons fresh tarragon leaves *or* ½ teaspoon dried
½ cup dry white wine
1 tablespoon finely chopped Italian flat-leaf parsley
4 salmon steaks, 6–8 ounces each
2 tablespoons melted butter for parchment paper

Have on Hand
Parchment paper
Egg glaze: 1 yolk mixed with 1 tablespoon water

Serves 4

Preheat oven to 375 degrees.

1. Melt 3 tablespoons butter in a heavy saucepan and, when foam subsides, add onion and shallots and sauté quickly until tender but not

brown. Add carrots, mushrooms, and tomatoes; season with salt, pepper, and tarragon, and stir to mix. Add white wine and cook over moderately high heat until wine is evaporated. Reduce heat, cover, and simmer 10–12 minutes. Remove from heat, add parsley, and stir to mix. Taste to adjust seasoning if necessary.

2. *To Prepare Parchment Paper:* Cut sheets of parchment paper wide enough to fold over and leave a 1½-inch border around each salmon steak. For each steak, fold a sheet in half, then cut off hard edges to round them. Open paper and brush each piece of parchment with melted butter. Place salmon steak on one half next to the fold. Continue with remaining steaks. Lightly season each steak with a sprinkle of salt and pepper. Divide and distribute the vegetable mixture evenly over each steak. Fold paper over to enclose fish. Starting at the top and working with about 1 inch at a time, make pleatlike folds around the edge. Hold a finger on fold as you make the next. Each fold seals the one before. Fold the end several times to secure it closed. With a pastry brush, brush egg glaze along pinched edges of parchment to seal it. Repeat procedure on remaining parchment packages. Can be done ahead to this point.

Salmon en Papillote, wrapping the fish in parchment paper

Step 1 Step 2 Step 3

3. Place parchment-covered salmon on a cookie sheet on middle rack of oven and bake 12–14 minutes. Serve in the paper bag; you cut one open first, so that your guests can follow suit. Parsleyed new potatoes are a suitable accompaniment.

To Prepare Ahead
Follow steps 1 and 2 up to several hours ahead and refrigerate. Bring to room temperature and complete step 3 before serving.

Note: Vegetable mixture can be prepared up to one day ahead and refrigerated in a suitable container.

POACHED SALMON STEAKS WITH MUSHROOM BÉARNAISE

When the occasion arises and fish is the star of your dinner party, this complete do-ahead preparation will set you at ease.

6 salmon steaks cut about 1
    inch thick
¾ cup water
1 cup white wine
1 medium onion, thinly
    sliced
6 peppercorns
3 sprigs Italian flat-leaf
    parsley
1 bay leaf

Béarnaise Sauce
4 tablespoons tarragon
    vinegar
⅛ teaspoon powdered mace
8 peppercorns
3 egg yolks
½–¾ teaspoon coarse
    (kosher) salt

10 tablespoons unsalted
    butter, cut into 10
    equal slices
½ teaspoon tomato paste

Garnish
¾ pounds fresh snow-white
    mushrooms, wiped
    clean, trimmed, and
    finely sliced
1 tablespoon grated orange
    rind
2–3 teaspoons grated lemon
    rind
½–¾ teaspoon coarse
    (kosher) salt
Freshly ground pepper

Serves 6–8

Preheat oven to 350 degrees.

1. Place salmon steaks in a 2-quart oblong Pyrex baking dish. Pour on water, wine, onion, peppercorns, bay leaf, and parsley. Cover with buttered parchment paper. Place in a preheated oven and bake 6–8 minutes. At this point fish will not be fully cooked. Remove from oven and lift steaks from liquid onto a cutting surface. Pour all the liquid ingredients into a saucepan.

2. Divide salmon steaks in half and carefully trim as well as possible of all bones and skin. Add trimmings to poaching liquid. Reduce poaching liquid to ¼ cup by simmering briskly over moderate high heat. Strain and set aside.

3. In the meantime, arrange the trimmed steaks neatly in a buttered baking dish and set aside.

4. *To Prepare Béarnaise Sauce:* In a nonaluminum saucepan combine vinegar, mace, and peppercorns over moderate heat and bring to a boil. Reduce liquid to 1½ tablespoons. Strain into a small mixing bowl. Add 3 egg yolks and whisk into vinegar mixture until creamy. Return mixture to saucepan and season with salt. Place pan over low heat and beat in butter 1 tablespoon at a time until mixture is smooth and thick. It may be necessary to lift the pan occasionally to cool the mixture so that it does not curdle. Add reduced poaching liquid, stir to mix, and remove from heat.

5. Place a layer of sliced mushrooms over salmon steaks. Spoon on sauce to cover completely. Sprinkle over orange and lemon rind and season with a light sprinkle of salt and pepper. Can be prepared ahead to this point. Cover with buttered parchment paper.

6. Before serving, put into a preheated 350-degree oven 10–15 minutes or until heated through. Place under broiler to glaze and color slightly.

To Prepare Ahead
Follow steps 1 through 5 early in the day and refrigerate covered with plastic wrap. Bring to room temperature and complete step 6 before serving.

TORTA DE SALMONE

There was both surprise and delight when I first ate a slice of this buttery tuna mousse encased in smoked salmon in Venice, Italy. I promise you—it will star at your next brunch. Just be sure to have the salmon cut into paper-thin slices long enough to line your mold.

¾ cup unsalted butter (12 tablespoons)
2 7-ounce cans tuna in oil, drained (reserve 1 tablespoon or so of oil)
2 tablespoons fresh lemon juice
¼ teaspoon freshly ground white pepper
1 cup mayonnaise, preferably homemade
1 teaspoon fresh chervil leaves *or* ¼ teaspoon dried
2 teaspoons capers
12–18 slices smoked salmon, depending on width salmon is cut (should be about 2 inches wide at center)

Garnish
Several sprigs of fresh dill
1 cucumber, peeled and cut into thin rounds
10–12 toast points
1 bunch watercress, washed and spin-dried

Have on Hand
6-cup ring mold or loaf pan
Plastic wrap

Serves 10–12

1. In a large mixing bowl, cream butter with a large wooden spoon until light and fluffy.

2. In another bowl, mash tuna with a fork, using 1 tablespoon or so of the oil to help soften. Add tuna to creamed butter and work it in until fully incorporated. Season with lemon juice and pepper.

3. Work the mixture with a large wooden spoon, beating it until light and fluffy. The more you work it, the lighter it gets in both color and texture. Add mayonnaise, chervil, and capers, and stir to mix. Taste to adjust seasoning.

4. Line a mold with a large enough piece of plastic wrap to leave approximately a 2–3-inch overhang all around after pressing into the

corners of mold. Lay strips of smoked salmon to line mold evenly, overlapping them slightly.

5. Cut any remaining pieces of salmon into small pieces and stir into tuna mousse. Spoon mixture into the lined mold. If any salmon strip ends come over edge of mold, fold them over onto tuna mousse, then bring up plastic wrap overhang to completely cover. Refrigerate for several hours or overnight. Can be completely prepared to this point up to two days ahead.

6. Unwrap plastic covering, then place a serving platter over mold to invert and unmold. Carefully pull off plastic wrap and discard. Arrange several fresh dill sprigs over top of mousse. Place overlapping slices of cucumber and toast points around base of mold on a bed of watercress—or use watercress to fill center, if a ring mold was used. Keep refrigerated until ready to serve. If left standing at room temperature, butter in mousse will soften and it will be difficult to slice. To serve, cut into slices with a serrated knife.

To Prepare Ahead
Follow steps 1 through 5 up to two days ahead. Refrigerate covered in mold. Complete step 6 just before serving.

MISTY FRIED SHRIMP WITH MUSTARD-FRUIT SAUCE

A beer batter for shrimp is something that has been familiar to many of us for a long time. The batter was classic and I taught it in its original recipe any number of times. It was a cooking-school favorite and remained unchanged until I met Elizabeth Andoh and she introduced me to her "Misty" Fried Shrimp. She uses transparent dried noodles known in Japanese as harusame *(literally, "spring rain"). It may be more familiar to us on market shelves as Chinese bean-thread noodles.*

When the shrimp are dipped into the bean-thread coating and deep-fried, they look like little white clouds with shrimp tails and work beautifully with the mustard-fruit sauce. Elizabeth's approach is lighter and the coating stays crisper than batter-fried—to me this recipe is today.

3 ounces harusame (Chinese bean-thread noodles)
30 raw extra large shrimp (16–18 count)
¼ cup flour
½ teaspoon coarse (kosher) salt
¼ teaspoon sansho (Japanese fragrant pepper)
2 egg whites
Enough vegetable oil for deep frying
Watercress for garnish (optional)

Mustard-Fruit Sauce
¾ cup orange marmalade
4–5 tablespoons fresh lemon juice
2 tablespoons fresh orange juice
3–4 teaspoons grated horseradish (preferably fresh)
½–¾ teaspoon powdered ginger
½ teaspoon coarse (kosher) salt
½–1 teaspoon dry English mustard

Serves 10–12

1. Snip noodles with sharp scissors into ¼–½-inch lengths. For ease of preparation, use food processor fitted with steel knife. Run the machine empty and feed the noodles in *small* batches through the feed tube, covering opening after each addition. Process about 10 seconds. You should have about ⅔–¾ cup of pieces. Set aside.

2. Carefully remove shells from body of shrimp, leaving tail intact. With a sharp paring knife, make an incision along back and lift out intestinal vein. Wash shrimp thoroughly under cold running water and drain on paper toweling.

3. Combine flour, salt, and pepper in a paper bag or plastic container with a cover. Toss shrimp in container until lightly coated.

4. Beat egg whites until foamy but not stiff. Dip shrimp into egg whites, then immediately into noodle pieces and place one layer deep on a jelly-roll sheet lined with wax paper. Set aside.

5. Heat oil to about 325 degrees and test with a bit of bean thread noodle, which should sink slightly, rise to the surface, and puff out, though not color. Fry the shrimp a few at a time for 2 minutes or until opaque. The noodle coating will hardly color. It should remain pale, like the morning mists it is named after. Drain fried shrimp on paper toweling. Serve hot or at room temperature with mustard-fruit sauce.

6. *Mustard-Fruit Sauce:* Combine all sauce ingredients in a mixing bowl, food processor, or blender, and stir or process to mix. If using a food processor, be careful not to purée, just process with one or two quick on/off pulses until ingredients are combined.

7. *To Serve:* This makes a spectacular first course to a dinner when served individually. Spoon a puddle of mustard-fruit sauce into the center of a dessert- or salad-size plate. Arrange 2 or 3 shrimp so that bodies meet in center of sauce and tail ends face outer edges of each dish. Garnish with sprigs of watercress if desired.

For cocktail parties, cover a large serving tray with crisp watercress, place a small dish of mustard-fruit sauce in center and arrange fried shrimp over greens.

To Prepare Ahead

Steps 1, 2, and 6 may be done up to one day ahead. Refrigerate covered in suitable containers. Bring to room temperature and complete remaining steps up to thirty minutes before serving.

Note: Since the mustard-fruit sauce can be prepared even weeks ahead, I would suggest you make it first and refrigerate it in a suitable container.

TARAMASALATA

A nifty little hors d'oeuvre. This delectable Greek appetizer, made from carp roe, is used as a spread on toast points or crisp slices of French bread or as a dip for crudités.

½ cup crumbed white bread
4-ounce jar tarama (carp roe)
2 tablespoons grated onion
Freshly ground white pepper
3 eggs

½ cup fresh lemon juice
1½ cups vegetable oil
1 head Boston lettuce,
    lemon slices, Greek
    black olives for garnish

Yields 3½ cups

1. Cut away crusts from a small loaf of French or white bread and pull into crumbs. Pack into a 1-cup measure. Pour cold water over bread and let soak 3–4 minutes. Squeeze bread in hands until very dry. Place in workbowl of food processor fitted with steel knife or in a blender. Add tarama, grated onion, and pepper and process or blend to mix until it becomes a paste. Stop machine and push down sides with a rubber spatula as necessary.

2. Add eggs one at a time and process or blend to mix.

3. With machine running, add lemon juice and oil alternately until mixture is thick but of spreading consistency. Taramasalata should have the texture of a light, creamy mayonnaise.

4. *To Serve:* Rinse whole head of lettuce, keeping the leaves intact, then turn upside down on paper towels to drain. Pull out center leaves of head so the lettuce looks like a petal-edged bowl. Place on a serving dish. Spoon tarama into center of the "bowl" and surround with lemon slices. Top each slice with a black olive and accompany with very thin slices of toasted French bread or toast points. Or simply spread on thin crisp toasted slices of French bread, decorate with a thin sliver of black olive, and serve.

To Prepare Ahead
Follow steps 1 through 3 up to three to four weeks ahead and refrigerate in suitable containers. Follow step 4 to use as a spread or a dip.

Note: Tarama, made from carp roe, is available in 4- and 8-ounce jars. If using less than the full jar, pour in a little oil to cover remaining portion and refrigerate. It will keep for a month.

DEVILED SHRIMP AND MELON

Stretch your culinary imagination with this fine example of nouvelle cuisine. The sweet cool fruit contrasts delightfully with the creamy spiciness of the shrimp.

1 pound raw small shrimp
(28–32 count), in the
shell
½ cup flour
Freshly ground pepper
¼ teaspoon paprika
½ cup vegetable oil
1 clove garlic, finely
chopped
1 tablespoon chili sauce
½ teaspoon coarse (kosher)
salt
1 teaspoon tomato paste

1–1½ teaspoons curry
powder
½ cup yogurt
2 tablespoons light or heavy
cream
1 ripe cantaloupe, cut into 8
even-sized wedges
Juice of 1 lime
1 tablespoon finely chopped
Italian flat-leaf parsley
1 bunch watercress for
garnish

Serves 4–6

1. Carefully remove shells from body of shrimp. With sharp paring knife, make an incision along the back and lift out the intestinal vein. Wash shrimp thoroughly under cold running water and drain on paper toweling.

2. Combine flour, pepper, and paprika in a paper bag or plastic container with cover. Toss shrimp in bag or in covered container until well coated.

3. Heat oil in an 8- or 9-inch skillet until it begins to ripple slightly (375 degrees). Watch it closely. Put in several pieces of shrimp at a time and fry on both sides until opaque, about 1 minute. Shrimp will cook very quickly. Be careful not to overcook, or they will toughen. Remove with slotted spoon as they are done and allow to drain on paper toweling.

4. Pour off and discard all but 1 tablespoon oil from skillet. Add garlic, chili sauce, and salt, and cook, stirring, 2 minutes. Stir in tomato paste and curry powder and cook for another 1–2 minutes.

5. Transfer chili-sauce mixture to a mixing bowl, then gradually whisk in yogurt and cream until smooth. Gently fold cooked shrimp into chili-sauce mixture and toss to coat.

6. With a knife, cut melon into 8 equal wedges and remove skin. Cut each wedge lengthwise into 3–4 thin slices and fan in an overlapping

arrangement on 8 individual plates. Sprinkle lime juice over melon slices. Divide shrimp mixture equally at the point of the fan of melon slices and sprinkle with chopped parsley. Garnish each plate with several sprigs of watercress.

To Prepare Ahead
Follow steps 1 through 5 up to one day ahead. Refrigerate, covered. Cut melon wedges up to several hours ahead and refrigerate covered with plastic wrap. Complete step 6 before serving.

SHRIMP PROVENÇAL

My students enthusiastically and quickly respond to this dish. Their joy is in the familiarity of the combination of ingredients and the foolproof procedure by which it is cooked.

1 pound raw shrimp in their shells, 22–25 count
3 tablespoons olive oil
2 cloves garlic, finely chopped
2 tablespoons finely sliced scallions, white and light green part only
2 pounds ripe tomatoes in season, peeled, seeded, and cut into shreds, *or* 1 can (1 pound, 12 ounces) whole tomatoes, drained
1 teaspoon coarse (kosher) salt
Freshly ground pepper
2–3 tablespoons finely chopped Italian flat-leaf parsley

2 teaspoons fresh thyme leaves *or* ¾ teaspoon dried
2 teaspoons fresh chopped basil leaves *or* ½ teaspoon dried
1½ teaspoons fresh oregano leaves *or* ½ teaspoon dried
Pinch sugar (optional)
3 tablespoons unsalted butter
¾ pound fresh snow-white mushrooms, rinsed clean and quartered

Have on Hand
Stainless steel 12-inch Dutch sauté or other 12-inch skillet

Serves 4–6

1. Remove shells from shrimp and discard. With a small paring knife, make an incision along the top curve of shrimp to remove intestinal vein. Rinse thoroughly and pat dry with paper toweling. Set aside.

2. In a large, heavy 12-inch stainless steel Dutch sauté pan or other 12-inch skillet, heat olive oil. Stir in garlic and scallion slices and sauté quickly without browning. Add tomatoes, salt, pepper, parsley, and herbs. Simmer briskly about 15–20 minutes until mixture has reduced and thickened slightly. Be certain mixture is not watery. Taste to adjust seasoning if necessary. Add sugar at this point if you feel it is needed. Keep tomato mixture warm over very low heat.

3. Melt 1 tablespoon of the butter in another skillet and, when foamy, sauté mushrooms over moderately high heat 2–3 minutes. Season with a dash of salt and pepper and transfer to tomato mixture. If any mushroom liquid has accumulated in pan, reduce it to about 1 tablespoon and pour into tomato mixture. Can be made ahead to this point.

4. Add remaining butter to skillet mushrooms were cooked in and, when foamy, add shrimp and sauté 3–4 minutes, stirring with a wooden spatula. The moment shrimp are opaque, they are done. Be careful not to overcook.

5. Transfer shrimp immediately to the warm tomato-mushroom mixture, stir to mix, and bring just to the edge of a boil. Remove from heat and serve at once. Delicious over rice or pasta.

To Prepare Ahead
Follow steps 1 through 3 up to one day ahead. Refrigerate, covered, in a suitable container. Bring to room temperature and complete steps 4 and 5 before serving.

POACHED STRIPED BASS WITH TOMATO VINAIGRETTE

I think poaching a whole fish is a lovely way to present it. It makes an admirable and elegant first course at a dinner party and a superb main dish at lunch or dinner buffet.

3½–4-pound whole striped bass, salmon, or snapper with head and tail on
8–10 cups Court Bouillon

Tomato Vinaigrette
¼ cup finely chopped Italian flat-leaf parsley
2 tablespoons finely chopped fresh basil leaves *or* 1 teaspoon dried
2 tablespoons Dijon mustard
3 tablespoons imported red wine vinegar
½ teaspoon coarse (kosher) salt
Freshly ground pepper
⅓ cup imported extra virgin olive oil

3 pounds fresh plum tomatoes, skinned, seeded, and shredded *or* 2 cans (1 pound, 12 ounces each) whole tomatoes, drained, seeded, and shredded

Watercress or curly parsley for garnish
Bretonne-Vegetable Garnish (optional) (recipe follows)

Have on Hand
Fish poacher or large roasting pan with rack (see *Note*)
Cheesecloth
Kitchen string

Serves 10–12 as first course or 6–8 as main course

Note: I recommend a fish poacher; however, if you are using a roasting pan, it should be as deep and narrow as possible. Prepare court bouillon in a separate saucepan, as recommended and transfer hot liquid to the roasting pan. Place wrapped fish in roasting pan on a rack to support it and cover securely. In this case, it would be best to bake it in a preheated 350-degree oven, using the fish-timing reference (see Index) as a guide.

1. Have fish dealer clean whole fish and remove gills and scales, leaving head and tail on.

2. Bring court bouillon to a boil, then allow to simmer 20–30 minutes before poaching fish.

3. In the meantime, wrap fish in a double thickness of cheesecloth

long enough to extend beyond fish at both ends. Twist ends of cloth to make "handles" and tie with kitchen string to secure. Lower rack into poaching liquid. If necessary add additional water to just barely cover fish. Cover and cook over moderate heat keeping liquid at a lazy surface bubble 18–20 minutes. Liquid must never boil. Timing fish will depend on its size (10 minutes per inch measured in height at its thickest point). When done, allow fish to cool in liquid for 5 minutes.

4. Carefully lift up rack and let fish drain into poacher. Transfer to a large platter or cookie sheet. Clip and discard strings and open cheesecloth, spreading it out around fish, but leaving fish on it. With a small sharp knife, make an incision in skin at base of tail and carefully roll it back in strips up toward the head. Discard. Scrape away tiny bones along backbone of the fish and discard. With aid of cheesecloth, gently roll fish over right onto serving platter and repeat cleaning procedures on other side. When finished, clean away any debris from exposed areas of the platter. Can be completely made ahead to this point.

5. *Tomato Vinaigrette:* Put parsley, basil, mustard, vinegar, salt, and pepper in a mixing bowl, and beat vigorously with whisk. Add oil gradually, whisking constantly until mixture is thoroughly blended. Add tomatoes and stir to mix. Set aside.

6. *To Present Fish:* Cover the eye with several sprigs of parsley or watercress or completely cover the head with chopped parsley and for the eye, place a round of carrot slice which can be fished out of the court bouillon. Spoon on tomato vinaigrette to completely cover body of fish. Place any additional sauce in a serving bowl. Decorate platter with lots of watercress or curly parsley, which in itself is very attractive. Or for a special added touch, prepare the Bretonne-Vegetable garnish that follows. This special arrangement finishes the dish in an extraordinary way.

7. *To Serve Fish:* A heavy backbone separates body of fish. With two large serving spoons (one supports the other) scoop and lift servings of fish and sauce from bone. When fish from one whole side of bone has been served, grasp bone at the tail end and lift up. The bone will come up in one solid piece; it will be necessary to break it at the opposite end. Discard bone and serve remaining fish underneath with additional sauce.

To Prepare Ahead
Follow steps 1 through 4 up to one day ahead. Cover loosely with a tent of plastic wrap and refrigerate. Follow step 5 up to one day ahead and refrigerate in a suitable container. Complete step 6 before serving.

BRETONNE-VEGETABLE GARNISH

A surprise ending to my Poached Striped Bass with Tomato Vinaigrette.

Bretonne Sauce
2 tablespoons unsalted butter
1 large onion, peeled and
    finely chopped
2 teaspoons chopped fresh
    basil leaves *or* ¾
    teaspoon dried
1 teaspoon fresh thyme
    leaves *or* ¼ teaspoon
    dried
1–2 teaspoons fresh lemon
    juice
¼ teaspoon coarse (kosher)
    salt
Freshly ground pepper

1 pound green beans,
    blanched*
2 red pimentos, cut into
    ¼-inch strips
¼ pound fresh snow-white
    mushrooms, quickly
    rinsed and thinly sliced
2 lemons, scored and thinly
    sliced
2 hard-cooked eggs, cut into
    wedges
¼ cup tiny black niçoise
    olives

Vegetable Garnish
Watercress, washed and
    spin-dried

1. Melt butter in a skillet and, when foam subsides, sauté onion quickly until tender but not brown. Add remaining sauce ingredients, stir to mix, and remove from heat. Set aside.

2. Place crisp watercress on platter completely surrounding fish. Divide beans into 4 separate bundles and place evenly around edge of platter. Crisscross pimento strips over beans to "bow" them and spoon the Bretonne sauce dressing over the beans. Arrange overlapping slices of mushrooms attractively between green-bean bundles. Border platter with lemon slices topped with egg wedges and sprinkle on olives for additional color.

To Prepare Ahead
Follow step 1 up to one day ahead and refrigerate, covered in suitable container. Crisp-cook beans and hard-cook eggs up to one day ahead and refrigerate separately in suitable containers. Complete step 2 up to several hours before serving. Refrigerate, loosely covered with plastic wrap, then bring to room temperature before serving.

SKEWERED SESAME SHRIMP

This interesting shrimp hors d'oeuvre is easily prepared—just marinate overnight, skewer, broil, and wait for the raves.

1½ pounds large shrimp
   (22–25 count)
⅓ cup dark soy sauce
⅓ cup dry white wine
Freshly ground pepper
1½–2 teaspoons finely
   chopped fresh ginger
1 tablespoon sesame oil
½ cup sesame seeds

Optional Garnish
2-ounce package cellophane
   bean-thread noodles
Pea pods, blanched*

Have on Hand
8–10 wooden skewers
   soaked in cold water
   for 10 minutes before
   using

Serves 10–12

Preheat broiler.

1. Carefully remove shell from body of shrimp, leaving tail intact. With a small paring knife, make an incision along the back and lift out intestinal tract. Rinse shrimp in a colander and dry on paper towels.

2. In a mixing bowl, combine soy sauce, wine, pepper, ginger, and oil, and stir to mix. Add shrimp, toss to coat, and marinate several hours or overnight. Cover bowl with plastic wrap and refrigerate.

3. Spread sesame seeds in a large flat plate and set aside. To spear shrimp, lift from marinade one at a time, curl tail end into curve of shrimp like a snail and run point of skewer through heavier portion of body first, catching the tail, then through the outer curve. This will prevent the tail from dangling. Place 4–5 shrimp on each skewer and dip into sesame seeds to coat both sides. Can be done ahead to this point.

4. Broil shrimp in preheated broiler about 3 inches from source of heat for about 2 minutes on each side, turning once. Serve on a nest of deep-fried cellophane bean-thread noodles and garnish with pea pods if desired.

To Prepare Ahead

Follow steps 1 through 3 up to one day ahead. Refrigerate covered. Prepare cellophane noodle nest and pea pod garnish up to several hours ahead. Skewer the shrimp and complete step 4 just before serving.

Note: Optional Garnish . . . Sesame Shrimp on a bed of deep-fried cellophane noodles makes a dramatic presentation. To deep fry the cellophane noodles, heat about 2 cups of vegetable oil in a wok or large skillet. Remove noodles from package and separate to spread the noodle threads, then drop them all at once into hot oil. The threads will expand into a great big white cloud on contact with the hot oil. Remove immediately with a strainer-skimmer in one large mass and transfer to paper towels to drain. Without breaking it up, place on a round serving platter and set aside. This can be prepared many hours before you grill the shrimp. Just before you are ready to serve, arrange shrimp on the cloudlike nest of noodles and tuck in pea pods.

SHRIMP WITH MANGO AND ROSEMARY

Cool jumbo shrimp and colorful sweet mango slices combine to compose a salad at lunch or a first course at dinner. The beautiful spiky and pungent leaves of rosemary flavors the vinaigrette and makes an ideal garnish.

12 raw jumbo shrimp in
   shells with tail on
Court Bouillon

Vinaigrette
2 shallots, finely chopped
1 tablespoon Dijon mustard
½ teaspoon coarse (kosher)
   salt
Freshly ground pepper
2 teaspoons fresh rosemary
   leaves *or* ¾ teaspoon
   dried
2 tablespoons red wine
   vinegar

6 tablespoons light, fruity
   olive oil

To Finish
1 bunch watercress, washed
   and spin-dried
2 ripe mangoes, peeled and
   sliced thin
4 2-inch sprigs fresh
   rosemary for garnish
   (curly parsley sprigs if
   rosemary is not
   available)

Serves 4

1. Cook shrimp in court bouillon 4–5 minutes. Be careful not to overcook or shrimp will be tough. Drain and allow to cool. Carefully remove and discard shell from body of each shrimp, leaving tail portion intact. Set aside.

2. *Prepare Vinaigrette:* Place chopped shallots in a mixing bowl or chop shallots finely in workbowl of food processor fitted with steel knife.

Add mustard, salt, pepper, rosemary, and vinegar, and stir or process to mix. Gradually add oil in a thin stream into the bowl or through feed tube of processor and mix or process until mixture is thoroughly blended. Taste to adjust seasoning if necessary.

3. Divide watercress and place on four oversized lunch plates. Mangoes are sometimes difficult to work with. Cut long thin slices away from large pit, then taper slices so they are neat. Arrange 3 slices of mango and 3 jumbo shrimp in a fan design on bed of watercress. Spoon about 2 tablespoons of dressing over shrimp on each plate. Garnish salad with a sprig of rosemary gracefully straddling fruit slices. Serve at room temperature. Makes a wonderful luncheon dish preceded by a chilled fruit soup.

To Prepare Ahead
Follow steps 1 and 2 up to several hours ahead. (Do not spoon vinaigrette on shrimp. Keep sauce separate until ready to serve.) Refrigerate arranged plate, lightly covered with plastic wrap, and complete step 3.

TRUITE FARCI ET PORTO

The vegetable julienne added to the fish mousse stuffing gives new dimension to this dish.

4 even-sized brook trout,
    about 12 ounces each
1 cup white wine (approx.)
½ cup tawny port (approx.)
3 whole shallots
Coarse (kosher) salt
Freshly ground pepper
⅓ cup Crème Fraîche or
    heavy cream
2 tablespoons unsalted
    butter, softened

Farci
½ pound haddock or
    flounder fillets
2 egg whites
½ cup heavy cream, chilled

1 teaspoon coarse (kosher)
    salt
Freshly ground white pepper

Julienne
2–3 carrots, washed, peeled,
    and trimmed
2 ribs celery, washed and
    trimmed
2 tablespoons unsalted butter

1 large bunch curly parsley
    for garnish

Have on Hand
Parchment paper
2-quart rectangular Pyrex or
    ceramic baking dish

Serves 8

Preheat oven to 375 degrees.

1. Have fish dealer clean out stomach and remove gills and heavy backbone of trout, leaving skin, head, and tail intact. Spread open on work counter and if any small bones remain, salt the area well and pull away with your fingertips as well as possible. Rinse and set aside.

2. *To Prepare Mousse Forcemeat:* Cut away the reed-thin bony line from the center of the fillets and discard. Cut fillets into 1-inch pieces, place in workbowl of food processor fitted with steel knife or a blender, and process until coarsely ground. Whisk egg whites until frothy. With machine running, pour egg whites through feed tube of processor or into blender in a slow, steady stream, then gradually add cream until mixture is a smooth purée. If mixture is very thick, add a little more cream. Season with salt and pepper and process to mix.

3. Open fish on work counter and stuff each one with an equal amount of mixture, smoothing it with a rubber spatula.

4. *Prepare Julienne:* Cut carrots in half lengthwise, then cut into thirds. Place each piece flat side down and with a chef's knife, cut into julienne strips. Cut celery into thirds, stack, and cut into julienne strips.

5. Melt 2 tablespoons butter in a heavy skillet. When foam subsides, sauté julienne strips about 2 minutes, turning to coat as they cook. Add enough water to barely cover vegetables and cook at a brisk simmer 8–10 minutes until most of the liquid is evaporated. Cool. Distribute about ⅓ of vegetable julienne evenly over mousse and season very lightly with just a sprinkle of salt. Reserve remaining vegetables in skillet and set aside. Reshape fish to enclose mousse and carefully place them side by side in a buttered baking dish. Can be done ahead to this point.

6. Pour on wine and port and sprinkle with shallots. Season lightly with salt and pepper. Cut a length of parchment paper to fit the inside of the baking dish, butter one side of paper, and gently place over fish to cover.

7. Bake fish in preheated oven 20 minutes. Remove paper and set aside, then carefully transfer fish to a warm serving platter, placing them parallel to each other. Arrange reserved vegetables, filling in spaces between fish. Cover with buttered parchment and keep warm in a 180-degree oven.

8. Pour liquid from baking pan into a small saucepan and reduce by half. Add crème fraîche or heavy cream to juices, then gradually swirl in softened butter to incorporate. Taste to adjust seasoning if necessary. Remove fish from oven. Pour on warm sauce and circle platter with bunches of curly parsley. Cut fish into halves or thirds for serving.

To Prepare Ahead
Follow steps 1 through 5 up to one day ahead and refrigerate, covered. Bring to room temperature and complete steps 6 through 8 just before serving.

PAN-FRIED SHRIMP

I have particularly enjoyed garlicky pan-fried shrimp in their shells at a New York Chinatown restaurant. They are delicious served with warm pan juices. Chopsticks or fingers seem the proper way to go; just dismantle shrimp and enjoy in messy pleasure. I have found they are even better, cold, the next day. They are firmer and seem to take on even more of the herb flavor. This makes an excellent appetizer any time—particularly at an outdoor summertime gathering.

1½ pounds extra-large raw
   shrimp in their shells
   (16–18 count)
2 tablespoons peanut or
   vegetable oil
1 1-inch piece fresh ginger,
   finely chopped
2–3 scallions, white and
   light green part only,
   thinly sliced
2 red or green peppers, cut
   into ½-inch dice

1 large clove garlic, finely
   chopped
2 tablespoons finely chopped
   Italian flat-leaf parsley
1 tablespoon chopped fresh
   marjoram *or* ½
   teaspoon dried
½ teaspoon coarse (kosher)
   salt
Freshly ground pepper
2 teaspoons sesame oil

Serves 6–8

1. Place shrimp in a colander. With a sharp paring knife, make a slit along the upper curve of the shrimp right through the shell and slightly into the body from the head end to the tail. Lift out the intestinal vein and discard, being careful not to remove shell. Continue until all are done. Rinse under a spray of cold water, then spread on a clean kitchen towel and pat dry.

2. In a heavy 12-inch skillet, heat oil, add ginger, scallions, and red peppers, and sauté quickly without burning ginger and scallions. Add shrimp, garlic, and herbs. Sauté 3–5 minutes, stirring and turning shrimp as they turn pink in their shells and become completely opaque. Season with salt and pepper, then drizzle over sesame oil. Stir through quickly and remove from heat. Transfer shrimp to a platter and serve hot or cold in their shells.

To Prepare Ahead
Follow steps 1 and 2 up to one day ahead. Serve this colorful dish garnished with Scallion Flowers on a white platter.

5

ALL MANNER OF MEAT

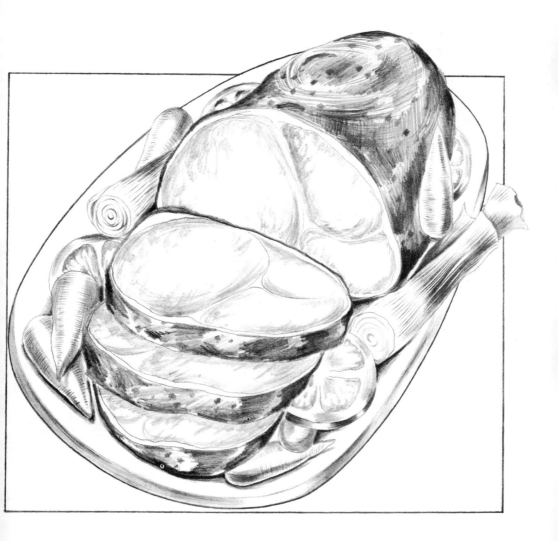

M eats in general have received a great deal of bad publicity of late. But to my mind there has been considerable overreaction concerning the harmfulness of meat in the American diet. Carefully chosen and prepared properly, meat can be a nutritious, tasty, and economical addition to one's diet.

Sometimes I hear myself saying I could almost become a vegetarian. When I teach certain classes in the spring or early summer where we prepare salads and use marvelous fresh produce or work with protein-rich pasta, I don't think about meat very much. There are times, however, when nothing satisfies me or makes me feel quite so well fed as when eating a perfectly grilled hamburger or a thick, juicy roast. But my objective in this book is to open new ideas in cooking to you and lift your eating habits out of the ordinary and into the more interesting possibilities available to you.

When storing in the refrigerator, remove meat from its package, place in a dish or container so that it lies flat, and make a tentlike covering of wax paper. Use within a day or so.

To store in the freezer, remove store wrapping and wrap securely in high-quality (heavily coated) freezer paper. Seal with freezer tape, wrapping carefully to avoid air pockets or exposed surfaces. Mark clearly with an appropriate permanent marking pen, indicating the item, the amount frozen or the number of people it will serve, and the date frozen, so your inventory may be checked from time to time. It is important that you do not allow meat to stand in the refrigerator for several days before freezing.

BEEF

How to Choose: USDA grades Prime and Choice indicate aging to ideal maturity and assures the highest-quality, most tender and flavorful beef. In these quality grades, cuts such as shells, sirloin, and porterhouse are best for grilling, while standing rib roasts and fillets are well suited for roasting. These top grades assure you of the best and most consistent results when properly cooked. Other cuts of beef, such as top and bottom rounds, chuck or rump roasts are best used for braising, stewing, pot roast, and so forth. In Prime and Choice grades, the beef should be light cherry red in color and the flesh firm and fine-grained. It is well marbled (streaked) with little veins of fat and has a smooth, creamy layer of fat at the edges.

Avoid beef that is dark in color and has little or no marbling, with a yellowish tinge to the fat. This indicates lower grades of beef such as Standard, Commercial, and Utility, which are used mainly for processed meat products. Of course, as with all meats, your selection should be free of bruises and discoloration.

Years ago—and perhaps still—the ultimate dinner-party table featured a glamorous roast tenderloin (fillet) of beef. The fillet can be simply slipped into the oven to cook itself. It's not intimidating to serve; nearly everyone likes beef; the boneless cut requires no complicated carving; and a single fillet will feed up to ten people. Unfortunately, very few cooks have the skills to bring this relatively bland piece of meat alive.

Over the years, various suggestions have been made by some good cooks I know for preparing a fillet. One of my favorites is a simple embellishment for Tenderloin of Beef. It consists of shallots, crushed black and green peppercorns, and a bit of Cognac, with some of its own fat trimmings ground up in the food processor and rubbed into the meat. It is delicious hot and a very practical meat served cold in thin overlapping slices on a buffet.

London broil is the name used for any number of different cuts of meat that are broiled or grilled, then sliced for serving. It is generally produced from a top sirloin or flank steak, but it can be cut from other areas also. A marinated and grilled flank steak produces the best London broil most consistently. Served with a flair, it is an economical and delicious beef cut for a dinner party or large group.

When it comes to steaks, I would rather buy a skirt steak, the diaphragm muscle that skirts the inside of the rib cage. It is modest in price compared with other beef cuts, boneless, and very flavorful. Shell steaks must be absolutely Prime cut or top-quality Choice and then well-seared in a very hot oven. I think sirloin or porterhouse are mediocre unless they are charcoal-grilled. Try this quick and easy skirt steak procedure: Trim excess fat, then cut the lengthy strip of skirt steak into 3- or 4-inch squares. Either pan-sauté them in butter with shallots and red wine vinegar, or grill them without further embellishment.

This brings to mind another idea for cooking skirt steaks: Combine them with chicken and sausage for a mixed grill. Serve this juicy selection of charcoaled meats with Frankie Hazan's garlicky Skordalia.

Aficionados would say that grinding your own meat is the best way to a hamburger. This, of course, means having access to a meat grinder or a food processor. As for me, I do not hesitate to use my food processor. For best results, trim fat very well, cube the meat into 1-inch squares, and place in the processor workbowl only as many cubes as will reach the top of the steel knife. Process with six or seven quick on/off turns of the cover or pulser, and the meat should be evenly chopped. If some of the cubes do not chop well enough, stop the machine, redistribute the meat, and pulse once or twice more. Be cautious not to overprocess, or the meat will become mushy. The whole procedure takes five to seven seconds. You will thrill at the difference in taste between your own fresh-ground hamburger and the packaged store-bought kind. Grinding your own meat gives you control of fat content; however, markets today are required to state percentage of fat to lean on ground-meat labels; 75–89 percent lean is considered ideal. Some fat is necessary for a juicier, tastier hamburger. The cut of meat I prefer, whether grinding myself or having it ground at the butcher, is chuck.

SAUTÉ OF BEEF BOURGUIGNON

It's tried and true and it goes a long way. What sets it apart is serving it with crisp, freshly made croutons.

5 pounds boneless top of
   beef chuck
Approximately ⅓ cup flour
   for dredging meat
2–3 dashes cayenne
3 tablespoons vegetable oil
3 tablespoons unsalted butter
1 teaspoon coarse (kosher)
   salt
Freshly ground pepper
3 shallots, finely chopped
3 cups red burgundy
1 tablespoon tomato paste
2 cloves garlic, finely
   chopped
1 cup Basic Chicken Stock
   or Beef Stock or broth
18–20 small white onions,
   peeled and left whole
2 teaspoons fresh thyme
   leaves *or* ½ teaspoon
   dried

2 teaspoons fresh marjoram
   leaves *or* ½ teaspoon
   dried
3 sprigs Italian flat-leaf
   parsley and 1 bay leaf,
   tied together with
   kitchen string
1 pound fresh mushrooms,
   trimmed, wiped clean,
   and halved
Fresh croutons and finely
   chopped parsley for
   garnish (recipe follows)

Have on Hand
5½ quart Dutch sauté pan or
   12-inch skillet with
   cover

Serves 8–10

1. Have butcher cut meat into 1½-inch cubes. Place meat in a colander and sprinkle on flour plus several dashes of cayenne and toss to coat. In a heavy Dutch sauté pan heat oil with 2 tablespoons butter and, when foam subsides, add meat in batches and sauté briskly until nicely browned on all sides. Remove meat from pan as it is done and set aside. Continue to sauté remaining meat until all done. Season with a light sprinkle of salt and pepper.

2. Pour off accumulated fat and add remaining 1 tablespoon butter to skillet. Place over moderate heat and, when foam subsides, add shallots and sauté quickly until tender but not brown. Pour in burgundy, bring to a boil over high heat, and with a wooden spatula stir to deglaze pan drippings; then reduce by half.

3. Add tomato paste and garlic and stir into drippings. Add stock, onions, herbs, and sautéed beef with accumulated meat juices and stir to mix. Cover pan and simmer gently for 1 hour. Can be made ahead to this point.

4. About 15 minutes before you are ready to serve, add mushrooms to meat and onions and simmer to cook mushrooms (and to warm the meat through as this dish is ideally made a day or more in advance). Taste to adjust seasoning if necessary. When meat is tender and vegetables are cooked, with a slotted spoon remove them to a warm serving platter; then reduce liquid in the pan until it has thickened slightly. Pour it on meat and vegetables. Surround Beef Bourguignon with fresh croutons and sprinkle meat with a good bit of chopped parsley. Serve immediately.

To Prepare Ahead
Follow steps 1 through 3 up to several days ahead and refrigerate in a suitable container. Or prepare up to several weeks ahead and freeze. Bring to room temperature and complete step 4 just before serving.

Croutons
8–10 slices day-old firm
    white bread
Vegetable oil for deep frying

Trim crusts from bread and cut into triangles. Place enough oil in a small skillet to reach about halfway up sides. Heat oil to about 375 degrees and add croutons in batches. Deep-fry until a light golden brown. Remove and drain on paper towels to dry. Can be made up to several hours prior to serving.

STEAK AU POIVRE

This simple, classic French recipe will give you the opportunity to practice the techniques of sautéing and deglazing, with impressive results.

4 shell or club steaks, about
    ½ inch thick
¼ cup peppercorns, coarsely
    cracked (see *Note*)
3 tablespoons olive oil
1½ tablespoons unsalted
    butter
⅓ cup Cognac
⅓ cup heavy cream

½ teaspoon coarse (kosher)
    salt

Have on Hand
Batticarne* (meat pounder)
12-inch skillet

Serves 4

Note: Crack peppercorns by placing them inside a large folded square of wax paper and crushing them with a rolling pin.

1. Trim steaks of excess fat. Place between sheets of wax paper and pound to ¼ inch thick with flat side of meat pounder.

2. With heel of your hand, rub scant teaspoon crushed peppercorns into each steak, spreading them as evenly as possible. Then drizzle ½ tablespoon olive oil over each. Refrigerate, covered with plastic wrap, if doing up to several hours ahead. Bring to room temperature (about 1 hour) before cooking.

3. Place 4 dinner plates in a 180-degree oven to warm. Coat bottom of a heavy 12-inch skillet with remaining tablespoon of oil and place over moderately high heat. When oil is hot but not smoking, sauté 2 steaks at a time (or as many as can comfortably fit in the pan without crowding) approximately 2½–3 minutes on each side. Transfer to a warm serving dish in one layer (never stack) as they are done. Cook remaining steaks and sprinkle lightly with salt.

4. Melt butter in the pan and add Cognac. With a flat wooden spatula, stir to scrape up pan drippings over high heat, to reduce Cognac by half. Stir cream into pan juices. With tongs, return steaks to the skillet, turning them over in the sauce once or twice to heat through quickly. Serve immediately on warm plates.

To Prepare Ahead
Follow steps 1 and 2 up to several hours ahead. Complete steps 3 and 4 before serving.

Serving Hint: If you're so inclined, this is a spectacular dish to prepare and serve at table from a chafing dish. Simply organize yourself and have all your ingredients—and guests—at hand.

PRIME RIBS OF BEEF

Every so often I will see a splendid 2- or 3-rib first-cut rib roast in my supermarket meat counter. If my eye is caught by its cherry red meat surrounded with a border of creamy white fat and unmarred by large fatty pockets, I can hardly resist. It is an expensive cut. There are times, however, that at the busy market I frequent this special cut is offered at a good price. Once in a great while I do indulge in prime ribs.

4-pound first-cut standing rib
    roast (2–3 ribs)
2–3 cloves garlic, finely
    chopped

2 tablespoons sweet paprika
1 tablespoon coarse (kosher)
    salt

Serves 4–6

Preheat oven to 350 degrees.

1. With a long slicing knife, cut off top layer of fat without cutting into meat, in one or two pieces as well as possible and set aside.

2. In a mixing bowl, combine garlic, paprika, and salt, and stir to mix. With fingertips, rub seasoning all over top and sides of meat. Return fat slices to conform to original position, wiping your hands ''clean'' on this fat.

3. Stand rib roast in sturdy roasting pan and roast in preheated oven 18–20 minutes per pound for rare. Remove meat from oven and insert an instant thermometer into the thickest part of the meat without touching the bone. Temperatures should read: 100 degrees for rare; 115 degrees for medium rare; or 140 degrees for medium. When done, remove and discard layers of fat and let stand on a ridged board 10 minutes before carving into slices for serving.

To Prepare Ahead

Follow steps 1 and 2 early in the day or up to several hours ahead. Complete step 3 before serving.

GRILLED TENDERLOIN OF BEEF

1 whole beef fillet, trimmed
  weight 3½–4 pounds
3–4 shallots, finely chopped
2 teaspoons crushed black
  peppercorns

2 teaspoons green
  peppercorns, in brine,
  not vinegar, drained
  and crushed
1 tablespoon brandy
2 tablespoons soy sauce

Serves 8–10

1. Trim the fillet of all visible fat and sinew. Discard sinew and reserve the fat. Cut fat into small pieces and grind with shallots in workbowl of food processor fitted with steel knife or have fat ground at the butcher's; then combine in a mixing bowl with shallots. Add black and green peppers and brandy, and process or stir to mix. Rub this pasty mixture into the meat, covering all surfaces. Allow to marinate several hours or overnight. Can be done ahead to this point.

2. Just before cooking, rub soy sauce all over meat.

3. *To Grill:* Preheat your grill, whether charcoal or gas, and wait for the coals or briquettes to have an ashen coating before you start to cook. Set gas at highest setting. Using tongs and a spatula, carefully place the fillet on the grill. Cover and cook about 5–6 minutes, then turn and cook covered an additional 5–6 minutes. Uncover and cook 6–7 minutes longer on each side. Baste meat with marinade drippings each time you turn it. For rare, meat should be springy to the touch; when tested with an instant thermometer, it will read 120–125 degrees.

To Roast: Preheat oven to 400 degrees. Place meat in a shallow roasting pan, then put into oven and roast until crusty brown outside and pink within, about 35–40 minutes; when tested with an instant thermometer, it will read 120–125 degrees.

4. *To Serve:* Allow meat to rest 8–10 minutes before carving, then carve into thin, even slices. Serve warm from a buffet or at table. A fillet of beef makes great party fare on a cold buffet and one that can be done completely ahead. Grill and carve up to several hours before serving, then arrange overlapping slices on a garnished platter.

To Prepare Ahead
Follow step 1 up to one day ahead. Follow steps 2 through 4 just before serving.

FEGATO ALLA VENEZIANA
Calf's Liver Venetian Style

Harry's Bar on the Grand Canal in Venice serves this piquant liver sauté. The liver is cut into medallion-size pieces and is cooked in a way that is reminiscent of Chinese stir-fry.

1¼ pounds calf's liver cut
    ½ inch thick
Flour for dusting
4 tablespoons unsalted butter
2 tablespoons vegetable oil
2 medium red onions, thinly
    sliced

1 teaspoon coarse (kosher)
    salt
Freshly ground pepper
6 tablespoons balsamic
    imported red wine
    vinegar

Serves 3–4

Note: Balsamic vinegar is available in most specialty kitchen and food shops. Its robust taste is essential to the success of the dish.

1. Remove any membrane or veins from liver slices. Then, with your knife at a 45-degree angle, cut each slice approximately into a 2-inch medallion. (This resembles a small scallop of veal.) Dust the slices with a bit of flour tapped through a sieve and set aside.

2. In a 12-inch heavy skillet, melt 3 tablespoons of the butter and the oil over moderately high heat. When foam subsides add the onions and sauté 3–4 minutes until limp and lightly colored. Do not brown. With slotted spoon, remove to a side dish and set aside.

3. Add remaining butter to skillet, turn up heat a bit, and, when butter is hot, add liver medallions. Quickly sauté liver 3–4 minutes, turning frequently with the aid of a slotted spoon and spatula. Cook until pieces are crisp around the edges and a light golden brown. Sprinkle with a bit of salt and a good grinding of pepper. Without removing liver medallions, pour vinegar into skillet and quickly deglaze by scraping up pan juices with a wooden spatula. Return onions to pan and toss with liver to coat. Cook, stirring and tossing an additional 1–2 minutes until liver is just pink within. Serve immediately with a boiled or baked potato.

To Prepare Ahead
Follow step 1 up to thirty minutes ahead. Complete steps 2 and 3 just before serving.

ZWIEZELROSTBRATEN

2 rib or club steaks, ¾ inch
    thick, well trimmed
½ teaspoon coarse (kosher)
    salt
Freshly ground pepper
1 tablespoon vegetable oil
2 tablespoons Worcestershire
    sauce
Dash Tabasco sauce

Sautéed Onions
3 tablespoons vegetable oil

2 tablespoons unsalted butter
2 Bermuda onions, very
    thinly sliced
Coarse (kosher) salt

1 ripe fresh tomato, halved,
    and parsley sprigs for
    garnish

Have on Hand
Batticarne* (meat pounder)

Serves 2

1. Place steaks between sheets of wax paper and pound until ½ inch thick. Sprinkle each steak lightly with salt, several grinds of pepper, oil, Worcestershire, and Tabasco. With hands, rub mixture well into the meat. Allow to season up to 2 hours. Refrigerate, covered, if necessary.

2. Heat 1 tablespoon of the oil and 1 tablespoon of the butter in a heavy skillet. When hot, add half the onions and sauté over moderately high heat to brown and crisp, stirring occasionally. With slotted spoon transfer to a side dish. Add additional 1 tablespoon oil and remaining 1 tablespoon butter to pan and sauté to crisp remaining onions. Transfer as above. Do not cook all the onions at once or they will steam rather than crisp. Sprinkle lightly with salt and set aside. Before cooking steaks, wipe skillet clean if necessary.

3. Place 2 dinner plates in a 180-degree oven to warm just before you are ready to cook steaks. Heat remaining tablespoon oil in skillet over moderately high heat and quickly sauté steaks about 3–5 minutes on each side for rare or medium rare. They should be well seared but pink inside. Divide onions over each steak and transfer to heated plates as they are done. Garnish with tomato halves and top with parsley sprigs. Serve at once.

To Prepare Ahead
Follow step 1 up to several hours ahead. Complete steps 2 and 3 just before serving.

VEAL

How to Choose: Quality veal comes from young cows and the best quality has an unmistakable pale pinkish hue with creamy white fat. Poorer quality of veal is usually a darker red or brownish and it usually has much less fat. The texture of the flesh is also soft and not as springy as good-quality veal.

Of all the meats available to the home cook, one of my personal favorites is veal. More than with almost any other meat, however, the success of the finished veal dish depends not only upon the skill of the cook, but also upon the talent of the butcher. Delicate veal scallopines are incomparable when sautéed quickly and served with a light sauce made from deglazed pan juices.

The very best veal scallopine is cut from the top round of the leg and is rather costly. In general, the public expects veal scallopine to be cut "from the leg." Unless it is cut properly by a knowledgeable butcher, the scallops can be tough and shrink a lot when cooked. Round medallions of veal are also used as scallopine and are cut from the eye of the veal loin.

Since veal has few juices, it can be dry unless certain precautions are taken during cooking. For instance, when cooking scallopines, lightly dust with flour, doing this just before cooking and only with the exact number of scallopines you can cook at one time. Those pieces on the counter waiting to be sautéed should not be floured yet, since they will exude their precious juices as they stand and you will end up braising the meat instead of sautéing it.

The shoulder, tied and rolled; eye of the loin; or leg of veal are used for roasts. However, I generally do not recommend roasting veal because the meat has such a delicate structure and such minute amounts of fat. I prefer to braise or poach it, as in one of my favorite company dishes, Poached Veal with Crème Fraîche Sauce. The delicately cooked veal is presented in thin overlapping slices and blanketed with a satiny creamy sauce made from a reduction of the poaching liquid, mushrooms, wine, and Crème Fraîche.

The shoulder is an economical cut of veal which can be used in a wonderful veal stew. If you like the do-ahead convenience of beef stew but think it a bit too earthy for a "company dish," you (and your pocketbook) will be delighted with the elegance of Veal à la Suisse, which uses shoulder and neck meat.

VEAL CHOPS WITH 20 CLOVES OF GARLIC

It is well known that favorite recipes are those remembered from childhood. My mother's braised veal chops and onions, peppery with cayenne, are the foundation for my love of this recipe. The strength of the garlic, when used whole, unpeeled, and blanched, is diluted. Until you pop a braised whole clove of garlic into your mouth, you'll never believe the incredible subtlety of its flavor.

4–6 rib veal chops, cut 1 inch thick and well trimmed
Flour for dredging meat
6 tablespoons clarified butter*
Coarse (kosher) salt
Freshly ground pepper
½ cup dry white wine
1½ cups Classic Chicken and Veal Stock or broth

20 cloves of garlic, unpeeled, lightly crushed with flat blade of a chef's knife or cleaver
2 tablespoons Crème Fraîche or heavy cream
Finely chopped parsley or snipped chives for garnish

Serves 4–6

1. Lightly dust 2–3 veal chops at a time with flour on both sides, tapping off excess. Flour only as many chops as you can cook at one time, since meat will exude precious juices on standing if floured ahead. Heat clarified butter in a heavy 12-inch skillet. When butter foam subsides, add the floured chops without crowding pan and sear over moderately high heat 3–4 minutes on each side until golden brown. Transfer chops to a platter large enough to hold them in a single layer and sprinkle lightly with salt and pepper. Dust remaining chops with flour, sauté until golden brown on both sides, and transfer to side dish. When all the chops are done to this point, pour off and discard cooking fat.

2. Add wine and stock to skillet and with a wooden spatula scrape to deglaze drippings in the bottom of the pan. Return chops to skillet with accumulated juices in side dish. Spoon liquids in pan over meat and scatter the unpeeled garlic cloves over and around the chops. Cover and simmer 25 minutes, turning once.

3. Transfer chops to a platter, one layer deep, and set aside. With a wooden spatula, mash the garlic cloves into the liquids, then, over

moderately high heat, reduce by half, stirring occasionally. Strain sauce into a small bowl, pressing down hard with a wooden spoon to extract the garlic purée and to remove the skin. Scrape purée from sieve into liquid. Return chops to skillet, pour on sauce, cover, and simmer over low heat about 5–10 minutes to warm chops. Stir in cream to enrich sauce and taste to adjust seasonings if necessary. Transfer chops to a warm serving platter, overlapping them slightly, garnish with a sprinkle of chopped parsley or snipped chives, and serve immediately.

To Prepare Ahead
Follow steps 1 and 2 up to two hours ahead. Return chops to pan and let stand covered at room temperature. Complete step 3 just before serving.

FLORENTINE GRILLED VEAL CHOPS

4 first-cut rib veal chops,
    sliced ¾ to 1 inch
    thick
2 teaspoons finely chopped
    garlic

1 tablespoon fresh chopped
    rosemary leaves *or* 1
    teaspoon dried
Tuscan extra virgin olive oil

Serves 4

1. Trim chops of excess fat along the bone and discard.
2. Spread ½ teaspoon chopped garlic and ¾ teaspoon fresh (or ¼ teaspoon dried) rosemary on both sides of each chop; then drizzle on a little oil to coat. Let stand up to 1 hour before cooking. (If you have the time, seasoning ahead is a convenience. However, they are equally good seasoned just before cooking.)
3. Place the chops 3–4 inches under a preheated broiler or grill over ashen hot coals 5–6 minutes on each side, until they are lightly charred on the outside and faintly pink on the inside. If chops are very thick, be sure meat is cooked through near the bone. Sprinkle with salt and pepper, if desired, and serve immediately.

To Prepare Ahead
Follow steps 1 and 2 up to several hours ahead. Complete step 3 just before serving.

ESCALOPES DE VEAU MORNAY

I particularly enjoy teaching this recipe because of the variety of techniques employed. The discussion begins with the veal. I prefer to have it cut from the top round of the leg, which gives you longer slices. Each scallopine is pounded lightly with a batticarne, and little knife cuts are made along the edges, spaced about one inch apart, to prevent shrinkage during cooking. A salpicon of mushroom is prepared to top the sautéed slices of veal, then a Mornay sauce to blanket the mushroom mixture completely. The juices in the pan the veal is sautéed in are deglazed and strained for the final sauce. It is not only a superb lesson but a fine company dish which can be made completely ahead.

8–10 large scallops of veal, preferably cut from the top round of the leg
Flour for dredging meat
3 tablespoons clarified butter*
2 tablespoons vegetable oil

Light Brown Sauce
2 shallots, finely diced
1 tablespoon flour
1½ teaspoons tomato paste
½ cup dry sherry
¾ cup Basic Chicken Stock or broth
¾ to 1 teaspoon coarse (kosher) salt
Freshly ground pepper

Salpicon
3 tablespoons unsalted butter
¾ pounds fresh mushrooms, rinsed and thinly sliced
2 shallots, finely chopped
½ teaspoon coarse (kosher) salt

Freshly ground pepper
1 tablespoon flour
½ cup Basic Chicken Stock or broth
2 tablespoons dry sherry
½ pound boiled ham, finely diced

Mornay Sauce
2 tablespoons unsalted butter
2½ tablespoons flour
1¼ cups warm milk
¼ teaspoon coarse (kosher) salt
Freshly ground pepper
1 cup grated Gruyère cheese

Finely chopped parsley or snipped chives for garnish

Have on Hand
Batticarne* (meat pounder)

Serves 8

1. Pound the veal scallops between sheets of wax paper with a

batticarne. With the tip of a paring knife, knick the edges of the scallopine spaced about 1 inch apart. This will help reduce shrinkage when cooking. Lightly dust 2–3 scallops at a time with flour on both sides, tapping off excess. Flour only as many scallops as you can cook at one time, since meat will exude juices on standing if floured ahead. Heat 2 tablespoons clarified butter and 2 tablespoons oil in a 12-inch heavy skillet. Sauté veal very quickly, about 1 minute on one side; turn and sauté ½ minute on other side until lightly golden. Transfer scallops to large cookie sheet, one layer deep. Be careful not to stack veal pieces on top of each other or they will steam and become soggy. Dust remaining veal scallops with flour, sauté as above, and set aside.

2. *To Prepare Light Brown Sauce:* In the same skillet the veal cooked in, melt remaining butter and sauté shallots quickly until tender. Stir flour into drippings for 1 or 2 minutes. Add tomato paste and stir into flour mixture. Add sherry, bring to a boil, and reduce by half. Pour in stock and bring to a simmer, season lightly with salt and pepper, and cook 3–4 minutes longer. Strain mixture into a small saucepan and set aside.

3. *To Prepare Salpicon:* Melt 3 tablespoons butter in a clean skillet and, when foam subsides, quickly sauté mushrooms and shallots. Sprinkle with salt and pepper, add flour, and stir through with a wooden spoon. Add stock and sherry. Bring mixture to a boil, reduce heat, and simmer until liquid is absorbed. Remove from heat, add ham, stir to mix, and set aside.

4. *To Prepare Mornay Sauce:* Melt butter in small heavy saucepan, add flour all at once, stirring with a whisk or a wooden spoon to incorporate butter. Cook about 2 minutes, being careful not to brown mixture. In the meantime, in another saucepan, heat milk to the edge of a boil. Add hot milk to sauce all at once, stirring vigorously over moderate heat until mixture is smooth and thick. Season lightly with salt and pepper and stir in cheese until it melts. Sauce will be quite thick. Remove from heat and set aside.

5. Arrange sautéed scallops of veal one layer deep on a jelly-roll pan or cookie sheet. Spoon some of mushroom mixture on top of each scallopine and spread evenly, leaving approximately a ½-inch border of meat all around. To blanket veal with Mornay sauce, scoop up some sauce with a large oval spoon and let it fall from the side of the spoon passing once over the veal scallop in one direction. I recommend this be made early in the day of serving. Do not refrigerate. Let sit at room temperature. A word of caution: Leave uncovered until cheese topping becomes firm, then place a tent of lightly buttered parchment over veal.

Veal will remain free from dust and can later go directly into the oven to heat through.

Preheat oven to 300 degrees.

6. When ready to serve, place jelly-roll pan containing veal in the oven and heat about 15 minutes. Be careful not to overcook or veal will dry out. In the meantime, place saucepan containing brown sauce over moderate heat and simmer until hot and bubbly. Taste to adjust seasoning if necessary. Pour sauce into a warm serving platter. Lift each veal scallop with a metal spatula and lower into sauce, arranging it nicely. Sprinkle with finely chopped parsley or snipped chives to garnish and serve immediately.

To Prepare Ahead

Follow steps 1 through 5 up to several hours ahead or early in the day. (Step 3, salpicon preparation, can be done up to one day ahead and refrigerated in a suitable container.) Complete step 6 just before serving.

VEAL À LA SUISSE

An elegant stew, whose flavor becomes even more delectable after the stay of a night or two in the refrigerator.

4 pounds boneless veal
    (neck or shoulder)
4 tablespoons vegetable oil
4 tablespoons unsalted butter
Flour for dredging meat
Coarse (kosher) salt
Freshly ground pepper
3–4 shallots finely chopped
2 tablespoons flour
1 teaspoon tomato paste
1½ cups Basic Chicken
    Stock or broth
1 cup dry white wine
Scant teaspoon coarse
    (kosher) salt
Freshly ground pepper

½ cup heavy cream
    (optional)
¾ pound fresh mushrooms,
    quickly rinsed clean,
    trimmed, and halved or
    quartered
1 tablespoon finely chopped
    Italian flat-leaf parsley
    for garnish

Have on Hand
5½-quart Dutch sauté pan
    with cover or 5-quart
    enamel-over-iron
    covered saucepan

Serves 6–8

Note: If doubling or tripling recipe, for 8 pounds of meat use 2 cups of chicken stock or broth, 1½ cups of wine, and ¾ cup heavy cream. For 12 pounds of veal, use 2½ cups of chicken stock or broth, 2 cups of wine and 1 cup of heavy cream.

1. Have butcher trim and cut veal into approximately 1½-inch cubes. I frequently prefer to do this job myself, since I will be careful to cut away more fat and less meat than a butcher might do. In a large heavy saucepan, heat oil with 2 tablespoons of the butter. Flour as many pieces of meat as you can cook at one time by placing them in a colander, sprinkling with flour, and tossing to coat. When butter and oil are hot, sauté lightly floured veal without crowding pan. Cook quickly, stirring occasionally to brown lightly on all sides. With a slotted spoon remove meat to a large platter as it is done and continue cooking until all meat is sautéed. Sprinkle lightly with salt and pepper and set aside.

2. Add remaining 2 tablespoons butter to same pan and, over moderate heat, using a wooden spatula, deglaze pan juices by scraping up the bits in the bottom. Add shallots, stir, and cook quickly until tender but not brown. Add tomato paste, stock or broth, and wine, and stir to mix, then simmer slowly until liquids reduce by half.

3. Return meat to pan, season with additional salt and pepper, and simmer with cover slightly ajar 1½ hours. At the end of this cooking time, if stew seems soupy, with a slotted spoon transfer all of the meat to a side dish and slowly reduce the liquid in the pan over moderate heat until it thickens slightly. Then return meat to pan.

4. About 20–25 minutes before meat is done, add mushrooms to veal mixture, gently stir to mix in, and finish cooking. Taste to adjust seasoning.

5. Several minutes before serving add the cream and stir through to warm. Garnish with a sprinkle of chopped parsley and serve with Potato-Vegetable Galette and Buffet Tomatoes Mimosa.

To Prepare Ahead

Follow steps 1 through 3 up to two days ahead. Refrigerate, covered. Bring to room temperature and follow step 4 up to several hours ahead. Complete step 5 just before serving.

POACHED VEAL WITH CRÈME FRAÎCHE SAUCE

Don't be put off by the long list of ingredients. This elegant company dish can be almost completely prepared ahead. The veal is poached early in the day, then the poaching liquid is reduced in plenty of time for the final sauce preparation. The veal, thus ready, can be left standing on a ridged carving board covered with a tent of parchment. Reheat the sauce, warm the veal in a slow oven, carve, and arrange on a heated platter to serve.

2 carrots, trimmed and
    scrubbed clean
1 large leek, trimmed, split,
    and washed thoroughly
1 rib celery, trimmed and
    rinsed

Bouquet Garni
2–3 sprigs Italian flat-leaf
    parsley
1 bay leaf

2 quarts or more water to
    barely cover veal
2 cups dry white wine
2 tablespoons fresh tarragon
    leaves *or* 2 teaspoons
    dried
1 teaspoon coarse (kosher)
    salt
½ teaspoon freshly ground
    pepper
3–3½ pounds boneless fillet
    of veal

¾ pound fresh mushrooms,
    quickly rinsed clean,
    trimmed, and cut into
    ½-inch slices
Water to cover mushrooms
3 tablespoons unsalted butter

¼ teaspoon coarse (kosher)
    salt

Crème Fraîche Sauce
2 teaspoons grainy Dijon
    mustard
1 cup Crème Fraîche
1 cup reduced poaching
    liquid
⅓ cup reduced mushroom
    liquid
1½ teaspoons fresh lemon
    juice
2 teaspoons fresh tarragon
    leaves *or* ½ teaspoon
    dried
4 tablespoons unsalted butter
Freshly ground pepper to
    taste
1 egg yolk
2 teaspoons arrowroot

Finely chopped parsley for
    garnish

Have on Hand
6–7-quart Dutch oven or
    enamel-over-iron
    casserole
Parchment paper

Serves 8–10

1. The most elegant cut of meat for this dish is the center cut of a boneless fillet of veal. See Herbed Veal Roast.

2. Place 2–3 quarts water in a Dutch oven or heatproof casserole. With kitchen string, tie vegetable and bouquet garni ingredients into a bundle and add to water with wine, tarragon, salt, and pepper. Bring to the edge of a boil, reduce heat, and simmer briskly with cover ajar 35–40 minutes. Add veal, which should be barely covered by the liquid, and adjust heat as necessary to maintain a lazy surface bubble 45–50 minutes. Simmer with cover ajar and check the liquid from time to time. Do not allow the liquid to boil too fast or simmer too slowly. Turn meat over once or twice. Meat should be a pale pink in the center when done, or insert an instant thermometer for a reading of 120 degrees.

3. While veal is cooking, poach mushrooms in a small saucepan with enough water to barely cover. Add butter and salt, bring to a boil, then simmer gently 5–6 minutes. Remove mushrooms with a slotted spoon and transfer to a side dish. Reduce mushroom liquid in saucepan to ⅓ cup, watching this reduction carefully, and set aside.

4. When veal is done, transfer to a ridged carving board, cover with a tent of parchment paper, and set aside. Reduce poaching liquid to 1 cup over moderate heat. After broth has reduced by about half, it is advisable to transfer the liquid and its contents to a smaller saucepan and continue to reduce until desired 1 cup has been reached. Combine with mushroom liquid and set aside.

5. *To prepare Crème Fraîche Sauce:* In a heavy saucepan, combine mustard and crème fraîche. Stir to mix, then, over moderate heat, whisk in combined veal and mushroom stocks, lemon juice, and tarragon. Simmer briskly 15–20 minutes, whisk in the butter 1 tablespoon at a time, then season with freshly ground pepper. Taste to adjust seasoning if necessary. Let stand, covered, at room temperature if made many hours ahead.

6. Place egg yolk in a small dish or bowl. Add arrowroot and stir to mix. Add 2–3 tablespoons of the hot liquid and stir into yolk mixture. Gradually return to the sauce, whisking all the time until mixture thickens slightly. Add the mushrooms to sauce, stir to mix, and keep warm over very low heat.

7. If veal has been standing at room temperature several hours or more, transfer to an oven-going platter before carving, cover with buttered tent of parchment, and warm in a 300-degree oven 15–20 minutes. Meanwhile reheat sauce.

8. *To Serve:* Pour some of warm sauce onto a heated serving platter. Carve poached veal into thin, even slices and arrange overlapping on

the platter. Spoon over additional sauce with mushrooms to blanket the meat. Sprinkle with finely chopped parsley for garnish. Pass remaining sauce from a heated sauceboat. Serve at once.

To Prepare Ahead
Follow steps 1 through 5 early in the day. Let stand covered at room temperature. Complete steps 6 through 8 before serving.

HERBED VEAL ROAST

This well-flavored veal recipe started life in my test kitchen as a cold veal roast to be used for summer buffet dinners. Served on a platter in very thin overlapping slices, it became a favorite of family and friends. The recipe below resulted from their enthusiastic suggestions that "some like it hot."

To obtain the cut of veal I prefer for this recipe, I call on my friendly butcher. Specialty butchers call this particular piece of meat a boneless fillet of veal. It runs from the shoulder through the loin chops and includes the rib-chop portion. It is expensive; however, you will only need approximately 3–3½ pounds to feed up to ten people, as there is very little fat and no bone. The shoulder end of the fillet has natural openings for the herb stuffing. While the meat is more solid in the rib and loin portion, there are separations along the sides of the chop area. Cut through the fatty tissue to create pockets. Should this cut not be accessible to you, use a whole breast of veal, which is also an economical choice. Have the butcher remove the meat in one solid piece and trim off as much fat as possible. The bones, of course, are an extra dividend and can be used for stock.

2 heaping tablespoons fresh
    rosemary leaves *or* 1
    teaspoon dried
1 tablespoon fresh sage
    leaves *or* ¼ teaspoon
    dried (see *Note* below)
1½ tablespoons fresh thyme
    leaves *or* ½ teaspoon
    dried
1 tablespoon chopped Italian
    flat-leaf parsley

3 medium cloves garlic,
    finely chopped
3–3½-pound veal roast
2 teaspoons green
    peppercorns, packed in
    water
Coarse (kosher) salt
Freshly ground pepper
2 tablespoons unsalted butter
3 tablespoons vegetable oil

1–2 carrots, scrubbed, rinsed, and thinly sliced

1 small onion, peeled and sliced

1 medium leek, trimmed, washed thoroughly, and thinly sliced, white and light green part only

½ cup dry white wine

2 cups Classic Chicken and Veal Stock or broth

2–3 ripe tomatoes, peeled, seeded, and coarsely chopped, *or* 1 cup canned tomatoes, drained and shredded

2–3 tablespoons finely chopped parsley or snipped chives for garnish

Serves 8–10

Note: If fresh sage is not available, I prefer to use the dry leafy sage rather than the powdered, which gives a distorted intense flavor.

Preheat oven to 325 degrees.

1. Combine herbs in mixing bowl. Add garlic and stir to mix. Place meat on work counter. With your fingers, spread combined herbs and garlic as far into crevices of meat as possible. Scatter in green peppercorns and sprinkle with salt and pepper.

2. If using fillet of veal, bring up sides of meat together, enclosing dressing. If using breast of veal, roll up like a jelly roll to secure stuffing. In either case, tie up meat like a sausage with a long length of kitchen string.

3. Put 1 tablespoon of the butter and 2 tablespoons of the oil in a heavy enamel-over-iron casserole or Dutch oven. Heat fat and, when hot, sear meat on all sides, turning with the aid of the string. Do not pierce with fork. Remove meat from pan; pour off and discard fat. Add remaining butter and oil to pan, melt, and, when butter is foamy, add vegetables, toss to coat, and simmer with cover ajar until tender, 5–7 minutes, stirring constantly and being careful not to brown. Add wine to vegetables in pan and stir to deglaze drippings. Slowly reduce wine by half. Return meat to pan, pour on stock, and sprinkle lightly with salt and pepper. Place in preheated oven. Cover pan and roast veal for approximately 1 hour and 15 minutes. Breast of veal will take longer— about 2 hours. Tested with an instant meat thermometer, veal should reach an internal temperature of 155 degrees. Remove meat from pan when done and allow to rest on carving board and set aside.

4. Add tomatoes to ingredients in pan and stir to mix. With a wooden spatula, scrape bottom of pan to deglaze drippings and reduce liquid to

about 1½ cups. Strain vegetables and liquid into a saucepan, pressing down hard on vegetables with a wooden spoon to extract juices. Scrape purée from under sieve into sauce and keep warm over low heat.

5. *To Serve Hot:* In the meantime, remove strings from meat and with a sharp knife carve into thin, even slices. Arrange in overlapping slices on a warm serving platter. Pour the hot strained juices over meat. Sprinkle with chopped parsley or snipped chives.

To Serve Cold: Slice and place meat on a platter as above. Strain juices directly over meat. Refrigerate several hours or overnight, during which time juices will congeal into a light natural aspic. At that point, cover lightly with a tent of plastic wrap. Just before serving, sprinkle with chopped parsley or snipped chives.

To Prepare Ahead
If serving cold, complete all the steps up to one day ahead and refrigerate, then serve at room temperature. If serving hot, follow steps 1 and 2 early in the day. Complete step 3 up to two hours ahead. Complete steps 4 and 5 just before serving.

LAMB

How to Choose: USDA Choice grade lamb is the predominant grade of lamb available in the market today. Look for young lamb that is finely grained and pinkish-red in color. Lamb that is soft and fleshy to the touch and has a brown tinge should be avoided.

The best lamb is available early spring through midfall. Americans who do not care for lamb have probably eaten mutton or something close to old lamb. Imaginative, health-conscious cooks have sought out lighter, subtler, and more interesting alternatives to the once ubiquitous ''beef and potatoes.'' Of all the alternatives, lamb has been perhaps the most neglected. The most familiar lamb dishes are chops, roast leg, or stew.

One of my favorite ways to prepare lamb is Rack of Lamb Persille, an exquisite company dish. This may be seasoned ahead, ready to pop into a very hot oven for a brief period of time. It is easy to slice and frees the hostess to enjoy her guests or attend to more complicated dishes.

For exotic barbecue fare, try the Gigot St. Tropez. The leg is boned and butterflied, then dressed in a fresh, tarragon-scented, mustardy marinade. This has become a traditional summertime favorite among my students, as I teach it in a special grill class.

GIGOT ST. TROPEZ

I will never forget sitting harborside in a restaurant in St. Tropez some years ago and being intrigued by the wonderfully subtle taste of tarragon in the lamb dish I ordered. It has become an ideal barbecue favorite for me and my students to serve at an outdoor dinner party. (This does not preclude oven roasting in cooler weather for an indoor dinner.) There is a melting, fork-tender quality to the meat that is derived in part from the excellent marinade and in part from the slow, smoldering heat of the ashen hot coals that penetrates its interior.

1 7–8-pound leg of lamb, boned and butterflied

Marinade
3–4 large shallots, finely chopped
2 tablespoons fresh tarragon *or* 2 teaspoons dried, crumbled
2 teaspoons fresh thyme *or* ¼ teaspoon dried, crumbled
2 teaspoons fresh oregano *or* ¼ teaspoon dried, crumbled

1 tablespoon Dijon mustard
1 tablespoon grainy Dijon mustard
½–¾ teaspoon coarse (kosher) salt
Freshly ground pepper
2 tablespoons tarragon vinegar
4–5 tablespoons light, fruity olive oil

5–6 cloves garlic smashed with the broad side of a knife

Serves 8–10

1. Have butcher bone and butterfly the lamb for roasting. Remove large inside sinews and heavy pieces of fat. Trim off all but a thin layer of fat surrounding the meat.

2. *To Prepare Marinade:* Place shallots, tarragon, thyme, oregano, mustards, salt, pepper, vinegar in a mixing bowl or workbowl of food processor, and stir or process to mix. Gradually add oil in a thin stream into the bowl or through feed tube and whisk or process to mix until mixture is thoroughly blended. Taste to adjust seasoning if necessary.

3. Place lamb in a nonmetallic dish, pour the marinade over it, and spread to coat both sides of meat. Let marinate several hours or up to one day ahead, turning once or twice. Cover loosely with plastic wrap and refrigerate. Bring to room temperature before cooking.

4. *To Grill:* Preheat your grill, whether charcoal or gas, and wait for the coals or briquettes to have an ashen coating before you start cooking. Set gas at highest setting. Toss the mashed garlic cloves into the coals and place the meat on the grill. Cover and cook 6–7 minutes; uncover and cook 7–8 minutes longer. Turn meat over and repeat covered and uncovered cooking times. The entire cooking time is about 30–35 minutes. Baste meat with marinade each time you turn it. Use an instant meat thermometer* if you like. (I do not like using the type of meat thermometer that probes the meat all during the cooking time, as precious juices will be lost.) Insert instant thermometer into the meat's thickest part for a reading—120 degrees for rare; 135 degrees for medium (more than that and it is just like an old shoe). Transfer to a carving board. Let meat rest for 5 minutes, which allows juices to recede back into it. With a sharp knife, carve long, thin slices across the grain.

To Roast: Preheat oven to 450 degrees. Adjust rack to center of oven. Scatter garlic cloves along the bottom of a roasting pan. Put the meat on top. Reduce oven temperature to 400 degrees before putting in meat. Roast for 30 minutes, then reduce oven temperature to 350 degrees. Add a little water to cooking juices in pan. Baste meat from time to time with reserved marinade. Cook for a total of 35–40 minutes. (See thermometer cooking time above.)

To Prepare Ahead
Follow steps 1 through 3 up to two days ahead. Complete step 4 just before serving.

RACK OF LAMB

One of the reasons a rack of lamb is such a popular restaurant offering is the ease and swiftness with which this luxury cut of meat can be prepared. When it is properly cooked, there is nothing more succulent. The topping of either the persillade or the crushed juniper-berry mixture will add incomparable flavor and texture. I have made the classic persillade coating for years and it is still a favorite. However, the juniper berries, gin, herbs, and grainy Dijon mustard permeate the meat, giving it a unique and fragrant flavor.

RACK OF LAMB WITH JUNIPER BERRIES

2 racks of lamb, about 2¼
  pounds each, or 7–8
  chops on each rack,
  trimmed
1 tablespoon juniper berries
  (available in specialty
  food shops)
2 cloves garlic, finely
  chopped
1 tablespoon snipped fresh
  rosemary leaves *or* ¾
  teaspoon dried
1 tablespoon gin

1 tablespoon grainy Dijon
  mustard
2–3 teaspoons fresh lemon
  juice
½ teaspoon coarse (kosher)
  salt
Freshly ground pepper

Have on Hand
Shallow roasting pan just
  large enough for racks
Aluminum foil

Serves 6

1. Have butcher remove chine bone and partially saw through the backbone of racks for easy slicing. Have him remove all surface fat from top of ribs, leaving a very thin layer, which may be scored. Finally, have him trim fat from ends of bones to expose them. In addition to the butcher's trimming, remove the layer of fat under the top flap of meat by using a sharp slicing knife and cutting parallel to the bone under this top layer of meat. Be careful not to separate this flap from the main "eye" portion of each rack.
Preheat oven to 475 degrees.

2. Place berries between sheets of wax paper and crush them with a rolling pin or bottom of heavy pan. Place in a mixing bowl, add all remaining ingredients, and stir to mix. Rub mixture over all surfaces of meat.

3. Place in shallow roasting pan, interlacing the exposed rib ends to support each other. Cut a 2–3-inch strip of aluminum foil long enough to wrap around interlaced bone ends and cover loosely, shiny side down, to prevent from burning. Roast 12–14 minutes, reduce heat to 400 degrees, and roast 15 minutes longer, or until an instant meat thermometer reads 130–135 degrees for rare or 145–150 for medium, or when meat feels springy to the touch when poked lightly. Ideally, the lamb should be served with a crusty, well-browned surface. Transfer the racks to a carving board and carve between each rib to serve. Serve with Timbale of Lettuce Chiffonade.

RACK OF LAMB PERSILLÉ

2 racks of lamb, about 2¼
    pounds each, or 7–8
    chops on each rack,
    trimmed
¼ cup finely chopped Italian
    flat-leaf parsley
1 tablespoon snipped fresh
    rosemary leaves *or* ¾
    teaspoon dried
2 teaspoons fresh thyme
    leaves *or* ¼ teaspoon
    dried
1 teaspoon coarse (kosher)
    salt

8 tablespoons (1 stick)
    unsalted butter, melted
2–3 cloves garlic, finely
    chopped
2 tablespoons Dijon mustard
1 cup toasted Bread Crumbs

Have on Hand
Shallow roasting pan just
    large enough for racks
Aluminum foil

Serves 6

1. Have butcher remove chine bone and partially saw through the backbone of racks for easy slicing. Have him remove all surface fat from top of ribs, leaving a very thin layer, which may be scored. Finally, have him trim fat from ends of bones to expose them. In addition to the butcher's trimming, remove the layer of fat under the top flap of meat by using a sharp slicing knife and cutting parallel to the bone under this top layer of meat. Be careful not to separate this flap from the main "eye" portion of each rack.

2. In a mixing bowl, combine 1 tablespoon of the parsley with rosemary, thyme, and salt. Rub the mixture into all surfaces of the meat as well as possible. Can be done ahead to this point.
Preheat oven to 475 degrees.

3. In a mixing bowl, combine melted butter, garlic, mustard, remaining parsley, and bread crumbs, and stir to mix. When cool, divide and press bread-crumb mixture onto meaty part of each rack.

4. Place in shallow roasting pan, interlacing the exposed rib ends to support each other. Cut a 2–3-inch strip of aluminum foil long enough to wrap around interlaced bone ends and cover loosely, shiny side down, to prevent them from burning. Roast 12–14 minutes, reduce heat to 400 degrees, and roast 15 minutes longer, or until an instant meat thermometer reads 130–135 degrees for rare or 145–150 for medium, or when meat feels springy to the touch when poked lightly. Ideally, the lamb should be served pink with a crusty, well-browned surface. Transfer the racks

to a carving board and carve between each rib to serve. I frequently serve this with Zucchini-Tomato Gratin.

To Prepare Ahead
Follow steps 1 and 2 up to one day ahead. Cover with plastic wrap and refrigerate overnight. Bring to room temperature before completing steps 3 and 4.

CHICKEN

How to Choose: What's in a name when it comes to a chicken? All chicken sold at retail is Grade A. However, the only factor worth considering is freshness. There is a question as to just how fresh. A chicken killed and eaten the very same day will not be tender. Fresh-killed chickens need a chance to chill thoroughly at least twenty-four hours to be properly tender. Look for chickens that have a soft, smooth skin without any dry patches and are free of bruises and blood spots. Skin color is the result of diet, and shades of quite pale to bright yellow are common.

When buying chickens in a market, you must be absolutely sure it is a market with a steady, fast turnover, since chicken is very perishable.

I cook chicken several times a week and yet I am never bored with it, since there are so many ways I enjoy preparing it. In fact, it is a staple in my own home. When I talk of chicken, it is as meat; it is a light meat—light in color and light to digest. Time was when chicken was a Sunday treat. Today it is one of our most economical meats, as well as an excellent source of protein. And most of all, it is extremely versatile.

Roast Chicken: Roast chicken is a simple dish, yet the fact remains that, when perfectly done, it is also probably one of the world's most superb dishes. It can be a satisfying culinary accomplishment, since it is easily achieved by the home cook. Simplicity aside, it affords a useful bonus. After the chicken has been carved, you are left with the carcass for your stockpot.

When correctly trussed, timed, and roasted, chicken will cook to perfection and remain moist, retaining its juices. (Be careful not to prick the skin when working with chicken.) At the exact point of juiciness, there is bound to be a touch of pink at the joint of the dark meat. To overcome the pink, if you must, return the thigh and leg pieces to the roasting pan (having first poured off the fat) and roast for a few minutes longer. Or place pan on top of the burner and cook the thigh and leg pieces for a few minutes while deglazing drippings in roasting pan with any liquid of your choice (see Poulet Rôti au Vinaigre de Framboise or French Roast Tarragon Chicken).

Another way with chicken that I can guarantee will become an absolute and frequent favorite is Grilled Chicken Breasts with Two Mustards. You only have to turn to the recipe to see why.

LITTLE DRUMSTICKS WITH VINEGAR SAUCE

Jean and Pierre Troisgros, creators of the three-star Les Frères in Roanne, France, were in themselves a winning combination. Here is a version of their winning and inspired chicken appetizer as served to me when I dined there several years ago.

16 chicken wings

Vinegar Sauce
3 tablespoons unsalted butter
2–3 cloves garlic, finely
    chopped
2–3 shallots, finely chopped
¾ cup dry white wine
3 tablespoons tarragon
    vinegar
3 medium-sized ripe
    tomatoes, peeled,
    seeded, and chopped *or*
    1 cup canned whole
    tomatoes, drained,
    seeded, and chopped
¼ teaspoon tomato paste
Coarse (kosher) salt
Freshly ground pepper

To Coat and Fry Wings
1 egg lightly beaten with 1
    tablespoon cold water
¾ cup dry toasted Bread
    Crumbs
1½–2 cups vegetable oil for
    deep frying

Garnish
Lots of curly parsley,
    washed, spin-dried,
    heavy stems removed
Lemon wedges

Have on Hand
Skillet for deep frying
Aluminum foil

Serves 8–10

1. Cut wings in half at the joint. Use only the part that resembles a small drumstick. Trim and discard excess fat and skin. Reserve or freeze other half for stockpot or other use.

2. Hold wing half at meaty end, clutching it with a paper towel so that it doesn't slip. With a sharp paring knife start to scrape the skin and meat at the base of the bone upward toward the heavier end. When you have scraped all the meat around the bone, turn the meat inside out with your hands, pulling it upward over the joint so that it resembles a closed tulip.

3. *Prepare Vinegar Sauce:* In a 12-inch skillet, melt butter and, when foam subsides, add garlic and shallots and sauté briefly until tender, being careful not to brown. Add wine, turn up heat and bring to the edge of a boil. Reduce heat to moderate and simmer until wine is reduced by half. Add tarragon vinegar and cook for 2–3 minutes longer. Add tomatoes and tomato paste. Sprinkle lightly with salt and pepper, then simmer 12–15 minutes. Taste to adjust seasoning if necessary. Can be made ahead to this point and reheated—or keep warm and then place in an attractive bowl for serving if passing a tray or serving buffet.

4. In a small bowl or soup plate, beat egg with water. Place bread crumbs in a flat plate. Dip each "drumstick" into the egg mixture and allow excess to drip off. Then roll in bread crumbs to coat, and tap off excess. Transfer one layer deep to a cookie sheet or piece of aluminum foil. Continue until all are done.

5. Heat oil in a frying pan or deep fryer. When fat is hot but not smoking, put 4 or 5 pieces of chicken into oil at one time and fry over moderate heat until cooked through and golden brown on both sides, turning once. With a strainer-skimmer or a slotted spoon, remove "drumsticks" as they are done and drain one layer deep on a double thickness of paper towels. When wings are thoroughly drained, wrap ends of bone with strips of aluminum foil. Line a tray or serving platter with lots of curly parsley. Place bowl of sauce in the center of the platter, then arrange "drumsticks" over the parsley surrounding the sauce. Serve at room temperature and pass with cocktail napkins (sauce is for dunking) or place a small pool of sauce on a salad or dessert plate and arrange 2 "drumsticks" on the plate with the meaty portion in the sauce and the foil-covered bone extending to the rim of the plate.

To Prepare Ahead
Follow steps 1 through 3 up to one day ahead. Refrigerate separately in suitable containers. Bring to room temperature and complete steps 4 and 5 before serving. Warm sauce, but serve fried chicken-wing halves at room temperature.

ALL MANNER OF MEAT
CHICKEN MARENGO

In this great company or family dish, succulent morsels of chicken are flavored by tomatoes and herbs. It is extra special when served in a brioche case.

½ cup flour
1½ teaspoons coarse (kosher) salt
Freshly ground pepper
2 teaspoons fresh tarragon leaves *or* ½ teaspoon dried
2 teaspoons fresh basil leaves *or* ½ teaspoon dried
2 teaspoons fresh thyme leaves *or* ½ teaspoon dried
¼ teaspoon paprika
5 whole chicken breasts, skinned, halved, and boned (10 boneless pieces) (see *Note* below)
¼ cup light, fruity olive oil or peanut oil
4 tablespoons unsalted butter
1 cup dry white wine

2 tablespoons tomato paste
1 cup Basic Chicken Stock or broth
1 can (1 pound, 12 ounces) whole tomatoes, drained, halved, and seeded. Reserve about ½ cup tomato liquid. Do not use canned tomatoes packed with purée
¾ pound fresh mushrooms, quickly rinsed clean, trimmed, and halved or quartered
2 cloves garlic, finely chopped
1 tablespoon finely chopped Italian flat-leaf parsley
Curly parsley or watercress for garnish
Party Brioche (optional)

Serves 10–12

1. Combine flour, salt, pepper, herbs, and paprika in a large plastic food-storage bag.

2. Rinse and dry chicken breasts, then cut into approximately 1½-inch pieces. Place chicken pieces into bag containing seasoned flour. Close bag securely and toss to coat in the herb mixture.

3. Add oil and butter to a large heavy skillet, and place over moderate heat. When butter foam subsides sauté chicken pieces in batches and cook briefly, stirring occasionally with a wooden spatula, until just golden on all sides. With a slotted spoon transfer chicken pieces to a casserole as they are done, and set aside.

4. Add any remaining seasoned flour to the fat in skillet chicken cooked in and, with a wooden spatula, stir to cook about 1½ minutes. Gradually add wine, stirring to deglaze drippings in bottom of pan, and reduce by half over moderate heat. Stir in tomato paste and stock or broth and simmer, stirring occasionally, until the sauce is smooth and thick.

5. Pour liquid over chicken in casserole, scraping out any residue with a rubber spatula. Add tomatoes, mushrooms, and garlic, and with a large wooden spatula stir to mix ingredients carefully. Liquid should barely cover chicken mixture. If necessary, add up to ½ cup of reserved tomato liquid. Taste for salt and pepper and adjust seasoning if necessary. Can be done ahead to this point.

Preheat oven to 350 degrees.

6. Cover casserole and bake in preheated oven 30–40 minutes or until chicken is tender. Sprinkle with chopped parsley and serve at once.

7. *If Serving Party Brioche:* Slice off the topknot of the brioche and set aside. To hollow out brioche, cut a ring around the inside rim with a serrated bread knife, then scoop out this inside portion with a large kitchen spoon. (Enjoy scooped-out portion of the bread in any way or at any time.) Place hollow brioche on a heated serving platter and spoon piping-hot chicken mixture into the hollow, filling it to overflowing. Spoon additional chicken mixture around the base of the brioche and lean topknot lid attractively against brioche case. Fill in any spaces on the platter with curly parsley or watercress.

Serving Chicken Marengo in a Party Brioche

Step 1

Step 2

Step 3

To Prepare Ahead

Follow steps 1 through 5 up to two days ahead. Refrigerate, covered. Bring to room temperature and complete steps 6 and 7.

Hint: Many of my students have successfully frozen this dish. If you freeze it, I would suggest that you do not add mushrooms at the end of step 5 and that you freeze chicken mixture in a suitable container. Defrost and return to room temperature, add mushrooms to mixture, and complete as above.

Note re Chicken: I know many of you probably buy boneless chicken breasts, but you are better off buying whole chicken breasts with skin and bone on. Otherwise you pay higher prices and probably end up with less meat. Have the butcher pull off the skin and remove the keel bone. He should do this for you at no extra charge. The rest is easy: Simply push the meat away with your thumb or a paring knife, starting at the heavy, more solid side of the bone, and with knife scrape away from the thinner rib bones. Trim off and discard excess fat. The bones, of course, may be used for making stock.

CHICKEN BREASTS IN GELATIN LA SCALA

1 rib celery with leaves, rinsed and halved
1 bay leaf, crumbled
1 clove garlic, unpeeled and left whole
1 red onion, peeled and quartered
6 peppercorns
1 tablespoon coarse (kosher) salt
4 whole chicken breasts, halved

½ cup dry white wine, chilled
1 envelope unflavored gelatin
Freshly ground pepper
2 teaspoons fresh rosemary leaves *or* ½ teaspoon dried

Boston lettuce leaves
8 thin slices prosciutto
Tomato slices for garnish

Serves 6–8

1. Place celery, bay leaf, garlic, onion, salt, and peppercorns in a 4-quart saucepan with about 2½ quarts water. Bring to a boil over high heat and add salt. Reduce heat to a brisk simmer, put in the chicken breasts and poach gently 14–15 minutes.

2. With a slotted spoon, transfer chicken breasts to a side dish. Allow to cool, remove and discard skin, then carefully cut the meat from the bone in one piece. Continue until all are done and set aside. Return accumulated bones to saucepan and cook, uncovered, at a brisk simmer until liquid is reduced to about 1½ cups. Skim and discard fat, then strain stock into a small bowl.

3. In the meantime, pour wine into a glass measuring cup or small bowl and sprinkle the gelatin over it. Let stand until gelatin absorbs the liquid, then stir into the hot broth to dissolve. Season broth with freshly ground pepper and rosemary and stir to mix. Allow to cool. Put into the refrigerator to cool completely. Be careful not to let aspic gel at this point.

4. Line a large round platter with lettuce leaves and arrange chicken breasts on it, placing them in a circle like the spokes of a wheel. Or arrange on a lined oval platter, side by side. Drape each breast with a slice of prosciutto. Coat with a thin layer of aspic and put into refrigerator to set. Keep applying additional coats of aspic as each layer sets. Refrigerate in between these applications. Should the aspic in the bowl set at any point, soften it by placing the bowl in a basin of warm water just until aspic becomes liquid again. When chicken breasts are nicely glazed, return to refrigerator and chill several more hours or overnight. When aspic is firm, cover with a tent of plastic wrap. Can be made completely ahead to this point.

5. Serve at room temperature garnished with tomato slices.

To Prepare Ahead
Follow steps 1 through 4 up to two days ahead. Refrigerate covered with plastic wrap. Complete step 5 before serving.

A Note About Aspic: An aspic should be crystal clear. If your stock should become cloudy, beat 1 or 2 egg whites, add to stock, and bring to a boil. The albumen in the egg whites will solidify the impurities and bring them to the surface. Simmer stock gently 2–3 minutes. Pass the clear liquid through a paper towel-lined sieve, being careful not to disturb the foamy scum, which is to be discarded.

CHICKEN VIROFLAY

*This was one of the first classic preparations I learned when I studied at
the Cordon Bleu in London. I hardly had one foot back on home territory
when I assembled the dish for my waiting family. Jet lag notwithstanding,
I was eager to work while the procedure of boning a whole chicken was
still fresh in my mind. The dish was spectacular then, as it is today. After
the chicken is boned, stuffed, and sewed, reform by molding it in your
hands to its original shape and truss. When this succulent roasted chicken
is served at tableside, people marvel to see it carved without a struggle
over the bones.*

1 roasting chicken, about
    3½ pounds, boned*

Stuffing
1 pound loose fresh spinach,
    fibrous stems and
    blemished leaves
    removed
4 tablespoons unsalted butter
2 shallots, finely chopped
1 cup fresh Bread Crumbs
½ pound boiled ham, diced
2 egg yolks
1 tablespoon finely minced
    Italian flat-leaf parsley
2 teaspoons fresh thyme
    leaves *or* ¾ teaspoon
    dried
½ teaspoon coarse (kosher)
    salt

Freshly ground pepper
2 tablespoons unsalted
    butter, softened

To Finish
1 apple, unpeeled and sliced
1 cup Basic Chicken Stock
    or broth
1 cup dry white wine
2 tablespoons Crème Fraîche
    or heavy cream
Watercress for garnish

Have on Hand
Trussing needle
Kitchen string
Boning knife

Serves 6

Preheat oven to 375 degrees.

1. After boning chicken*, rinse it clean and pat dry with paper towels.

2. Wash spinach in several changes of lukewarm water to clean the
leaves of dirt and sand. Transfer to a heavy saucepan with about 1 inch
of water. Cover tightly and cook 3–4 minutes, stirring occasionally until
tender. Drain and refresh by fanning* or briefly running under cold water
to set color and stop the cooking. With your hands, squeeze spinach to
remove moisture, then place in a clean kitchen towel and squeeze very
dry. Place on a wooden board and chop coarsely.

3. In a skillet melt butter and, when foam subsides, sauté shallots quickly until tender but not brown. Add spinach, stir to mix, and cook 1 minute longer. Transfer to a mixing bowl and add bread crumbs, ham, egg yolks, parsley, thyme, salt, and pepper.

4. Spread chicken, skin side down, on work surface and sprinkle lightly with coarse salt. Thread trussing needle with a length of kitchen string and start to sew chicken along back, starting at tail and sewing only about ⅔ of the way up. Do not detach string, which will be used to finish. Pack in all the stuffing, spreading it to distribute evenly, then continue sewing up toward the neck area. It may be necessary to push stuffing back into the cavity of the chicken as you sew. Secure string well at neck end. Truss* chicken, keeping its original form intact, then rub all over surface of skin with 2 tablespoons softened butter.

5. Place chicken on a rack in a shallow roasting pan and put in the sliced apple and stock. Roast in preheated oven about 1 hour and 10 minutes, basting every 15 minutes or so. Carefully turn chicken over in roasting pan about every 20 minutes, ending with breast side up to brown it nicely. Try not to tear the skin or pierce the chicken as you rotate it. Breast meat should be springy to the touch when done. Be careful not to overcook. Transfer to a warm serving platter. Straddle 2 burners with the roasting pan and skim off surface fat and discard. Pour wine into pan and, over moderately high heat, using a wooden spatula, mash apple slices as you deglaze drippings in bottom of pan and reduce liquid by half. Strain contents into a small saucepan and with back of a wooden spoon, press down hard to extract juices. Stir in crème fraîche or cream and keep warm over low heat.

6. In the meantime, remove trussing strings from chicken and garnish platter with crisp watercress. Carve at the table and pass the sauce around.

To Prepare Ahead
Follow steps 1 through 3 up to one day ahead. Follow steps 4 and 5 up to two hours ahead, cutting roasting time by fifteen minutes if done ahead. Finish last fifteen minutes of roasting to brown the chicken and complete step 6 just before serving.

POULET DE BRESSE GRILLÉ

When I visited and observed in the professional kitchen of Père Bis, a Michelin Guide three-star restaurant in Talloires, France, I was captivated by a well-charred honey-glazed chicken. It was so succulent and spectacular-looking that I decided to develop a recipe that would re-create the experience. The beurre vinaigre is an embellishment and added only as an extra touch if desired.

2 3–3½-pound chickens

Deviling Sauce
2–3 cloves garlic, finely
   minced
½ cup Dijon mustard
¼ cup honey
1 tablespoon lemon juice
½ teaspoon freshly ground
   pepper
½ cup vegetable oil

Beurre Vinaigre (optional)
2 tablespoons butter
3–4 shallots, finely chopped
2 tablespoons red wine
   vinegar
Freshly ground pepper
½ cup Mock Demi-Glace
2 tablespoons Crème Fraîche
   or unsalted butter
   (optional)

Bunch of watercress for
   garnish

Serves 6–8

1. Butterfly chickens. Have butcher remove backbones. (Save along with giblets for stock.) Place chicken flesh side up, and bend carcass sharply backward with both hands on either side of breast until chicken lies flat. Repeat with second chicken. Trim chickens of excess fat, pinfeathers, etc. Rinse clean and pat dry with paper toweling. Sprinkle lightly with salt on both sides. Place butterflied chickens on a platter large enough to hold them in one layer.

2. *To Prepare Deviling Sauce:* Place garlic, mustard, honey, lemon juice, and freshly ground pepper in a mixing bowl or workbowl of a food processor fitted with a steel blade, and stir or process to mix. Gradually add oil in a thin stream into the bowl or through feed tube and whisk or process to mix until mixture is thoroughly blended. Taste to adjust seasoning if necessary.

3. Pour all of marinade over chickens and spread to coat. Let marinate several hours or up to one day ahead, turning once or twice. Cover loosely with plastic wrap and refrigerate. Bring to room temperature before cooking.

4. *To Grill:* Preheat your grill whether charcoal or gas and wait for the coals or briquettes to have an ashen coating before you start to cook. Set gas at highest setting. Using tongs and a spatula, carefully place the butterflied chickens on the grill skin side up. Cover and cook 5–6 minutes. Uncover and cook 6–7 minutes longer. Carefully turn chickens over, placing them flat on the grill. Repeat covered and uncovered cooking times. Total cooking time is about 25–30 minutes. Baste with reserved marinade each time you turn. Skin of chicken should be well charred with the meat remaining moist. If chicken skin is charred and meat is not cooked through, put into a 180-degree oven 10–15 minutes longer to complete the cooking.

To Broil: Preheat broiler. Arrange marinated chicken, flesh side down, on a broiler rack. Broil 5–6 inches from source of heat, about 8 minutes on one side and 10 minutes on the other. Chicken should brown nicely. However, if it begins to burn, it may be necessary to adjust rack and lower broiling pan. To be sure chicken is cooked through, turn off broiler and set oven to 350 degrees. Allow to roast on middle rack 10 minutes longer. Total cooking time should be 25–30 minutes.

5. Transfer chickens to a large warm serving platter. Arrange them neck to neck, garnished with a crisp bunch of watercress where they meet. For serving, cut through joints with a sharp slicing knife or kitchen shears. If desired, serve with a little beurre vinaigre spooned over individual portions.

Beurre Vinaigre: Melt butter in a small saucepan. Add shallots and sauté quickly until tender but not brown. Add vinegar and cook until liquid is almost evaporated but shallots are still moist. Add demi-glace and stir until it is liquid. Whisk in the crème fraîche or butter over very low heat. Keep warm. If preparing ahead (up to 2 hours), cover surface of sauce with a disk of buttered wax paper to prevent skin from forming. Taste to adjust seasoning if necessary.

To Prepare Ahead
Follow steps 1 through 3 up to one day ahead. Cover loosely with plastic wrap and refrigerate. Bring to room temperature before cooking and complete through step 5. See beurre vinaigre for prepare-ahead directions.

POLLO ALLA GIANNINO'S

Giannino's is a well-known restaurant in Milan. These boneless stuffed chicken breasts are a lighter and more flavorful variation of the classic Cordon Bleu recipe.

4 whole chicken breasts,
    skin on, boned and
    halved
2 tablespoons Dijon mustard
Coarse (kosher) salt
Freshly ground pepper
1 tablespoon dried oregano
2 tablespoons finely chopped
    shallots
8 thin slices boiled ham
¾ cup grated Gruyère
    cheese
Flour for dredging chicken
⅓ cup vegetable oil
3 tablespoons clarified
    butter*

Sauce
½ cup dry white wine
1 cup Basic Chicken Stock
    or broth
2–3 tablespoons fresh lemon
    juice
Coarse (kosher) salt
Freshly ground pepper

Fresh watercress for garnish

Have on Hand
Batticarne* (meat pounder)

Serves 6–8

1. Buying whole chicken breasts with skin on and bone in is practical and economical. I find that boneless chicken breasts are generally minimally sized and maximally priced. So do your own boning. Have butcher remove the keel bone and split the breasts in half, then bone them. With a sharp paring or boning knife, start to scrape against the heavier portion of the bone and push the flesh away from the rib bones until breast is free. Trim and discard excess fat and place skin side down on work counter. Release the chicken fillet where it is attached to breast and flip it over to make breast wider. Pound the meat lightly with a batticarne to flatten and to make it approximately the same thickness. Spread the flesh side of each breast with ¾ teaspoon Dijon mustard and sprinkle lightly with salt, pepper, and a scant ½ teaspoon of the oregano. Scatter approximately ½ teaspoon of the shallots over each. Cover with a slice of ham and top with a thin layer of grated cheese.

2. Tuck in the short ends of breasts, then fold long sides over to enclose package neatly. Cup your hands and roll breasts over, skin side

up, and transfer to a shallow pan. Continue to stuff and roll chicken breasts until all are done. Set aside. Can be done ahead to this point.

3. Just before cooking stuffed chicken breasts, coat lightly with flour by tapping the flour through a sieve directly over the breasts. Lift each breast and tap off excess.

4. In a large heavy skillet, heat oil with butter. When foam subsides, sauté chicken breasts a few at a time over moderately high heat until golden brown on all sides. Do not worry if they open slightly when you turn them, as they can be reshaped. As they are done, transfer one layer deep to a shallow pan to catch the juices.

5. *To Prepare Sauce:* Pour off all but 2 tablespoons of fat in skillet. Sauté remaining 2 teaspoons shallots in hot fat. Add wine and stir with a wooden spatula to deglaze the drippings in bottom of pan, then reduce by half over moderately high heat. Add chicken stock, lemon juice, and seasonings, and stir to mix. Strain sauce into a bowl, pressing shallots with a wooden spoon to extract juices.

6. Return the chicken breasts one layer deep to skillet and pour on sauce.

7. Cover pan with a tight lid and simmer over very low heat 18–20 minutes. Transfer to a warm serving platter. Serve with freshly cooked escarole or garnish with watercress.

To Prepare Ahead
Follow step 1 up to one day ahead. Refrigerate covered. Follow steps 2 through 6 up to several hours ahead. Let stand at room temperature. Complete step 7 just before serving.

POULET RÔTI AU VINAIGRE DE FRAMBOISE

3½-pound roasting chicken
½ teaspoon coarse (kosher) salt
Freshly ground pepper
2 tablespoons light olive oil

3 tablespoons unsalted butter
3 tablespoons finely chopped shallots or scallions
⅓ cup raspberry vinegar

Serves 4

Preheat oven to 400 degrees.

1. Trim chicken of excess fat, pinfeathers, etc. Rinse, then pat dry with paper towel and season with a light sprinkle of salt and pepper, inside and out. Truss* chicken.

2. Pour 2 tablespoons olive oil in a shallow roasting pan. Be careful not to use an oversize pan for one chicken. Place over moderate heat and brown carefully and slowly until golden on all sides, 12–15 minutes. Place pan in oven and roast 20 minutes on one side, basting occasionally. Turn over and continue roasting another 15 minutes. Turn again so breast side is up, and roast, still basting every 5 minutes or so, 15–20 minutes longer. Remove trussing string and place on a carving board. Pour off and discard fat in roasting pan. Do not wash pan at this point.

3. With a slicing knife, carve chicken into 8 sections, removing legs and wings, then thighs, and finally breast meat from carcass. Transfer to a serving dish. If thighs are still slightly pink, return to pan and cook 5 minutes longer in oven or sauté on top of stove in roasting pan. Add to remaining chicken on a warm serving platter.

4. Add butter and shallots or scallions to solidified juices in pan. Stir with a wooden spatula, scraping bottom until butter melts. Add raspberry vinegar and deglaze bits in bottom of pan, stirring and scraping until vinegar is reduced by half.

5. Just before serving, return chicken pieces to pan and warm through with raspberry vinegar sauce, spooning on juices. Serve with hot buttered noodles if desired.

To Prepare Ahead
Follow step 1 up to one day ahead. Complete steps 2 through 5 before serving.

GRILLED CHICKEN BREASTS WITH
TWO MUSTARDS

This is a delicious quickie that when carefully cooked can be a masterpiece. Whenever I prepare it as a special company dish, I prefer to keep the breast whole, which makes a nice presentation. However, when I serve it to my family, I usually cut the breasts in half.

4 whole chicken breasts, on the bone	2 tablespoons fresh lemon juice
Coarse (kosher) salt	Freshly ground pepper
4–5 large shallots, finely chopped	4 tablespoons light fruity olive oil
2 tablespoons grainy mustard	Dry toasted Bread Crumbs
2 tablespoons Dijon mustard	

Serves 4–6

1. Have butcher flatten chicken breasts and remove keel bone. Leave breasts whole or cut in half as you wish.

2. Trim excess chicken fat from breasts and discard. Rinse clean and pat dry with paper toweling. Sprinkle both sides of breasts lightly with salt and place in a shallow dish, skin side up, one layer deep.

3. Place shallots in a mixing bowl or chop finely in workbowl of food processor fitted with steel knife. Add mustards, lemon juice, and several grinds of pepper, and whisk or process to mix. Gradually add oil in a thin stream into bowl or through feed tube of processor and whisk or process to mix until mixture is thoroughly blended. Mixture is loose and in a sense is a marinade. Divide and spread evenly over chicken breasts. Can be done ahead to this point.

4. If chicken breasts were refrigerated, bring to room temperature before cooking either on an outdoor grill or in the oven broiler.

To Grill: Preheat your outdoor grill whether charcoal or gas and wait for the coals or briquettes to have an ashen coating before you start to cook. Set grill at medium-heat setting. Using tongs or a spatula, carefully lift chicken breasts from marinade, place skin side up, and cook, covered, 5 minutes on each side, turning once. Turn skin side up and sprinkle with a coating of crumbs and cook 10 minutes, uncovered. Turn pieces over and cook an additional 3–4 minutes. Baste with remaining sauce as pieces are turned. Skin should be charred and crisp. If breasts are not fully cooked through and skin has already charred, place in a 300-degree oven for 8–10 minutes to complete cooking.

To Broil: Preheat oven broiler. Line a shallow roasting pan with aluminum foil, shiny side down. Arrange chicken breasts in single layer, skin side up, directly on foil and place pan about 3–4 inches from source of heat. Broil 5–6 minutes on one side. Turn pieces, baste with mustard drippings, and broil 3–4 minutes on other side. Turn skin side up, basting again with drippings, sprinkle each breast with a coating of crumbs, and broil 1–2 minutes longer. Serve immediately.

To Prepare Ahead

Follow steps 1 through 3 up to one day ahead. Refrigerate, covered. Bring to room temperature before cooking.

ROAST CAPON WITH SAUTÉED FRUITS

8-pound capon
½ cup dry white wine
¼ cup brandy or Cognac
Coarse (kosher) salt
Freshly ground pepper
½ cup Basic Chicken Stock
    or broth

A Selection of Fruits . . . 1,
    2, or More
1 ripe pineapple
1 or 2 Golden Delicious or
    Cortland apples
2 tablespoons lemon juice
2–3 navel oranges
3 tablespoons unsalted butter
½ cup seedless red or green
    grapes
Freshly ground pepper

Sauce to Nap the Capon
¼ cup dry white wine
½ cup Basic Chicken Stock
    or broth
1 cup Crème Fraîche or
    heavy cream
1–2 tablespoons fresh lemon
    juice
Coarse (kosher) salt
Freshly ground pepper

1–2 tablespoons finely
    chopped parsley for
    garnish

Have on Hand
Kitchen string or trussing

Serves 10–12

1. Trim capon of excess fat, pinfeathers, etc. Rinse quickly, then pat dry with paper toweling. Up to one day before roasting, place capon in a large mixing bowl, pour on white wine, brandy or Cognac, a light

sprinkle of salt, and freshly ground pepper. Cover with plastic wrap and marinate overnight in the refrigerator.

Preheat oven to 400 degrees.

2. Before roasting, lift capon from marinade and pat dry with paper toweling. With a long length of kitchen string truss* the capon and place on a rack in a roasting pan. Bring to room temperature, add ½ cup stock to pan, and roast, breast side up, in oven 20 minutes. Reduce temperature to 350 degrees and roast 1 hour longer, basting with pan juices from time to time. It may be necessary to add some stock or water to pan from time to time. Turn capon breast side up in the final 30 minutes of cooking to brown evenly.

3. While meat is roasting, prepare fruits. Slice off top and bottom of pineapple. Run a knife between fruit and inside wall to free pulp, then cut away core or use a pineapple corer. Cut ½-inch-wide slices lengthwise, then cut slices into 2-inch lengths and set aside. Peel the apple or apples, core, then cut into ½-inch wedges, or use an apple divider. Sprinkle apples with lemon juice to prevent discoloration and set aside. Peel oranges, removing all the skin right down to the flesh; then, with a small sharp paring knife, cut out orange segments between the membranes. Set aside.

4. Melt butter in a skillet and, when foam subsides, add apple wedges and sauté 1–2 minutes. Add pineapple slices, orange sections, and grapes and toss gently to mix. Sauté with apples 30–40 seconds longer just to warm fruits. Season with a sprinkle of fresh pepper to bring out the flavor of the fruits, and remove from heat.

5. When capon is done, transfer to a ridged carving board, remove strings, and let rest about 10 minutes. Pour off and discard fat from roasting pan. Place pan over moderate heat, add wine and stock and, with a wooden spatula, stir to deglaze drippings in bottom of pan. Add crème fraîche or heavy cream and simmer briskly until liquid has reduced by half and has thickened slightly. Season with lemon juice, salt and pepper, stir to mix, then taste to adjust seasoning if necessary. Keep warm.

6. Carve capon by first cutting off the wings, then the legs and thighs, and finally the breast meat in long thin slices as you would a turkey. As you carve each section, transfer it to a heated serving platter. Pour on hot sauce and surround with sautéed fruits. Sprinkle with a bit of chopped parsley for added color and serve immediately.

To Prepare Ahead

Follow step 1 up to one day ahead. Follow steps 2 through 4 up to 2 hours ahead. Fruits and sauce can stand at room temperature. Reheat gently just before serving, then complete steps 5 and 6.

CHICKEN LA ZARAGOZANA

La Zaragozana is a famous restaurant in Spain. The descendants of the family moved to Cuba and finally to Puerto Rico, where I first tasted this deliciously piquant and beautifully presented chicken dish.

2 frying chickens, cut into 8
    pieces
Coarse (kosher) salt
1 can (6 ounces) frozen
    orange juice
    concentrate, diluted to
    half strength
3 large cloves garlic, finely
    chopped
¼ cup finely chopped Italian
    flat-leaf parsley
¾ cup dry sherry
½ cup golden raisins
⅓ cup flour for dredging

1 tablespoon paprika
¼ cup light, fruity olive oil
8 tablespoons (1 stick)
    unsalted butter
1 cup Basic Chicken Stock
    or broth
2–3 fresh sprigs of thyme *or*
    1 teaspoon dried
2 teaspoons coarse (kosher)
    salt
Freshly ground pepper
⅓ cup slivered almonds,
    lightly toasted

Serves 6–8

1. Trim chicken parts of excess fat, pinfeathers, etc. Rinse, then pat dry with paper towel and season with a light sprinkle of salt. Combine orange juice, garlic, and parsley in a deep bowl, add chicken pieces, and turn to coat in the marinade. Marinate chicken several hours or overnight. Cover and refrigerate if doing ahead and bring to room temperature before proceeding with the cooking.

2. Pour sherry over raisins in a small bowl to plump them; leave 30 minutes, then drain; reserve sherry and set aside.

3. Combine flour and paprika in a large plastic food-storage bag. Lift chicken from marinade, allowing excess to drip off, and place 2–3 chicken pieces at a time in bag containing seasoned flour. Close bag securely and shake to coat in the mixture. Arrange floured chicken parts one layer deep on a sheet of wax paper or a cookie sheet. Continue until all are done and set aside.

4. In a 12-inch heavy skillet, heat oil with 4 tablespoons of the butter. When foam subsides, add chicken a few pieces at a time (do not crowd pan) and fry until golden brown on both sides. Transfer to a side dish. Continue until all chicken is done.

5. Pour off fat from pan, being careful to retain drippings. Add

remaining 4 tablespoons butter to pan and, over moderate heat, stir with a wooden spatula to deglaze drippings. Add sherry and bring to a boil; add reserved marinade, stock, and thyme. Season to taste with salt and pepper and stir to mix. Cook at a brisk simmer to thicken the sauce slightly. Taste to adjust seasoning if necessary. Return chicken to skillet with accumulated juices, spooning over pan juices.

6. Cover and cook at a low simmer for 45 minutes or until chicken is tender. Transfer to a warm serving dish and garnish with a sprinkle of sherried raisins and toasted almonds.

To Prepare Ahead
Follow step 1 up to one day ahead. Follow steps 2 through 5 up to several hours ahead. Complete step 6 before serving.

FRENCH ROAST TARRAGON CHICKEN

1 roasting chicken, 3–3½ pounds
4 tablespoons unsalted butter
1 tablespoon fresh tarragon leaves *or* ¾ teaspoon dried
2 teaspoons fresh rosemary leaves *or* ½ teaspoon dried
1 teaspoon coarse (kosher) salt

1½ cups Basic Chicken Stock or broth
2 tablespoons additional butter or Crème Fraîche (optional)
Watercress for garnish (optional)

Have on Hand
Kitchen string

Serves 4–5

Preheat oven to 400 degrees.
1. Trim chicken of excess fat, pinfeathers, etc. Rinse, then pat dry with paper towel and season with a light sprinkle of salt.

2. With a wooden spoon cream butter in a mixing bowl, add seasonings, and stir to mix. Smear a small amount of the seasoned butter all over the inside of the chicken. Truss* chicken and smear remaining seasoned butter all over bird.

3. Place breast side up on a rack in a roasting pan with ½ cup stock or broth. Roast in oven 55 minutes–1 hour, basting from time to time. It may be necessary to add a little more stock or water to roasting pan

if liquid should evaporate. After 20 minutes turn breast side down for 20 minutes, then finish roasting breast side up to crisp and brown the skin.

4. I generally undercook my chickens, since I find the breast meat tends to become very dry. I use the following checks for doneness: Poke a couple of fingers into the breast meat, which should spring back if meat is properly cooked. Be careful not to overcook. You may also gently pierce the thigh bone with a fork and juices should run clear. If a little pink appears in the juice, do not be concerned, as chicken will continue to cook in its own heat before carving. Remove from oven and place on a carving board. Allow to rest 6–8 minutes. Set aside.

5. Pour off fat from roasting pan and discard, then straddle 2 burners with pan. Pour stock or broth into pan and, over moderate heat and using a wooden spatula, stir to deglaze drippings in the bottom of pan. Strain liquid into a small saucepan and reduce by half over moderately high heat. Swirl in butter or crème fraîche to thicken and enrich sauce if desired. Keep warm over low heat.

6. *To Serve:* Remove and discard trussing string and carve the chicken. Transfer to a warm serving platter and spoon on sauce. Garnish with watercress (optional) and serve with Carrots With Raspberry Vinegar.

To Prepare Ahead
Follow steps 1 and 2 up to several hours ahead. Refrigerate covered with a tent of plastic wrap. Bring to room temperature before roasting, then complete remaining steps before serving.

PROCESSOR PÂTÉ MAISON

The addition of giblets and herbs lends a subtle yet exciting flavor to this simple no-bake version of a classic chicken-liver terrine.

6 tablespoons unsalted butter
2 tablespoons finely chopped
    onion
2 tablespoons finely chopped
    shallots
⅓ pound chicken livers,
    trimmed, rinsed, and
    patted dry
Giblets from 2 chickens
¾ teaspoon coarse (kosher)
    salt
Freshly ground pepper

2 tablespoons Cognac
2 tablespoons white wine
    vinegar
2 hard-cooked eggs
1 tablespoon fresh thyme *or*
    ¾ teaspoon dried
1 tablespoon fresh marjoram
    or ¾ teaspoon dried
Tomato Rose for garnish
French Croutons or toast
    triangles for serving

Serves 6–8

1. In a large nonaluminum skillet, melt 5 tablespoons of the butter; add onion and shallots and cook over moderate heat 3–4 minutes, stirring occasionally, until tender. Transfer to workbowl of food processor fitted with steel blade and allow to cool.

2. Meantime, melt remaining tablespoon butter in the same skillet over brisk heat. When butter foam subsides, add the livers without crowding and sauté quickly until crisp and brown on the outside while still pink within. Season with salt and pepper. Pour Cognac and vinegar over livers and cook quickly until moisture has evaporated. Allow to cool thoroughly before adding to workbowl containing onion-shallot mixture. (If livers are added while still hot, mixture will probably curdle.)

3. Coarsely chop hard-cooked eggs and add to cooled livers and onion-shallot mixture. Add thyme and marjoram and process until mixture is smooth and thoroughly blended. Taste to adjust seasoning if necessary. Spoon into a covered crock, onion-soup bowl, or small soufflé dish. Garnish with a tomato rose. Cover and chill until ready to serve.

To Prepare Ahead
Follow steps 1 and 2 up to two days ahead. Refrigerate until ready to serve.

DUCK

How to Choose: Today's consumer has a difficult time judging the quality of duck in the supermarket. Duckling is mostly available to us frozen. Even though fresh duck is available more and more, it is almost impossible to tell how fresh it is, since most are sold in vacuum packs. Look for ducks, fresh or frozen, that are plump, with light, transparent fat and a moist, clean skin free of blotches. Since ducklings are difficult to raise in the harsh winter months, the season for domestic duck is April through November.

I am very fond of duck. Because of the generous layer of fat under its skin duckling has been a much maligned and frequently mistreated member of the poultry family. Some good cooks I know complain about cooking duckling. They can never get the skin crisp enough with the flesh still moist after cooking. Here is a technique that allows fat to drip out, in which the fork just pricks the skin, never touching the flesh underneath at all: With a fork, take long shallow running stitches through the surface of the duck's skin, coming in and out without piercing the meat. There are those who say not to prick the duckling at all, simply roast it in a very hot oven so that all the fat is rendered.

I have worked out a method for precooking ducks which I find very effective for a variety of reasons. You can precook the duck in a conventional oven; however a rotisserie, oven spit roaster, or a convection oven, which permits an air flow of dry heat to completely circulate, gives the most satisfactory results. This method crisps the skin more quickly in the initial stages of cooking while the meat within is still quite rare. Precooking can be done early in the day and even the day before. Since boning a raw duck is a difficult procedure, precooking it facilitates boning, making feasible those seemingly complicated nouvelle cuisine recipes that use boneless meat. With this in mind turn your attention without delay to the classic Duck Breasts and Legs in Vinegar and Green Peppercorn Sauce or the Sautéed Duck Breasts and Legs in Red Wine and Cassis Sauce.

The precooking also enables you to cut the duckling in halves and quarters to remove excess fat and the heavy bones, leaving in just wing and thigh bone. The bones and trimmings can help you to prepare a wonderful sauce. Everything is done ahead and the trimmed duck portions are appealing to serve. Simply slip the meaty duck halves or quarters into the oven with a bit of white wine (a restaurant technique) to finish roasting, then serve with the delicious Cassis Sauce from the Napa Valley for a memorable duck dinner.

PREROASTED DUCK

2–3 ducks, 4½–5 pounds   Coarse (kosher) salt
   each

Preheat oven to 325 degrees.
   1. Cut off and discard excess skin and fat from duck necks and cavity. Rinse ducks and dry well. Reserve giblets for stock. Use liver for pâté if desired or freeze for future use. With a long-tined fork, take long, shallow running stitches through the surface of the duck skin, coming in and out without piercing the meat. Season ducks with a light sprinkling of salt.
   2. Place ducks breast side up on an adjustable rack in a roasting pan and roast 10 minutes per pound or 40–50 minutes for a 4–5-pound duck. To accommodate more than one, turn ducks on their sides, reversing them halfway through the roasting. Remove pan from oven and pierce skin as above; drain and set aside. Pour off and discard fat from pan. (The French claim duck fat makes the best fried potatoes.)
   3. When ducks are cool enough to handle, halve them with poultry shears or sharp knife. (Actually, you will need both to facilitate the boning.) Turn ducks on your work counter breast side down. With shears, cut along both sides of backbone to remove. Set aside. Breast side up, cut through the center of the duck so that you have two halves. There is a natural separation between the breast and the thigh. Cut between these sections starting at the lower portion of the thigh. (In both instances, this starting point is diagonally opposite the wing.) If you start cutting at exactly the right point, you will have a V-shape at the lower portion of the breast when that section is separated from the thigh completely.
   Remove wings from breasts by cutting through the joints. With a sharp knife at a 45-degree angle, start to scrape against the bone to remove breast meat, being careful to keep it in one solid piece. Trim each section of excess bone and fat.
   Transfer carcass bones and wings to a clean roasting pan and reserve for stock.
   Put boned breasts and thighs in a single layer on a foil-lined cookie sheet or roasting pan. Can be done up to one day ahead to this point and refrigerated securely covered with foil. Use as directed in recipe of your choice.

SAUTÉED DUCK BREASTS AND LEGS IN RED WINE AND CASSIS SAUCE

The beauty of this recipe is that the ducks can be marinated and the sauce prepared up to two days ahead.

3 Preroasted Ducks

Marinade
3 cloves garlic finely
   chopped
3–4 shallots finely chopped
2 tablespoons finely chopped
   Italian flat-leaf parsley
1 teaspoon fresh thyme
   leaves *or* ¼ teaspoon
   dried
1 tablespoon coarse (kosher)
   salt
Freshly ground pepper

Red Wine and Cassis Sauce
2 cups Basic Duck Stock
2 tablespoons sugar
¼ cup dry red wine
2 tablespoons cassis
2–3 tablespoons Crème
   Fraîche or heavy cream

To Finish
4 tablespoons clarified
   butter* to sauté ducks
½ cup dry white wine

Serves 6

1. With a sharp knife, score duck breasts by making 2–3 angled incisions through the skin and fat. Set aside.

2. Combine garlic, shallots, parsley, thyme, salt, and pepper on a sheet of wax paper. Coat sections of duck meat by rolling them in the mixture and arrange in a glass or earthenware baking dish in one or two layers. Set aside.

3. Heat duck stock to a simmer.

4. In a separate saucepan, combine sugar and red wine and stir to dissolve sugar. Bring to the edge of a boil, then simmer briskly until sugar caramelizes, about 2–3 minutes. Add cassis, hot duck stock and crème fraiche or heavy cream and stir to mix. Taste to adjust seasoning if necessary. Keep warm.
Preheat oven to 375 degrees.

5. *Preparation of Duck Legs and Thighs:* Heat 2 tablespoons butter in a heavy skillet. When butter sizzles, add duck leg/thigh sections, 2–3 at a time, and sauté over moderately high heat 3–4 minutes on each side until lightly seared; transfer to a baking dish skin side up in one layer and cover with foil. Put in preheated oven and bake about 25–30

minutes until tender or when meat springs back at the touch of a finger. Remove from oven and place on a grill pan large enough to hold all duck pieces in a single layer. Set aside. Can be done up to 1 hour ahead.

6. *Preparation of Duck Breasts:* To prevent splattering, clean your skillet and heat remaining 2 tablespoons butter in it. When butter sizzles, add 2–3 duck breasts at a time; do not crowd pan. Sauté over moderately high heat about 2–3 minutes on each side. Add to grill pan skin side up as they are done. Interior of breast meat should be faintly pink. Moisten duck pieces with a light sprinkle of white wine. Can be done up to 1 hour ahead.

Turn the broiler on to highest heat.

7. *Final Grill:* Place the grill pan with all the duck pieces under the broiler, about 3 inches from source of heat, 1–2 minutes to crisp skin. Watch carefully that meat does not burn. Put one breast and leg-thigh section on each warm dinner plate. Pour on several spoonfuls of sauce. Serve hot with Timbale of Lettuce Chiffonade or Purée of Parsnips and Carrots.

To Prepare Ahead

Follow steps 1 and 2 up to two days ahead. Cover with plastic wrap and refrigerate. Follow steps 3 and 4 up to several hours ahead. Reheat sauce and keep warm. Bring duck to room temperature before completing steps 5 and 6.

DUCK BREASTS AND LEGS IN VINEGAR AND GREEN PEPPERCORN SAUCE

3 Preroasted Ducks

Marinade-Coating
2 cloves garlic, finely
    chopped
¼ cup finely chopped Italian
    flat-leaf parsley
1–2 teaspoons fresh snipped
    chives (optional)
1 teaspoon coarse (kosher)
    salt
Freshly ground pepper
¼ teaspoon dry English
    mustard

⅛ teaspoon cayenne
¼ cup dry toasted Bread
    Crumbs
½ cup melted unsalted
    butter

Sauce
2 cups Basic Duck Stock
2 tablespoons sugar
¼ cup red wine vinegar
¼ cup green peppercorns,
    packed in water

Serves 6

1. With a sharp knife, score duck breasts by making 2–3 angled incisions through the skin and fat. Set aside.

2. Place duck breasts and leg/thigh sections in a glass or earthenware baking dish in one layer (use 2 baking dishes if necessary). Combine all the marinade-coating ingredients in a mixing bowl and stir to mix. Spoon equal amounts of marinade-coating over duck pieces and pat with fingertips to coat each piece. Set aside.

3. Heat duck stock to a simmer.

4. In a separate saucepan, combine sugar and vinegar and stir to dissolve sugar. Bring to the edge of a boil, then simmer briskly until sugar caramelizes, about 2–3 minutes. Watch carefully—sugar can burn. Add green peppercorns and hot duck stock and stir to mix. Taste to adjust seasoning if necessary. Keep warm.

Preheat oven to 375 degrees.

5. *To Roast Duck Legs/Thighs:* Arrange duck legs/thighs on a rack in a roasting pan. Just before cooking ducks, drizzle a little melted butter over them. Roast in preheated oven 30–35 minutes until tender. Remove from oven and keep warm.

Turn broiler to high heat.

To Grill Duck Breasts: When the coils are flame red, place duck breasts on a broiler pan skin side up, about 3–4 inches from source of heat and grill about 3 minutes on each side. Remove from broiler. Serve one breast and leg/thigh section on each warm dinner plate and pour peppercorn-vinegar sauce around the meat.

To Prepare Ahead
Follow steps 1 and 2 up to three to four hours ahead. If necessary, cover with plastic wrap and refrigerate. Follow steps 3 and 4 up to two hours ahead. Reheat before serving. If refrigerated, bring ducks to room temperature and complete step 5.

DUCK AU POIVRE VERT

3 tablespoons clarified
   butter*
3–4 shallots, finely chopped
½–¾ cup dry red wine
1½ cups Basic Duck Stock
3 tablespoons green
   peppercorns (packed in
   water)
⅓ cup Crème Fraîche or
   heavy cream

6 Preroasted Duck breasts,
   skin removed
1 teaspoon coarse (kosher)
   salt
Freshly ground pepper
Flour for dredging
1 tablespoon finely chopped
   parsley

Serves 4

1. Heat 1 tablespoon of the butter in a large heavy saucepan and sauté shallots for a few seconds until tender. Add wine and stock and bring to a boil over high heat. Lower the heat just a bit and reduce the liquids by half, maintaining a lazy surface bubble at all times.

2. Scatter peppercorns on a sheet of wax paper. Mash them with side of a chef's knife and stir into sauce. Add crème fraîche or heavy cream to warm sauce and stir to mix. Taste to adjust seasoning if necessary. Keep warm.

3. Season duck breasts lightly with salt and pepper; then dredge in flour to coat, tapping off excess.

4. Heat remaining 2 tablespoons butter in a large heavy skillet and, when it sizzles, put in duck breasts, 2–3 at a time; do not crowd pan. Sauté over moderately high heat about 1½ minutes on each side. Transfer to a warm platter one layer deep as duck breasts are done, and sauté remaining breasts. Interior of meat should be faintly pink with a crisp outside. Keep warm in a 180-degree oven.

5. Slice duck breasts at an angle, cutting them crosswise into 3–4 pieces. Spoon several tablespoons of hot sauce onto warmed serving plates, arrange 4–6 slices of duck meat in center of plate, and sprinkle meat with parsley. Serve at once with Gratin Dauphinois.

To Prepare Ahead
Follow step 1 up to one day ahead. Refrigerate, covered, in suitable container. Bring to room temperature when ready to serve; warm through and complete step 2. Just before serving, complete steps 3 through 5.

6

A PASTA WORKSHOP

Pasta is being called the food for the eighties. I call it food for all seasons.

There is such variety in pasta that one can never grow bored with it. It has been said that one would have to spend a whole year in Italy to experience all the different pastas—an idea that I find very agreeable! Most assuredly, there is more to pasta than spaghetti and meatballs.

The enormous interest in pasta has spawned an industry. There are pasta machines galore, long wooden pins for rolling pasta and special boards to roll it on, racks for drying it out, canisters for storing it, and pots to cook it in. There is even a spaghetti measure—a round plastic disk containing four holes of various sizes to insure perfect pasta portions. We eat it hot or cold in a multitude of shapes and use it in a diversity of recipes. We make it ourselves or buy it "fresh" or commercially prepared.

Pasta is here to stay and is recognized as one of the most healthful foods to eat. It is low in fat and offers bulk in proportion to calorie content. In this country, we tend to think of pasta as being heaped on a platter and heavily sauced. In Italy I have learned to eat pasta in smaller quantities, thereby satisfying my appetite to a point where I don't require anything more than a simple grilled meat or an uncomplicated fish dish with a fresh vegetable.

Dry Imported Pasta: The best imported pasta in both flour and texture is from Naples and Arbruzzo and is available in many specialty food stores throughout the country. Don't think of this as second-class pasta just because it is commercial. It is desirable and acceptable and is important to the correct sauce.

While different shapes of pasta will blend harmoniously with different sauces, an important consideration is not to overwhelm. A sauce with texture, such as a meat sauce, works best with a tubular pasta or shells that can "catch" the sauce. Alfredo Sauce (a delicate cream sauce) would not suit heavy commercial grooved rigatoni or tubetti (little tubes), as the pasta would overwhelm the sauce. They would cancel each other out. On the other hand, a rich tomato sauce with sausage or a hot, spicy sauce would compete with a fresh tagliatelle (fettuccine) or taglierini (a fine thin pasta), the texture of which is too delicate to stand up to the sauce. In Italy, for instance, it is not just Carbonara Sauce, but Spaghetti alla Carbonara. Italian cooks would never prepare this sauce with fresh pasta. Only a sturdy dry commercial spaghetti would be used . . . and the marriage is complete.

Dry Domestic Pasta: All the sizes and shapes of dry imported pasta—and more—are available in domestic commercial brands. The shopper can choose from domestic pasta in long strands, such as spaghetti (in varieties of thicknesses), linguine, fettuccine, lasagna, and so forth. Or shaped pasta may be found, such as shells, bows, twists, tubetti, orzo, to name a few. Even the freezer compartment of your market will yield ravioli, cannelloni, manicotti, and tortellini, among others.

Fresh Pasta: Whatever the proportions, a basic recipe for fresh pasta can be made into many different shapes. Among them are tagliatelle, taglierini, spaghetti, lasagna—one can go on ad infinitum. Basic proportions can be doubled and tripled for larger quantities. Unbleached all-purpose flour is preferable for making fresh pasta. This type of flour is not unlike the flour used in making fresh pasta in Italy.

Since the best dry commercial pasta is prepared from semolina flour, why then, you might ask, isn't it used in the best homemade? It is because semolina is a very hard wheat flour and would result in very tough pasta. There is some fresh pasta made with semolina in certain parts of Italy. This is for a specially shaped pasta that has to be tough, since it must cook for a long time in combination with other ingredients. Softer pasta would fall apart.

You might enjoy making some of the colored pastas, which require nothing more than the simple addition of a finely chopped precooked vegetable.

Spinach is probably the most frequently used ingredient to color pasta green. Tomatoes, beets, carrots, and even mushrooms can be incorporated into the basic recipe to be hand-rolled or rolled by machine.

After the vegetables are precooked and chopped, take care to squeeze out all of their moisture as thoroughly as you can. Despite this cautionary step, you will undoubtedly need to incorporate additional flour to compensate for the extra moisture in the vegetables (see Pasta Verde and Pasta Rossa).

Making pasta is fun and making colored pasta is even greater fun. Especially when the results are the pink fettuccine (made from beet pasta) afloat in a light sauce of cream and cheese (Alla Panna), topped by deep green blanched broccoli flowerets.

To successfully cook one pound of pasta, bring 5–6 quarts of water to a boil with 1½–2 tablespoons coarse (kosher) salt added. Add the pasta all at once to the turbulently boiling water. As the pasta strands go into the water, press down and stir gently with a wooden spoon until they are submerged and separated. It is important to cook pasta in plenty of boiling water so it can swirl around freely as it cooks and rid itself of all its starch. Cover the pot and quickly return the water to a boil, being careful not to let it boil over. Remove the cover when the water surface returns to a lively surface bubble.

Cooking time depends on the type of pasta you are cooking: about 30 seconds for freshly made and up to approximately 8 minutes for dry commercial pasta. Fresh pasta should cook up light. Dry commercial pasta should be al dente, or tender, but toothsome to the bite. It is important that you taste pasta as it cooks.

The instant the pasta is done, drain it in-a colander, shaking it quickly to remove all the water. No time should be wasted between draining the pasta and saucing and serving it. Like a well-puffed soufflé, it must be served the moment it is cooked. Undercook pasta just slightly, since it will continue to cook in its own heat from the time it goes from pot to plate. Be sure to keep your pasta plates warm in a 180-degree oven while the pasta is cooking.

It is absolutely unnecessary to run cold water over the pasta to wash away the starch. The ample cooking water takes care of that. In addition, you would cool off your pasta and stop the cooking process—fine for cold pasta, but not so fine if it is meant to be served hot.

Another "no-no": Never add oil to the water when cooking any kind of pasta. Just add salt. If oil is in the water, it will coat pasta and cool off the water as well. Then, when pasta has been drained, it will not be able to absorb the sauce, which will slide off. This, of course, would be disastrous.

When I discuss the final serving of pasta, I advise my students to have their sauce "ready" in a pan before the pasta is done. Alla Panna cream sauce takes but a few minutes to make. Shortly before the water is boiling for the pasta, I will reach for a large twelve-inch stainless steel or enamel skillet, prepare my sauce so that it is "ready" to receive the cooked and drained fettuccine, and quickly toss to coat evenly. For a different type of sauce, a simple tomato, for instance, may be kept warm in a small saucepan. An uncooked Pesto may be held in a small mixing bowl. Drain the pasta and without delay return it to the large pot it cooked in. (Placing sauce on top of plain boiled pasta is actually an American custom. The Italian-European way is to toss the two together before serving.) Add sauce at once and quickly toss with two forks or a spoon and fork to coat.

HOMEMADE PASTA
BASIC RECIPE

1½ cups all-purpose flour
2 large eggs
1 tablespoon olive oil
Pinch salt

Pastry scraper
Sieve
Pasta machine

Have on Hand
Pasta board

Yields ¾ pound

PASTA VERDE

2 cups flour
2 large eggs
1 tablespoon olive oil

Pinch salt
⅓ package frozen spinach,
　　cooked and drained

PASTA ROSSA

When preparing Pasta Rossa, substitute 2 tablespoons finely chopped cooked beet for spinach. The beet must be cooked until soft, peeled, then chopped extremely fine. Do not use the processor or blender for either beet or spinach, as texture will be too mushy. Gather chopped vegetable into a clean towel and squeeze until very, very dry.

1. *Technique for Preparing Basic Pasta in the Pasta Machine:* Place flour in a mound on a large wooden board. Make a well in center of mound deep and large enough to beat and hold eggs, oil, and salt.

2. Carefully beat egg mixture with a fork until blended. Then gradually incorporate flour from inside lower portion of well to prevent batter from flowing out. When a heavy paste has formed, mix in as much flour as needed until mixture becomes crumbly. Toss mixture back and forth with sides of your hands to make a soft dough that is no longer sticky. Like people, flour reacts to the weather. On a damp day you will need

a little bit more flour, but if the weather is dry, less flour is necessary. Gather dough into a ball and set aside. With a pastry scraper, clean your board by scraping away any dry bits of dough, then sift the remaining flour through a sieve back onto your board before you start to knead.

3. With clean hands, knead the dough *very gently* with the heel of your hand by folding, turning, and pressing on a lightly floured surface. I find that many students tend to knead with too much pressure. Continue kneading gently until the dough is smooth and supple—about 3–4 minutes. Any remaining flour should be passed through the sieve again and kept to coat dough as you knead and thin the pasta in the machine.

Making fresh pasta

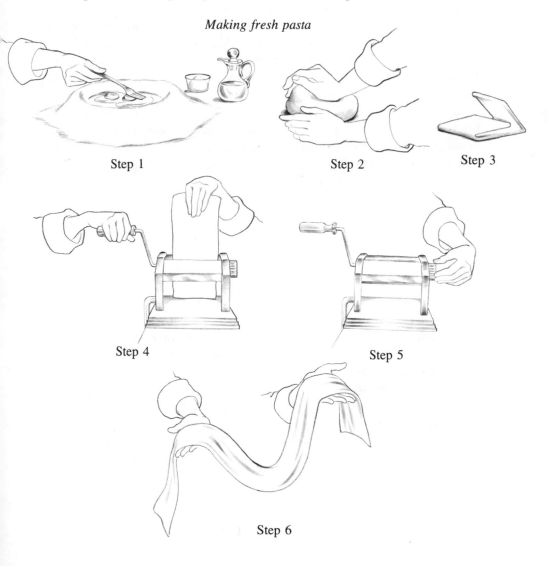

Step 1

Step 2

Step 3

Step 4

Step 5

Step 6

4. *To Prepare Pasta Verde or Pasta Rossa:* Technique is exactly the same as for basic pasta made in the pasta machine. Additional flour will be necessary to incorporate into the dough during kneading to compensate for extra moisture from spinach or beets, as in quantity of flour shown in Spinach Pasta recipe.

5. A pasta machine has a set of rollers, a detachable cutting portion, and an adjustable knob on the side of the machine to vary the width of the rollers. Clamp the machine to your table and adjust rollers to widest setting. The detachable handle is used to turn rollers in the main part of the machine or inserted into the side of the cutting portion of the machine to cut either the wide or narrow strands of pasta.

6. *To Roll the Dough:* Cut dough in half and work with one piece at a time, covering second piece with a clean kitchen towel to prevent drying. Be sure your board is lightly coated with flour. With your fingertips, flatten dough, then pass it between the rollers. Dough will be rather moist and unevenly textured at this point. Lightly flour one side of dough, tapping off excess. Fold strip into thirds like puff pastry, floured side out, and press down to flatten. Repeat, passing dough between rollers on the open side to push out air. Then flour, fold, press, and roll 5 or 6 more times until dough is very smooth and elastic. At this point dough is ready to thin.

7. Adjust the knob on the side of the machine up one notch, decreasing gap between rollers. It is no longer necessary to fold pasta; however, dust with flour as necessary. (Remember, the weather can affect the texture as you work the dough.) Continue to move the notch up once each time you pass dough through machine. Each time you decrease gap between rollers, the sheet of pasta will be longer and thinner. Continue thinning until pasta reaches the thickness desired. Some machines will successfully go to the last notch; others might cause dough to tear. I advise using caution beyond the next to the last notch. When the long sheet of pasta has emerged through the final rollers, carefully pull out the layer to its full length, stretching it over your arms, then transferring it to a clean white sheet or kitchen towels placed across your worktable to dry. Repeat steps 5 through 7 with remaining half of dough. Pasta is now ready to cut into tagliatelle (fettuccine, wide cutting portion) or taglierini (narrow cutting portions) after it has dried at least 10 minutes. Drying time is approximate and will be governed by weather conditions.

8. When ready to cut, be sure pasta sheet is still malleable and not too dry and brittle. Pass sheet through on either the wide or the narrow setting as desired. To cut spaghetti, pass pasta through the rollers as in step 7 but stop when you arrive at the fourth notch (number 4 on the

machine) which leaves the sheet a little thicker. When the pasta is sufficiently dry, pass it through the narrow cutting section, which will give you a rounded spaghetti shape. Carefully lift the cut pasta with both hands under it and transfer to a lightly floured, towel-lined baking sheet, gently separating the strands to dry.

9. *To Prepare Lasagna and Cannelloni Squares:* With a fluted ravioli cutter, cut sheet of pasta into 4-inch squares as soon as it has come through the final rollers. The squares are now ready to precook. If you are questioning the use of 4-inch squares for lasagna—it works. There is absolutely no resemblance to the long, heavy, boxed variety.

10. *To Store Pasta:* If I am not going to use the cut pasta the same day, I cover it with another clean towel and let it stand overnight to dry completely. It can then be kept 2–3 weeks by storing in a large plastic bag securely closed and kept in a cool dark cupboard.

11. *To Precook Squares:* Bring a large kettle of salted water to a boil. Fill a mixing bowl with cold water and 2 tablespoons oil and put it near the pot. Spread several clean kitchen towels on a work area nearby. You are now ready to precook pasta. Put 3 or 4 squares of pasta into the boiling water for several seconds. They will rise almost immediately to the top. With a strainer-skimmer or a slotted spoon, transfer the squares into the cold water to stop the cooking. Lift each square out of the water as though a picture were being developed and transfer one layer deep to the towels. Allow squares to dry 20–30 minutes. They are now ready to fill and roll for cannelloni or to layer for lasagna.

12. *To Prepare Tortelli, Agnolotti, or Ravioli:* Work with one sheet of pasta at a time, since dough *must remain moist* and flexible to seal the fillings tightly. When working with one sheet, keep remaining dough covered with a towel to prevent drying. Place small mounds of filling at regular intervals (according to your recipe) halfway up sheet. Bring unfilled half up and over filled half so that opposite edges meet. With fingertips press firmly between filling and along edges to seal. Using fluted ravioli cutter, cut into squares with filling centered in each square. Separate filled squares and transfer to a lightly floured towel-lined cookie sheet one layer deep. Do not allow pieces to touch, as dough is probably still very moist and they will stick to each other. Repeat process with remaining dough and filling. These pasta packages can be made early in the day, sprinkled very lightly with flour, and covered with another towel. They may also be frozen at this point. To flash-freeze, place one layer deep on a cookie sheet in freezer, uncovered. When the filled pasta squares are completely frozen, about 30 minutes, transfer to freezer bags

or containers, securely tied or covered, and freeze. Do not thaw before ready to cook. Drop frozen pasta squares into boiling salted water for a little longer than recipe specifies.

13. *To Roll Dough by Hand:* After you have made the basic pasta, divide in half as in steps 1 through 3. Roll each piece on a lightly floured surface until it is almost translucent and thin enough to cut—about ⅛ inch thick. Roll dough up like a jelly roll. Using a sharp knife, cut into ⅛- or ¼-inch widths as desired. Separate strands and allow to rest on a lightly floured towel-lined baking sheet to dry.

AGNOLOTTI ALLA PANNA

These meat-filled pasta packages resembling ravioli are from the Piedmont, a region of northwestern Italy.

2 recipes Basic Pasta

The Filling
1 pound loose fresh spinach,
    fibrous stems and
    blemished leaves
    removed, washed in
    several changes of
    lukewarm water to
    remove sand
2 tablespoons unsalted butter
½ pound ground raw
    chicken
½ pound ground raw veal
1 teaspoon coarse (kosher)
    salt
Freshly ground pepper
1 tablespoon fresh marjoram
    leaves, chopped, *or* ½
    teaspoon dried,
    crumbled

⅛ teaspoon grated nutmeg
2 eggs, lightly beaten
¼ pound prosciutto,
    chopped
5 tablespoons freshly grated
    Parmesan cheese

The Sauce
6 tablespoons unsalted butter
1½ cups heavy cream
½ teaspoon coarse (kosher)
    salt
Freshly ground pepper
Freshly grated nutmeg
⅔ cup freshly grated cheese

Have on Hand
Pastry or feather brush
Fluted ravioli cutter

Serves 6–8
Yields approximately 60 pieces

1. Put ½ inch water in a heavy saucepan with cover. Bring to a boil and add spinach. Cover and cook 3–4 minutes, stirring occasionally. Drain spinach well, then squeeze very dry in a clean kitchen towel. Chop fine on a wooden board and place in a mixing bowl.

2. Melt butter in a skillet and sauté the chicken and veal just until they lose their color. Do not overcook or brown. When cool, add to the spinach. Add remaining filling ingredients, stir to mix, and set aside.

3. Make Basic Pasta recipe. Roll out one sheet of pasta at a time. Place 1 teaspoon of spinach mixture at 1½-inch intervals halfway up the sheet. Dip pastry brush in water. Brush between fillings and along edges. Bring the unfilled half up and over filled half so that opposite edges meet. Press firmly between fillings and along edges to seal. Using a fluted ravioli cutter, cut into squares with filling centered in each square. Separate filled squares and transfer to a lightly floured towel-lined cookie sheet, one layer deep. Do not allow pieces to touch, as dough is moist and they will stick to each other. Repeat process with remaining dough and filling.

4. Just before you are ready to cook the pasta, prepare the sauce: In a 12-inch stainless steel or enameled cast-iron skillet, melt butter and add 1 cup of the heavy cream. Simmer over moderate heat 3–4 minutes, stirring occasionally until mixture thickens slightly. Season with salt, pepper, and nutmeg, and turn off heat.

5. When ready to cook pasta, bring 5–6 quarts water to a rolling boil, adding 2 tablespoons coarse (kosher) salt to water. Slip in agnolotti all at once, stirring gently to separate. Cover and return water to a boil. Remove cover and cook about 1 minute or until agnolotti rise to the surface. Drain immediately and transfer to a warm platter.

6. In the meantime, warm sauce with remaining cream, stir in cheese and taste to adjust seasoning if necessary. Spoon sauce over agnolotti and serve immediately on warm plates. Pass extra cheese if desired.

To Prepare Ahead
Follow steps 1 through 3 up to one day ahead. Complete steps 4 and 5 just before serving.

CALSONES

When Mom suggested she would prepare this dish for me following a bad siege of the flu, I thought, "Calzone? That's Italian." She quickly corrected me for not remembering a dish from my childhood and how quickly it nourished us back to health. Calsones are a cheese-filled crescent-shaped package similar to the Italian Agnolotti made with noodle dough. The dish is of Spanish origin. No doubt my Sephardic ancestors added the feta-cheese topping while living in their adopted country, Greece.

Filling
1 pound farmer cheese
2 eggs, lightly beaten
½ teaspoon coarse (kosher) salt
Freshly ground pepper

Noodle Dough
1 egg
¼ teaspoon salt
Water

2–2¼ cups all-purpose flour

Melted unsalted butter
¼ pound feta cheese
1 tablespoon chopped fresh mint leaves *or* 1 teaspoon dried

Have on Hand
2½-inch round cookie cutter
2-quart shallow baking dish

Serves 8–10

1. In a mixing bowl, mash farmer cheese gently with a fork; add the 2 eggs, salt, and pepper, and stir to mix. Set aside.

2. *Noodle Dough:* Put the egg in a 1-cup liquid measure. Add salt and fill remainder of cup with water. Stir to mix.

3. Place egg mixture in a mixing bowl and gradually add 2 cups of the flour, slowly absorbing it into the liquid until the mixture is thick and pasty. Lightly sprinkle work surface with additional flour and knead dough very gently for just a few minutes, incorporating remaining flour as necessary. Cover dough with a tea towel and allow to rest 10 minutes. This will make it easier to roll and stretch.

4. Spread a clean sheet or tea towels on work surface. Cut dough in half and roll out each half into circles about 10 inches in diameter. Place the rounds of dough on the sheet or towel, cover, and let rest another 10 minutes.

5. Take up edges of dough in your fingertips and gradually stretch and pull very gently to rectangular shape about 18–20 inches long, or egg-noodle thin. Dough should not be paper thin as is strudel dough.

6. About 1½ inches from bottom edge of dough, drop rounded teaspoonfuls of filling in a single row spaced about 1 inch apart. Working very lightly with fingertips, lift bottom edge and fold up and over cheese to enclose, keeping cheese close against the fold. To form crescent-shaped calsones, place cookie cutter over each covered mound, allowing half the circle to cover the mound and the opposite half of the cutter pressed against the work surface. Cut through with firm pressure. Seal edges by pressing lightly with fingertips. Transfer them as they are done to a corner of a lightly floured sheet or towel. With a sharp knife, cut across bottom edge of dough to make an even line and set cut strip aside, covered. Continue to fill and shape calsones.

7. When calsones have been shaped from half the dough, gather up excess strips, form into a ball, roll out into another round, cover, and let rest. Meanwhile repeat stretching, filling, and cutting second round of dough. When remaining excess strips of dough have been rolled, rested, and stretched, continue shaping calsones in the same manner, using the remaining cheese mixture.

8. Bring 6 or 7 quarts of salted water to a rolling boil. Put in all calsones, cover, and quickly return to a boil. Reduce heat, but allow water to maintain a gentle, rolling boil and cook 20–30 minutes until tender, with cover ajar. Drain in a large colander until all liquid is gone, shaking off excess.

Preheat oven to 350 degrees.

9. Transfer to a 2-quart glass or ceramic heatproof serving dish. Pour on melted butter. Place in a preheated oven 15 minutes to heat through. Sprinkle on crumbled feta cheese and mint and serve immediately.

To Prepare Ahead

Complete filling and steps 1 through 8 up to one day ahead. Refrigerate in a suitable container covered with plastic wrap. Before you are ready to serve, drain excess liquid that has accumulated in container and complete step 9.

LAYERED PASTA WITH WILD MUSHROOM AND TOMATO SAUCE

This truly spectacular dish is an adaptation from Ristorante Arnaldos near Parma, Italy.

2 recipes Basic Pasta
4–5 quarts water
2 tablespoons coarse
    (kosher) salt
2 tablespoons oil

Béchamel Sauce
3 tablespoons butter
3 tablespoons flour
2 cups milk
Salt and pepper

¼ teaspoon grated nutmeg
1 cup grated Parmesan
    cheese

Wild Mushroom and Tomato
Sauce (recipe follows)

Have on Hand
2 2-quart lasagna pans
Foil or parchment paper

Serves 10–12

1. Prepare basic pasta recipe according to lasagna directions.

2. Bring water to a boil and add salt. Meanwhile, fill a mixing bowl with cold water and 2 tablespoons oil and place on counter near the saucepan. Place a towel-lined cookie sheet near the bowl.

3. When water is boiling, slip 2 or 3 squares of pasta into pot for several seconds. As they rise to the surface, transfer each to the bowl of cold water with a strainer-skimmer and allow to cool; then transfer to the towel-lined cookie sheet and arrange one layer deep to drain. Continue cooking all squares until they are done. Layer additional lightly dampened towels over pasta squares as necessary to hold them all.

4. *To Prepare Béchamel Sauce:* In a heavy saucepan, melt butter, then add flour all at once. Stir the butter-flour mixture about 2 minutes over low heat being careful not to brown. In the meanwhile, heat milk in a separate saucepan and bring to the edge of a boil. Remove butter-flour mixture from heat and gradually add hot milk, stirring all the time. At first sauce will be very thick and porridgelike; then it will become liquid. Return saucepan to heat and allow mixture to come to the edge of a boil, stirring gently until it thickens to a smooth cream. Season with salt, pepper, and nutmeg and stir to mix. Add grated cheese and cook, stirring, until cheese melts. Remove from heat.

5. *To Assemble:* Lightly butter both baking-serving pans. Arrange pasta squares slightly overlapping to completely cover bottom of each pan. Divide the béchamel sauce equally and spread evenly to completely

cover all pasta in each pan. Cover sauce with remaining pasta squares and dot with butter. Can be done ahead to this point.
Preheat oven to 350 degrees.

6. When ready to serve, cover with parchment paper or foil and bake in a preheated oven about 20 minutes to warm through.

7. Heat mushroom-tomato sauce while the pasta is baking. Remove baking dishes from oven. Cut pasta into 3-inch squares and transfer individual squares to warmed plates. Place one large spoonful of sauce centered over each pasta square and serve immediately as a first course.

To Prepare Ahead
Follow steps 1 through 5 up to one day ahead. Refrigerate, covered with foil or plastic wrap. Bring to room temperature, then complete steps 6 and 7 just before serving.

WILD MUSHROOM AND TOMATO SAUCE

2 ounces dried Italian
    porcini mushrooms
2–3 shallots, finely chopped
1 tablespoon vegetable oil
¼ pound fresh mushrooms,
    thinly sliced
3 tablespoons unsalted butter
¼ pound pancetta (see
    Note), coarsely
    chopped
1 can (1 pound, 16 ounces)
    whole tomatoes with
    their liquid

¼ teaspoon coarse (kosher)
    salt
Freshly ground pepper

Have on Hand
Cheesecloth
2 mixing bowls

Yield 1½ cups

Note: There are several recipes in this book that call for pancetta. Pancetta is the same cut as bacon but is not smoked. It is cured with salt and pepper, like prosciutto. Do not substitute bacon if pancetta is not available. If you must substitute, prosciutto is the choice. Pancetta's popularity is growing; however, at the moment it may be found only in ethnic specialty shops. Generally speaking, I prefer not to use bacon in cooking at all. I like it only for breakfast with eggs. The taste of bacon is very strong and will mask the subtleties of flavor that I so enjoy achieving in cooking.

1. Place porcini mushrooms in a small bowl with warm water to cover and soak at least 30 minutes. Reach into the bowl and lift out mushrooms, shaking them free of sand, then transfer to a fresh, clean bowl. Line a strainer with several thicknesses of cheesecloth and pour soaking liquid through and over mushrooms. Rinse cheesecloth under running water to remove dirt. Porcini mushrooms are very sandy and must be rinsed several times. Repeat cleaning procedure 2 or 3 times, discarding excess sand left behind each time. Reserve concentrated mushroom liquid. Cut mushrooms into julienne strips and set aside.

2. In the meantime, sauté the shallots quickly in oil and butter until translucent. Add the fresh mushrooms and cook 2–3 minutes, stirring occasionally, until tender.

3. Add pancetta and continue to cook a few minutes until crisp, stirring occasionally.

4. Remove seeds from tomatoes and then add tomatoes with their liquid to mixture, breaking them up in the pan with the side of a spoon. With paper toweling, blot the porcini mushrooms and add to tomato mixture with ¼ teaspoon salt, some freshly ground pepper, and half of reserved porcini liquid. Cook, uncovered, at a gentle simmer 30–35 minutes, stirring occasionally. Mixture will absorb most of the liquid and be a moderately thick sauce when done.

To Prepare Ahead
Follow steps 1 through 4 up to one day ahead. Refrigerate, covered, in a suitable container. Warm through before serving. Sauce can also be used over cooked fusilli or penne.

Note: Remaining porcini mushroom liquid may be used in soup stock or discarded.

FETTUCCINE ALLA PANNA

This is fettuccine with a classic butter-and-cream sauce. I prefer to use Crème Fraîche, which gives a nice thick texture and a nutty flavor to the sauce.

6 tablespoons unsalted butter
1½ cups Crème Fraîche or
    heavy whipping cream

¾ teaspoon coarse (kosher)
    salt
Freshly ground pepper
Several dashes freshly grated
    nutmeg

2 tablespoons coarse
    (kosher) salt for
    cooking water
1 pound fettuccine—
    preferably fresh (see
    Basic Pasta)
¾ cup freshly grated
    Parmesan cheese

Serves 4–6

1. Just before you are ready to cook the pasta, prepare the sauce. In a 12-inch stainless steel or enameled cast-iron skillet, melt butter and add one cup crème fraîche or cream. Simmer over moderate heat 3–4 minutes, stirring occasionally, until mixture thickens slightly. Season with salt, pepper, and nutmeg, and turn off heat.

2. Bring 5–6 quarts water to a rolling boil and add salt. Add fettuccine all at once, stirring to separate strands. Return immediately to a boil and cook 30 seconds to several minutes according to freshness of your pasta, or additional time according to package directions.

3. Just before the pasta is ready, turn heat on "low" under sauce to warm it. As soon as pasta is done, drain thoroughly in a colander and transfer to the cream mixture. Toss quickly in the sauce. Add remaining cream, stir in ½ cup cheese and taste for seasoning. Serve immediately on warm plates. Pass additional cheese if desired.

To Prepare Ahead
Follow step 1 up to ½ hour before. Complete steps 2 and 3 before serving.

PASTA VONGOLE ALLA VENEZIANA
(Linguine with clam sauce Venetian style)

36 littleneck clams in their
shells
Olive oil
4 large cloves garlic, finely
minced
3–4 tomatoes, peeled,
seeded, and coarsely
chopped *or* 1 can (1
pound) whole
tomatoes, drained and
seeded
1 hot dried red pepper, cut
in half, seeded and
snipped with kitchen
scissors
Freshly ground black pepper
1 tablespoon fresh oregano
or ¾ teaspoon dried

2 tablespoons fresh basil *or*
1 teaspoon dried
¼ cup finely chopped Italian
flat-leaf parsley
½ cup dry white wine
Reserved strained clam
liquor
1 pound imported
commercial linguine
2 tablespoons coarse
(kosher) salt

To Finish
4 tablespoons butter
½ cup Mock Demi-Glace
(optional)
Freshly ground pepper

Serves 6–8

1. Shuck clams with their liquor into a bowl. If you cannot handle opening the clams yourself, ask your fish dealer to do it for you, reserving liquor and clams in a container. Reach into container and lift shucked clams from their liquor, shaking them free of sand as you remove them. Chop clams coarsely and set aside. Strain liquid through a sieve lined with a double thickness of cheesecloth. Repeat straining 3–4 times to get rid of sand.

2. Cover bottom of a large skillet with about ¼-inch depth of olive oil and place over moderate heat. Add garlic and cook briefly to soften. Do not allow garlic to brown. Add prepared tomatoes, snipped hot pepper, ground pepper, oregano, basil, and parsley, and stir to mix. Simmer for 5 minutes.

3. Add wine and clam liquor; bring to a boil and reduce liquids by half. Can be prepared ahead to this point.

4. Shortly before you are ready to serve, bring several quarts of water to a rapid boil. Add salt and slip in linguine. Return liquid to boil. Separate spaghetti strands with a large fork and cook at a brisk simmer about 8 minutes. Taste pasta for doneness after about 6–7 minutes. Pasta should be al dente, or have a slight resistance when bitten into.

5. After linguine has been cooking 3–4 minutes, add chopped clams to sauce and cook an additional 5 minutes (no longer) until pasta is ready.

6. In the meantime, heat ½ cup demi-glace in a small saucepan and swirl in butter. If not using glace, just melt butter.

7. Drain spaghetti in a colander, shaking it to get rid of excess liquid. Add to clam sauce and stir quickly with two large forks to mix. Transfer to a warm platter, then drizzle on demi-glace and lots of freshly ground pepper. Serve at once.

To Prepare Ahead
Follow step 1 up to one day ahead. Follow steps 2 and 3 early in day. Let sauce stand in skillet covered. Complete steps 4 through 7 before serving.

PAGLIA E FIENO

How fortunate I was to study many years ago with that incredible teacher of northern Italian cooking Marcella Hazan. It was the first time I had eaten Paglia e Fieno, a most extraordinary pasta dish. Here is my adaptation.

2 ounces dried porcini
    mushrooms
6 tablespoons unsalted butter
2 tablespoons finely chopped
    shallots
Coarse (kosher) salt
Freshly ground pepper
6 ounces ham, thinly sliced
    and cut into thin
    julienne strips
1½ cups heavy cream or
    Crème Fraîche

2 tablespoons coarse
    (kosher) salt for
    cooking water
½ pound Basic Pasta, cut
    into fettuccine
½ pound Pasta Verde, cut
    into fettuccine
⅔ cup freshly grated
    Parmesan cheese

Serves 6–8

1. Place porcini mushrooms in a small bowl with warm water to cover and soak at least 30 minutes. Reach into bowl and lift out mushrooms, shaking them free of sand, then transfer to a clean bowl.

Line a strainer with several thicknesses of cheesecloth and pour soaking liquid through and over the mushrooms. Rinse cheesecloth under running water to remove dirt. Porcini mushrooms are very sandy and must be rinsed several times. Repeat cleaning procedure 2 or 3 times, discarding sand left behind each time. Reserve concentrated mushroom liquid. Cut into thin even strips and set aside.

2. In a 12-inch skillet, melt 4 tablespoons of the butter until foamy. Add shallots and cook, stirring occasionally, until translucent, being careful not to brown. Add mushroom pieces, stir into butter, and cook over moderately high heat until mushrooms have absorbed butter. Season lightly with a sprinkle of salt and a grinding of pepper. Reduce heat, add ham and 1 cup of the cream, stirring rapidly. Simmer a few minutes until cream thickens slightly. Add about ¼–⅓ cup of reserved mushroom liquid and stir to mix. Taste to adjust seasoning if necessary and remove from heat. Cover and set aside. Can be made ahead to this point.

3. In a large stockpot, bring 6–7 quarts of water to a boil; then add 2 tablespoons salt. Return skillet containing sauce ingredients to a very low heat while pasta cooks. Select a large pasta bowl or platter that can later accommodate all the pasta, and put in the remaining 2 tablespoons of butter and the remaining ½ cup cream. Place on top of stockpot over boiling water for several minutes. This will keep your plate warm and melt the butter into the cream. Remove serving dish before cooking pasta. With water at a full rolling boil, put in plain pasta first and, seconds later, add spinach pasta, as it cooks faster. Stir quickly with a wooden pasta fork to separate strands, then cover for several seconds until the water returns to a boil. Cook 30–40 seconds to several minutes, depending on freshness of pasta. As soon as pasta is done, drain thoroughly in a colander, transfer to warm sauce in skillet, and toss quickly. Transfer to melted butter and cream in the warm serving platter, sprinkle with cheese, toss quickly, and serve immediately.

To Prepare Ahead
Follow Steps 1 and 2 up to one hour ahead and complete step 3 before serving.

ORZO PILAF

Orzo is a rice-shaped pasta indigenous to Greek cooking. A trick I learned from Mom is to toast it first for a nuttier flavor.

To Toast Orzo
Spread orzo in a jelly-roll pan. Place in a preheated 375-degree oven and toast about 10 minutes to color lightly. Remove from oven and redistribute orzo, returning it to the oven to color more evenly another 5–6 minutes.

1 medium onion, thinly sliced	2 cups whole tomatoes, drained and coarsely chopped
2 tablespoons vegetable oil	
1 clove garlic, finely chopped	1 teaspoon coarse (kosher) salt
2 cups orzo	Freshly ground pepper
3 cups Basic Chicken Stock or broth	

Serves 6–8

1. Place onion slices and oil in 12-inch skillet, and simmer over moderate heat, stirring occasionally, 3–4 minutes until onions are tender but not brown. Add garlic. Cook very briefly, being careful not to burn. Add toasted orzo and stir to distribute through onion mixture.

2. In a separate saucepan, bring stock to the edge of a boil. Add to orzo mixture with tomatoes, salt, and pepper, and stir to mix.

3. Return liquid to a boil. Then reduce to a simmer and cook covered, stirring occasionally, 15–20 minutes until liquid is absorbed and the orzo is tender. Serve immediately.

To Prepare Ahead
Follow step 1 up to one hour ahead. Complete steps 2 and 3 before serving.

PASTA PRIMAVERA, ORIENTAL STYLE

The increasingly popular cold pasta salad is combined here with oriental treatment of vegetables. It makes a choice dish for a spectacular buffet.

1 head broccoli, heavy stalks and leaves removed, cut into "little trees"

3–4 narrow, firm zucchini, scrubbed clean, ends discarded and sliced at an angle into 1-inch slices

5–6 fresh carrots, scrubbed clean, and peeled if necessary, ends discarded and sliced at an angle into 1-inch slices

1 pound green beans, stacked and cut at stem end only, leaving tail on, cut in thirds at an angle

1 pound snow peas, rinsed, ends V-notched

14–16 spears asparagus in season, tender and young; cut at an angle into thirds

Dressing

3–4 scallions, trimmed and thinly sliced (white and light green part only)

2 tablespoons finely cut julienne strips of fresh ginger

¼ teaspoon dry English mustard

2 teaspoons fresh basil leaves sliced into ribbons, *or* ½ teaspoon dried

1 teaspoon fresh thyme leaves *or* ½ teaspoon dried

4 tablespoons dark soy sauce

6 tablespoons tarragon vinegar

4 tablespoons sesame oil

6 tablespoons peanut oil

1 pound dry imported commercial spaghetti

2 tablespoons coarse (kosher) salt for cooking water

Have on Hand

Strainer-skimmer or slotted spoon

Serves up to 25

1. Blanch* vegetables.
2. When all the vegetables are cooked, be sure they are completely dried before combining. Set aside.

3. *To Make Dressing:* Combine scallions, ginger, mustard, basil, thyme, soy sauce, vinegar, and oils in a mixing bowl or workbowl of a food processor and stir or process to mix. Add oil in a slow steady stream into mixing bowl or through feed tube of processor and whisk or process until mixture is thoroughly blended. Set aside.

4. Bring 5–6 quarts of water to a rolling boil and add salt. Put spaghetti in all at once and stir to separate strands. Return immediately to a boil, then cook at a brisk simmer about 8 minutes until tender and firm to the bite. Drain in a colander and rinse under a spray of cold water to stop the cooking. Transfer to a clean kitchen towel and pat dry to absorb excess moisture. Place in a mixing bowl and pour on dressing. Toss gently to coat pasta and taste to adjust seasoning if necessary. Can be done ahead to this point.

5. Up to several hours ahead, toss pasta gently in a bowl to redistribute dressing. Then add vegetables and toss very gently to combine evenly. Transfer to a serving bowl, making sure that there is a representative distribution of vegetables over surface of pasta. Serve at room temperature.

To Prepare Ahead
Follow steps 1 through 4 up to one day ahead. Refrigerate pasta and vegetables separately in suitable containers. Complete step 5 up to several hours ahead. Refrigerate, covered with plastic wrap, if necessary and bring to room temperature before serving.

SPAGHETTI ALLA CARBONARA
IN A CHAFING DISH

For Spaghetti alla Carbonara one must use only a dry imported commercial spaghetti, which is strong enough to stand up to the spicy sauce. If you enjoy serving with a flair, prepare it tableside, which is the way I first experienced it many years ago in Sicily.

6 ounces pancetta (see
   Index) or prosciutto,
   sliced ⅛ inch thick
4 tablespoons unsalted butter
2 whole eggs
2 egg yolks
¾ cup grated Parmesan
   cheese
1 pound dry imported
   commercial spaghetti
2 tablespoons coarse
   (kosher) salt for
   cooking water
1 tablespoon olive oil

1 small hot red pepper cut in
   half, seeded and
   snipped with kitchen
   scissors
½ cup heavy cream
Coarse (kosher) salt and
   freshly ground pepper
   to taste
Extra cheese for serving

Have on Hand
Chafing dish or 12-inch
   skillet

Serves 4–6

1. Cut pancetta into small pieces and sauté in a skillet until crisp. Remove with slotted spoon and set aside in a small dish.

2. In a mixing bowl, cream butter until soft and fluffy. Set aside. In a separate bowl, beat eggs and egg yolks and whisk until whites and yolks are combined. Add ½ cup grated cheese to beaten eggs and set aside.

3. When ready to serve, bring 5–6 quarts water to a rolling boil and add salt. Put spaghetti in all at once, stirring to separate the strands. Return immediately to a boil, then cook at a brisk simmer 6–7 minutes until slightly tender but firm to the bite. Remember that the spaghetti will cook for another minute or so in a chafing dish or a skillet just before serving. As soon as it is done, drain in a colander.

4. In the meantime, combine oil and hot pepper in a chafing dish or skillet and heat briefly, stirring the hot pepper into the oil. The moment pasta is done, drain and transfer to the mixture; add cream, butter, egg-and-cheese mixture, and pancetta, tossing with abandon to melt butter and to warm cheese and other ingredients. Sprinkle very lightly with salt

and pepper to taste. Serve at once on warm plates. Pass additional cheese if desired.

To Prepare Ahead
Follow step 1 up to one hour ahead. Follow steps 2 through 4 before serving.
   Suggestion: Organize and set up ingredients for a smooth presentation.

COLD PENNE SALAD

Sun-dried tomatoes, a new and interesting specialty-store food, combine with quality commercial pasta for an unusual cold pasta salad.

2 tablespoons coarse
   (kosher) salt for
   cooking water
3 cups dry imported
   commercial penne or
   rigatoni
½ cup San Remo tomatoes,
   thinly sliced
2 tablespoons liquid from jar
   of tomatoes
1 medium red onion
10–12 fresh basil leaves,
   stacked and sliced ¼
   inch wide, *or* 1
   teaspoon dried basil,
   crumbled

1 tablespoon fresh oregano
   leaves *or* 1 teaspoon
   dried, crumbled
1 tablespoon finely chopped
   fresh Italian flat-leaf
   parsley
½ teaspoon coarse (kosher)
   salt
2 tablespoons freshly grated
   Parmesan cheese

Serves 10–12

1. Bring 4–5 quarts water to a boil and add salt. Put in pasta all at once, stirring to separate. Return immediately to a boil and cook 8–12 minutes, depending on the brand, or until tender, but firm to the bite. Stir occasionally to keep pasta from sticking. Drain under cool running water, then shake in colander and transfer pasta to a clean kitchen towel to absorb excess moisture. Put into a mixing bowl and add tomatoes.

2. Peel and halve onion; cut flat side down into paper-thin slices. Add to pasta in bowl with remaining ingredients. Toss gently to distribute all

ingredients and to coat pasta. Taste to adjust seasoning if necessary. Transfer to an attractive glass or earthenware serving bowl and serve at room temperature.

To Prepare Ahead
Follow steps 1 and 2 up to one day ahead. Refrigerate, covered with plastic wrap, until ready to serve.

SPAGHETTI ALLA BOLOGNESE

I prize this northern Italian dish as prepared for me by the chef of the SS Michelangelo many years ago before the food processor. I have written the recipe with its original directions; however, all of the vegetables can be prepared in the processor.

2 tablespoons olive oil
3 tablespoons unsalted butter
1 medium onion, finely diced
1 fresh carrot, scrubbed clean and finely diced
1 rib celery, rinsed, trimmed, and finely diced
⅛ teaspoon ground cloves
¾ pound chopped beef
1½ cup Beef Stock or broth
1 teaspoon tomato paste
1 teaspoon coarse (kosher) salt
Freshly ground pepper

¼ teaspoon freshly grated nutmeg
2–3 chicken livers, rinsed, fatty particles removed
½ pound fresh mushrooms, wiped clean, trimmed, and thinly sliced
2 slices prosciutto, coarsely chopped
1 pound dry imported commercial spaghetti
2 tablespoons coarse (kosher) salt for cooking water
¼ cup light cream (optional)

Serves 4–6

1. In a saucepan, heat olive oil with 2 tablespoons of the butter. When butter foam subsides, add onion, carrot, celery, and cloves. Sauté 4–5 minutes over moderate heat, stirring occasionally with a wooden spoon. Add beef, breaking it up in pan with the side of the spoon, and

brown well. Add stock, tomato paste, salt, pepper, and nutmeg. Stir to mix and simmer gently, uncovered, over low heat 45 minutes.

2. In a skillet, heat remaining 1 tablespoon butter until foamy and sauté chicken livers until crisp on both sides. Remove from skillet, chop, and set aside. In same skillet, add mushrooms and sauté over moderately high heat 3–4 minutes, shaking pan. Turn off heat. Add reserved chopped livers and prosciutto to mushrooms in pan and set aside. When meat sauce is done, add mushroom mixture and stir to mix. Can be made ahead to this point.

3. Bring 5–6 quarts water to a rolling boil and add salt. Put spaghetti in all at once, stirring to separate. Return immediately to a boil and cook at a brisk simmer about 8 minutes until tender and firm to the bite. Drain thoroughly in a colander and return quickly to pot the pasta was cooked in. Pour sauce on and toss with abandon to coat completely. Transfer to a warm serving platter and drizzle on a little cream, if desired. Serve immediately.

To Prepare Ahead
Follow steps 1 and 2 up to one day ahead. Refrigerate, covered, in suitable container. Bring to room temperature, reheat meat sauce, and complete step 3 before serving.

Note: Food Processor Directions: If using a processor, place onion in workbowl fitted with steel knife and process until finely chopped. Remove and set aside. Cut carrots and celery into 1-inch pieces. Place in workbowl fitted with steel blade and process with quick on/off pulses until coarsely chopped. Remove and set aside. Replace steel knife with slicing blade. Prepare mushrooms for slicing and process with light pressure to thinly slice.

SPAGHETTI PRIMAVERA

*Part of the fun of this dish is selecting the freshest vegetables in season
and enjoying it all year long—not only in the spring.*

Vegetables
1 head broccoli, heavy stalks
  and leaves removed,
  cut into "little trees"
2 narrow, firm zucchini,
  scrubbed clean, ends
  discarded, sliced at an
  angle into 1-inch slices
6–8 spears asparagus in
  season—tender, young
  spears cut at an angle
  into 1-inch pieces
½ pound green beans,
  stacked and cut at stem
  end, only tail left on,
  cut into 1-inch pieces
  at an angle

Amatriciana (Tomato) Sauce
3 tablespoons vegetable oil
1 large onion, finely
  chopped
2 cloves garlic, finely
  minced
½ pound pancetta (see
  Index), coarsely
  chopped
2 pounds plum tomatoes,
  skinned, seeded, and
  coarsely chopped *or* 1
  can (1 pound, 12
  ounces) whole
  tomatoes, drained and
  coarsely chopped

½ teaspoon crushed, dried
  hot pepper
½ teaspoon coarse (kosher)
  salt

Alla Panna Sauce (Alfredo)
4 tablespoons unsalted butter
¾ to 1 cup heavy cream
½ cup freshly grated
  Parmesan cheese

Spaghetti
2 tablespoons coarse
  (kosher) salt for
  cooking water
1 pound dry imported
  commercial spaghetti
⅓ cup pine (pignoli) nuts,
  toasted, for garnish

Have on Hand
Strainer-skimmer or slotted
  spoon

*Serves 8–10 for first course or
6 for dinner*

1. See Index for vegetable cooking and blanching procedures. You may wish to increase vegetable cooking time slightly for this recipe. When all the vegetables are cooked, be sure they are completely dried. Set aside.

2. *To Make Amatriciana (Tomato) Sauce:* Heat oil in a skillet; add onion and sauté quickly until translucent. Add chopped garlic and cook for 1 minute longer. Add pancetta and cook for several minutes until slightly crisp. Add tomatoes, hot pepper, and salt. Cook over medium heat, uncovered for about 25 minutes, stirring occasionally. Remove from heat and taste to adjust seasoning if necessary. Can be done ahead and reheated later.

3. *To Make Alla Panna (Alfredo) Sauce:* Just before you are ready to cook the pasta, prepare the final alla panna sauce. Choose a 12-inch stainless steel or enameled cast-iron skillet you can serve from. Melt butter in skillet and add cream and simmer over moderate heat for 3–4 minutes, stirring occasionally until mixture thickens slightly. Keep warm.

4. While pasta is cooking, combine reheated tomato sauce with prepared vegetables and warm cream sauce. Add cheese and stir to mix thoroughly. Keep warm.

5. Bring 5–6 quarts water to a rolling boil and add salt. Put the spaghetti in all at once, stirring to separate strands. Return immediately to a boil and cook at a brisk simmer about 8 minutes until tender and firm to the bite. Drain thoroughly in a colander. Return immediately to the pot it was cooked in and add sauce-vegetable mixture. Toss gently and quickly to coat pasta thoroughly. Transfer to a warm serving platter and garnish with toasted pine nuts. Serve immediately.

To Prepare Ahead
Follow steps 1 and 2 up to one day ahead. Refrigerate covered in suitable containers. Bring vegetables to room temperature and reheat tomato sauce before completing steps 3 through 5.

PESTO GENOESE

Fresh basil is probably one of the easiest things to grow. Give it plenty of room and sunshine in your garden or window (it does very well as a pot plant) and stand aside. The scent derived from this savory herb is reason enough to have it around, but blended into a smooth paste for a pesto sauce, it is incomparable. The basil leaf grows on long stems and one small plant can grow three feet high with leaves up to 3 inches long. Cut stems as needed. Cut completely before the frost and store leaves in a glass jar, layered in coarse (kosher) salt for use during the winter. Or make large batches of pesto and freeze to enjoy all winter long. Some will insist that authentic pesto should only be made in a marble mortar claiming the texture of the finished sauce is superior. Perhaps so. However, the modern food processor or blender will make a superb pesto.

3 cups fresh basil leaves
2–3 cloves garlic
⅓ cup pignoli nuts
½ teaspoon coarse (kosher)
    salt
Freshly ground pepper to
    taste
½–⅔ cup light olive oil

½ cup freshly grated
    Parmesan cheese
2 tablespoons butter,
    softened
1 pound fettuccine
2–3 tablespoons of the pasta
    cooking water

Serves 6

1. If the size of the basil leaves varies greatly, gently tear the larger leaves into 2 or 3 pieces. Without crushing basil, lightly pack into measuring cup. Set aside.

2. Put the garlic cloves into workbowl of food processor fitted with knife blade or into an electric blender and process until finely chopped. Add basil leaves, pignoli nuts, salt, and pepper, and process with several on/off turns or blend until ingredients are combined. Scrape mixture down sides of bowl with rubber spatula as necessary.

3. Add oil in a thin stream through feed tube of processor or small hole in the cover of blender and blend until mixture is smooth. You can prepare ahead to this point and freeze or store in a tightly covered container and refrigerate for up to 3 days.

4. When ready to sauce your pasta, stir cheese and butter into the pesto.

5. Bring 5–6 quarts salted water to a boil. Add fettuccine, stir with a fork to separate strands, and return water to a boil immediately. If pasta is freshly made it will cook within 20 seconds; or if commercially dried, in up to 8 minutes. Just before draining pasta, add 2–3 tablespoons

cooking water to pesto and stir to mix. Transfer pasta to a warm platter, toss with pesto sauce, and serve immediately on warm plates.

To Prepare Ahead
Follow steps 1 through 3 up to several days ahead and refrigerate—or up to several months ahead and freeze. Complete steps 4 and 5 just before serving.

SPAGHETTI ALLA PUTTANESCA

The Italian word puttanesca *means a woman of dubious character. For me, the dish means something delicious with a character all its own.*

2 tablespoons olive oil
2 cloves garlic, finely chopped
2 pounds ripe tomatoes, peeled, seeded, and coarsely chopped *or* 1 can (2 pounds, 3 ounces), drained, seeded, and coarsely chopped
2 tablespoons fresh basil leaves *or* 1 teaspoon dried
Freshly ground pepper

1 tin (2 ounces) flat anchovy fillets, drained and chopped
3 tablespoons capers
½ cup black olives (preferably Greek), pitted and halved
2 tablespoons coarse (kosher) salt for cooking water
1 pound dry imported commercial spaghetti
2 tablespoons olive oil

Serves 4–6

1. Heat oil in a skillet and quickly sauté garlic, being careful not to brown. Add tomatoes, basil, and several grinds of pepper. Stir to mix and simmer 30 minutes. Keep warm.

2. Combine anchovies, capers, and olives in a small dish or bowl and set aside. Can be done ahead to this point.

3. When ready to serve, bring 5–6 quarts of water to a rolling boil and add salt. Put spaghetti in all at once, stirring to separate strands. Return immediately to a boil, then cook at a brisk simmer about 8

minutes until tender but firm to the bite. Drain pasta thoroughly in a colander.

4. Transfer to a warm serving platter. Drizzle on olive oil and warm tomato sauce and toss with abandon. Garnish with anchovy, caper and olive mixture and serve immediately on heated plates.

To Prepare Ahead
Follow steps 1 through 2 up to one day ahead. Refrigerate, covered, in suitable containers. Complete steps 3 and 4 just before serving.

VERMICELLI WITH UNCOOKED TOMATO SAUCE

This fresh uncooked sauce recipe works best in summer when local ripe tomatoes and fresh basil are available. Served over a warm pasta, it makes a fine summer lunch or light supper dish that totally satisfies.

1–1½ pounds fresh ripe tomatoes (preferably plum)
2 cloves garlic, finely chopped
1 red onion, cut into paper-thin slices
½ teaspoon coarse (kosher) salt
Freshly ground pepper
3 tablespoons chopped fresh basil *or* 2 teaspoons dried
2 tablespoons balsamic red wine vinegar

⅓ cup extra virgin olive oil
2 tablespoons coarse (kosher) salt for cooking pasta
1 pound fresh or imported commercial spinach vermicelli
1 tablespoon extra virgin olive oil for tossing cooked spaghetti
1 tablespoon finely chopped Italian flat-leaf parsley, for garnish

Serves 4–6

1. *To Prepare Sauce:* Plunge 2–3 tomatoes at a time into boiling water 10–20 seconds. Remove with slotted spoon and cool quickly under a spray of cold water. With the tip of a knife, remove skin. Cut each in half crosswise, hold in palm of your hand and squeeze gently to remove and discard seeds. Repeat with remaining tomatoes, then cut

into ½-inch strips. Place tomatoes in a large glass or earthenware mixing bowl (not metal). Add garlic, onion, salt, pepper, basil, vinegar, and the ⅓ cup of oil, and very gently toss to mix. Can be made ahead to this point.

2. Just before serving, bring 5–6 quarts water to a boil and add salt. If pasta is dried commercial, it will be necessary to cook anywhere from 8–12 minutes depending on the brand. If pasta is freshly made, it will cook in anywhere from 30 seconds to 3 minutes. Taste for doneness in either case prior to the specified cooking time.

3. Drain pasta quickly and transfer to a warm serving platter. Drizzle on a little oil and toss very well. Pour tomato mixture lengthwise over the spaghetti, leaving an exposed edge of green pasta on either side. Top with chopped parsley and serve immediately on warm plates.

To Prepare Ahead

Follow step 1 up to one day ahead. Refrigerate covered. Bring sauce to room temperature and complete steps 2 and 3 just before serving.

SPINACH FETTUCCINE WITH SCALLOPS AND BASIL SAUCE

4 tablespoons unsalted butter
1–2 tablespoons finely
    chopped shallots
1 pound sea scallops,
    halved, sinews
    removed, *or* tiny bay
    scallops in season
1¼ cups Crème Fraîche or
    heavy cream
Freshly ground pepper
1 pound Pasta Verde, cut
    into fettuccine—
    preferably fresh

2 tablespoons coarse
    (kosher) salt for
    cooking water
½ cup fresh basil leaves,
    stacked and thinly
    sliced
Several fresh basil leaves for
    garnish (optional)

Serves 4–6

1. Just before you are ready to cook pasta, prepare sauce: In a 12-inch stainless steel or enameled cast-iron skillet, melt 1 tablespoon of the butter. Add shallots and sauté briefly until tender, about 30–40 seconds. Add remaining butter, melt, then add scallops. Cook at a bare simmer, stirring, about 2 minutes. With a slotted spoon transfer scallops to a side dish. Add crème fraîche or heavy cream and simmer over moderate heat 3–4 minutes, stirring occasionally, until cream thickens slightly. Sauce should lightly coat back of a spoon. Season with pepper and turn off heat.

2. Bring 5–6 quarts water to a rolling boil and add salt. Put fettuccine in all at once, stirring to separate strands. Return immediately to a boil and cook 30 seconds to several minutes, according to freshness of your pasta—or additional time, according to package directions.

3. Meanwhile, return scallops and accumulated juices to cream sauce in skillet, add basil, and simmer just long enough to warm the sauce.

4. As soon as pasta is done, drain thoroughly in a colander and transfer to a warm serving platter. Spoon on scallop-cream sauce and top with fresh basil leaves.

To Prepare Ahead
Follow step 1 up to thirty minutes ahead. Complete steps 2 through 4 just before serving.

7

POTATOES, RICE, AND BEANS

P otatoes, rice, and beans, to me, play the same role at mealtime. I wouldn't serve them together as side dishes, but individually they provide the starchy portion of a meal.

PASSIONATE ABOUT POTATOES

At the mere mention of potatoes, people think fattening. The potato is one of nature's most complete foods. A baked or boiled potato, unadorned, contains 80–90 calories. Think about having an extra helping of potatoes rather than an extra serving of meat. Potatoes are a carbohydrate; meat, although a protein, is a concentrated source of calories and fat.

Potatoes originated in Peru, dating from prehistoric times. They were introduced to Europe in the fourteenth and fifteenth centuries. The potato was considered poisonous as well as a curiosity in many lands partly because of its bulbous and irregular shape. Ireland was one of the first European countries to recognize and cultivate the potato. This "bread of the poor," however, would one day cause the terrible Potato Famine of 1846 in Ireland, when the entire year's crop was lost.

Many a French restaurant menu will feature a potato dish termed *à la parmentier*. Antoine Auguste Parmentier, a French pharmacist, discovered the potato while a war prisoner in Germany in 1771. His love for the tuber was so great that he prevailed upon Louis XVI for permission to plant potatoes in a sandy field outside of Paris . . . "Marie Antoinette wore potato flowers in her hair" (*Wise Encyclopedia of Cookery*). If you should ever drive through the eastern end of Long Island where acres and acres of potato fields abound, you can see these lacy white blossoms that bloom before the harvest.

Most varieties that grow in the United States are marketed in one of four ways: "all-purpose potatoes," "Idaho/baking potatoes," "new potatoes," or "sweet/yams." In general, potatoes should be firm, relatively smooth, and of a regular shape. Store in a cool dark bin, but do not refrigerate. If temperatures fall below 40 degrees, the starch will convert to sugar and produce an undesirable sweet taste when cooked. Potato surface can turn green from exposure to light and discolored areas, in general, can be bitter or even toxic.

All-Purpose Potatoes: These are best for boiling, mashing, creaming, or in salads. They have a waxy texture and hold shape when cooking. All-purpose old or mature potatoes are those that have been stored and are available in winter. They are particularly good for pancakes, dumplings, and salads with dressings because they have lost their moisture and are more absorbent. They are perfect for Potato-Vegetable Galette, the crusty, golden brown potato pancake with a sandwich of tender braised vegetables.

Idaho/Baking Potatoes: Quality is the best of anything—even a perfect potato. A properly baked potato, split open to make way for a bit of sweet butter to sink into its mealy depths, is for me one of the riches of the table. To bake potatoes, force metal skewers through them lengthwise. This will help them cook more quickly and evenly.

New Potatoes: Leave the thin skins on these tender potatoes. They are more perishable than the all-purpose or baking potatoes, so use within several days of purchase. I love the little "news" just scrubbed and simply boiled or in the Pommes—boiled, then roasted in their jackets until buttery-crisp.

Sweet/Yams: There are two types of sweet potatoes. One has pale yellow flesh and is dry and mealy when cooked. The other (yams) is also a type of sweet potato and has deep orange flesh and a sweeter, moister interior.

Buy firm, thick, well-shaped potatoes, tapering at the ends. They are best cooked one or two days after purchase and kept in dry, cool (55–60 degrees) storage. They are somewhat perishable and refrigeration and dampness damages them.

As with regular potatoes, it is best to cook sweet potatoes in their skins, which not only preserves nutrients but makes them easier to peel than when raw. Sweet potatoes can sometimes be fibrous, so if you are mashing them, I suggest you put them through a food mill or a ricer.

Sweet potatoes are delicious mashed hot with just some salt, pepper, and milk. And a sweet potato casserole fragrant with cinnamon, nutmeg, and mace sums up thoughts of a ritual Thanksgiving food.

I almost never peel potatoes, but if you must peel, drop pared potatoes into a bowl of cold water to prevent darkening. I cut potatoes into french-fry sticks by hand or in a food processor with well-scrubbed skin still on. Whichever shape you choose, the small amount of skin clinging to the potato has a "today" look. The nutrients just beneath the skin are an important bonus in addition to the attractive appearance when potato skins are left on.

All need not be lost even when a recipe calls for peeling. Many potato preparations call for preboiling the potatoes—for mashing or salads, for example. I always boil potatoes in their skins; if it should then be necessary to peel them, I do it after cooking, and I love the surprise of the following "non-recipe." (It is a "non-recipe" because there are no specific measurements.) Spread peels in a baking pan; if a little potato is sticking to them, all the better. Lightly season with a sprinkle of lemon juice and a hint of Worcestershire, Tabasco, oil, salt, and freshly ground pepper. Then place in a 400-degree oven 20–25 minutes until lightly browned, with crisped edges. Move peels around pan every now and then to cook evenly. They are so good that family and friends are lucky to get any at the end of the cooking time. I feel a strong temptation to nibble each time I open the door to redistribute them.

CHÂTEAU POTATO FANS

2 pounds tiny new red
    potatoes
6 tablespoons clarified
    butter*

Coarse (kosher) salt
Freshly ground pepper
Coarse (kosher) salt for
    cooking water

Serves 6–8

1. Scrub and peel potatoes with vegetable peeler. Trim ends so they simulate an olive shape. To permit potato to fan easily, trim a thin slice off one of the ends. With a small paring knife, carefully cut ⅛-inch slices, starting at the flat end and cutting toward, but not through, the opposite end.

2. Bring 4–5 cups salted water to a boil. Drop in potatoes and cook in the briskly simmering water 3–4 minutes. Drain and pat dry with paper toweling. Spread slices of each potato to fan. Can be done ahead to this point.

Preheat oven to 450 degrees.

3. In a heavy skillet heat butter and when foam subsides, add potatoes, stirring them gently to coat. Turn occasionally with a wooden spatula 3–4 minutes until golden on all sides and sprinkle with salt and pepper. Transfer to gratin dish and bake in preheated oven for 20–25 minutes until crisp.

To Prepare Ahead

Follow steps 1 and 2 up to one day ahead. Refrigerate in suitable container. Bring to room temperature and complete step 3.

Making Château Potato Fans

Step 1

Step 2

POTATOES NORMANDE

This is another version of Gratin Dauphinoise made different by the addition of tender sautéed sweet onions. As an option, add a bit of diced boiled ham (about ¼ pound) to the potato layers.

4 tablespoons unsalted butter
1 large or 2 medium onions, peeled and thinly sliced
1–2 cloves garlic, finely chopped
2½ pounds boiling potatoes, peeled
1 teaspoon coarse (kosher) salt
Freshly ground pepper

1 cup milk
¼ cup freshly grated Parmesan cheese
¼ cup freshly grated Swiss Gruyère cheese

Have on Hand
Shallow earthenware or porcelain baking dish

Serves 8–10

Preheat oven to 375 degrees.

1. In a skillet, melt 2 tablespoons of the butter and, when foam subsides, add onion slices and sauté until translucent and tender, being careful not to brown. Add garlic and stir to mix.

2. Cut potatoes into ⅛-inch-thick slices or slice in workbowl of food processor fitted with thin slicing blade, using light pressure.

3. Butter a baking dish and spread ⅓ of potatoes on bottom. Spread ½ of the onion-garlic mixture over potato layer and season with a light sprinking of salt and pepper. Arrange additional ⅓ of potatoes over first onion layer and place remaining onions and garlic over this second layer of potatoes. Sprinkle lightly with salt and pepper. Top with remaining potatoes and season with another light sprinkle of salt and pepper.

4. In the meantime, bring milk to the edge of a boil and pour it over potatoes. Spread combined cheeses over top and dot with remaining butter.

5. Place on middle shelf of preheated oven and bake 45–50 minutes or until top is crusty and golden brown. Serve hot.

To Prepare Ahead
Follow steps 1 through 5 up to several hours ahead. Let stand at room temperature, covered with a tent of buttered parchment. Just before serving, warm through in a 350-degree oven 15–20 minutes, covered with the buttered parchment to prevent further browning.

POMMES DE PROVENCE

This "cousin" to Gratin Dauphinoise begins in a similar way with potato slices cooked ahead in milk, then layered with cream or stock and seasonings and baked. In place of the cheese, herb mixtures are added, making for a less rich but nonetheless stunning climax.

4–5 boiling potatoes, about 2 pounds
Enough milk to cover potatoes

Persillade
2 cloves garlic, finely chopped
2–3 tablespoons Italian flat-leaf parsley, finely chopped

1½ teaspoons herbes de Provence *or* ½ teaspoon each dried

marjoram, basil, and thyme
½ teaspoon coarse (kosher) salt
Freshly ground pepper
½–¾ cup Crème Fraîche or heavy cream
¼ teaspoon nutmeg
2 bay leaves

Have on Hand
9- or 10-inch porcelain quiche or other gratin dish, well buttered

Serves 6–8

Preheat oven to 375 degrees.

1. Peel and rinse potatoes and slice about ⅛ inch thin, or slice in a food processor fitted with slicing blade, using light pressure. Put into a saucepan and pour on just enough milk to barely cover. Place over moderate heat, bring to a boil, then simmer 12–15 minutes until tender but firm and not falling apart.

2. With a slotted spoon, transfer half the potatoes to the buttered baking dish. Combine garlic and parsley to make the persillade. Layer half the persillade, half the dry herb mixture, a sprinkling of salt and pepper, and half the cream. Spoon on remaining potatoes and repeat layering. Finish with a sprinkle of nutmeg and tuck bay leaves under some potato slices.

3. Place in preheated oven and bake 40–45 minutes until top is crusty and golden. If top looks dry, spoon over a thin layer of crème fraîche or heavy cream. Return to oven and bake an additional 5–6 minutes until surface is glazed. If necessary, slide under the broiler for a minute or two to color the top. Remove bay leaves and discard.

To Prepare Ahead
Follow steps 1 and 2 up to several hours ahead. Complete step 3 up to one hour before serving.

POMMES FONDANTE

The classic preparation known as savonette requires peeling and trimming new potatoes until they are small olive shapes, then slowly cooking them in water until crisp and buttery. Leaving the skins on is newer, infinitely easier to do, and results in one of the simplest and most successful potato dishes I teach.

3 pounds small, even-sized,
    unpeeled new potatoes
Cold water
1–2 teaspoons coarse
    (kosher) salt
1 stick (8 tablespoons)
    unsalted butter

1–2 tablespoons finely
    chopped parsley

Have on Hand
Flameproof gratin dish or
    12-inch oven-going
    skillet

Serves 10–12

Preheat oven to 425 degrees.

1. Scrub potatoes clean. Arrange in baking dish or skillet just large enough to hold them in one layer. Add cold water to barely cover potatoes and sprinkle lightly with salt. Cut thin slices of cold butter over tops of potatoes and slowly bring water to a boil over moderate heat.

2. Transfer baking dish or skillet to lower third of preheated oven and bake 45 minutes. Water should be almost evaporated. Remove from oven and, with tongs, carefully turn each potato. Return to oven and bake 45–60 minutes longer or until they are golden brown and crisp.

3. Sprinkle with chopped parsley and serve immediately. This is great at a barbecue or an informal buffet.

To Prepare Ahead
Follow steps 1 and 2 up to two hours before serving. Potatoes can be kept warm in a turned off oven.

SPICED SWEET POTATO PIE

In Food, *Waverly Root wrote about "a recipe for potato pie whose other ingredients included cinnamon, nutmeg, mace, grapes, and dates, which would be a little hard to reconcile with white potatoes." I was thoroughly inspired.*

4½–5 pounds yams or sweet potatoes
Coarse (kosher) salt for cooking water
4 tablespoons unsalted butter, plus 1–2 tablespoons extra butter to top pie before baking
1 cup milk, scalded
½ teaspoon ground cinnamon

¼ teaspoon freshly ground nutmeg
¼ teaspoon ground mace
1 cup halved seedless sweet red or green grapes
1 cup pitted dates, each one cut into 4–5 thin slices

Have on Hand
Food mill or potato ricer

Serves 16–18

Preheat oven to 375 degrees.

1. Scrub potatoes thoroughly. Bring 4 quarts of salted water to a boil in a large saucepan. With slotted spoon, lower potatoes into water and cook at a brisk simmer with cover ajar until potatoes are tender, about 30–40 minutes. The smaller the potatoes, the quicker they will cook. Remove to a colander as they are done and start to peel while waiting for remaining potatoes to cook through. Discard peel, cut potatoes into 1-inch chunks, and purée in batches in a food mill or potato ricer over a large mixing bowl.

2. Cut the 4 tablespoons of butter into small pieces and add to hot potato purée. Gradually add hot milk while beating with a large wooden spoon until mixture is smooth and fluffy. Season with cinnamon, nutmeg, and mace, and stir to mix. Add grapes and dates and stir into potato mixture until thoroughly incorporated.

3. Butter a 2-quart baking dish and spoon in potato mixture in an even layer. Cut remaining 1 or 2 tablespoons butter into small pieces and dot over top of pie. Can be done ahead to this point.

4. Bake in preheated oven 20 minutes. Serve very hot.

To Prepare Ahead

Follow steps 1 through 3 up to two days ahead. Refrigerate, covered, in baking dish. Bring to room temperature and complete step 4 before serving.

GRATIN DAUPHINOISE

2½ pounds boiling potatoes
Enough milk to cover
　　potatoes
2–3 cloves garlic, finely
　　minced
Coarse (kosher) salt
Freshly ground pepper
¾–1 cup Crème Fraîche or
　　heavy cream

½ cup freshly grated
　　Parmesan cheese
Unsalted butter

Have on Hand
11-inch fluted porcelain
　　quiche or other shallow
　　baking dish

Serves 6–8

Preheat oven to 350 degrees.

1. Peel and rinse potatoes and slice about ⅛ inch thin, or slice in a food processor fitted with slicing blade, using light pressure. Put in a saucepan and pour on just enough milk to barely cover. Place over moderate heat, bring to a boil, then simmer 12–15 minutes until tender but firm. Drain in a colander.

2. Butter a baking dish. Transfer half the potatoes to dish and spread evenly. Sprinkle with half the garlic, a light touch of salt, and several grinds of fresh pepper. Spoon on half the heavy cream or crème fraîche. Repeat second layer with remaining garlic, seasonings, and cream. Sprinkle cheese over top layer and dot with butter.

3. Bake on a cookie sheet 30–35 minutes or until top is a crusty golden brown and bubbly. Serve hot.

To Prepare Ahead

Follow steps 1 and 2 up to several hours ahead. Let stand at room temperature. Complete step 3 before serving.

POTATO-VEGETABLE GALETTE

A potato galette is basic to a French cook's repertoire. When it calls for a sandwich of a vegetable julienne, it becomes a bit more ambitious. There are times when I just do a potato galette excluding the vegetable mirepoix.

Mirepoix
3 shallots, finely chopped
2 large carrots, scrubbed and trimmed
1 leek, trimmed, cut in half lengthwise, rinsed well, white and light green part only

6 tablespoons clarified butter*
1½ teaspoons coarse (kosher) salt

Freshly ground pepper
2½ pounds boiling potatoes, peeled and rinsed
1 tablespoon butter
1 tablespoon finely chopped Italian flat-leaf parsley

Have on Hand
12-inch T-Fal skillet

Serves 6–8

Note: For Potato Galette, a simplified version of this recipe, see below.

1. With a chef's knife, finely chop shallots and set aside. Halve carrots lengthwise and cut across into thirds. Cut leek halves into 1½-inch pieces across. Place vegetables flat side down on a cutting board and, using a chef's or slicing knife, and working with one piece at a time, cut into thin julienne strips. Set aside.

2. In a heavy saucepan with a cover, heat 3 tablespoons of clarified butter and, when foam subsides, add vegetables and stir to coat. Season with a scant ½ teaspoon of the salt and several grinds of pepper. Cook, covered, over low heat to braise 8–10 minutes, stirring occasionally. Be careful not to brown vegetables.

3. Grate potatoes into a mixing bowl. Cover with cold water and drain ·in a colander. Transfer to a clean kitchen towel, fold over ends, and pat dry. Place in a second clean dry towel, lift up and twist the ends to squeeze out any excess moisture. Potatoes should be absolutely dry.

4. Heat remaining 3 tablespoons of the clarified butter in T-Fal skillet, tilting pan to completely coat bottom and sides. When butter is foamy, put in half the grated potatoes and, with a fork, spread to edges of pan and pack down firmly. Distribute mirepoix in an even layer over potatoes, leaving about ½-inch edge of potatoes showing. Add remaining potatoes,

spreading them carefully with a fork to cover but not disturb vegetable mixture. Form a smooth dome with no straggly loose strands around the edges. Sprinkle with salt and pepper and dot around sides of pan with the tablespoon of butter. Cover skillet securely with foil and cook over moderate heat 25–30 minutes or until the bottom is browned and crisped. While it is cooking, shake the pan gently over heat so that galette does not stick.

5. Before inverting potatoes, make certain that the edges detach from sides of the pan. Put a plate face down over the pan. Holding plate firmly, reverse pan and turn out galette. Return pan to heat and carefully slide galette into it to cook other side. Dot top with additional tablespoon butter and a light sprinkle of salt and pepper. Cook, uncovered, 20 minutes until bottom is crisp and brown. Transfer to a heatproof serving platter.

6. *To Serve:* Garnish with finely chopped parsley and cut into wedges like a pie. Serve at once.

To Prepare Ahead
Follow steps 1 through 5 up to several hours ahead. Cover galette with a piece of buttered parchment and let stand at room temperature. Place in a 200-degree oven 10–15 minutes to warm. Then complete step 6.

Potato Galette	1½ teaspoons coarse
3 pounds boiling potatoes	(kosher) salt
6 tablespoons clarified	Freshly ground pepper
butter*	

Follow steps 3 through 6, excluding the vegetable-mirepoix instructions. (When cooking the potatoes, use 4 tablespoons butter initially, then dot top with remaining 2 tablespoons.)

RICE—THE PERFECT ACCOMPANIMENT

We throw rice at brides and grooms and sometimes wonder why. One theory is that rice, a symbol of fertility, will keep away evil spirits and that by feeding it to the spirits, the couple is assured of a fruitful marriage. Another theory is that the souls of bridegrooms are bribed with rice to prevent them from being fickle. Whatever some primitive cultures might suggest, rice is perhaps the most universally known and eaten food.

I like the easy style of rice. I find when I teach my classes, there is a timidity and temerity which is undeserved about cooking rice. As a life-sustaining nourishment, its virtues are many. It:

- stores well—is convenient, versatile and economical
- is easy to cook, no peeling, scraping, or washing
- provides much nourishment at little cost
- is nonallergenic and virtually free of sodium and salt
- is low in fat and cholesterol
- is easily digested and not fattening if eaten in moderation
- combines well with innumerable foods.

Milled or converted rice includes long, short, and medium grains. The hull, germ, outer bran layers, and some inner bran layers have been removed. They are ready to cook and should not be washed. Long-grain rice, when properly cooked, tends to separate into light fluffy grains and is especially suited for salads, curries, pilaf, stews, and side dishes. The particles of short- and medium-grain rice tend to cling together, and I favor it only when a molded pudding or rice ring is called for. I see no need for precooked or instant rice at all. My basic white rice is so easy to prepare, I can't imagine anything more instant than that.

With nutritional concerns greater than ever, rice in its rough state, that is to say brown or unpolished rice, is becoming extremely popular and many people will only eat brown rice. Since only the outer hull and small amount of bran is removed, brown rice contains more nutritive elements than white. In addition to its nutritional benefits, it has a nutlike flavor and a chewy texture.

A rice dish which I have become familiar with from my study and travels in Italy is the true risotto of the river Po, which runs through the northern part of that country. Riso means rice in Italian, but an authentic risotto should be made with those pearly white grains, preferably Italian arborio-type rice, available in this country in specialty food stores. The rice is prepared similarly to pilaf. The grains are added to some fat in a pan, and the liquid, usually a hot broth, is slowly incorporated until completely absorbed by the rice. This can take 20–25 minutes of constant stirring. The wonderful smells wafting from the pan as you cook it until it is creamy and toothsome is worth the effort. Ask a family member or a friend to share the stirring while sipping a glass of wine and enjoying a chat. Or, if you're alone, a good book will help pass the time. The rice can be deliciously combined with the earthy and pungent porcini mushroom or with seafood or just some freshly grated Parmesan cheese.

Wild rice, our nation's oldest crop, a delicacy very much favored by connoisseurs, is really not a true rice but the seeds that are beaten out of reedlike water plants that grow along the banks of lakes and rivers. Found and harvested by hand, it is understandably expensive. The good news is that wild rice is highly nutritious, supplying protein, carbohydrates, vitamin C, iron, and potassium. One cup of wild rice has only 130 calories. Its unique flavor and texture allows it to combine well with other ingredients, stretching the food and thereby making it more affordable. It works extremely well in casseroles and as a stuffing. One of my favorite ways is the colorful and crunchy Wild Rice Salad.

There are some valuable rice by-products available to the consumer. Rice oil extracted from the rice bran (which is another by-product) is fine for cooking and is extremely low in cholesterol. Rice flour is ground milled rice. Since rice is nonallergenic, rice flour would be particularly valuable to those who are allergic to wheat-flour products.

Whichever rice you decide to cook, there are many brands available to you. Before you buy, know your needs. Decide which is the best type for the dish you want to cook.

To store uncooked rice, transfer the boxed contents to a glass container with a tight-fitting lid. I keep a collection of rice and beans stored in mason jars on open shelves away from direct sunlight and heat. It is an attractive area of the kitchen.

Some do's and don'ts with rice:

- Do not wash and rinse milled rice, which causes loss of flavor and vitamins (exception: brown rice and wild rice).
- Do not lift lid when boiling rice, or steam will escape and lower cooking temperature.
- Do not stir rice after it comes to a boil. This could make the grains gummy.
- When rice is cooked, simply lift it gently with a fork to fluff it. Do not stir.
- Holding cooked rice: If rice is completely cooked before you are ready to eat, cover with a lightly dampened cloth placed directly on

top of rice, and replace lid to keep in heat and moisture; or transfer rice to a steamer set in a pan of simmering water. Cover and keep warm. Fluff with a fork when ready to serve.

Leftover cooked rice keeps well in the refrigerator for several days. Store, covered, in a crockery or glass bowl. Cooked rice can be used for Chinese fried rice and rice salads and even freezes well. Allow to cool after cooking and freeze in suitable containers.

Methods of cooking rice include top of the stove, double boiler, and oven bake. All methods are similar, since rice cooks in liquid until it is absorbed. Oven bake would necessitate the use of a covered casserole or baking dish as opposed to a saucepan or a skillet.

Many people have their own way of cooking rice. Whatever the "one and only" way is, the ultimate goal is to achieve thoroughly cooked, plump, fluffy, and separate grains.

RISOTTO WITH DRIED WILD MUSHROOMS AND SAFFRON

A gastronomic specialty from northern Italy. In a traditional Italian meal, a pasta or a risotto is served as a separate course. This is beautiful food.

1 ounce dried Italian porcini mushrooms
4–4¼ cups Basic Chicken Stock or broth
4 tablespoons unsalted butter
2 tablespoons olive oil
1 medium onion, finely chopped

1 cup imported Italian arborio rice
4 tablespoons freshly grated Parmesan cheese
Salt and freshly ground pepper
Pinch of saffron powder

Serves 3–4

Note: Total cooking time to combine rice and broth will be approximately 20–25 minutes.

1. Place mushrooms in a small mixing bowl. Bring 1½ cups stock or broth to the edge of a boil and pour it over mushrooms. Allow mushrooms to soak in the liquid about 30 minutes. Reach into bowl, shake mushrooms free of sand and dirt, then transfer to another clean

small bowl. Line a strainer with several thicknesses of cheesecloth, secure over bowl, and pour soaking liquid through and over mushrooms. Rinse cheesecloth under running water to remove dirt. Porcini mushrooms are very sandy and must be rinsed several times. Repeat cleaning procedure 2 or 3 times, discarding excess sand left behind each time. Reserve the concentrated mushroom liquid/broth. Cut mushrooms into julienne strips and set aside.

2. Add mushroom broth to stock or broth in a saucepan. Bring to the edge of a boil and keep at a slow, steady simmer. It is essential to the success of this dish that broth be boiling hot when added to rice.

3. In a separate 2½–3-quart saucepan, melt 2 tablespoons of the butter with the oil and, when foam subsides, add onion and sauté gently until translucent but not brown. Add rice and stir until it is well coated, 2–3 minutes.

4. Add ½ cup of simmering broth to rice and stir constantly over moderate heat with a wooden spoon until liquid is absorbed. Be sure to maintain moderate heat at all times when adding liquid to rice. Add remaining hot broth a ladleful at a time and continue to stir. Broth must be totally absorbed before each addition of liquid.

5. After 10–12 minutes, add reserved mushrooms with some broth and continue to cook as above until all liquid is used. Just before rice is creamy but still al dente, add remaining 2 tablespoons butter, cheese, salt, and pepper to taste while still over heat. Remove from heat, stir in saffron, and serve immediately.

To Prepare Ahead
Follow step 1 up to several hours ahead. Follow steps 2 through 5 just before serving.

INSALATA DE RISO

*This is a colorful and tasty dish that would make a perfect accompaniment
to grilled meats or an addition to a cold buffet.*

1½ cups converted rice
3⅓ cups water
1 small onion, peeled and
　left whole
2 tablespoons fresh lemon
　juice
½ cup fresh or frozen peas
1 medium red pepper, cut
　into small dice
3 scallions, trimmed and
　thinly sliced, white and
　light green part only
1 teaspoon coarse (kosher)
　salt for cooking water

Dressing
1 tablespoon Dijon mustard
1 teaspoon coarse (kosher)
　salt
Freshly ground pepper
2–3 tablespoons finely
　chopped Italian flat-leaf
　parsley
1½ tablespoons freshly
　chopped dill
3 tablespoons white wine or
　herb vinegar
9 tablespoons light, fruity
　olive oil

Serves 10–12

1. Put rice in a 2½-quart saucepan and pour on cold water. Place
onion on top of rice. Bring to a boil over high heat, reduce heat, and
simmer rice, covered, about 15 minutes. Check under lid at end of
cooking time to see if rice has absorbed all the water but is still moist.
If there is still liquid in the pot, cover and cook 1–2 minutes more.
Water must be completely absorbed. Remove from heat and let stand,
covered, 10–12 minutes or until rice is dry. Remove onion and discard.
Add lemon juice to rice and fluff with a fork. Spread rice on a large
plate or cookie sheet to cool. When completely cool place in a bowl,
cover with plastic wrap, and chill for several hours or overnight.

2. *To Prepare Dressing:* In a mixing bowl, combine mustard, salt,
pepper, herbs, and vinegar. Stir to mix with a wire whisk. Gradually
whisk in oil in a slow steady stream until mixture is thoroughly blended.
Set aside.

3. If using fresh peas, cook 3–4 minutes in salted boiling water, or
defrost frozen peas and cook 1–2 minutes in salted boiling water. Drain
and dry in a clean kitchen towel. Set aside.

4. Pour dressing over rice. Add cooked peas, red pepper, and scallions.
Fluff the rice with two forks to distribute the ingredients. Serve at room
temperature.

To Prepare Ahead
Follow steps 1 through 4 up to two days ahead. Refrigerate, covered.
Bring to room temperature before serving.

BASIC WHITE RICE

*Such an easy rice to prepare . . . yet I notice my students reaching for pen
and paper every time I talk about cooking plain boiled rice. I frequently
cook rice this way. If I use it to accompany a Chinese main dish, I never
add salt and butter. Sometimes I will add a little sweet butter when it
accompanies other dishes.*

1 cup long-grain rice
2¼ cups cold water

Serves 4

Place rice in a 2-quart saucepan and add water. Bring to a boil over
high heat, cover pan tightly and reduce heat to a simmer. Cook rice 15
minutes over moderate heat, then remove from heat. Do not stir. Look
under lid; you will see in the surface of the rice little open pockets here
and there. These hollow areas are known as "fish eyes" in Chinese
cooking terminology. Rice should appear moist without any visible
amount of liquid. If, after 15 minutes of cooking, there is liquid still
bubbling over rice, cover and cook 3–5 minutes longer until water is
completely absorbed. Cover pan, as rice will continue to cook in its own
heat for an additional 10 minutes. Rice will be perfectly cooked, with
fluffy separate grains, and will remain hot another 20 minutes. Do not
stir at any time after cooking or rice will stick to bottom of pan. Serve
hot.
   Note: For Parsleyed Lemon Rice simply add to cooked basic white
rice 1 tablespoon or so of finely chopped Italian flat-leaf parsley, the
grated rind of one lemon, and a little sweet butter to taste. Stir gently
to mix and serve hot.

To Prepare Ahead
Prepare up to forty-five minutes before serving.

WILD RICE SALAD

In some circles wild rice is thought of as the star of truly American food. This crunchy, nutty Wild Rice Salad is certain to star whenever you serve it. The procedure for cooking the rice may seem unorthodox, but it is simple to do, always results in a tender but firm chewy texture, and retains important nutrients.

½ pound wild rice
1 red pepper, cored, seeded, and cut into tiny dice
¼ cup very thinly sliced white of scallion
2 tablespoons finely chopped Italian flat-leaf parsley

Dressing
2–3 large shallots, finely chopped

1 tablespoon Dijon mustard
2½–3 tablespoons imported red wine vinegar
½ teaspoon coarse (kosher) salt
Freshly ground pepper
7–8 tablespoons imported light, fruity olive oil

Have on Hand
Fine sieve

Yield 4½ cups

1. Place rice in a large fine sieve and rinse under cold running water. Put rice in a saucepan. Add fresh cold water to cover to a depth of about 1 inch (or up to the first knuckle on your thumb). Bring just to the edge of a boil over moderately high heat. Reduce heat, then cook, uncovered, at a brisk simmer 18–20 minutes or until kernels have "blossomed," adjusting heat as necessary. Remove from heat, cover tightly, and let stand 3–4 hours or overnight. Rice will have absorbed most of water and should be tender but still crunchy. Drain in a fine sieve, transfer to a clean kitchen towel, and pat dry. Place in a mixing bowl with red pepper, scallions and parsley. Fluff with a fork as you gently toss to mix. Set aside.

2. *Prepare Dressing:* Place shallots in a mixing bowl. Add Dijon mustard, vinegar, salt, and pepper, and stir to mix. Add oil in a slow, steady stream and whisk until mixture is thoroughly blended. Pour dressing on rice and gently stir to combine thoroughly. Transfer to an attractive serving dish or bowl and serve at room temperature.

To Prepare Ahead
Follow steps 1 and 2 up to one week ahead. Cover with plastic wrap and refrigerate. Bring to room temperature before serving.

TO EACH HIS OWN "SHELL" BEAN

Beans are an edible variety of legumes, some of which were covered in the Vegetable text. We will concern ourselves with dried beans in this section.

Of all the bean varieties, shell beans are too often ignored and misunderstood. They have a marvelous potential, but are noticeably missing from many a contemporary cook's larder. Many people openly voice a dislike for beans. Is it their presoak and lengthy cooking? Because they cause flatulence? Or because, like potatoes and rice, they are considered heavy and starchy? The lowly bean was considered less than elegant in the Great Depression—another possible reason people shun it today.

We are familiar with Boston baked beans and chili con carne, black bean soup, and perhaps the exotic French flageolets. But once you've tasted a hearty and flavorful Tuscan Bean Soup; a Spanish onion, tomato and bean casserole; a light French lentil salad; or fresh, buttery red pinto and kidney beans indigenous to Southwestern and Mexican cooking, I hope shell beans will take their place in the forefront of your culinary imagination.

Dry shell beans are widely available commercially packaged in almost any food market, which guarantees reliably clean and even-sized beans. They are sometimes available loose in ethnic and specialty food stores. Nevertheless, I suggest that beans be purchased in a market with a good turnover. Beans do have a lengthy shelf life, but the drier they are, the longer they take to cook. They are an inexpensive food and, like rice and potatoes, are extremely versatile and good meal stretchers. Add some whole to a leftover soup, or purée and add to a soup for body and thickness. When the meat from a stew is gone, combine the leftover liquid or sauce with cooked beans for another meal. Add cold cooked beans to an antipasto platter or to a salad for texture and color.

Beans date back to antiquity and their varieties are numerous. Supermarket shelves, however, will feature just a handful such as Great Northerns, marrow, pinto, kidney, pea, lentil, black beans, garbanzos or chick-peas, and so on. Dry shell beans require very little storage space. Like rice, they store well in glass jars with tight-fitting lids.

Dry shell beans should be rinsed in a colander and picked over to remove stones and dehydrated kernels. I like to presoak them. Place in a crockery or glass bowl with enough fresh water to cover about 1½ inches above the surface of the beans. It is not necessary to refrigerate them during this time unless your kitchen is *very* hot. I do not add anything to the water—salt, baking soda—not anything. The next day beans can be simmered slowly at your convenience or whenever you plan on being around long enough to check the water level as the beans cook. Some nutritionists will suggest that the soaking water be used for cooking. The soaking liquid leaches relatively few nutrients and so the choice is yours. Thorough soaking and cooking beans to the point of tenderness will diminish their possible flatulent effects.

The amount of time it takes to cook beans varies from one kind of bean to another and their freshness. If they are reasonably fresh and contain some moisture, they will cook more quickly. If they have been stored for a long period of time, they will take longer to cook. You can't tell from looking at a dry bean just how old it is. Recipes for cooking dry beans are a guide; you must taste as you cook to know when the bean are tender. Cook just enough beans for the recipe or the occasion; they are best when freshly cooked. It is best to add salt to the bean cooking water toward the end of the cooking time or beans will be tough.

You can eliminate a long or overnight soak by utilizing the quick-cook method. Rinse beans well and pick them over; then put in a pot with cold water to cover or with water three times the volume of the beans and bring to a rapid boil, covered; reduce heat and let boil gently one minute. Remove from heat and let stand covered one hour. They are ready to cook. Return beans to heat in their cooking water, cover, and bring back to the boil; reduce heat, maintaining a lazy surface bubble at all times, and simmer until tender.

As with pasta and rice, it is important to cook beans in enough liquid to keep grains from sticking. Whichever cooking method you choose, remember that beans will swell, absorbing water as they cook. Be sure to check water level several times to make certain there is still enough water for cooking.

Whenever I cook certain bean dishes, for instance Cannellini and Shrimp, and there is still liquid left when the beans are tender and ready to eat, I drain them and save the liquid. I transfer the liquid to a small saucepan and reduce it until it is almost a glaze, about ½–1 cup, then carefully fold it through the beans for added flavor with a good bit of nutrition thrown in. I would not suggest this process when cooking black beans, as their flavor is very strong. Another use for the stock from cooked beans is as a base for a soup or a stew. This stock contains a rich supply of vitamin B and minerals. Beans (except soybeans) are notably low in fat and have no cholesterol. Bean cookery is especially important in the diet of vegetarians, since beans are unrefined and supply a great deal of protein to supplement a meatless diet.

CANNELLINI AND SHRIMP

1 cup fresh cannellini beans,
    soaked overnight in
    cold water to cover
1½ quarts water for cooking
    beans
1 tablespoon coarse (kosher)
    salt
2 teaspoons fresh sage
    leaves *or* ¼ teaspoon
    dried leaf sage (not
    powdered)
2 large cloves garlic, left
    whole
1 tablespoon olive oil

8–10 large shrimp, cooked
Sprigs of curly parsley for
    garnish

Vinaigrette
Coarse (kosher) salt
Freshly ground pepper
1 teaspoon grainy Dijon
    mustard
1½ tablespoons imported red
    wine vinegar
4–5 tablespoons imported
    Italian olive oil

Serves 6–8

1. Drain beans, then rinse in cold water and place in a large saucepan with 1½ quarts of fresh water, salt, sage, garlic, and oil. Bring just to the edge of a boil, then adjust heat and simmer very slowly 1½–2 hours with cover ajar. Raise and lower heat as necessary to maintain a lazy surface bubble at all times and cook until just tender. Be careful not to overcook or beans will fall apart.

2. With a slotted spoon, transfer beans into a mixing bowl and allow to cool. Transfer bean liquid to a smaller saucepan and simmer briskly over moderately high heat to reduce to 1 cup. Cool, then add to beans and set aside.

3. Cut shrimp into ½-inch dice and add to beans.

4. In a small mixing bowl, combine a light sprinkling of salt and pepper with mustard, vinegar, and oil, and whisk until mixture is thoroughly blended. Pour over the bean mixture and toss *very gently* to mix, being careful not to break beans. Taste to adjust seasoning if necessary. Transfer to a serving dish and serve at room temperature.

To Prepare Ahead
Follow steps 1 through 4 up to one day ahead. Cover with plastic wrap and refrigerate. Bring to room temperature, garnish with parsley sprigs just before serving.

CUBAN BLACK BEANS WITH CRÈME FRAÎCHE, CAYENNE, AND TOMATO

It's not really a soup; yet it's more than just a side dish. It's a satisfying bean dish made with a Sofrito, a mixture of onions, peppers, garlic, and tomato, and works extremely well as a first course served in a small soup bowl. Top it with a dollop of crème fraîche or sour cream, a sprinkle of cayenne and a bit of tomato, and it's food for today.

1 package (1 pound) black beans
1 small whole green pepper, rinsed
1 small whole onion, peeled

Sofrito Sauce
3 tablespoons olive oil
2 onions, peeled and finely chopped
2 green peppers, trimmed, seeded, rinsed, and finely diced
3 cloves garlic, peeled and finely chopped
3 tablespoons red wine vinegar
1 cup dry red wine

⅔ cup Basic Tomato Sauce
1 bay leaf
¼ teaspoon cayenne pepper
½ teaspoon cumin powder
1 teaspoon coarse (kosher) salt
Freshly ground pepper
1–1½ cups reserved bean liquor
1½–2 cups Basic Chicken Stock or broth

Garnish
About ½ cup Crème Fraîche or sour cream
Cayenne pepper
1 large ripe tomato, peeled, seeded, and shredded

Serves 6–8

1. Rinse the beans well and pick over them to remove any foreign particles. Place in a large mixing bowl. Add enough cold water to come about 2 inches above level of beans, and let stand overnight.

2. Next day, drain the beans well and place in a 5–6-quart saucepan with green pepper and onion. Add fresh cold water to cover to a depth of about 3 inches above the beans. Bring to a boil and, with cover ajar, cook over moderate heat about 1½–2 hours. Keep control of heat, checking occasionally to see that the water maintains a brisk simmer. It may be necessary to adjust heat up or down from time to time. When the beans are still a little firm but almost tender, remove from heat. Lift out green pepper and onion and discard. Place a large sieve over a bowl and drain beans. Reserve bean liquid in bowl. Return beans to rinsed-out saucepan and set aside.

3. *To Prepare Sofrito:* In the meantime, heat oil in a 12-inch skillet or a saucepan. Put in chopped onions and diced green pepper and sauté until onions are translucent, about 7–8 minutes, stirring occasionally. Stir in the garlic and cook 30–40 seconds longer. Add wine vinegar and red wine, bring to a boil, then reduce heat to a simmer. Add tomato sauce, bay leaf, cayenne, cumin, salt, and pepper, and simmer with cover ajar 15 minutes. Remove bay leaf and discard.

4. Add sauce to drained beans in saucepan, then reserved bean liquid and stock, and stir gently to mix. Simmer with cover ajar, stirring occasionally, about 1 hour until beans are completely tender. If liquid has been absorbed while beans are cooking, add additional bean liquid or stock. Beans should not be dry; they should be completely coated with sauce and with just enough liquid to keep them moist.

5. *To Serve:* Divide into 6 or 8 soup bowls. Spoon a dollop of crème fraîche or sour cream over the top, sprinkle each dollop with a dash of cayenne and dot with a bit of shredded tomato. Serve immediately, piping hot.

To Prepare Ahead
Follow step 1 up to two days ahead. Follow steps 2 through 4 up to one day ahead, cover, and refrigerate in a suitable container. Bring to room temperature, place in a saucepan, and simmer, covered, stirring occasionally until heated through. Complete step 5 before serving.

Note: If doing ahead, it may be necessary to add more stock to recipe. The cooked bean mixture will thicken on standing overnight in the refrigerator.

FEJONES

Frijoles, fagioli, or feijoada—any way you say it, it all adds up to a centuries-old Sephardic Jewish bean stew. It was a hot meal prepared for the sabbath. The beans were never soaked, just rinsed and picked over for stones and grit, then left to simmer in a pot over hot ashes overnight. Family tales tell me that New England Boston baked beans were based on this dish. Ship captains learned it from Jewish immigrants. In bad weather cooking flames could start a fire on board; consequently the pot of beans was buried in hot ashes to provide food while at sea. However history has adapted it (cholent from eastern European Jews and of course the famous French cassoulet), to me it is a simple bean casserole, one that my sisters and brother remember much like the proverbial kettle of soup simmering at the back of the kitchen stove. It is a comforting and sustaining dish that I thoroughly enjoy preparing on a blustery winter day. The beans do not have to be soaked overnight. A simple stew of chopped onions, some meat on a bone, seasonings, and a bit of tomato sauce is prepared and water and beans are added. It is stirred just once to bring everything together, then cooked at the very barest simmer your range can adjust to. "To be good," my mother says, "the beans should cook very slowly and for a long time." The beans will layer as they cook. These layers should never be disturbed in any way. If they are, the beans will split and become pasty. The long cooking time is also a convenience. One can come and go, then return to a rich and flavorful bean stew. Complete this high-protein meal with a bowl of hot rice and a crisp green salad.

1 pound Great Northern
    beans
2 tablespoons vegetable oil
2 onions, finely chopped
½ cup Basic Tomato Sauce
    or canned tomato sauce
1½ pounds chuck steak with
    bone
2 sprigs fresh thyme *or* ¼
    teaspoon dried

2 quarts water
1–2 teaspoons coarse
    (kosher) salt
1 large whole red pepper,
    rinsed
1 tablespoon finely chopped
    flat-leaf Italian parsley

Serves 6–8

1. Rinse beans well and pick over carefully to discard stones and grit. Set aside.

2. Heat oil in a 5½-quart stainless steel saucepan or enameled iron casserole and, when hot, put in onions and sauté over moderate heat, stirring occasionally, until translucent. Cut meat into 2-inch squares and add with bone to onion; then cook, stirring meat until it loses its red

color. Add tomato sauce, thyme, and water, and bring to a boil. Add beans and salt. Stir once to combine ingredients and return to the edge of a boil. Let cook with water maintaining a lazy surface bubble about 10 minutes or until some beans float to the top of liquid. Reduce heat to the barest simmer and cook with cover ajar for a minimum of 4 hours and up to about 8 hours. After an hour or two, check under lid to see if liquid is being absorbed. There should be enough liquid to just cover beans at all times. If beans are exposed above the surface of liquid add enough hot water to cover them. At this point gently place the red pepper on top to cook with beans. (It adds flavor and a fantastic aroma.) Continue to cook over very low heat. The beans can be left to cook right up to the time you are ready to eat them. Just before serving, remove red pepper and, if desired, trim and cut into coarse dice and add to beans. Sprinkle with chopped parsley and serve hot over rice.

To Prepare Ahead
Follow steps 1 and 2 up to one day ahead. Let cool, refrigerate in covered pot, bring to room temperature, and then heat through in a 250-degree oven.

MME. JEANETTE PEPIN'S
SALADE DE LENTILLES

To Mme. Pepin, with my everlasting thanks for a well-made and deliciously different salad.

1 cup lentils
4 cups cold water
1 onion stuck with one clove
3 shallots, finely chopped
1 clove garlic, finely
    chopped
Pinch thyme
1 bay leaf
½–¾ teaspoon coarse
    (kosher) salt
Freshly ground pepper

Dressing
1½ tablespoons Dijon
    mustard
3 tablespoons imported red
    wine vinegar
6–8 tablespoons imported
    light, fruity olive oil

2 tablespoons finely chopped
    parsley for garnish
    (optional)

Serves 4–6

1. Rinse lentils in a colander and place in a heavy stainless steel or enamel saucepan. Add water, clove-pierced onion, shallots, garlic, thyme, bay leaf, salt, and pepper, and bring to a boil. Reduce heat and simmer with cover ajar, maintaining a lazy surface bubble. Cook 20–25 minutes until most of the liquid has evaporated and lentils are tender but still firm.

2. Drain lentils in a large sieve, discarding the liquid. Remove onion and bay leaf and discard. Transfer mixture to a ceramic or glass bowl.

3. Place mustard in a mixing bowl with vinegar. Whisk in oil in a slow steady stream to incorporate. Add to lentils while still warm to help them absorb dressing. Stir very gently with a rubber spatula to combine ingredients. Refrigerate several hours or overnight.

4. Garnish with a sprinkle of chopped parsley if desired and serve at room temperature.

To Prepare Ahead
Follow steps 1 through 3 up to several days ahead. Refrigerate, covered, in a suitable container. Complete step 4 before serving.

8

EGGS, THE KITCHEN WORKHORSE

Eggs are reliable and economical and can be simple or elegant. There are quail eggs and duck eggs, ostrich eggs and peacock eggs. In fact, all of life has one thing or another to do with the egg. However, it is the chicken egg that most often graces our table. With eggs on hand, one can always be certain of something to eat at any time of the day. They can be transformed into a variety of tempting entrees for lunch and supper or provide the staple breakfast.

Freshness and quality are important in all food, but the freshness in eggs has always been thought of as something of a mystery. There is a great deal of technical advice offered on how to tell a fresh egg by using such methods as candling or placing an egg in water with a solution of salts, but I believe the whole matter should be a simple one: I start by shopping in markets where I have confidence.

How fresh is fresh? Eggs are at the very least several days—and perhaps even months—old (cold storage), when we purchase them. Dating on cartons, when you can find it, is determined from the time the eggs were packaged, not when the eggs were laid. I always open a carton of eggs and check to see if any are visibly broken, and even if they look perfect, I will run my fingers over them and gently roll them in place to determine unseen breakage which might cause them to stick to the egg carton. Cracked and broken eggs are a matter of serious health concern, as any bacterial entry into the egg can cause salmonella infection.

A simple way to determine freshness of eggs is to hold one in your hand. You can feel, as well as hear, a rattle which suggests a less than fresh egg. Although fragile in appearance, an egg should feel solid. Another obvious way to test for freshness is by smell and taste. Like fresh-picked corn, the flavor of a fresh egg is incomparable and it is odor free. Freshness is of prime importance in the poaching of eggs. The white of the egg, or albumen, should be thick and stand high and close around the domed yolk. Older whites will be runny and fall away from the yolk during poaching.

Eggs are still useful, however, when they are not absolutely fresh. Older egg whites, for instance, can be beaten to a greater volume than very fresh ones, and hard-cooked eggs are easier to peel when they are at least four to five days old. This should not be a matter of great concern, however, since it is unlikely most of us will be confronted with the problem of having access to newly laid eggs.

The most fundamental preparations in egg cookery include cooking eggs in their shells, poaching, scrambling, and shirring. Yet as basic as they may appear, there are numerous ways in which the cook can handle these operations. Whether one starts an egg in boiling water or in cold to soft- or hard-cook an egg is not that critical as long as care is taken in either circumstance. And certainly in the more complicated dishes, such as omelets, frittatas, soufflés, etc., it is all the more important to exercise care.

To Hard-Cook: I prefer to hard-cook an egg by gently slipping it into a saucepan with just enough cold water to cover, then bringing it to a simmer. At no time should the water be boiling furiously, since this will make the egg tough and rubbery and cause an unpleasant greenish ring around the yolk. Cook it from three minutes for a tender soft-cooked egg to about twelve minutes for a firmer hard-cooked egg. Remove with a slotted spoon, run quickly under cold water, then tap the rounded end of the egg against the side of the sink. Gently roll against the counter or between the palms of your hands to crack the remaining shell and peel.

It is here I would like to tell you about the hard-cooked egg from my Sephardic background that graces our Passover (Seder) table. Whenever I describe the six-hour cooking process, I am titillated by the wide-eyed amazement that is certain to follow. Place a dozen or more eggs in a large saucepan with cold fresh water to cover. Add a cupful or so of loose onion skins (the peel you would ordinarily throw away), then float a doubled or tripled square of cheesecloth over everything. With cover ajar, bring slowly to the edge of a boil over moderate heat. Simmer, maintaining a lazy surface bubble, for about six hours. Watch the water level carefully. If it begins to fall below that of the eggs, add additional water to cover. When ready to eat, the shells and white of the egg will have turned a lovely shade of orangy-brown, the yolks, despite their lengthy cooking, are tender, and the flavor, for those of you lucky enough to remember it, is reminiscent of the unlaid egg found in a freshly killed chicken.

To Beat Egg Whites: Like anything else in life, one learns cooking from doing. Think of each time you beat egg whites as a learning experience. The various stages along the beaten path are extremely helpful in indicating just when "stiff, not dry" peaks form.

The whites can be beaten with an electric hand mixer, in the bowl of an electric mixer, or by whisk in a copper bowl. Whichever method you choose, the whites should be beaten with the utmost of care until stiff *but not dry* peaks form. Master the art of the perfectly beaten egg white and enjoy the security that goes with the skill. Egg whites are best separated when they are cold; however, to achieve maximum volume, they are best beaten at room temperature, but never too warm. Whenever I separate eggs, I start out with three bowls: a large, clean bowl to beat the whites in; a bowl to slip the yolks into; and a very small bowl, or even a dessert dish, to catch the whites initially. In this way, if a yolk should break into a white, you can use that egg for another purpose. Since even a trace of yolk in the whites inhibits their expansion while beating, using the three-bowl method when working with large numbers of eggs eliminates that risk.

The bowl in which egg whites are to be beaten must be absolutely clean. Use stainless, glass, or copper only, since plastic will absorb fats and aluminum will discolor the whites. I will add a pinch of salt or cream of tartar to the egg whites if using other than a copper bowl. A copper bowl, however, should be rinsed out with a little lemon juice before using and wiped clean.

When you whip, if cream of tartar or salt is called for, add it just at the point where the egg whites become foamy. This will help increase their volume. As you whisk, look for a smooth texture, and when you slowly lift out the beaters, egg whites will pull into peaks that gleam. Correctly beaten egg whites will stay firmly in the bowl and not slide. Overbeaten egg whites will break down and no longer be fluffy and shiny.

The amount of time to beat egg whites properly is dependent on many variables, such as temperature and size of egg whites, type of equipment used for beating, and the vessels they are beaten in. Here are a few specifics:

Beating egg whites in a copper bowl with a large balloon-shaped whisk that fits into the curve of the bowl will take anywhere from two to eight minutes depending upon how many whites are being beaten and whose strong arm is doing the beating.

In the bowl of an automatic mixer, at moderately low speed, beating egg whites could take approximately two to three minutes, again depending upon the number of whites being beaten. An automatic electric mixer is ideal and very practical to use, since you can be doing something else while the machine is working for you.

If you are using a portable hand mixer and beating egg whites in a mixing bowl, it could take about four to five minutes for them to reach the properly beaten stage.

The market and demand for utensils change so rapidly that it is hard to keep up. For instance, one can purchase a copper-bowl liner for the automatic mixer, which will speed up the beating time. Several small appliance manufacturers are now producing battery-operated whisks of various sizes and shapes which are also useful.

To illustrate in depth the versatility of eggs, the following pages include recipes for omelets, frittatas, quiches, crêpes, and savory soufflés. But before turning to specific recipes, I have included some general comments about the preparation of the most popular egg dishes.

Omelets: Escoffier said that omelets are a "scrambled egg enclosed in a coating of a coagulated egg." An omelet, as we know it, is a creamy, light wrapper frequently encasing a flavorful filling. In the preparation of omelets, the egg batter is poured into the foaming butter; the eggs are then quickly stirred back and forth with a fork to prevent sticking. It might be a good idea, therefore, to have a pan just for the purpose of doing omelets. A brand of nonstick surface, such as T-Fal, is highly recommended. The pan does not need any seasoning whatsoever. Aluminum would be acceptable to use also, but will not work as well as iron or T-Fal. Do not use stainless or other nonporous materials.

Frittatas: All my life my Mother would make a Spanish omelet. Until I went to Italy, I didn't realize it was a frittata. Frittata is a popular Italian egg dish always consisting of a good number (about six to eight) beaten eggs. Mixed into it might be anything from a cooked vegetable or combination of vegetables to leftover pasta. It cooks slowly on both sides and the results are a firm, pie-shaped egg dish, which is served hot or cold—and most often as an appetizer. Giuliano Bugialli introduced me to the delights of a frittata, using leftover fettuccine, and for that I am forever grateful. It will probably never happen that you have leftover Fettuccine Alla Panna, but if you should, chop it up, add it to some beaten eggs, and prepare a delicious frittata following techniques outlined in my Spinach Frittata.

Quiche: For many of us, quiche was our first introduction to French cooking. Originally it was a custard made with eggs and cream, and all the additions that followed were simply variations on a theme.

Although other dishes have come along to replace the quiche, it is still a practical and pleasing idea. But like all recipes, you should carefully consider your ingredients, looking only for the freshest, and rule out convenience pie crusts and inferior cheeses. Whenever I teach my Mushroom Quiche or Tomato Quiche they are enthusiastically received. I have decided to include them along with my other egg-based recipes to remind you of their delicious possibilities. And remember, one doesn't always have to include a pastry crust when preparing a quiche. See the delectable Crustless Leek Quiche for a different approach.

Crêpes: Crêpes are very thin pancakes made from a light batter poured sparingly into a pan and cooked briefly. They can be simple, just folded and sprinkled with confectioners' sugar, or grand, as in crêpes Suzette. Their fillings include everything from savory to sweet. Like the ubiquitous dumpling, crêpes appear in many ethnic kitchens and similar preparations result in blintzes, manicotti, and so forth, and yet our first introduction was most likely credited to French cuisine.

The equipment I prefer to use in the preparation of crêpes is the traditional iron skillet and not the electric crêpe-maker gadgets, which I think are nonsense. If you use them, you will come up with nothing more than dried-out crêpes with a border that resembles starched lace.

The best equipment in which to make crêpes is the iron pan from France which has been seasoned. To season, simply pour plain vegetable oil to a depth of ½ inch into the skillet. Place it over heat and allow to warm until a blue haze appears over the surface or the top of oil begins to ripple slightly. Never leave and go off to do something else while the oil is heating, as it may catch fire. The moment the oil is hot, remove pan from heat. Allow oil to cool just long enough to pour it off and reserve to repeat procedure. Now, pour salt completely over the lightly oiled surface and let salt sit in the pan for 1 hour or more. Wipe clean with paper toweling, discarding salt. I recommend that the entire procedure be repeated a second time before you prepare your first crêpe.

Soufflés: There are innumerable kinds of soufflés. There are savory soufflés made with purées of meat, fish, shellfish, and vegetables. Chicory, leek, sorrel, and even brain soufflés make up some of the more unusual. And, of course, there are sweet soufflés.

In the preparation of a soufflé, the main ingredient is usually combined with a base for a white sauce (a roux or a bouille). Egg yolks are added to the basic preparation, which can usually be made ahead and held in a warm-water bath at this point. The sauce is then carefully folded into stiffly beaten egg whites. Perhaps the most important aspect of soufflé preparation is the beating of the egg whites and the oven temperature. Follow instructions outlined above for beating egg whites and make certain your oven is calibrated correctly for all your baking procedures.

THE PLAIN BASIC OMELET

The noncook in the family can become a Sunday cook with this one.

2 eggs
1 tablespoon water
1 tablespoon unsalted butter
Coarse (kosher) salt
Freshly ground pepper

Dash of Tabasco sauce

Have on Hand
8-inch T-Fal or iron skillet

Serves 1

1. In a mixing bowl, beat eggs and water vigorously with a whisk just until they combine, being careful not to overbeat. As you lift whisk, mixture should fall in threads.

2. Heat a T-Fal or well-seasoned omelet pan over medium-high heat until hot, add butter, and swirl to coat bottom and sides. Remember that speed is of the essence when making omelets, since they take only a minute or two.

3. Pour eggs into hot pan and immediately stir with a fork in a circular motion, shaking pan back and forth with other hand to keep eggs loose.

4. As eggs begin to set, quickly push in sides with fork, tilting pan slightly to allow uncooked portion to run out to the edges. Control heat at all times. If necessary, remove pan from heat for the seconds it will take to adjust heat.

5. Tilt pan at a 20-degree angle and start to roll omelet away from handle to opposite edge of pan. Pause briefly to season and/or fill moist uncooked side with desired filling.

Tilting the pan to roll out an omelet

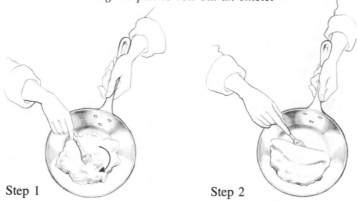

Step 1   Step 2

6. Now change position of pan so that your working hand can grip handle with palm up, making it easier to flip omelet over. Tilt pan at a 45-degree angle to roll omelet in one motion onto a warmed plate so that it folds over on itself, seam side down.

Note: When you become more proficient, you can double the recipe and serve 2 people. If feeding more than 2, this is a quick procedure and you can probably turn out several in a very short time. I don't recommend making more than a 4-egg omelet at one time.

Step 3

FINES HERBES FOR BASIC OMELET

1 tablespoon finely chopped
    Italian flat-leaf parsley
1 tablespoon fresh tarragon
    leaves *or* 1 teaspoon
    dried

2 teaspoons snipped chives
    or ½ teaspoon dried

Combine ingredients in a dish. Add to Basic Omelet.

PARMESAN AND FINES HERBES FOR BASIC OMELET

Use Fines Herbes filling with the addition of 1 tablespoon finely grated Parmesan cheese. Add to Basic Omelet.

SPINACH FRITTATA

1 pound loose fresh spinach,
    fibrous stems and
    blemished leaves
    removed
4 tablespoons olive oil
1 medium onion, finely
    chopped
1 clove garlic, peeled and
    halved
½ teaspoon coarse (kosher)
    salt
½ teaspoon freshly ground
    pepper
⅛ teaspoon freshly ground
    nutmeg

5 eggs
3 tablespoons grated
    Parmesan cheese
1 tablespoon fresh basil
    leaves *or* 1 teaspoon
    dried
2 teaspoons fresh thyme
    leaves *or* ½ teaspoon
    dried
1 tablespoon finely chopped
    Italian flat-leaf parsley

Have on Hand
10-inch T-Fal or iron skillet

Serves 6–8

1. Wash spinach in several changes of lukewarm water to clean leaves of dirt and sand. Dry well with paper toweling, then with scissors cut into ribbons.

2. Heat 3 tablespoons oil in a 10-inch skillet or omelet pan, add onion, and cook until tender but not brown. Add garlic with spinach to skillet and stir to mix. Allow to simmer over low heat about 20 minutes, stirring occasionally. Add salt, pepper and nutmeg and taste to adjust seasoning. Remove garlic and discard. Set aside.

3. In a mixing bowl whisk together eggs, cheese, and herbs.

4. Thoroughly drain liquid from spinach mixture and add to beaten eggs in bowl. Stir to mix until all ingredients are incorporated.

5. Add 1 tablespoon oil to skillet spinach cooked in and heat gently. When hot, pour in egg mixture.

6. As eggs are beginning to set, push them from edge of pan and tilt slightly, allowing some uncooked egg mixture to run to the edges. When eggs are set and frittata is well detached from bottom of pan, put a plate face down over pan. Holding plate firmly, reverse pan and turn out frittata.

7. Return pan to the heat. Carefully slide frittata into pan to cook other side. After 2 minutes, slide frittata onto a warm serving dish.

8. To serve, cut into wedges like a pie. Serve hot or cold.

To Prepare Ahead

Follow steps 1 through 7 up to one day ahead. Refrigerate, covered in plastic wrap. Bring to room temperature and complete step 8.

SUGGESTED FILLINGS FOR BASIC OMELET

PEPPER, TOMATO, AND MUSHROOM FILLING

2 red or green peppers
2 ripe tomatoes, peeled,
    seeded, shredded
2 tablespoons vegetable oil
1 tablespoon unsalted butter

½ pound fresh mushrooms,
    quickly rinsed clean,
    trimmed, and thinly
    sliced
¼ teaspoon coarse (kosher)
    salt
Freshly ground pepper

Yields 1½ cups

Preheat broiler to high.

1. Place peppers on a foil-lined cookie sheet and broil about 3–4 inches from source of heat until skin blisters and blackens. Turn peppers over as necessary to char evenly on all sides. It is difficult to tell how long it will take. When the peppers blacken, they themselves will tell you when they are ready to be turned. The aroma is that distinctive. Transfer to a paper bag, close bag securely, and let stand a minute or two to steam. Remove peppers one at a time and with tip of small paring knife, loosen charred skin. Remove and discard. Scrape out seeds, then slice peppers into ¼-inch-wide strips. Set aside.

2. Bring 2–3 cups water to a boil in a saucepan. Plunge tomatoes into boiling water 20–30 seconds. Remove with slotted spoon and fan to cool or cool under cold running water briefly. With the tip of a knife, remove skin, which will slip off easily. Cut in half crosswise, hold in palm of hand and squeeze gently to remove and discard seeds. Slice into ¼-inch shreds and set aside.

3. In a skillet, heat oil and butter. When butter foam subsides, add mushrooms and cook over moderately high heat, shaking pan back and forth several minutes until moisture evaporates. Add tomatoes and peppers and cook 3–4 minutes longer. Season to taste with salt and pepper.

Note: Can be prepared up to two days ahead, refrigerated in a suitable container, and used as filling for an omelet or in a frittata.

STUFFED EGGS BÉCHAMEL

10 hard-cooked eggs, peeled
    and cooled
2 teaspoons Dijon mustard
2 tablespoons unsalted
    butter, softened
4 ounces cream cheese,
    softened
½ teaspoon paprika

Béchamel Sauce
1⅓ cups milk
1 small onion, quartered
6 peppercorns
¼ teaspoon mace

1 bay leaf
2 tablespoons unsalted butter
2 tablespoons flour
½ teaspoon coarse (kosher)
    salt
Freshly ground pepper

Lots of curly parsley,
    washed and spin-dried,
    for garnish

Have on Hand
Pastry bag with small star
    tip

Serves 10 or more

1. With a sharp knife cut eggs firmly in half lengthwise and scoop out yolks into a mixing bowl. With a fork, mash yolks very well to make certain they are free of lumps before combining with additional ingredients. Add mustard, butter, cream cheese, and paprika. Stir to mix until ingredients are thoroughly combined and set aside.

2. *Béchamel Sauce:* In a saucepan heat milk with onion, peppercorns, mace, and bay leaf. Bring to the edge of a boil and remove from heat. Strain into a small bowl.

3. In a heavy saucepan, melt 2 tablespoons of butter over moderate heat. Add flour all at once and stir to mix. Simmer for 2 minutes, stirring occasionally. Remove saucepan from heat and gradually add hot milk, whisking constantly to prevent lumps from forming. Return pan to moderate heat and stir gently until mixture comes to the edge of a boil and thickens. Season with salt and pepper. Reduce heat to a simmer and cook 8–10 minutes, stirring occasionally, until the sauce is smooth and thick and cooked through. Taste to adjust seasonings if necessary. Allow to cool a bit, then combine with the yolk mixture and stir to mix until thoroughly blended.

4. Fit a large decorating bag with a small star tip and fold the bag over to make a collar. Place in a tall glass or jar to support it and fill with Béchamel mixture. Pipe rosettes into egg halves by resting bag in one hand and exerting some pressure with working hand. Starting at outside edge, follow outline of egg and make concentric circles until you finish in center. Arrange on a platter of curly parsley.

To Prepare Ahead

Follow steps 1 through 4 up to one day ahead. Refrigerate eggs one layer deep on a platter covered with a tent of plastic wrap. Store parsley in a separate container to keep crisp. Arrange eggs on the parsley-lined platter and serve at room temperature.

GIULIANO BUGIALLI'S FRITTATA OF GREEN TOMATOES

With Giuliano Bugialli's permission, I have reprinted from his book The Fine Art of Italian Cooking *this wonderful frittata with a minor change: I substituted wheat germ for the flour—not that I'm such a health nut, but it gives a nice crispy texture to the tomatoes and a measure of good health.*

4 large or 6 medium green
    tomatoes
½ cup plus 1 tablespoon
    olive oil
1 cup wheat germ
Salt and freshly ground
    pepper
6 eggs

Have on Hand
10-inch T-Fal or other
    seasoned nonstick
    skillet

Serves 6

1. Wash tomatoes very well and cut into ½-inch slices.

2. Heat the ½ cup oil in a frying pan. (Do not use more, as tomato slices should not be completely covered.) While oil is heating, "flour" tomato slices with wheat germ.

3. When oil begins to sizzle, place only as many tomato slices in pan as will make a single layer. Sauté until golden brown on both sides, then transfer to paper toweling to drain; sprinkle with salt and pepper. Fry remaining tomato slices the same way.

4. Beat eggs very lightly with a pinch of salt and set aside.

5. Heat the 1 tablespoon of olive oil in an omelet pan. When it is hot, add tomato slices to pan. (The slices are reduced in size from having been sautéed, so they should all fit in one layer.) Pour eggs over tomato slices. When eggs are well set and frittata is well detached from the bottom of pan, place a plate face down over pan. Holding plate firmly,

reverse pan and turn out frittata. Return pan to flame. Carefully slide frittata into pan to cook other side. After 1 minute, reverse frittata onto a serving dish. It may be served either hot or at room temperature.

A MANY-LAYERED SPINACH AND MUSHROOM CRÊPE

A different twist to serving crêpes.

14–16 prepared crêpes

Vegetable Filling
1 pound loose fresh spinach,
    fibrous stems and
    blemished leaves
    removed
¾ pound fresh mushrooms,
    rinsed clean, trimmed,
    and thinly sliced
2 tablespoons unsalted butter
Coarse (kosher) salt
Freshly ground pepper

Mornay Sauce
3 tablespoons unsalted butter
2 tablespoons flour
2 cups milk
½ to ¾ coarse (kosher) salt
Freshly ground pepper
¾–1 teaspoon dry mustard
1 cup grated Swiss Gruyère
    cheese

Have on Hand
Round heatproof platter

Serves 8–10

Preheat oven to 350 degrees.

1. Wash spinach carefully in several changes of lukewarm water to clean leaves of dirt and sand. Transfer spinach to a large heavy saucepan with about ½ inch salted water. Cover tightly and cook 3–4 minutes, stirring occasionally, until tender. Drain and refresh by fanning* and briefly running under cold water to stop the cooking. With your hands, squeeze spinach to remove moisture, then place in a clean kitchen towel and squeeze very dry. Place on a wooden board and chop coarsely. Transfer to a small bowl and set aside.

2. Trim mushroom stems and discard stem ends. To clean mushrooms place in a colander; then, with fingertips, quickly toss under a spray of cold running water. Gather up mushrooms in a clean kitchen towel and pat gently to get rid of excess moisture. Cut into thin slices, then sauté in melted butter over moderate heat about 2–3 minutes until just tender.

Season with a light sprinkle of salt and freshly ground pepper. Place in a dish and set aside.

3. In a heavy saucepan, melt butter over moderate heat, then add flour and stir constantly for about 2 minutes. Meanwhile, in another saucepan, bring milk to the edge of a boil. Off heat, gradually add hot milk to the butter-flour mixture, whisking constantly until sauce is smooth. When approximately half of liquid has been added, return saucepan to moderate heat and whisk in remaining milk, whisking until mixture comes to a boil. Add salt, pepper, mustard, and cheese, and stir to mix. Simmer over low heat, stirring occasionally, 10–12 minutes until cheese melts and sauce is bubbly and thick. Taste to adjust seasoning if necessary.

4. Stir 3–4 tablespoons sauce into the 2 vegetables separately. Can be done ahead to this point. If doing ahead, cover surface of Béchamel with a square of buttered parchment to prevent a skin from forming.

5. Lightly butter a heatproof serving dish to assemble crêpes. Place one crêpe on bottom of buttered dish. With a large kitchen spoon spread 2–3 tablespoons of each vegetable mixture alternately between the crêpes until all the filling and crêpes are used. Top with a crêpe and cover with a sheet of buttered parchment. Set aside.

6. Just before ready to serve, place dish containing layered crêpes in a preheated oven and bake for 15 minutes. When hot, spoon warm sauce on top crêpe crisscross fashion, allowing it to fall to rim of dish. Spoon additional sauce around base of crêpes and serve immediately. Cut into wedges for serving.

To Prepare Ahead

Follow steps 1 through 4 up to one day before. Store cooked vegetables and sauce separately in suitable containers and refrigerate. Bring vegetables and sauce to room temperature. Follow step 5 up to several hours ahead. Just before ready to serve, reheat sauce and complete step 6.

Note: If sauce is refrigerated for advance preparation, it will probably become quite thick. To thin, transfer to a small saucepan with a rubber spatula. Stir in just enough milk to loosen to a pouring consistency, then warm through just before serving, stirring occasionally.

THE TERRINE OF THREE CUSTARDS
(A pâté of tomatoes, spinach, and cheese)

In 1977 on my first trip to Roger Verge's Moulin de Mougins, this magical, delicate vegetable terrine appeared. Knowing there wasn't any gelatin used, I asked M. Verge how the layers stayed intact. He simply answered, "It works!" Well, it does, and it is work, but I compare it with doing a gelatin mold and waiting for each layer to set. The difference in this case is that this sets in the oven rather than in the fridge.

4 tablespoons light olive oil or peanut oil

2 shallots, finely chopped

2 pounds ripe tomatoes *or* 1 can (1 pound, 12 ounces) whole tomatoes, drained, seeded, and chopped

1 tablespoon tomato paste

½ teaspoon coarse (kosher) salt

1 teaspoon fresh thyme leaves *or* ¼ teaspoon dried

2 teaspoons fresh basil leaves coarsely chopped *or* ½ teaspoon dried

6 whole eggs

2 egg yolks

1 cup Crème Fraîche

½ cup grated Parmesan cheese

1½ pounds loose fresh spinach, fibrous stems and blemished leaves removed

1 large clove garlic, peeled

⅛ teaspoon freshly ground nutmeg

½ cup grated Swiss Gruyère cheese

Freshly ground pepper

Sprigs of curly parsley for garnish

Have on Hand

3 mixing bowls

1-quart loaf terrine, lightly buttered

Bain-marie*

Serves 10–12

1. Heat 2 tablespoons olive or peanut oil in a skillet. Add shallots and sauté quickly, being careful not to brown. Add tomatoes, tomato paste, ¼ teaspoon of the salt, thyme, and basil. Simmer slowly over low heat, stirring occasionally, 10–12 minutes until moisture has evaporated. To absorb any excess moisture, transfer mixture to a sieve lined with paper toweling and let drip, but do not push mixture through. Allow to cool, transfer to a mixing bowl, and combine with 2 beaten eggs and

1 egg yolk, ¼ cup of the crème fraîche and ¼ cup Parmesan cheese. Stir to mix. Taste to adjust seasoning if necessary.

2. Pour tomato mixture into prepared loaf pan. Place terrine in a shallow baking pan with enough hot water to come ⅔ of way up sides of mold (bain-marie). Bake in preheated oven 25–30 minutes, until a knife inserted in center comes out clean. Remove from oven. Leave water-filled bain-marie in oven to keep hot.

3. Wash spinach in several changes of lukewarm water to clean leaves of dirt and sand. Place in a covered saucepan with about ½ inch of water. Bring to a boil, add a bit of the salt, and simmer, covered, 3–4 minutes, stirring occasionally. Drain and fan* to cool or refresh quickly under cold running water. Squeeze out moisture with hands until almost dry, then chop coarsely.

4. In a clean skillet, heat remaining 2 tablespoons oil with garlic for about a minute. Add chopped spinach, season with remaining ¼ teaspoon salt and nutmeg, and cook, stirring with a wooden spoon, until moisture is completely evaporated. Remove garlic and discard. Transfer to a mixing bowl and when cool, add 1 beaten egg, 1 egg yolk, ¼ cup crème fraîche, and remaining ¼ cup cheese. Stir to mix. Taste to adjust seasoning and set aside.

5. In another mixing bowl, combine remaining 3 eggs and beat with ½ cup crème fraîche, ½ cup grated Gruyère cheese, and a slight sprinkling of salt and pepper. Taste to adjust seasoning if necessary.

6. Pour egg-cheese mixture over firm tomato layer in terrine, place in bain-marie, and bake 15–20 minutes until set or until a knife inserted in the center comes out clean. Remove from oven and allow to cool. Let water-filled bain-marie remain in oven to stay hot. Add more hot water to bain-marie if necessary.

7. Finally, pour in spinach mixture over previously set layers and return to bain-marie. Bake 20–25 minutes longer or until completely firm. Remove from oven and allow to cool completely. Cover and refrigerate up to 1 week before unmolding.

8. *To Unmold:* Loosen sides by drawing an ordinary kitchen knife between terrine and inside of pan. Place a serving platter over the top of mold and invert. Garnish with sprigs of curly parsley and cut into slices for serving.

To Prepare Ahead
Follow steps 1 through 7 up to one week ahead. Refrigerate, covered. Follow step 8 before serving.

POACHED EGGS PROVENÇAL

The poached eggs are bedded down on a simple tomato sauce and topped with a light sprinkle of grated cheese. It's simple to prepare and colorful to present for brunch or a light supper.

2 tablespoons white vinegar
6 eggs
1 tablespoon olive oil
1 large clove garlic, finely
  chopped
5–6 plum tomatoes, peeled,
  seeded, and shredded
½ teaspoon coarse (kosher)
  salt
Freshly ground pepper
Dash cayenne
1 tablespoon fresh basil
  leaves, finely chopped,
  or ¼ teaspoon dried

¾ teaspoon fresh thyme
  leaves *or* ¼ teaspoon
  dried
5–6 tablespoons grated
  Swiss Gruyère cheese

Have on Hand
Gratin or porcelain quiche
  dish, lightly buttered

Serves 6

Preheat oven to 350 degrees.

1. *To Soft-Poach Eggs:* Bring 2–3 cups of water to a rapid boil. Add vinegar. Poach only 2–3 eggs at one time and have them ready in small individual dishes so they may be added to water at approximately the same time. When water is boiling rapidly, slip in eggs while rotating surface of the water with the back of a large kitchen spoon to help draw whites around yolk. Remove pan from heat and count to 30. With a slotted spoon, flip to roll eggs over one at a time. Let stand in water about 2 minutes longer. Remove with slotted spoon and drain on paper toweling. Repeat procedure with remaining eggs.

2. Place oil in saucepan over moderate heat. Add garlic and cook quickly being careful not to burn. Add tomatoes, salt, pepper, cayenne, and herbs, and stir to mix. Simmer only 4–5 minutes to retain the texture of tomatoes. Taste to adjust seasoning if necessary.

3. Transfer tomatoes to prepared dish and spread to edges in a thin layer. Arrange poached eggs in a single layer over tomato mixture. Season eggs lightly with a little salt, pepper, and cayenne, and sprinkle grated cheese over top. Can be made ahead to this point.

4. Place in preheated oven and bake 10–12 minutes until cheese melts. Serve hot.

To Prepare Ahead
Follow steps 1 through 3 up to one day ahead. Refrigerate, covered with plastic wrap. Bring to room temperature and complete step 4 just before serving.

CRÊPES
(Multipurpose crêpes)

1 cup all-purpose flour
2 eggs, lightly beaten
½ cup milk
1 cup water
½ teaspoon coarse (kosher)
　　salt

1 tablespoon oil
1 teaspoon unsalted butter

Have on Hand
Seasoned 7-inch iron slope-
　　sided crêpe pan

Yields 16–18 crêpes

1. *Hand Method:* Sift flour into a mixing bowl and make a well in center. Pour in beaten eggs, milk, water, salt, and oil. With a fork or a whisk, gradually incorporate flour from inner wall into combined liquids just until you have a smooth, creamy batter. Cover bowl and let rest 1 hour or more, which will help batter spread more evenly when cooked. Whisk for a few seconds before proceeding.

Processor/Blender Method: Combine all ingredients except butter in workbowl of processor or blender (it isn't necessary to sift flour) and process or blend to mix. With a rubber spatula, scrape down pasty bits of flour that have stuck to sides of the workbowl or blender. Let crêpe batter rest in container for 1 hour or so, then process or blend a few seconds before proceeding. Batter should be consistency of heavy cream. If it thickens on standing, whisk or blend in a teaspoon or so of water.

2. Place skillet over moderate heat for a few seconds, then add butter. Tilt and rotate pan over heat to coat bottom with melted butter. Pour off any excess butter into batter and stir it in.

3. Return pan to heat. When butter sizzles, you can begin to cook crêpes. Ladle about 3 tablespoons of batter into pan and quickly rotate the pan until batter coats bottom before it sets.

4. Cook each crêpe until very lightly browned and edges are bubbly. Carefully slide a metal spatula under the crêpe and flip it over. Cook about 10–20 seconds longer or until light brown spots appear on underside. This "second" side is less attractive than the first, which I refer to as the lacy side. Transfer crêpes as they are done to a platter, slightly overlapping and lacy-side up until they cool completely.

5. If not using immediately, stack crêpes with a square of wax paper between each one, beginning and ending with wax paper. Then wrap entire stack in aluminum foil to securely cover and freeze. Or cover with plastic wrap and refrigerate overnight. Use as directed in recipes.

To Prepare Ahead
Follow steps 1 through 4 up to one day ahead and refrigerate, or up to one month ahead and freeze.

CRUSTLESS LEEK QUICHE

Dry toasted Bread Crumbs
4–8 leeks, about 1 pound
3 tablespoons unsalted butter
½ teaspoon coarse (kosher) salt
Freshly ground pepper
2 ounces cream cheese, softened
½ cup Crème Fraîche
½ cup heavy cream
2 whole eggs plus 1 egg yolk

2 tablespoons finely chopped Italian flat-leaf parsley
5–6 tablespoons finely grated Parmesan cheese
2 ripe tomatoes, peeled, seeded, and shredded *or* 1 cup canned whole tomatoes, drained

Have on Hand
10- or 11-inch porcelain quiche or gratin dish

Serves 6–8

Preheat oven to 350 degrees.
1. Prepare a well-buttered quiche or gratin baking dish with enough bread crumbs to coat completely.

2. Trim off root end of each leek. Remove any outer soft bruised layers and discard. Cut off and discard tough green leaves (good for the stockpot) at top of still tender light green portion just above whites. Holding the bottom, insert a paring knife into center and lift it right up through top. Then, holding top together, cut down to split leek in two. To clean, fan leek halves one at a time under cold running water until all the sand is removed, then reform layers. Place halves in a basin of cold water and allow to soak 10–15 minutes. Transfer to a clean kitchen towel and pat dry so that all moisture is absorbed. Stack 2 or 3 halves on a cutting board and cut into ¼-inch slices or slice in workbowl of food processor fitted with slicing blade, using full pressure. Set aside.

3. Melt butter in a heavy skillet and, when foam subsides, add leeks. Cook slowly and carefully over low heat about 20–25 minutes, stirring occasionally with a wooden spatula, scraping down sides of pan to cook leeks evenly.

4. Combine cream cheese, crème fraîche, heavy cream, whole eggs and yolk, parsley, and Parmesan cheese in a mixing bowl or in workbowl of food processor fitted with steel knife and stir or process to mix. Add leeks and tomatoes and fold through mixture to distribute evenly. Taste to adjust seasoning if necessary.

5. Pour leek mixture into the prepared baking dish, scraping the bowl clean, then level with a rubber spatula. Bake in a preheated oven 35–40 minutes until top is lightly browned or until knife inserted in center comes out clean. Slice into wedges as you would a quiche and serve warm.

To Prepare Ahead
Follow steps 1 through 4 up to one day before and refrigerate, covered. Bring to room temperature and complete step 5 just before serving.

PETITE ZUCCHINI SOUFFLÉS WITH SAUCE AURORE

I have taught these individual soufflés many times and always to the delight of my students. One student decided to prepare them for a party to which I was invited. The surprise was that there were more than eighty people at this party and she prepared at least two soufflés for everyone. Yes . . . they can not only be made ahead but frozen ahead. They are most successfully made in little individual aspic molds found in specialty kitchenware shops.

1 pound small firm zucchini
Coarse (kosher) salt
5 tablespoons butter
3 tablespoons flour
1 cup hot milk
1½ teaspoons coarse
   (kosher) salt
Freshly ground pepper
3 egg yolks
¾ cup grated Swiss Gruyère
   cheese
4 egg whites

Sauce Aurore
1 cup heavy cream
1 cup Basic Tomato Sauce

Have on Hand
12 well-buttered aspic molds
   or 8–10 3-ounce-
   capacity ramekins
Bain-marie*
11-inch fluted porcelain
   quiche baking dish or
   other gratin dish

Makes up to 12 3-ounce soufflés

Preheat over to 375 degrees.

1. Scrub zucchini clean; trim and discard ends. Shred on a hand grater or in workbowl of food processor fitted with shredding blade. If using processor, cut zucchini in lengths to fit the feed tube horizontally and process with light pressure to shred. Spread in a colander, sprinkle lightly with salt, and let stand 20 minutes or so.

2. When moisture has exuded, rinse zucchini under cold running water. Transfer to a clean kitchen towel and squeeze very dry.

3. In a heavy skillet melt 2 tablespoons of the butter and sauté zucchini, stirring occasionally, over moderately low heat 10–12 minutes until all moisture has evaporated and zucchini lightly colored.

4. *Prepare Béchamel:* In a heavy saucepan, melt the remaining 3 tablespoons butter over moderate heat, then add flour and stir constantly about 2 minutes. Meanwhile, in another saucepan, bring milk to the edge of a boil. Off heat, gradually add milk to butter-flour mixture. When approximately half the liquid has been added, return saucepan to moderate heat and whisk in remaining milk, stirring, until mixture reaches

the edge of a boil. Season with salt and pepper and stir to mix. Reduce heat and allow to simmer over low heat whisking the sauce occasionally about 10–12 minutes. Remove from heat and stir to cool slightly. Add egg yolks one at a time and stir to incorporate. Add prepared zucchini and ½ cup of the grated cheese and stir to mix.

5. In bowl of electric mixer or in a mixing bowl with portable beaters, whip egg whites at low speed until foamy. Add a pinch of salt, adjust speed to medium high, and continue beating until firm but not dry peaks form. With a large rubber spatula gently mix ¼ of the beaten egg whites into soufflé base to soften, then carefully fold in remaining whites.

6. Spoon the mixture into prepared molds, filling them about ¾ full. Transfer molds to a shallow baking pan and cover with a sheet of wax paper. Pour boiling water into pan to about ⅔ up sides of molds. Place pan in preheated oven and bake 20–25 minutes. Remove the well-puffed soufflés from oven and let stand in water bath 5 minutes or so. They will deflate on standing but will puff up again when returned to the oven later. Remove from water bath and when cool enough to handle invert the soufflés into a prepared dish.

7. Butter a porcelain quiche or gratin dish and spoon 2–3 tablespoons sauce Aurore in bottom of dish. Insert a kitchen knife around the edge of the molds; then place them on an angle, side by side in a circle around dish. Spoon remaining sauce over soufflés and sprinkle with remaining ¼ cup cheese. Can be prepared up to several hours ahead to this point. Refrigerate, covered with a light tent of plastic wrap, then bring to room temperature before returning to oven.
Preheat oven to 350 degrees.

8. Just before ready to serve, return soufflés to preheated oven and bake 20 minutes until they puff and swell and cheese is lightly colored and bubbly. Serve immediately.

To Prepare Ahead
Follow steps 1 through 6 up to one day ahead. Remove from molds and place in a shallow baking dish lightly covered with plastic wrap and refrigerate. Or flash-freeze after completing step 6. After the soufflés have baked the first time, cool and unmold. Place on a cookie sheet in one layer and freeze. When frozen solid, transfer to a covered freezer-going container such as Tupperware or securely wrapped food storage bags and return to freezer for up to one month. If refrigerated, bring to room temperature and complete steps 7 and 8. If soufflés are frozen, prepare the buttered baking dish with sauce Aurore, place frozen soufflés in dish, and top with remaining sauce and cheese. Put into a preheated

375-degree oven and bake 30–35 minutes until well puffed and thoroughly heated. Serve immediately.

Sauce Aurore

1. Place heavy cream in a small saucepan and cook over moderate heat until reduced by half. Adjust heat and watch carefully so that the cream does not boil over. Reduce heat to a simmer.

2. Add Basic Tomato Sauce, stir to mix, and keep warm over low heat until ready to serve.

To Prepare Ahead

Follow steps 1 and 2 up to two days ahead. Refrigerate, covered, in a suitable container. Bring to room temperature, add tomato sauce, and heat through before serving.

POACHED EGGS IN CHEESE SOUFFLÉ

Imagine your guests discovering the surprise of poached eggs enclosed in a light soufflé.

2 tablespoons white vinegar
3 eggs

Béchamel Sauce
2 tablespoons unsalted butter
1 scant tablespoon flour
1 cup milk, scalded
¼–½ teaspoon coarse
    (kosher) salt
Freshly ground pepper
Dash cayenne
4 egg yolks

1 cup plus 1 tablespoon
    grated Swiss Gruyère
    cheese
5 egg whites
¼ teaspoon cream of tartar

Have on Hand
1-quart soufflé dish, buttered
    and lightly sprinkled
    with additional grated
    Gruyère

Serves 6

Preheat oven to 450 degrees.

1. *To Soft-Poach Eggs:* Bring 2–3 cups of water to a rapid boil. Add vinegar. Have eggs ready in small individual dishes so they may be

added to water at approximately the same time. When water is boiling rapidly, slip in eggs while rotating surface of the water with the back of a large kitchen spoon, to help draw whites around yolk. Remove pan from heat and count to 30. With a slotted spoon, flip eggs over one at a time. Let stand in water about 2 minutes longer. Remove with slotted spoon and drain on paper toweling.

2. *Prepare Béchamel Sauce:* In a small heavy saucepan, melt butter, add flour, and stir to mix. Simmer mixture over low heat about 1–2 minutes. Remove pan from heat, gradually add hot milk, whisking constantly to prevent lumps from forming. Return pan to moderate heat and stir gently until mixture comes to the edge of a boil and thickens. Season with salt, pepper, and cayenne. Reduce heat to a simmer and cook 8–10 minutes, stirring occasionally, until the sauce is smooth and cooked through. Remove from heat.

3. Stir egg yolks into sauce one at a time, then add 1 cup of the cheese and stir to mix. Transfer to a bowl large enough to receive the beaten egg whites.

4. In bowl of automatic mixer or in a mixing bowl, beat egg whites at slow speed until foamy. Add cream of tartar, adjust to higher speed, and beat until firm but not dry peaks form. Gently mix ¼ of beaten egg whites into soufflé base to soften. Then carefully fold remaining whites into mixture. Transfer half of mixture into prepared soufflé dish. Arrange poached eggs in a single layer, then add remaining soufflé mixture. Smooth top and sprinkle on remaining tablespoon grated cheese. With tip of spatula, draw a circle about 1 inch from outer edge of soufflé dish.

5. Put into preheated oven and bake 10 minutes. Reduce oven temperature to 375 degrees and bake 10–12 minutes longer until well puffed and nicely browned. Serve immediately.

To Prepare Ahead
Follow steps 1 through 3 up to two hours ahead and let stand, covered, at room temperature. Complete steps 4 and 5 just before serving.

BANANA AND APRICOT
DESSERT CRÊPES

Within a few days of my opening Cooktique in 1976, an attractive Israeli woman came into the store to sign up for cooking classes. She loved to bake and was anxious to improve her knowledge of cooking and cooking skills. Yocheved Hirsch had been a nursery school teacher for twelve years and so the art of teaching was natural to her. Several years later she joined the teaching staff at Cooktique. She has been popular among her students who love her easy manner and simplification of recipes. Below is a version of her delicious banana crêpes.

16 prepared Crêpes

Fruit Filling
⅓ cup apricot preserves
2 tablespoons dark rum
4 large ripe bananas
2 teaspoons lemon juice
2–3 tablespoons softened
    butter

2 tablespoons sugar
Sour cream or Crème
    Fraîche (optional)

Have on Hand
13 × 9-inch Pyrex, lasagna,
    or other nonmetallic
    baking dish

Serves 8

Preheat oven to 350 degrees. Butter baking dish and set aside.

1. In a small bowl, combine apricot preserves and rum and stir to mix until smooth.

2. Peel bananas and cut them in half lengthwise through the inside curve so they lie flat. Slice each lengthwise cut in half so that you have 16 pieces. Sprinkle on lemon juice to prevent them from darkening.

3. Place crêpes lacy side down on wax paper. Spread a thin layer of apricot mixture evenly on each crêpe. Place banana cut side down on the lower third of each crêpe and roll up.

4. Arrange crêpes seam side down and close together in the baking dish. Dot with softened butter and sprinkle to coat with the sugar.

5. Place in preheated oven and bake 10 minutes, until golden. Serve warm, topped with a dollop of sour cream or crème fraîche if desired.

To Prepare Ahead
Follow steps 1 through 4 up to several hours ahead. Cover and let stand at room temperature. Complete step 5 just before serving.

9

PASTRIES, SAVORY AND SWEET

If there is one food preparation that benefits from repeated hands-on experience, it is the preparation of pastry. I have approached this chapter, which covers puff and pie pastry, pâte à choux, and phyllo dough, with the same care and thoroughness that I use with my students in the cooking school. I encourage you, too, to learn by doing and to feel in your fingertips your growing skills.

WORKING WITH PÂTE BRISÉE

Pâte brisée is a light, short pastry with a crisp crust when baked. It is easily made and is similar to pie crust, but the dough is richer. Prepare one or two batches ahead and refrigerate or freeze. Half of the following recipe will be enough for a 9-, 10-, or 11-inch tart or quiche pan. If you are planning to bake one quiche or tart, it would be practical to prepare the full recipe, use half, and freeze the remaining portion. It will be waiting whenever you are ready for another quiche or tart. Most fillings are simple to do and so with step 1 behind you, you're ahead of the game.

Preparing the dough in the processor is a quick and easy procedure. If you own one, you probably will never make pâte brisée any other way. I suggest that you first work the dough by hand until you feel comfortable with it and understand exactly what its texture looks and feels like at the different stages of development. When I prepare a quiche, I work with the salt and sugar quantities as listed below. However, when I prepare a fruit or dessert tart, I simply reverse the salt and sugar quantities, i.e., a pinch of salt and ½ teaspoon sugar.

BASIC PÂTE BRISÉE

2 cups all-purpose flour
½ teaspoon coarse (kosher)
    salt
Pinch sugar
8 tablespoons cold unsalted
    butter

3 tablespoons cold
    shortening
6 tablespoons ice water

Hand Method: In a mixing bowl combine flour, salt, and sugar. Cut butter into flour, then add shortening. With tips of fingers, two knives, or a pastry blender, blend flour and fat until mixture is a coarse meal. I prefer to work pastry by hand, lifting fat and flour with fingertips working swiftly to crumble mixture. This method aerates dough. Add ice water 1 tablespoon at a time, and gently work pastry and water with your hands, or stir with a fork, until you have a rough ball of dough. This rough mass should be moist but not wet. If, on the other hand, it is dry and crumbly, add water by droplets. Quickly work this into dough, being careful not to make it wet, which will cause shrinkage in baking. If dough is wet and you must work more flour into it, do so gently, since overworking will toughen pastry. Form a rough ball of dough by gathering the buttery particles in one hand, then transfer to a lightly floured work surface.

Fraisage (A blending of fat and flour with the heel of your hand): With the heel of your hand, gently push dough across work area. Cup your hands, gather dough and position it in front of you, then push it away from you one more time. This method, called fraisage, is the final blending of the fat and flour. Gather dough once again in cupped hands and gently form into shape of a large hamburger patty, flattening top a bit. With a knife, cut a crisscross on top of dough, which will relax it, making it easier to roll out. Cover with wax paper and chill 30 minutes to 1 hour before rolling out.

Food Processor Method: Fit workbowl of food processor with steel knife. Place flour, salt, and sugar in bowl, cover, and process with 2 quick on/off pulses just to mix. Remove cover and cut cold butter and shortening directly into bowl. Cover and process until mixture has consistency of tiny pebbles or coarse meal. If tiny lumps of butter are visible, this is fine. Stop the machine, measure ice water directly into a 1-cup liquid measure. Start machine and carefully pour liquid through feed tube in a steady stream. The moment the last drop is in, stop the machine even though ingredients in no way resemble a ball of dough. (Many food processor recipes will instruct you to "process until a ball of dough is formed." If a ball of dough is formed, your pastry will be tough.) Remove cover and steel knife and set aside. Empty contents of workbowl onto a lightly floured surface. If any dough sticks to the steel knife, slide it off carefully and add to mass of dough. Continue fraisage as above.

To Roll Dough and Fit a Baking Form: Use a removable bottom metal quiche pan, a flan ring (a metal ring placed directly on a cookie sheet), or a pie plate. If dough has had a sufficient rest in the refrigerator, it will be firm when you remove it. Place on a lightly floured surface, then with a rolling pin tap it gently before you start to roll. Roll to about ⅛ inch thickness. Roll from center out, then from the center in toward edge nearest you, turning dough as necessary to retain a fairly even round. Work quickly with light, even pressure. There is no need to exert a great deal of pressure when rolling, as this should be a gentle process.

Place rolling pin near top edge of dough at the point farthest from you. Lift edge of pastry over pin and roll pastry toward you to about center of circle. When you lift pin, half the pastry will be dangling from it. Carefully lower pastry into pan. If you are using a fluted quiche pan, be aware that it has sharp edges and can cut the pastry like a knife, so be extra cautious when lowering into a metal quiche pan. Slowly unroll pastry on pin away from you, allowing dough to "drape" into pan, which gives you some leverage when fitting dough inside the form. To guard against poking holes in pastry, press lower inside rim with the side of an index finger. There will probably be an uneven excess of pastry hanging over edge of pan. With a sharp knife, cut away enough dough to allow about a ½-inch overhang. With thumb and index finger, gently press dough against rim of pan to secure it, or press dough upward above rim to create a double thickness, which can be fluted with a pastry crimper, a fork, or your fingers. With the flat underside tines of a fork, prick bottom of shell, being careful not to make holes through pastry.

How to lift rolled dough onto a pin and fit into a baking pan

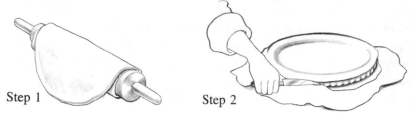

Step 1   Step 2

Bake Blind: To bake blind is to prebake a pastry shell without filling. Line the inside of unbaked dough with foil or parchment and weight down with metal weights or dried beans. This will prevent it from puffing up. Before baking any pastry, it is essential to preheat your oven to the specified temperature. The initial burst of heat sets pastry and controls length of cooking time. Preheat oven to 375 degrees, place weighted pastry shell on a cookie sheet, and bake 10–12 minutes. Remove from oven, carefully lift up foil containing weights, and set aside to cool for future use. Return pastry to oven 2–3 minutes to dry out bottom crust. Proceed with recipe.

PÂTE FROMAGE

I recall falling in love with this unusual cheese pâte in Paris when my talented and dear friend Gracieuse Rive-Georges prepared it for me. It is actually a quiche made with Boursault instead of cream.

½ recipe Basic Pâte Brisée
4 eggs, beaten
¼ pound Roquefort cheese,
    crumbled
1 package (5 ounces)
    Boursault cheese
¼ pound Swiss Gruyère
    cheese, grated
¼ teaspoon coarse (kosher)
    salt or less, according
    to cheeses

Freshly ground pepper

Have on Hand
1-quart Pyrex casserole
Egg glaze: 1 yolk beaten
    with 1 tablespoon
    water
Pastry brush

Serves 8–10

Preheat oven to 375 degrees.

1. Divide pâte brisée in half; roll half of it out on a lightly floured surface and fit into a 1-quart Pyrex casserole or 9-inch pie plate, allowing extra pastry to hang over sides. Lightly prick bottom of shell and set aside.

2. To beaten eggs in mixing bowl add Roquefort and mash in Boursault. Add grated cheese, season with salt and pepper, and stir to mix. Taste to adjust seasoning if necessary. Pour into uncooked pastry shell, scraping out all of mixture with a rubber spatula.

3. Roll out remaining half of dough and place over filling. Seal edges of pastry together around bowl. With a paring knife, trim excess pastry, leaving approximately a ¾-inch overhang. Crimp pastry neatly by scalloping or pinching edges.

4. *To Decorate Top Crust:* Chill remaining scraps of pastry until firm, then roll out. With a paring knife cut out several small leaf shapes. Score surface of leaves with dull side of knife and arrange decoratively in a cluster on top of pastry. Brush with egg glaze to cover completely, then bake in preheated oven 45–50 minutes or until puffed and golden.

5. If baked in casserole, run an ordinary kitchen knife between pastry and baking dish to loosen. Tilt, then gently slip the pie onto a heated platter. Can be done ahead to this point. Serve warm and slice into wedges like a pie.

To Prepare Ahead
Follow steps 1 through 4 early in the day. Let stand at room temperature, then heat through in a preheated 350-degree oven about 15 minutes and complete step 5 before serving.

MUSHROOM QUICHE

½ Basic Pâte Brisée recipe
1 tablespoon Dijon mustard
2½ tablespoons unsalted
    butter
3 scallions, trimmed and
    finely sliced, white and
    light green part only
½ pound fresh mushrooms,
    quickly rinsed clean,
    trimmed, and thinly
    sliced
1 cup heavy cream
¾ teaspoon coarse (kosher)
    salt

½ cup grated Swiss Gruyère
    cheese
2 eggs
Freshly ground pepper
Pinch freshly ground nutmeg
¼ cup grated Parmesan
    cheese

Have on Hand
9-inch fluted quiche pan
    with removable
    bottom,
    or pie plate

Serves 6–8

Preheat oven to 375 degrees.

1. See basic pâte brisée and prepare as specified, fitting the pastry into a 9-inch quiche pan or pie plate, then bake blind. When pastry cools, with a teaspoon spread mustard over bottom of partially baked shell and set aside.

2. In a skillet melt butter and, when foam subsides, sauté scallions gently for 2 minutes. Add mushrooms and cook 3–4 minutes, stirring occasionally. Add ¼ cup of the cream and, with cover ajar, simmer 15–20 minutes. Remove cover and reduce liquid slowly over moderate heat until moisture evaporates. Season with about ¼ teaspoon of the salt lightly sprinkled into mixture, and stir to mix. Spoon mushroom mixture into prepared pastry shell and sprinkle on 3 tablespoons of the Gruyère cheese. Set aside.

3. In a mixing bowl combine eggs, remaining cream, salt, pepper, and nutmeg. Stir to mix and taste to adjust seasoning if necessary. Pour custard over mushroom-cheese mixture in shell and top with remaining Gruyère and Parmesan cheese.

4. Bake in preheated oven about 25 minutes or until top is golden brown and puffed and a knife inserted into the center of custard comes out clean.

To Prepare Ahead

Follow step 1 up to one day ahead or one month ahead and freeze according to recipe. Follow steps 2 through 4 up to several hours ahead, warming through just before serving. Can be baked ahead and frozen and placed in freezer securely wrapped. When ready to serve, place frozen quiche in a preheated 425-degree oven 20 minutes until thoroughly warmed.

PISSALADIÈRE 1

There are two recipes for French-style pizza in this book. The recipe below, made with Basic Pâte Brisée, is topped with Basic Tomato Sauce, grated cheese, and anchovies. The other, Pissaladière 2, is made with a yeast dough. Once, with company coming, a last-minute decision was made to prepare the following recipe, as I had all the ingredients on hand. The Basic Pâte Brisée was in the freezer and the tomato sauce and cheese in the refrigerator. Within a short time I had the whole pizza baked with little or no fanfare.

½ recipe Basic Pâte Brisée
2 cups Basic Tomato Sauce
½ cup grated Swiss Gruyère
    cheese
1 tin (2 ounces) flat anchovy
    fillets, rinsed in cold
    water and dried on
    paper toweling

Have on Hand
12-inch-round pizza pan

Serves 6–8

Preheat oven to 375 degrees.

1. Prepare basic pâte brisée recipe according to directions and roll out. With aid of rolling pin, lift onto pizza pan and trim excess pastry from edge of pan, leaving a ½-inch overhang. Fold under to create a smooth edge. Weight down as directed, place in preheated oven, and prebake 10–12 minutes. Remove from oven and let cool slightly.

2. Spread on tomato sauce almost to rim. Sprinkle with grated cheese and form a spoke pattern of anchovies over cheese. Place in oven and bake 20–25 minutes until crust is golden brown and cheese is melted and bubbly. Cut into wedges and serve hot.

To Prepare Ahead
Follow steps 1 and 2 up to several hours ahead. Let stand at room temperature, covered with a tent of plastic wrap. Return to a preheated 350-degree oven 5–10 minutes to warm.

TOMATO QUICHE

It's wonderful. It's quite different from the ordinary cheese-and-bacon quiche. Topping it with tomatoes adds color, flavor, and an unusual touch.

½ recipe Basic Pâte Brisée
2 tablespoons Dijon mustard
2 tablespoons vegetable oil
1 onion, thinly sliced
1 cup grated Swiss Gruyère
  cheese
2 eggs
1 egg yolk
1 cup heavy cream
¾ teaspoon coarse (kosher)
  salt

Freshly ground pepper
¼ teaspoon freshly ground
  nutmeg
1 large ripe tomato cut into
  ¼-inch slices

Have on Hand
9-inch high-sided fluted
  quiche pan with
  removable bottom, or
  pie plate

Serves 6–8

Preheat oven to 350 degrees.

1. See basic pâte brisée and prepare as specified, fitting the pastry into a 9-inch quiche pan or pie plate, then bake blind. When pastry cools, with a teaspoon spread mustard over bottom of partially baked shell and set aside.

2. In a skillet heat oil and sauté onion slices until translucent, being careful not to brown. Scatter onion slices in shell and sprinkle on ¾ cup of the grated cheese. Place in preheated oven and bake 3–4 minutes just to melt cheese. Remove from oven and set aside.

3. In a mixing bowl combine eggs and yolk, cream, salt, pepper, and nutmeg, and stir to mix until smooth. Taste to adjust seasoning if necessary. Pour mixture into prepared shell and top with tomato slices arranged in a circle at the surface of the liquid and sprinkle on remaining cheese.

4. Return to oven and bake an additional 30–35 minutes until puffed and golden or until cake tester or a knife inserted in center of custard comes out clean. Remove from oven and, if using quiche pan with removable sides, release the pastry by scraping the dough overhanging top edge of pan. Remove outer rim of quiche pan by resting pan on a can or jar and allowing the sides of pan to fall to the counter. Transfer to warm serving platter, cut into wedges, and serve hot.

To Prepare Ahead
Follow step 1 up to one day ahead or one month ahead and freeze

according to recipe. Follow steps 2 through 4 up to several hours ahead, warming through just before serving.

WORKING WITH PUFF PASTRY

Regarded as the finest of all flaked pastries, puff is sadly reputed to be the most difficult to make. It is undoubtedly time-consuming, but its even-layered rising produces the crispest texture and the most tender and flaky effect. It is certainly one of the most versatile of pastries and can happily be used for a variety of sweet and savory dishes. It is ideal for hors d'oeuvres, as well as a multitude of delicious desserts. When working puff pastry, keep calm and cool; when it is prepared correctly with a light handling, the results are distinguished.

Start out with a good recipe. A balanced proportion of ingredients are necessary for lightness and richness. You don't need a marble slab, but correct handling is essential. Also, a cool working atmosphere is helpful, as with all pastries. If weather is hot or other cooking will be going on in your kitchen, make the pastry early in the morning or in the evening, when temperatures are lower. It is essential to keep fat chilled up to the point that you will be using it. You might even refrigerate your rolling pin and other equipment. Rinsing your hands under a cold tap also makes good sense. Give yourself plenty of time, especially if you are making it for the first time. If at any time during the process of making pastry the dough or fat gets too warm, stop immediately. Wrap dough in wax paper and chill in refrigerator for up to a half hour before starting again.

A light hand is necessary on the rolling pin because heavy rolling will break up the air pockets, expelling precious air. Rolling must be consistent and even, because uneven rolling will distort the shape of the rectangle. Fat will also become unevenly distributed. Rest periods between rollings are necessary to firm the dough by chilling. This, of course, makes the pastry easier to handle and gives a flakier texture. When cutting pastry for shaping, make clean, decisive cuts which avoid dragging it. A clean cut will ensure that the pastry rises with a maximum expansion. For an attractive, glossy appearance, pastry should always be glazed just before baking.

The final step to a light, crisp pastry is the baking. Oven temperature should generally be quite hot but will vary according to recipe.

Storage: Cooked pastry soon loses its freshness, but it can be prepared early in the day and covered with a tent of plastic wrap or foil. Refrigeration will harden the butter and result in toughness. Unbaked pastry in block form or cut shapes, and in some cases with filling, when wrapped airtight can be left in a freezer for up to 4 months.

RAPID PUFF PASTRY

I must credit Jacques Pépin for inspiring me to develop this recipe.

2½ cups all-purpose flour
10½ ounces (2 sticks plus 5
   tablespoons) unsalted
   butter, cut into 1
   teaspoon slices, cold
   from refrigerator

¾ teaspoon coarse (kosher)
   salt
¾ cup ice water

Yields 1½ pounds

1. Measure out flour and put into freezer for at least 30 minutes.

2. Cut butter and put into bowl of electric mixer or workbowl of food processor fitted with steel knife and place in refrigerator at least 30 minutes to chill butter and equipment.

3. Prepare a cold surface to work on by placing ice cubes on a cookie sheet and allowing it to sit on a marble slab or work table at least 30 minutes, thereby chilling work surface beneath it.

4. Combine butter, flour, and salt, and mix in bowl of electric mixer using flat paddle, or in workbowl of food processor fitted with steel knife, and mix or process until mixture is crumbly with tiny lumps of butter. This will take about 30 seconds. Add water and mix 5–10 seconds longer. (The shorter time applies to working with a food processor.)

5. Remove the ice-filled cookie sheet and discard icy water. Very lightly flour chilled work surface and rolling pin and turn dough out onto it. Gently spread dough across work area with heel of your hand to incorporate fat and flour. This is called a fraisage. With the aid of a pastry scraper, quickly shape dough into a rough rectangle. Now roll dough into an even rectangle about 18 × 8 inches. Fold dough in fourths; fold ends until they touch the middle; then fold dough in half.

This is a double turn. Give dough a quarter turn to the right so folded edge is perpendicular to you. Roll out again and do 2 more double turns. Wrap well with wax paper and foil and chill in refrigerator at least 1 hour.

6. The pastry should be worked very quickly. If at any time during rolling the butter becomes soft, stop immediately. Wrap dough in wax paper and chill in refrigerator 20–30 minutes before rolling out again. If you need to chill pastry between turns, indent it with the balls of your fingertips to indicate number of turns you have already made. When using pastry as directed in any recipe, be sure dough has been chilled at least 2 hours before rolling it out.

Making Rapid Puff Pastry

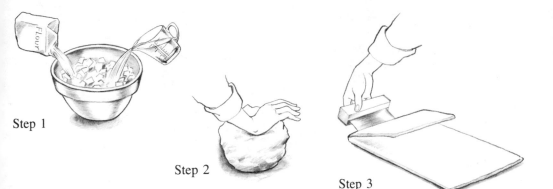

Step 1

Step 2

Step 3

Step 4

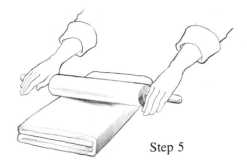

Step 5

DARTOIS

This double-crusted puff pastry recipe is in the shape of the classic pithiviers and has a savory filling. It is simple to make with the puff pastry on hand. When done, it is puffy, golden brown, and dramatic. When it is cut through for serving, the cheese oozes out over the herb-flavored layers of sweet tomato and ham. It makes a very satisfying brunch or luncheon dish.

1 recipe Rapid Puff Pastry
Dijon mustard
½ pound thinly sliced boiled
    ham
½ pound Swiss Gruyère
    cheese, grated
1 tomato, sliced paper thin
Coarse (kosher) salt
Freshly ground pepper
2 teaspoons fresh basil
    leaves, chopped, *or* ½
    teaspoon dried

Have on Hand
Sharp paring knife
14 × 17-inch cookie sheet
Egg glaze: 1 yolk mixed
    with 1 tablespoon
    water
Feather brush

Serves 8

1. Pastry should have 6 complete turns and a minimum of 2 hours' rest in the refrigerator before rolling out.

2. Take chilled pastry dough from refrigerator and cut in half. Wrap one half with wax paper and return to refrigerator. Sprinkle board lightly with flour and place remaining chilled pastry on it. Rapidly and with quick, light strokes, roll from center out and from center toward you to make a 10-inch circle about ¼ inch thick. Be sure to keep pastry of even thickness at all times. With the aid of the rolling pin, lift dough onto a baking sheet. If dough should contract, gently roll it back into shape right on baking sheet. Refrigerate about 20 minutes or until firm.

3. Remove chilled pastry round from refrigerator. Place a 9-inch form (cake pan or pot cover) centered on the pastry and mark a circle with the point of a small paring knife. Remove metal pattern and pastry trimmings. With the back of a spoon, spread a thin layer of mustard on surface of the pastry, leaving 1½-inch border all around. To form layers, arrange 2 slices of the ham over mustard, then sprinkle on a third of the grated cheese. Top with a third of the tomato slices and lightly season with a sprinkle of salt, pepper, and basil. Repeat layering until all ingredients are used.

4. Remove remaining pastry from refrigerator and roll out rapidly into a 10-inch circle. With the aid of your rolling pin, lift and place on top of filling, allowing an overhang. With lightly floured fingers, seal edges firmly and quickly to press out air pockets. Return to refrigerator for 20 minutes to firm the dough. When thoroughly chilled, remove from refrigerator and trim overhang of dough to meet edge of bottom layer. With a small paring knife, press edges all around pastry. Then, holding the knife vertically and using the tip, cut into edge to make scalloped indentations about 1 inch apart all around. To seal edges firmly, invert a bowl or baking pan that will fit over filling and press down. Refrigerate 15–20 minutes before baking.

Preheat oven to 450 degrees.

5. Just before baking, mark or score the surface of the pastry with a decorative design: With the tip of a sharp paring knife, cut down into dough, forming 8 wedges. Then slash short diagonal cuts centered between wedge marks. Lightly brush with a coating of egg glaze, being careful not to let glaze drip along scalloped border. When glazed and scored, place on middle rack in preheated oven and bake 20 minutes. Reduce heat to 400 degrees and continue to bake another 15–20 minutes. If top is browning too quickly, cover lightly with a tent of aluminum foil. Serve immediately cut into wedges like a pie.

To Prepare Ahead

Follow steps 1 through 4 up to one day ahead. Refrigerate, covered.

To Freeze: Follow steps 1 through 4 up to one month ahead. Flash-freeze on cookie sheet, uncovered. When pastry is frozen solid, wrap securely in aluminum foil with freezer wrap over it and freeze. If refrigerated, complete step 5; if frozen, unwrap and place without thawing into hot oven and complete step 5, increasing baking time an extra 5–10 minutes at each temperature.

RIS DE VEAU EN FEUILLETÉ
(Sweetbreads in puff pastry shells)

Ris—the name of the thymus gland of young calves and lambs is considered one of the most delicate products of butchery. Calf sweetbreads are what is mainly available to the home cook. When served in a puff pastry shell they are a much appreciated entree.

½ recipe Rapid Puff Pastry
1½ pounds calf sweetbreads, fresh and pale pink in color
4 tablespoons unsalted butter
1 carrot, trimmed, scrubbed, and thinly sliced
1 rib celery, trimmed, rinsed, and thinly sliced
1 leek, trimmed, well washed, and thinly sliced

½ teaspoon coarse (kosher) salt
Freshly ground pepper
2½–3 cups Classic Chicken and Veal Stock
1¼ cups white wine
⅔ cup Crème Fraîche or heavy cream

Have on Hand
Egg glaze: 1 yolk mixed with 1 tablespoon water

Serves 6–8

1. Pastry should have 6 complete turns and a minimum of 2 hours' rest in the refrigerator before rolling out. Roll chilled pastry into a large square or rectangle to about ¼-inch even thickness. Trim sides of pastry to make neat edges all around. If your pastry softens during rolling, return to refrigerator to chill and firm before proceeding. With a sharp knife or pizza cutter, cut firmly through the dough into rectangles about 4½ × 2 inches. Work rapidly and transfer rectangles to a cookie sheet about 1 inch apart. Cut decorative diagonal slashes over each strip with tip of a knife. Can be done ahead to this point and placed in refrigerator or freezer.

2. Soak sweetbreads in several changes of cold water for a minimum of 2 hours. Drain; cut away sinew and discard.

3. In a 5½-quart heavy saucepan, melt 2 tablespoons of the butter. When butter is foamy, put in vegetables and toss to mix. Cover and braise vegetables 7–8 minutes until tender. Place sweetbreads over vegetables, pour on stock and wine to cover; cover pan and cook at a bare simmer 35–40 minutes.

4. With a slotted spoon remove sweetbreads to a side dish and allow to cool. Separate pieces where they naturally break, carefully removing and discarding connective tissue. Place sweetbreads on a dish, cover with a clean kitchen towel, and weight down with a heavy refrigerated object (filled coffee can—bowl of fruit, etc.) and refrigerate 1–2 hours to firm them. Remove vegetables from saucepan and set aside.

5. In the meantime, reduce the cooking liquids remaining in saucepan to 1 cup. Skim off fat as liquid reduces.

6. Add crème fraîche or heavy cream to reduced liquid in saucepan and stir to mix over moderate heat. Swirl in remaining butter and stir to mix until mixture is thickened slightly. Add sweetbreads and vegetables to sauce and keep warm over low heat. Cover the surface of the liquid with a sheet of buttered wax paper to prevent a skin from forming. Can be done ahead to this point.

Preheat oven to 475 degrees.

7. *To Bake Puff Pastry Shells:* Brush chilled shells with egg glaze just before baking, making certain that none of glaze drips down sides of pastry. Bake on middle rack of oven 6–7 minutes. Reduce oven heat to 425 degrees and bake an additional 5–6 minutes until tops are golden brown and pastries have puffed.

8. Remove from oven and, while warm, split pastry horizontally where it separates naturally. Place the bottom slices on 6 or 8 dinner plates and spoon equal portions of sweetbreads and vegetables over each. Replace pastry tops and spoon additional sauce around shells. Serve at once.

To Prepare Ahead

For Pastry: Follow step 1 up to one day before serving and refrigerate on cookie sheet covered lightly with wax paper; or flash-freeze on cookie sheet and, when solidly frozen, transfer to freezer-going container and freeze. If refrigerated, complete step 7; if frozen, place without thawing into hot oven and complete step 7, increasing baking time 2–3 minutes longer at each temperature.

For Sweetbreads: Follow step 2 up to one day ahead. Refrigerate in suitable container. Follow steps 3 through 6 up to several hours ahead. Complete step 8 just before serving.

COQUILLES ST. JACQUES AU NATUREL

We all know about the convenience of having puff pastry on hand. This recipe was born in France during the height of the nouvelle cuisine and has been adapted for use as an elegant first course. I think you will be amazed at the simplicity of preparation of this splendid dish.

1 recipe Rapid Puff Pastry
1 large or 2 medium leeks, trimmed, white part only
2–3 carrots, scrubbed clean, trimmed
1 pound sea scallops, trimmed and cut into 2–3 crosswise slices
2–3 tablespoons fresh lemon juice

Coarse (kosher) salt
Freshly ground pepper
4 tablespoons unsalted butter

Have on Hand
10 coquille shells
2 large cookie sheets
Sharp paring knife
Egg glaze: 1 yolk mixed with 1 tablespoon water

Serves 10

1. Pastry should have 6 complete turns and a minimum of 2 hours' rest in the refrigerator before rolling out.

2. Lightly butter coquille shells and arrange them on your work area. Set aside.

3. Split leeks in half lengthwise and rinse under cold running water. Place halves in a basin of cold water and allow to soak 10–15 minutes. Transfer to a clean kitchen towel and pat dry. Place leek halves, flat side down, on work surface and cut crosswise into 2-inch lengths. Now slide knife along the layered pieces and slice into julienne.

4. A. Cut carrots into thirds, then slice, stack and cut into julienne.

B. *Processor Method:* Fit workbowl with julienne or shredding blade. Cut carrots to fit feed tube horizontally. Run machine and julienne or shred carrots with full pressure. Empty workbowl.

5. Combine vegetables and divide equally in buttered coquille shells. Divide scallop slices equally over the vegetables, then spoon about ¼ teaspoon of the lemon juice over each. Sprinkle lightly with salt and pepper and dot each shell with a teaspoon of butter.

6. Place 3–4 filled shells fairly close together on work counter. With a pastry brush, brush water around outside edges of each shell. Set aside.

7. Take chilled pastry from refrigerator and cut in half. Cover leftover dough with wax paper and return to refrigerator. Sprinkle board lightly

with flour and place chilled pastry on it. Rapidly and with quick, light strokes, roll from center out and from center toward you to an even ⅛-inch-thick circle. Be sure to keep pastry of even thickness at all times. With the aid of the rolling pin, lift dough and place over closely spaced filled shells. With a sharp paring knife, cut around each shell, leaving an overhang, and press pastry around the moistened edges of each shell. Tranfer to a cookie sheet and refrigerate. Continue to cover shells with remaining chilled pastry and refrigerate for several hours or overnight. *Preheat oven to 475 degrees.*

8. When pastry is chilled and firm, cut a small hole with the tip of a knife into each covered shell. Just before baking, place shells on a cookie sheet (you may need 2) and brush with egg glaze. Reduce oven temperature to 450 degrees, place cookie sheets on oven racks set at lower and upper third of oven and bake 5 minutes. Reduce oven heat to 425 degrees, reverse position of cookie sheets, and bake 12–15 minutes longer until pastry is crusty, well puffed, and golden brown. Serve at once.

To Prepare Ahead
Follow steps 1 through 7 up to one day ahead. Refrigerate, covered. Complete step 8 just before serving.

TARTE TATIN EN FEUILLETÉ

Tarte Tatin is not news; what is new, however, is the shape of the apples, how they are placed in the skillet and, of course, using puff pastry for the crust. When inverted, this tarte takes on a different look and the taste and texture is reminiscent of deliciously baked apples.

8–10 large apples (Golden
    Delicious or Winesaps)
4–5 tablespoons fresh lemon
    juice
5 tablespoons unsalted butter
¾ cup sugar
½ recipe Rapid Puff Pastry,
    turned 3 times and
    allowed to rest in
    refrigerator at least 2
    hours before using

Vanilla ice cream or freshly
    whipped cream
    (optional)

Have on Hand
9–10-inch heavy black iron
    skillet

Serves 8–10

Preheat oven to 425 degrees.

1. Peel and core apples. Leave one apple whole, then cut remaining apples in half vertically. Put all in a mixing bowl, sprinkle with lemon juice, and let stand while preparing the caramel, occasionally turning the halves.

2. An old-fashioned heavy black iron skillet will do the proper job of caramelizing the sugar. Be sure the pan is clean and dry. Melt butter in skillet; add sugar and stir into butter to coat bottom of pan. Cook over moderately high heat until mixture becomes a light caramel color. Remove from heat. Place the whole apple in center of skillet and stand apple halves vertically against it, forming rings to edge of the pan. Return to moderately high heat and cook until sugar turns a deeper caramel color. Gently move the pan back and forth over the burner so apples do not stick and the sugar does not burn. Remove from heat and allow to cool about 15 minutes.

3. Pour accumulated apple and lemon juices from bowl into a separate saucepan and cook over moderate heat until slightly thick. Drizzle syrup over tops of apples.

4. Be sure oven is quite hot before baking the tart. Roll out prepared pastry to approximately 12 inches in diameter. Lift pastry with the aid of a rolling pin, then lower to cover apples completely. Trim excess pastry to about 1 inch beyond edge of pan and then with fingers push pastry inside the pan, forming a border around apples. Prick pastry gently with a fork and brush surface lightly with water. Place skillet on middle shelf of oven and bake 20 minutes. Reduce heat to 375 degrees and bake 20 minutes longer. Turn oven off and let tart sit in oven for 10 more minutes. Remove from oven and unmold as soon as pan is cool enough to handle.

5. *To Unmold:* Place a serving platter over the skillet and invert. Serve with vanilla ice cream or a dollop of freshly whipped cream, if desired.

To Prepare Ahead

Follow steps 1 through 5 early in the day. Set aside lightly covered with a tent of wax paper until ready to serve.

WORKING WITH BASIC PÂTE À CHOUX

A basic pâte à choux, consisting of water, butter, flour, and eggs, is perhaps the simplest of all French doughs. The water and butter are placed in a saucepan, then brought to the edge of a boil. The flour is then stirred into the mixture all at once until a ball of dough is formed. Eggs are added one at a time until the dough is shiny and smooth. When the eggs are added, the pastry becomes very dense. This procedure has been, and I'm certain still is, being done by hand. As simple as the preparation is, however, using a food processor fitted with the steel blade or automatic mixer with a flat paddle will require less energy.

1 cup water
1 stick (8 tablespoons)
    unsalted butter, cut into
    pieces
1 cup sifted all-purpose flour
Pinch salt

4 eggs at room temperature

Have on Hand
14 × 17-inch cookie sheet
Optional: pastry bag and
    plain round tip

1. Place water and cut-up pieces of butter in a 2½-quart stainless or enamel saucepan and bring to a boil. Try to adjust heat so butter melts at approximately the same time as water reaches a boil. The moment water is boiling and butter melts, remove from heat and add flour with salt all at once. With a large wooden spoon, rapidly stir mixture into a doughy mass. Return the pan to moderate heat and stir vigorously 1 or 2 minutes until mixture forms a ball of paste and leaves sides of pan.

2. *Hand Method:* With a large wooden spoon, beat in eggs one at a time; each is absorbed into dough before next is added. Continue beating until all eggs are added and mixture is shiny and smooth. It is necessary to beat dough vigorously to incorporate as much air as possible to create light puffs. Use as recipe directs.

Food Processor or Automatic Mixer Method: Transfer dough to workbowl of food processor fitted with steel blade or into bowl of automatic mixer fitted with flat paddle. With machine on at low speed, add eggs one at a time through feed tube of processor or directly into bowl. Run machine between additions until eggs are thoroughly incorporated and mixture is shiny and smooth. Use as directed in recipes.

To Prepare Ahead
Follow steps 1 and 2 up to one day ahead. Refrigerate raw pâte à choux dough in a suitable container. Bring to room temperature and follow individual recipe directions.

BEIGNETS SOUFFLÉS

Another approach to working with pâte à choux. This deep-fried fritter
makes a light and appealing dessert when served with apricot sauce.

Use half Basic Pâte à Choux
    ingredients and proceed
    as directed in recipe
2 tablespoons dark rum

2 tablespoons kirsch or rum

Oil for deep frying
Confectioners' sugar

Apricot Sauce
½ cup apricot preserves
2 tablespoons superfine
    sugar

Have on Hand
Deep-frying thermometer
Frying pan or deep fryer

Serves 8–10

1. Add rum to basic pâte à choux recipe in mixing bowl, workbowl of food processor, or bowl of electric mixer. Stir or process to incorporate thoroughly. Taste to adjust seasoning if necessary. Chill batter for ½ hour.

2. *Apricot Sauce:* Meanwhile, in a small heavy saucepan, combine all sauce ingredients and slowly bring to a boil. Stir to mix with a wooden spoon. Allow to simmer, stirring occasionally, 3–4 minutes. Strain and keep warm. If you have an attractive little copper pot, this is a perfect time to use it. Can be made ahead to this point.

3. Pour enough oil into a frying pan or deep fryer to at least 2½ inches deep. Slowly heat oil to 375 degrees or when a cube of bread quickly browns or a drop of water sizzles. Scoop up a heaping teaspoon about the size of a walnut and drop into hot fat, pushing it off the spoon with tip of your finger or with another small spoon, maintaining its round shape as well as possible. Fry about 4 or 5 beignets at a time until golden brown. Do not crowd the pan, as too many beignets will cause oil temperature to drop and they will swell as they cook. When they are half done, turn them with a wooden spoon. They sometimes turn of their own accord. Cook as evenly as possible, then transfer to a paper-towel-lined cookie sheet to drain. Dust beignets with confectioners' sugar and serve warm with apricot sauce. Beignets can be kept in a warm oven up to 30 minutes before serving.

To Prepare Ahead
Follow step 1 and 2 up to one day ahead. Refrigerate separately in suitable covered containers. Complete step 3 up to thirty minutes before serving and reheat sauce.

GOUGÈRE WITH SAUCE BLANCHE

Gougère, a traditional dish from Burgundy, is made from pâte à choux combined with Dijon mustard and grated cheese and formed into a ring before baking. It makes an interesting appetizer served with a glass of burgundy, of course. When teamed with the Sauce Blanche below, it is a lovely luncheon or supper dish.

1 recipe Basic Pâte à Choux
2–3 teaspoons Dijon mustard
Dash cayenne
¾ cup freshly grated
    Parmesan or Swiss
    Gruyère cheese

Sauce Blanche (optional)
¼ pound fresh snow-white
    mushrooms, quickly
    rinsed, trimmed, and
    thinly sliced
Coarse (kosher) salt for
    cooking water
½ pound boiled ham, thinly
    sliced, *or* ½ pound
    cooked and cleaned
    shrimp

Béchamel Sauce (optional)
3 tablespoons unsalted butter
2 tablespoons flour
1½ cups hot milk
1 small onion
¼ teaspoon nutmeg
1 teaspoon coarse (kosher)
    salt
Freshly ground white pepper

Have on Hand
14 × 17-inch cookie sheet
Optional: pastry bag and
    plain round tip
Egg glaze: 1 yolk mixed
    with 1 tablespoon
    water

Serves 6–8

To Prepare Cookie Sheet: Lightly butter cookie sheet, then dust with flour, tapping off excess. With a 7- to 8-inch pot cover press in place the outline of a circle on the sheet. Set aside.

Preheat oven to 425 degrees.

1. Prepare basic pâte à choux as directed in recipe. Add mustard, cayenne, and cheese, and stir or process to mix. Taste to adjust seasoning if necessary.

2. Drop full rounded tablespoons mounding to about 1 inch high, one next to the other in a ring just outside the circle or pipe out 1-inch-high mounds through a pastry bag fitted with a plain round tube, following the marked circle. Brush tops with egg glaze and sprinkle remaining cheese on top of the ring. Bake in preheated oven 15 minutes, then reduce heat to 375 degrees and bake about 20–25 minutes longer until well puffed, crisp, and brown. The moment it is done, remove from

oven and with a sharp knife pierce sides of gougère in each puff around ring to let steam escape, otherwise it will be soggy. Return to turned off oven and let sit with door ajar. This will stay warm up to 30 minutes. Serve plain or with sauce blanche.

3. *Sauce Blanche:* In a heavy saucepan, bring 2 cups of salted water to a boil, reduce to a simmer, and blanch mushroom slices 30–40 seconds. Drain and fan* to cool quickly, then transfer to a clean kitchen towel and pat dry. Set aside.

4. Stack ham slices on work surface, cut into long thin strips, then dice tiny and set aside. If using shrimp, chop coarsely and set aside.

5. *Prepare Béchamel:* In a heavy saucepan, melt butter over moderate heat, then add flour, and stir constantly about 2 minutes. Meanwhile, in another saucepan, combine milk with onion and nutmeg and stir to mix. Slowly bring milk just to a boil, then discard onion. Off heat, gradually add hot milk to the butter-flour mixture, whisking constantly until sauce is smooth. When approximately half the liquid has been added, return saucepan to moderate heat and whisk in the remaining milk, whisking until mixture comes to a boil. Season with salt and pepper and stir to mix.

6. Reduce heat and allow to simmer over moderate heat, whisking the sauce occasionally, about 10–12 minutes, until thick and smooth. Remove from heat, stir in mushrooms and ham or shrimp. Taste to adjust seasoning if necessary. If doing ahead, place a buttered square of wax paper over sauce to keep a skin from forming. Remove paper and reheat just before serving.

7. *To Serve:* Cut gougère into 6 or 8 pieces and spoon warm sauce over them.

To Prepare Ahead
For Gougère: Follow step 1 up to one day ahead. Refrigerate raw pâte à choux dough in a suitable container. Bring to room temperature and complete step 2 up to several hours before serving. If desired, return to a 300-degree oven and heat through or serve at room temperature.

For Sauce Blanche: Follow steps 3 through 6 up to one day ahead. Refrigerate, covered, in a suitable container. Bring to room temperature and reheat the sauce, stirring occasionally just before serving. If sauce has thickened considerably on standing, add a little milk while stirring to warm until desired consistency is achieved.

WORKING WITH PHYLLO

Filled Greek pastries have become increasingly popular in the last ten to fifteen years. They are ubiquitous with caterers, but when the home cooks realized how simple they were to prepare, these "little pies" became a favorite appetizer. They are delicate but rich and filling, and for this reason I could never understand why they are served before a dinner. But they are perfect party fare when used at a large cocktail party, a brunch, or a late supper.

Because of my Sephardic heritage, Greek and Spanish cooking were a definite blend while I was growing up. My American Greek-born parents hungered for the traditional Greek dishes and my mother was blessed with a talent for fine cooking. So these *bourekas*, as I know them, were commonplace fare in our household and I never realized until many years later that they would be considered exotic food.

My mother still prepares her own phyllo dough, which generally consists of nothing but flour, water, oil, and a bit of salt. She also incorporates a small amount of yeast in the mixture, kneads it ever so briefly, then allows it to rest for ten minutes or so to relax the gluten in the dough. Adding the yeast, she claims, makes the dough easier to work and stretch. For years people have been able to buy phyllo dough, also called strudel leaves, in specialty food shops. Today it is available packaged in most markets. It is preferable to buy phyllo from a market with a quick turnover, since the phyllo should be fresh. Many markets will sell it frozen. If it is not carefully defrosted, the dough can dry out to an unworkable condition. Phyllo is packaged wrapped in a plastic tube and boxed. When ready to use, cut open the plastic tube, unroll on work surface, cover with a lightly dampened tea towel, and work with one sheet at a time. Use what you need for your recipe, reroll the unused portion, and slip it back into the plastic tube. Seal with Scotch tape, return it to the box, and freeze.

I never use butter when working with phyllo because it weights down the leaves. I use vegetable oil with a very light hand to moisten the dough. My mother's technique is as follows. Pour a small amount of vegetable oil into a dish or cup. Working with one sheet of phyllo at a time, dip the tips of your fingers into the surface of the oil, lift them out, and flick the oil onto the sheet of dough, covering the exposed surface. Or spinkle with a feather brush.

Traditionally, the phyllo leaves are cut, filled, and shaped into triangles or rolls, which is a practical and useful way to serve them. My mother offers a helping hand when she suggests placing the filling between lightly oiled layers of phyllo in a greased baking dish. Needless to say, this cuts down preparation time considerably. Her artistic finishing touch is to cut two or three sheets of phyllo dough in half crosswise and lift each sheet from the center like a hankie, and drop it over the top layer. These "hankie" toppings, adjacent to one another, give a rippling, airy effect. When baked, the sheets puff up to a golden brown. Be sure to sprinkle oil lightly on this final layer, too.

A box of phyllo dough is not a large investment. Some of the traditional fillings are really quite simple, so don't be intimidated by phyllo. It is one of the simplest of all pastries to work with. The results will be your reward.

TYROKOPITA
Greek Cheese Triangles

½ pound feta cheese
1 package (8 ounces) farmer
  cheese
4 ounces cream cheese,
  softened
3 eggs, lightly beaten
Freshly ground pepper
⅛ teaspoon freshly ground
  nutmeg

½ pound phyllo leaves

Have on Hand
Vegetable oil in small dish
  or cup
Goosefeather brush
Lightly greased baking sheet

Yields up to 25 triangles

Preheat oven to 375 degrees.

1. Into a mixing bowl crumble feta cheese, then add farmer cheese and cream cheese. With a wooden spoon stir well to mix. Add eggs, pepper, and nutmeg, stirring to mix thoroughly.

2. Remove phyllo from package. Unroll, divide in half, and return unused portion to refrigerator or freezer. With a sharp knife or scissors, cut into thirds lengthwise. Cover phyllo with a lightly dampened, not wet, tea towel to keep from drying out. Work with one sheet at a time, removing it from under towel to a work surface. Dip tips of your fingers into oil and flick oil onto sheet or dip a feather brush in oil and sprinkle

sheet very lightly. Be careful not to moisten with too much oil or final preparation will be heavy and greasy.

3. Place 2 rounded teaspoons of cheese mixture at one end of each strip. Working quickly to prevent dough from drying out, fold one corner over opposite edge, covering filling and forming a triangle. Fold this triangle again along the phyllo strip, then continue to fold to end of strip like the folding of an American flag. Repeat procedure using 1 strip at a time until all cheese mixture is used.

How to form phyllo triangles

4. As each triangle is shaped, place close together on a lightly greased cookie sheet and dot with a flick of oil.

5. Bake in preheated oven 15–20 minutes or until crisp and golden brown. Serve piping hot.

To Prepare Ahead

Follow steps 1 through 4 up to two months ahead. Freeze solid, uncovered, on a cookie sheet, then layer in a freezer-going container and seal securely. Do not defrost before baking. Place frozen triangles on a cookie sheet in a preheated 400-degree oven and bake 20–25 minutes. If they are browning too quickly, cover with a tent of foil. Or prepare up to one day ahead. Refrigerate covered on a cookie sheet and complete step 5.

Note: For a quick and easy preparation, I will sandwich the above filling ingredients between layers of lightly oiled phyllo dough and bake in a 2-quart Pyrex or earthenware baking dish.

1. Lightly grease a 2-quart baking dish.

2. Combine cheeses, eggs, and seasonings as above.

3. Cut phyllo leaves in half. Work with one sheet at a time. Transfer it from under towel to greased baking dish, allowing one end to come up over rim along each side of the dish. Overlap each one in the center so that layers of dough cover bottom of dish completely. Sprinkle each

sheet lightly with oil as you arrange 7 or 8 sheets across bottom. Add cheese mixture and with a large kitchen spoon spread to an even layer.

4. Place 6 or 7 sheets over filling, layering them as above. Finally, cut 7–8 sheets in half again, lift each sheet from the center like a hankie, one at a time, and drop it over the top layer. "Hankies" should be adjacent to one another. Sprinkle lightly with oil.

5. Bake in a preheated 350-degree oven about 25–30 minutes until puffed and golden brown. Cut into squares and serve hot.

To Prepare Ahead
Follow steps 1 through 4 up to one day or several hours ahead. Cover lightly with a tent of plastic wrap and refrigerate. Bring to room temperature and complete step 5 just before serving.

VARIATIONS OF FILLINGS IN PHYLLO DOUGH

SPANAKOPITA
Greek Spinach and Cheese Triangles

1 pound loose fresh spinach
   or 2 packages (10
   ounces each) frozen
   chopped spinach
½ pound feta cheese
1 container (8 ounces)
   ricotta cheese
2 eggs, lightly beaten
Freshly ground pepper
1 tablespoon finely chopped
   fresh dill *or* 1 teaspoon
   dried

½ pound phyllo leaves

Have on Hand
Vegetable oil in small dish
   or cup
Goosefeather brush
Lightly greased baking dish

Yields up to 25 triangles

Preheat oven to 375 degrees.
1. If using fresh spinach, remove fibrous stems and blemished leaves. Wash in several changes of lukewarm water to clean leaves of dirt and sand. Transfer spinach to a heavy saucepan with about ½ inch of water.

Cover tightly and cook 3–4 minutes, stirring occasionally, until tender. Drain and refresh by fanning* and briefly running under cold water to set color and stop the cooking. With your hands, squeeze spinach to remove moisture, then place in a clean kitchen towel and squeeze very dry. Place on a wooden board and chop coarsely. If using frozen spinach, defrost thoroughly and place in a clean kitchen towel and ring it to remove all moisture. Do not cook spinach if using frozen.

2. In a mixing bowl, combine chopped spinach with feta cheese, ricotta, eggs, pepper, and dill, and with a wooden spoon stir very well to mix.

3. Handle phyllo as in Tyrokopita step 2.

4. Place 2 rounded teaspoons of spinach mixture at one end of each strip. Working quickly to prevent dough from drying out, fold one corner over opposite edge, covering filling and forming a triangle. Fold this triangle again along the phyllo strip, then continue to fold to the end of the strip like the folding of an American flag. Repeat procedure using 1 strip at a time until all the spinach mixture is used.

5. As each triangle is shaped, place close together on a lightly greased cookie sheet and dot with a flick of oil.

6. Bake in preheated oven for 15–20 minutes or until crisp and golden brown. Serve piping hot.

To Prepare Ahead
Follow steps 1 through 5 up to two months ahead. Proceed as in Tyrokopita and freeze or prepare up to one day ahead, refrigerate, then complete step 6.

Note: For a quick and easy lasagna-style preparation see Tyrokopita for details.

BAKLAVA FINGER ROLLS

This is different from the usual baklava recipes in that no honey is used, making it less sweet and more palatable. My mother prepares her baklava only in this way, which is a simple, light, pickup version.

Filling
½ pound walnuts, finely
    chopped
½ cup sugar
1 teaspoon cinnamon
Dash ground cloves

Syrup
1 cup sugar
1 cup water

2 tablespoons lemon juice

½ pound phyllo leaves

Have on Hand
Vegetable oil in small dish
    or cup
Goosefeather brush
Lightly greased cookie sheet
Cake rack

Yields up to 36 pieces

Preheat oven to 350 degrees.

1. *To Prepare Filling:* In a mixing bowl, combine walnuts, sugar, cinnamon, and cloves, and stir to mix. Set aside.

2. *To Prepare Syrup:* In a heavy saucepan, combine sugar and water and bring to a boil. Add lemon juice and cook at a brisk simmer about 15 minutes until mixture is a light syrup. Keep warm over very low heat.

3. In the meantime, remove phyllo from package. Unroll, divide in half, and return unused portion to refrigerator or freezer. With a sharp knife or scissors, cut in half lengthwise. Cover the phyllo with a lightly dampened, not wet, tea towel to keeping from drying out. Work with one sheet at a time, removing it from under towel to a work surface. Dip tips of your fingers into oil and flick oil onto sheet, or dip a feather brush in the oil and sprinkle sheet very lightly. Be careful not to moisten with too much oil or final preparation will be heavy and greasy.

4. Place 1 rounded tablespoon of nut mixture along bottom third of each sheet. Lift bottom edge of phyllo over the mixture to cover, then fold in sides, envelope style, and continue to roll into a cylinder. Place seam side down on prepared cookie sheet. When all rolls are prepared, place pan in preheated oven and bake 12–15 minutes. Remove from oven when golden brown and crisp.

5. Place a cake rack on a jelly-roll pan. While rolls are still warm, use tongs to dip them one at a time into the hot syrup, allowing excess

to drip off. Place on cake rack to cool. Repeat procedure of coating rolls with syrup until done. When cool, arrange on a cake plate in graduated layers or store in a wax-paper-lined covered cookie tin for several weeks.

To Prepare Ahead
Follow steps 1 through 5 up to three to four weeks ahead. Serve at room temperature.

BOUREKIA ME KIMA
Greek Meat Triangles

3 tablespoons vegetable oil
2 onions, finely chopped
1 clove garlic, finely
    chopped
1 pound ground chopped
    lean beef
1 teaspoon coarse (kosher)
    salt
Freshly ground pepper
½ teaspoon ground
    cinnamon

½ teaspoon allspice
1 tablespoon dry vermouth
2 tablespoons tomato paste
½ pound phyllo leaves

Have on Hand
Vegetable oil in small dish
    or cup
Goosefeather brush
Lightly greased baking dish

Yields up to 25 triangles

Preheat oven to 350 degrees.

1. In a large skillet, heat oil, add onions, and cook until translucent. Add garlic and cook just a few seconds longer. Add meat to onion mixture and cook until meat has lost its red color, stirring occasionally. Season with salt, pepper, cinnamon, allspice, vermouth, and tomato paste, and stir to mix. Bring mixture to a boil and, with cover ajar, simmer about 20 minutes or until mixture has absorbed most of liquid. Remove from heat and cool completely.

2. Handle phyllo as in Tyrokopita step 2.

3. Place 2 rounded teaspoons of meat mixture at one end of each strip. Working quickly to prevent dough from drying out, fold one corner over opposite edge, covering filling and forming a triangle. Fold this triangle again along phyllo strip, then continue to fold to end of strip like the folding of an American flag. Repeat procedure using 1 strip at a time until all of meat mixture is used.

4. As each triangle is shaped, place close together on a lightly greased cookie sheet and dot with a flick of oil.

5. Bake in preheated oven 15–20 minutes or until crisp and golden brown. Serve piping hot.

To Prepare Ahead
Follow steps 1 through 4 up to two months ahead. Proceed as in Tyrokopita and freeze or prepare up to one day ahead; refrigerate, covered, then complete step 5.

Note: For a quick and easy lasagna-style preparation see Tyrokopita

10

THE BAKERY

I t doesn't take much to convince home chefs to do some home baking once a comparison is made between their results and the commercial kind. Home baking not only results in a superior product but allows one control of the ingredients. Lowering intake of salt, sugar, and additives is recognized today as a healthful approach to all nutrition. Baking at home provides one more opportunity to set and follow your own standards of nutrition. Whether you are an experienced baker or not, the step-by-step recipes in the Bakery section of this book will guide you along the path to successful home baking while pleasing the palates of your family and guests.

Ingredients: Flour is certainly the ubiquitous ingredient in baking, and one's choice of just the proper flour is governed by the recipe used and your experience.

Many cakes call for all-purpose flour, which is a blend of hard and soft wheats. Its high gluten content also makes it more desirable than others when baking breads.

The many different flours displayed on your market shelf will include unbleached, enriched, and self-rising all-purpose flour; cake flour; and self-rising cake flour. If cake flour is called for, do not substitute all-purpose for it. Each flour has its own characteristic and one may not necessarily serve in place of another. Be extra-careful when buying cake flours. Since this is not a frequent item on your marketing list, you might accidentally pick up self-rising rather than the plain cake flour. The self-rising contains salt and baking powder whose undetected presence will affect the outcome of your baking efforts.

All sugar used in this book is granulated sugar unless otherwise specified. When sprinkling confectioners' sugar over a cake, place a small amount in a strainer and tap the sides with fingertips. In this way you will be able to control the amount and direction of the sugar.

Measurements: It is essential to measure ingredients accurately. Use USDA standard measures, which are available in all specialty kitchenware shops and department stores. The plastic varieties of measuring cups and spoons, as well as other measures bought for aesthetic reasons, e.g., copper, do not conform to USDA standards. Many a cake or pastry has been ruined as a result of careless or inaccurate measuring.

Preparation of Pans: Use clean pans of standard sizes. Burned-on grease from former baking procedures can cause a burned cake the next time the pan is used.

Grease the pan with shortening or butter. Dust bottom of pan lightly with flour or bread crumbs by tilting the pan from side to side to coat evenly, then tap off and discard excess. Maida Heatter says, "Dusting with bread crumbs gives the outside of the finished cake a crisper texture."

To line a cake pan with wax paper, grease the pan, line with wax paper, and then grease the paper.

To fit a rectangular pan with wax paper, place pan on a piece of wax paper and draw an outline around the base of it with the tip of a small knife. Cut out the tracing with a pair of scissors and place the wax paper cut to conform with the pan's shape inside the bottom of the pan. Grease paper. After cake is baked, but while it is still warm, peel off wax paper from cake bottom and discard.

To fit a round cake pan or charlotte mold, tear off a length of wax paper approximately the width of the pan. Fold the sheet in half, then in half again into quarters, pressing hard along the folded edges to make a square. Make another fold so the two side edges meet, forming a triangle. Continue to fold from the point several more times until you have a long, narrow triangle. Now hold the triangle at the rough-cut end, positioning the point at the center of the baking pan and cut the paper with scissors where it lines up along the inside edge of the pan. Discard the portion of paper you are holding, and open remaining piece to a full round that should fit neatly inside your pan or mold. Of course, butter this paper as instructed above.

Fill pans according to recipe directions. Filling pans too full will result in hard, crusty edges with centers sunken in.

Accurate Oven Heat: Baking is the process of heating and drying and accurate oven heat is therefore an essential component of successful baking. You may have the best and most up-to-date equipment available, but oven temperatures can be thrown off and inaccurate. It is a good idea to buy an oven thermometer, available in specialty kitchenware shops, to give you the assurance you are baking at correct temperatures. If you have a gas oven and temperatures differ from a reliable oven thermometer's reading, the oven should be calibrated. Your local public utility will service a gas oven for you free of charge in most cases. An electric oven will require a service call to calibrate its temperature setting.

Never use aluminum foil to line oven racks or the floor of the oven, since it interferes with the proper distribution of heat. If two baking pans must be placed in the oven at one time, do not place them one over the other on two separate racks. Place them at catty-corner positions to one another, neither touching each other or the oven walls, to allow proper heat flow and to assure they will bake evenly.

Baking Techniques: CREAMING BUTTER AND SUGAR: When butter and sugar are creamed together sufficiently, the result will be neither sugary nor greasy. Work the butter first with the back of a wooden spoon or in an electric mixer, then add sugar until the two ingredients are thoroughly combined and are light in color with a fluffy texture.

FOLDING: Folding is a method by which two or more ingredients are combined very gently to incorporate air into the mixture. You will fold egg whites into a sauce or a batter for a soufflé or a cake, or fold whipped cream or a combination of cheeses for a pie or a cake. Lightness of handling is the key to the eventual lightness of the dish. You can fold into a batter using an electric mixer on the lowest speed, but to fold by hand is simple and satisfying, as you can feel the lightness when mixing and therefore remain in complete control of the process.

A large rubber spatula (domestic ones are best) is an essential tool with which to fold. With spatula, glide over the top of the mixture, then sweep down along the inside of the bowl and the ingredients to be combined. Bring the spatula up on the other side of the bowl, turning the bowl with one hand at the same time your working hand folds with the spatula. Folding must be done gently and carefully. Reckless stirring will remove the air from your batter and make it heavy.

PIPING ROSETTES OR A FILLING FROM A PASTRY BAG: Fold back a collar on a large pastry bag, drop in the metal tip, and fit it into the small opening at the bottom of the bag. Place bag in a tall milk glass or wide-mouthed jar, tip end down, so that it will stand independently. Fill the bag with whatever filling you are using—firmly whipped cream, pâte à choux dough, and so forth—to about ⅔ full. Set aside any extra filling. Pull up the collar and remove bag from glass or jar. Close the bag at the top so edges meet and press down toward the enclosed filling. Pleat or twist the bag at this point and tuck it between the thumb and forefinger of your working hand. Cradle the filled pastry bag in other hand, using it only to guide you, and exert pressure with your working hand to force the filling through the metal tip. Always hold the bag vertically and directly over the area you are working on so the placement is direct. To practice, whip up a cup of heavy cream until firm and pipe out rosettes by placing the pastry bag tip about ¼ inch above a plate or cookie sheet.

With working hand, exert pressure to create a 1-inch round of cream, making a slight circular movement; now bring the tip into the center of the round, release the pressure, and pull the bag up abruptly. This action will create a tiny peak at the top of the rosette, which is attractive when you are using whipped cream. If you prefer not to have this peak on another type of filling, simply flatten it down with the tines of a fork or the tip of a knife dipped in cold water. Or, tap the tip of the pastry bag down into the circle gently to flatten the peak.

Reading recipes carefully, perhaps once or twice at first, and proceeding with confidence and a sense of joyous challenge will result in baking that surpasses even your most ambitious dreams. I encourage your repeated attempts, knowing the results will be repeated successes and your reward will be in the tasting.

How to fit a pastry bag with a decorating tube and pipe out filling

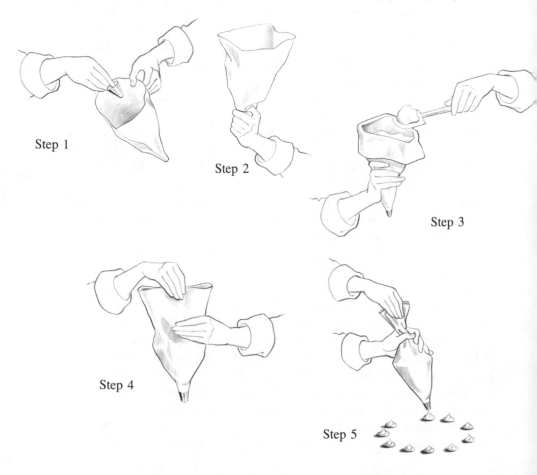

Step 1

Step 2

Step 3

Step 4

Step 5

BISCOCHO
(Greek Almond Cookie)

I was reminded of this wonderfully crisp little cookie—an everyday staple in my mother's kitchen—a number of years ago when I was introduced to Biscotti di Prato, the favorite "cookie" of Tuscany. "What an amazing similarity," I thought. "Now, why didn't I pay more attention to Mother!"

½ cup blanched almonds
3 eggs
¾ cup sugar
½ cup vegetable oil
1 teaspoon vanilla
2½ cups all-purpose flour
2 teaspoons baking powder
Equal mixture of sugar and
    cinnamon for topping
    (about ½ teaspoon
    each)

Have on Hand
11½ × 17½-inch flat
    cookie sheet
Egg glaze: 1 beaten white

Yields 6–7 dozen

Preheat oven to 375 degrees.

1. Place almonds on a cookie sheet and toast in oven 15 minutes until golden brown. When cool, put into workbowl of food processor fitted with steel knife or in batches in a blender and grind very fine. Set aside.

2. Combine eggs and sugar in a mixing bowl and beat with a large wooden spoon. Add oil and vanilla and continue beating until incorporated. Stir in 1 cup flour gradually. Slowly add remaining flour and baking powder and stir gently to mix. Add ground almonds and carefully fold into the dough. Dough will be soft and slightly sticky, but you should be able to handle it.

3. Butter a cookie sheet and lightly dust with flour. Take about ¼ of the dough and place it on a lightly floured work area. Then, with lightly floured hands, shape into a long, thin roll about 1½ inches in diameter. Place lengthwise on prepared cookie sheet. Shape remaining dough in the same manner into three additional rolls and place on cookie sheet, leaving a 1½–2-inch space between rolls. Brush tops of each roll with beaten egg white, then sprinkle each with sugar-and-cinnamon mixture.

4. Place in a preheated oven and bake 25–30 minutes. Remove from oven and cut with a serrated bread knife at a 45-degree angle every ½ inch or so to obtain the required oval shape.

5. Reduce oven temperature to 250 degrees and adjust oven shelves. It is necessary to dry cookies in oven after their initial baking. You will probably need two cookie sheets at this point. Place cookies, cut side up and very close together, on the cookie sheet. Return to oven 25–30 minutes until they are quite crisp and dry.

To Prepare Ahead
Follow steps 1 through 5 up to several weeks ahead. These cookies will keep very well in an airtight container. Use for snacking and dunking.

GÉNOISE BLUEBERRY ROLL

Garnish your platter or board with little mounds of extra blueberries edged with fresh mint leaves and you can see summer written all over this deliciously tangy génoise roll. A perfect end to a light summertime lunch or a dinner of salad or fish.

6 large eggs at room
    temperature
¾ cup sugar
1 teaspoon vanilla
Grated rind of 1 lemon
1 cup all-purpose flour
6 tablespoons unsalted
    butter, melted and
    cooled to room
    temperature
1 cup Crème Fraîche or
    heavy cream

2 teaspoons superfine sugar
2½ cups fresh blueberries
Confectioners' sugar

Have on Hand
11½ × 17-inch jelly-roll
    pan
Wax paper
Vegetable oil
Additional butter and flour

Serves 8–10

To Prepare Pan: Tear a length of wax paper to fit jelly-roll pan, leaving a slight overhang. Grease one side of paper with vegetable oil. Invert paper greased side down to adhere to pan and hold in place. Butter exposed side of paper, then dust with flour, tapping off excess.
Preheat oven to 350 degrees.
    1. Break eggs into a large mixing bowl or bowl of electric mixer. Add sugar, vanilla, and lemon rind, and beat mixture 10 minutes at moderate speed until it is triple in volume, pale yellow in color, and

falls off beaters in thick ribbons without sinking into batter. The success of this recipe depends on the lengthy beating.

2. Sift ⅓ cup of the flour at a time directly over the batter. With a large rubber spatula and a light hand, fold in flour as you rotate bowl in the opposite direction to the folding. Do this quickly and evenly, being careful not to deflate batter. Be sure to fold in any dry flour pockets. Add cooled melted butter, using the same folding procedure.

3. Pour batter into prepared jelly-roll pan and smooth out gently. Bake at once on middle shelf of preheated oven 20–22 minutes. Check cake after 18 minutes. The color should be a light golden brown and cake should spring back when touched. The sides will also begin to pull away from pan. Allow cake to cool in pan 5–10 minutes.

4. To remove cake, on your work counter spread a clean kitchen towel (not terry cloth), lightly moistened with tap water. Working quickly, hold onto sides of cake and pan, with potholders if necessary, and carefully tilt and lower pan toward towel until inverted. Lift off pan and carefully remove wax paper and discard. Aided by towel, roll up sheetcake lengthwise and let sit for about 10 minutes so it assumes a rolled shape. This cake will be quite firm and you should not have any difficulty with cracks or breaking.

5. In the meantime, chill a bowl and beaters 5–10 minutes. Whip chilled crème fraîche or heavy cream until firm. Add superfine sugar and stir to mix. Rinse berries quickly and pat dry in a clean kitchen towel.

6. Gently ease the cake back to a flattened position. With a rubber spatula scrape cream onto sheetcake and spread evenly, leaving a 1-inch border of exposed cake along the edge opposite you. Distribute 2 cups of the berries equally over cream. To reroll cake, use the length of the towel closest to you to help return it to its original rolled position. Lift the 2 ends of the towel under cake and transfer it, seam side down, to an elongated rectangular platter and refrigerate, lightly covered with plastic wrap, 3–4 hours until firm, or overnight. (I often serve my cake rolls on a wooden French bread board.)

7. Cut off ends with a serrated bread knife to expose rolled layers and sprinkle roll with confectioners' sugar just before serving.

To Garnish: Overlap some fresh mint or lemon leaves at either end of the cake on your serving platter and divide remaining berries and arrange mounds of the fruit over the leaves.

To Prepare Ahead
Follow steps 1 through 6 up to one day ahead. Complete step 7 before serving.

CHOCOLATE ROULAGE

This special-occasion cake has become a favorite dessert in our home during the Christmas season, but it is just as special all year long.

5 eggs
6 ounces imported
　　semisweet chocolate
¾ cup superfine sugar
3 tablespoons all-purpose
　　flour, sifted
¼ teaspoon cream of tartar
1 cup heavy cream, whipped
1 tablespoon rum
Confectioners' sugar
Additional ½ cup heavy
　　cream, whipped, for
　　rosette garnish
　　(optional)

Have on Hand
11 × 17-inch jelly-roll pan
Wax paper
Clean tea towel
Pastry bag
Star tip

Serves 10–12

To Prepare Pan: Tear a length of wax paper to fit jelly-roll pan, leaving a slight overhang. Grease one side of paper with vegetable oil. Invert paper greased side down to adhere to pan and hold in place, then grease exposed side.

Preheat oven to 375 degrees.

1. Separate eggs into 2 mixing bowls, or in bowls of electric mixer, and allow to come to room temperature. Set aside.

2. Melt chocolate in a heavy saucepan with 2 tablespoons cold water over very low heat, or place in a small metal bowl and melt in a 250-degree oven 15 minutes. When mixture looks soft, stir to a smooth cream. Set aside to cool.

3. Add sugar to egg yolks and beat until thick and light in color, about 2–3 minutes in electric mixer or 4–5 minutes by hand.

4. With a rubber spatula, gently blend the melted chocolate into egg-yolk mixture alternately with the flour.

5. With clean beaters, beat egg whites in bowl of electric mixer, or with portable mixer, at low speed until foamy. Add cream of tartar all at once and continue beating at high speed until firm but not dry peaks are formed. Be careful not to overbeat. With a large rubber spatula, gently fold beaten egg whites into chocolate mixture.

6. Pour batter into prepared jelly-roll pan and smooth out gently. Bake at once on middle shelf of preheated oven 20–22 minutes. Check after 16 or 17 minutes. When cake is done it should spring back when touched and sides will begin to pull away from the pan. Allow cake to cool in the pan 5–10 minutes.

7. To remove cake from pan, on your work counter spread a clean kitchen towel (not terry cloth), lightly moistened with tap water. Working quickly, hold onto sides of cake pan, with potholders if necessary, and carefully tilt and lower pan toward towel until inverted. Lift off pan and carefully remove wax paper and discard. Aided by towel, roll up sheetcake lengthwise and let sit for about 10 minutes so it assumes a rolled shape. When you unroll, do not be concerned if it cracks a bit. With palms of hands, push in from outside edges to close the gaps. Its natural moistness will keep it together.

8. In the meantime, chill a bowl and beaters 5–10 minutes and whip heavy cream until firm. Fold in rum.

9. With a rubber spatula scrape cream onto sheetcake and spread evenly, leaving a 1-inch border of exposed cake along edge opposite you. To reroll cake, use the length of the towel closest to you to help return it to its original rolled position. Lift the two ends of the towel under the cake and transfer it, seam side down, to an elongated rectangular platter and refrigerate, lightly covered with plastic wrap, 3–4 hours until firm, or overnight. When cake is firm, cut off unattractive ends with a serrated bread knife to expose rolled layers. (I like to serve my cake rolls on a French wooden board.)

10. *To Serve:* Sift confectioners' sugar by tapping through a sieve

Preparing Chocolate Roulage

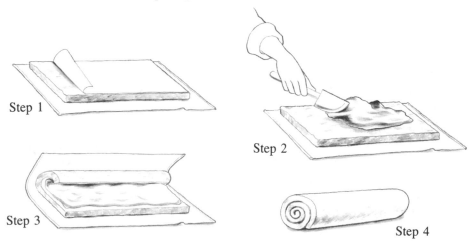

Step 1

Step 2

Step 3

Step 4

over top of cake. With a pastry bag fitted with a star tip, pipe out a row of rosettes along top of cake if desired.

To Prepare Ahead
Follow steps 1 through 9 up to one day ahead, or securely wrap in freezer paper and freeze up to one month ahead. Complete step 10 before serving.

CHERRY PRALINE TORTE

Two easy-to-prepare sponge layers are sandwiched with fresh cream and topped with a blanket of cherries, all huddled close together under a glistening praline apricot glaze.

4 large-size eggs at room
　　temperature
1 cup superfine sugar
¾ cup all-purpose flour,
　　sifted
1 tablespoon Kirsch

¾ cup heavy cream,
　　whipped
2 packages (10 ounces each)
　　frozen pitted cherries,
　　well drained
⅓ cup Praline Powder

Glaze
5 tablespoons apricot
　　preserves
3 tablespoons currant jelly
3 tablespoons cold water

Have on Hand
2 9-inch removable-bottom
　　layer cake pans
Double cake rack

Serves 8–10

To Prepare Pans: Butter cake pans, then lightly dust with flour or unseasoned Bread Crumbs.
Preheat oven to 350 degrees.

1. Place eggs in a mixing bowl or bowl of electric mixer and beat at low speed while adding sugar gradually. Adjust speed to medium and continue to beat mixture 3–4 minutes until batter is increased in volume and thick and pale in color.

2. Sift flour onto a piece of wax paper; then, with a large rubber spatula, carefully fold into egg mixture until thoroughly incorporated. Divide mixture between prepared cake pans. Place both pans on middle

shelf of preheated oven catty-corner to each other and not touching, to allow heat to circulate. Bake 25–30 minutes until top springs back when gently touched with fingertips and is golden brown. Remove from oven and allow to cool in pan 10–15 minutes.

3. Loosen sides of each cake by drawing an ordinary kitchen knife between cake and inside of pan. Place one pan at a time on top of a round, flat-top cylindrical object such as a coffee can, and allow metal ring of pan to drop to the counter. Insert a long metal spatula between cake and bottom of pan and slide each cake onto a double cake rack. Let cool completely.

4. With a cake tester or larding needle, poke several holes into surface of cakes and sprinkle 1½ teaspoons Kirsch over each.

5. In a small heavy saucepan, combine apricot preserves and currant jelly with cold water. Simmer over low heat 7–8 minutes until softened. Keep warm over very low heat. Glaze will become thick and unworkable if left standing at room temperature. If this should happen, reheat to soften.

6. In a cold bowl with cold beaters whip cream and spread over one sponge layer. Place the second layer over the cream to sandwich it. Spread a thin layer of warm glaze over top of cake; reserve remaining glaze. Place drained cherries on a double thickness of paper towels to absorb any excess moisture, then arrange very close together on top of cake.

7. Combine remaining glaze with praline powder and stir to mix. Coat cherries with this mixture by letting it fall from side of a large kitchen spoon over cherries. Allow some of the glaze to drop from the spoon down sides of cake.

To Prepare Ahead
Follow steps 1 through 7 up to one day ahead. Refrigerate. When cake is well chilled and glaze has hardened, place a loose tent of plastic wrap over the cake. When ready to serve, place on a doily-lined cake stand or platter. Use serrated knife to cut cake.

VIENNESE NUT TORTE

A dark, sweet, rich cake reminiscent of the classic Sachertorte but with a lighter touch.

5 eggs, separated
½ cup superfine sugar
2½ cups nuts ground to a
  coarse-fine texture
  (combination of
  blanched almonds,
  pecans, hazelnuts—see
  Note)
2 tablespoons dark rum
¼ teaspoon cream of tartar

Chocolate Cream Filling
2 ounces imported
  semisweet chocolate,
  broken into small
  pieces
1 cup heavy cream, whipped

Apricot Glaze
⅓ cup apricot jam
1 tablespoon dark rum

Chocolate Icing
4 ounces imported
  semisweet chocolate,
  broken into small
  pieces
5–6 tablespoons unsalted
  butter

Have on Hand
9 × 2½-inch springform
  pan
Long, narrow spatula

Serves 10–12

Note: If using hazelnuts, I suggest you toast them first in a 350-degree oven 10 minutes. Transfer to a strainer over a bowl and gently rub them with damp paper toweling to remove their skins as well as possible.
Preheat oven to 375 degrees.

Prepare Pan: Butter springform pan and dust with fine bread crumbs or flour.

Helpful Hint: Allow shelf space in refrigerator for cooling, steps outlined below.

1. Combine egg yolks and sugar in a mixing bowl or bowl of electric mixer and beat until thick and pale in color—about 3–4 minutes. Add ground nuts and rum and fold gently until thoroughly incorporated.

2. In a clean mixing bowl with clean beaters, beat egg whites at low speed until foamy. Add cream of tartar, adjust speed to high and beat until mixture takes shape and firm but not dry peaks form. With a large rubber spatula add ¼ of the beaten egg whites into nut mixture and stir to soften, then carefully fold in remaining whites. Pour into prepared pan, scraping bowl clean, then level mixture. Bake in preheated oven

for 10 minutes. Reduce oven heat to 325 degrees and bake 45–50 minutes longer. Cake is done when it pulls away from sides of pan or when a cake tester inserted into center comes out clean. Loosen sides of cake by drawing an ordinary kitchen knife between cake and sides of pan and remove springform sides. Place a rack over cake and invert. Remove bottom of pan and set aside and allow cake to cool on rack. When cool, cover with another rack and invert again to return to original upright position. Place bottom section of springform pan over top of cooled cake and invert so that bottom is up. It is necessary to split cake into two layers and I advise that you refrigerate or freeze for an hour or so at this point. When cake is firm, carefully cut in half horizontally with a sharp serrated bread knife and set aside.

3. Melt 2 ounces chocolate in heavy saucepan or in top of double boiler over very low heat. Remove from heat, stir to a smooth cream, and set aside to cool. In the meantime, whip heavy cream in a cold bowl with chilled beaters and stir in cooled chocolate. Spread over bottom layer and sandwich with top half of cake. Chill in refrigerator while preparing apricot glaze.

4. Place apricot jam in a small saucepan and simmer over low heat to soften. Add rum and stir to mix; remove from heat. With back of wooden spoon push the glaze through a strainer over top of cake and smooth it all over with a metal spatula. Refrigerate to set glaze.

5. To prepare icing, melt remaining 4 ounces chocolate with butter in top of double boiler or heavy saucepan over very low heat; then stir to a smooth cream. Cool to tepid.

6. To ice cake, cut wax paper into four 10 × 3-inch strips. Place them in a square at edges of a cake plate to keep it clean. Remove cake from metal base and place on serving plate protected by wax-paper strips. Pour approximately ¾ of the melted chocolate over top. Now hold plate in both hands and tip it back and forth gently so icing rolls over top and is perfectly smooth. Smooth remaining icing around sides of cake with a long metal spatula. Let cool 5–10 minutes, then remove wax-paper strips by carefully pulling them out one at a time by the narrow end. Refrigerate uncovered or keep cool until ready to serve.

To Prepare Ahead
Follow steps 1 and 2 up to one month ahead. Cover securely with freezer wrap and freeze. Follow steps 3 and 4 up to two days ahead. Chill to set the glaze, then cover lightly with plastic wrap. Complete steps 5 and 6 early in the day of serving and keep in a cool place, uncovered, to avoid disturbing frosting.

MERINGUE HAZELNUT TORTE WITH CHOCOLATE BUTTER CREAM

The classic use of hazelnuts, which adds to the crunchiness of the meringue, and the velvety-smooth richness of the butter cream combine to make a delicious triple-tiered dessert.

1¾ cups hazelnuts, ground to a very fine texture

Meringue
6 egg whites
Pinch of salt
¾ cup sugar
2 tablespoons flour
1 teaspoon vanilla extract

Chocolate Butter Cream
2 egg yolks
3 ounces imported bittersweet chocolate
2 tablespoons water
½ cup sugar
⅓ cup water

12 tablespoons unsalted butter, at room temperature

1 tablespoon cocoa for garnish
Additional coarsely chopped hazelnuts for garnish

Have on Hand
14 × 17-inch cookie sheet, well buttered and dusted with flour
Pastry bag and plain ½-inch round tip
Baking rack

Serves 8

Preheat oven to 350 degrees.

1. *To Toast and Prepare Nuts:* Place hazelnuts on a cookie sheet and toast in oven about 10 minutes or until lightly colored. Transfer to a sieve-lined bowl and rub with a tea towel to remove skins as completely as possible. Pick out clean nuts and set aside. (Some of the nuts may still have a bit of skin clinging to them, but this doesn't matter.) Place nuts in workbowl of food processor fitted with steel blade or in batches into a blender and chop with several on/off pulses until nuts are finely ground.

2. *To Prepare Meringue Layers:* Reduce oven to 325 degrees. In a clean mixing bowl with clean beaters, beat egg whites at low speed until foamy. Add salt, increase speed of beaters, and beat until peaks begin to curl softly. Gradually add 3 tablespoons of the sugar, then beat 1 minute more until meringue is stiff but smooth and glossy. Set aside.

3. Sift remaining sugar and flour together into a separate mixing bowl

and stir in ground hazelnuts. With a large rubber spatula, carefully fold sugar mixture, a little at a time, into meringue. Add vanilla, stir through gently, and set aside.

4. *Outline for Meringue Layers:* To make necessary circle outlines, place a 7- or 8-inch saucepan cover at the uppermost corner of prepared cookie sheet as close to the edge as possible. Carefully twist the cover in place to make a pattern. With the first circle to guide you, make two additional circles on cookie sheet.

5. Fit a large pastry bag with the round tip and fill with meringue mixture. With even pressure, pipe a neat outline of a circle, making concentric circles as you work toward center. Continue to make 2 additional layers.

Making coil layers for Meringue Hazelnut Torte

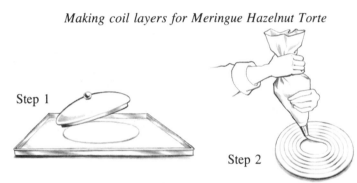

Step 1

Step 2

6. Place in preheated oven and bake 30–35 minutes until lightly browned and crisp to the touch. When done, remove from oven and, with the dull side of a paring knife, score the most perfect layer into 8 wedgelike sections while meringue is still warm. Allow layers to cool about 10 minutes on cookie sheet, then transfer to a rack to dry completely. Can be made ahead to this point.

7. *To Prepare Butter Cream:* Place egg yolks in a bowl of electric mixer or in a mixing bowl with hand beaters and whisk yolks until thick and pale.

8. Melt chocolate with 2 tablespoons water in a heavy saucepan or in top of a double boiler over simmering water. Remove from heat, stir to a smooth cream, and set aside to cool.

9. Combine sugar and water in a small saucepan and bring to a boil over moderately high heat. Allow to boil 1 minute, stirring to dissolve sugar. Reduce heat and let simmer about 10–12 minutes. If using a candy thermometer, clip onto side of pan, suspending tip in liquid but not touching bottom of pan. Cook until mixture reaches 220 degrees (the soft-ball stage). Sugar syrup should be of pouring consistency. If sugar

begins to color and has not yet reached 220 degrees, remove from heat and proceed with recipe.

10. As soon as syrup is ready, pour into beaten egg yolks in a thin stream. Continue beating until mixture cools.

11. Beat in softened butter, 1 tablespoon at a time, until thoroughly incorporated into mixture. Gently fold in cooled chocolate. If butter cream is too soft to spread onto meringue layers, refrigerate until it thickens slightly to spreading consistency.

12. *To Assemble Torte:* Set aside the scored layer. Divide butter cream and spread equal amounts over 2 remaining layers. Place one meringue layer over the other and top with the scored meringue circle. To decorate torte, tap cocoa powder through a sieve over top and sprinkle on the coarsely chopped hazelnuts.

To Prepare Ahead
Follow steps 1 through 6 up to two to three days ahead. Store in a large cookie tin or suitable covered container to keep crisp. Follow steps 7 through 11 up to one day ahead. Refrigerate, covered, in a suitable container. Complete step 12 early in the day and refrigerate until ready to serve.

LACE COOKIE CUPS

¾ cup pecans
½ cup white or brown sugar
⅓ cup light Karo syrup
1 stick unsalted butter
½ teaspoon salt
¾ cup all-purpose flour
Diced seasonal fruits
Assorted berries

Crème Fraîche

Have on Hand
2 14 × 17-inch aluminum
   cookie sheets
3 Chinese teacups without
   handles

Yield 10–12 cookie cups
To Prepare Cookie Sheets: Lightly butter cookie sheets, then dust with flour, tapping off excess.
Preheat oven to 300 degrees.

1. Place pecans on a cookie sheet and toast lightly in oven 5–6 minutes. Chop by hand or in food processor fitted with steel knife until medium fine. Set aside.

Adjust to preheat oven to 350 degrees. Adjust oven rack to lower third of oven.

2. In a heavy saucepan, combine sugar, syrup, and butter. Cook over moderate heat, stirring with a wooden spoon occasionally until butter melts. Add salt and flour and stir to mix with a wooden spoon. Remove from heat and add pecans. Stir to mix.

3. Spoon 2 teaspoons of batter for each cookie onto cookie sheet about 4 inches apart. With dampened fingers, pat mixture to an even, thin circle. Bake only 4 cookies on a sheet at one time, as they spread considerably. Place one cookie sheet at a time in lower third of oven. Bake 6–7 minutes until cookies are light brown and bubbly. Place teacups upside down on work counter, then remove cookies from oven and let stand 20–30 seconds before shaping.

How to form Lace Cookie Cups or Tulip Cookie Cups

Step 1   Step 2

4. With metal spatula, lift up one cookie at a time and gently place over teacup, pressing gently with fingers to form a tulip shape. It is important to work quickly, as cookies will cool and cannot be molded. If this should happen, return cookies to oven for a few seconds just to warm and soften them.

5. Form remaining cookies in batches on a clean prepared cookie sheet. Failure to use a freshly prepared cookie sheet will cause cookies to stick and crumble when you try to remove them. This batter stands well as you prepare each batch. Continue to bake cookie cups until batter is used up. Since lace cookie cups are fragile, carefully set them aside in one layer.

6. Just before serving, fill with an assortment of summer berries and top with crème fraîche.

To Prepare Ahead
Follow steps 1 through 5 up to two days ahead and store cookies in airtight containers, such as Tupperware. Cookies are fragile, so handle carefully.

Note: If weather is very hot and humid when you prepare these cookie cups, I advise baking them the same day as serving or they may lose their crispness.

MADELEINES

Madeleines are those wonderful little cakes made famous by Marcel Proust who found them "to look as though they had been moulded in the fluted scallop of a Pilgrim's Shell."

A madeleine pan is a baking utensil containing twelve shell-shaped molds. The following recipe will make enough batter to fill two pans.

6 tablespoons unsalted
    butter, plus additional
    1½ tablespoons to
    butter pans
3 eggs
⅔ cup granulated sugar
1 teaspoon vanilla
1 tablespoon grated lemon
    rind

1 cup all-purpose flour,
    sifted
Pinch of salt

Have on Hand
Two madeleine pans
Pastry brush
Wax paper

Yield 24 madeleines

Preheat oven to 375 degrees.

To Prepare Pans: In a small saucepan melt 1½ tablespoons butter and brush the fluted molds of the madeleine pans evenly. Dust pans with flour, tapping off excess and set aside.

1. In the same saucepan melt remaining 6 tablespoons butter and set aside.

2. In a mixing bowl with a portable hand mixer or in bowl of electric mixer, beat eggs at slow speed until foamy. Adjust speed to medium, add sugar, and beat about 8–10 minutes until egg mixture is thick and pale in color.

3. Sift flour and salt onto a square of wax paper and remeasure to 1 cup. Sift again directly over egg mixture in mixing bowl. With a large rubber spatula, carefully fold in until flour is completely incorporated. Add vanilla and lemon rind and fold into mixture. Lastly add melted butter, folding it in a little at a time until thoroughly incorporated. Do not allow prepared batter to stand.

4. Spoon the batter into the fluted shells to about ¾ full. If you added too much or too little, it's okay to scoop out or add additional batter. The batter will level itself. Place in preheated oven and bake 12–14 minutes until puffed and golden. Check halfway through baking. If necessary, reverse the position of pans so that madeleines brown evenly. Remove from oven and allow to cool about 5 minutes. With the tip of

a kitchen knife inserted between cakes and mold, lift out cakes and transfer them to a cake rack to cool completely.

To Prepare Ahead
Follow steps 1 through 4 up to two days ahead. Store in cookie jar or a covered tin.

Note: Madeleines are best served the same day they are baked, but will keep fairly crisp for several days (if they last that long) in a tightly covered cookie jar or tin.

TULIP COOKIE CUPS

These fluted, crispy cookies are a delicious container for your favorite sherbet, mousse, or ice cream.

⅔ cup confectioners' sugar
2 egg whites
4 tablespoons unsalted
    butter, melted
1 tablespoon heavy cream
1 teaspoon vanilla
5 tablespoons flour

Have on Hand
2 14 × 17-inch aluminum
    cookie sheets
3 Chinese teacups without
    handles

Yield 9–10 cookie cups

To Prepare Cookie Sheets: Lightly butter cookie sheets, then dust with flour, tapping off excess. Mark three circles on each, using a 6- or 7-inch pot cover, pressing it in place to make an impression.
Preheat oven to 325 degrees.

1. Combine confectioners' sugar and egg whites in a mixing bowl and stir to mix. Add butter, cream, and vanilla and stir to combine ingredients thoroughly. Sift flour directly into the batter, folding rapidly but gently with a rubber spatula.

2. Spoon approximately 1½ tablespoons batter into center of each circle. With back of a spoon, spread batter in a circular motion to edge to less than ⅛ inch thick.

3. Place one cookie sheet at a time on middle shelf in preheated oven and bake 6–7 minutes or until about 1 inch or so of the borders are golden brown.

4. Place teacups upside down on work counter, then remove cookies from oven. With metal spatula, lift up one cookie at a time and gently place over teacup, pressing gently with fingers to form a tulip shape. It is important to work quickly, as cookies will cool and cannot then be molded. If this should happen, return cookies to oven for a few seconds just to warm and soften them.

5. Form remaining cookies in batches on a clean prepared cookie sheet. Failure to use a freshly prepared cookie sheet will cause cookies to stick and crumble when you try to remove them. This batter stands well as you prepare each batch. Continue to bake cookie cups until batter is used up. Since tulip cups are fragile, carefully set them aside in one layer.

6. Just before serving, fill as suggested above or with Grapefruit Sorbet.

To Prepare Ahead
Follow steps 1 through 5 up to two days ahead and store cookies in airtight containers, such as Tupperware. They are fragile, so handle carefully.

Note: If weather is very hot and humid when you prepare these cookie cups, I advise your baking them the same day as serving or they can lose their crispness.

BREADS

Many people are intimidated by yeast, and baking bread seems like a tedious chore. And yet, baking bread gives one a sense of accomplishment and the wonderful feeling that you are contributing to your family's health. One can always purchase a pure bread in health-food stores, but baking your own gives it that extra ingredient called love. There are so many ways that one benefits by baking his or her own bread. First of all is taste—and everyone knows the best way to sell a house is to have a bread baking in the oven, its incomparable aroma permeating the air.

Yeast: The basis of all bread baking is the combination of flour and yeast. When one understands how to work with yeast, a living organism, all of the mystery is removed from bread baking.

There are two types of yeast: Fresh yeast that must be kept refrigerated; and dry, granular yeast. The most important thing to look for when purchasing yeast is the date on the package. Fresh yeast will last up to about two weeks in the refrigerator and the stamped date on dry yeast packages generally indicates a six-month shelf life. It is wise, however, to use it well within that stamped date.

To check that yeast is fresh, proof it by combining it with some or all of the liquid indicated in the recipe and 1 tablespoon or so of sugar. After about 5 minutes, fresh yeast will bubble and foam. You then proceed to use this mixture, following your recipe.

I don't always care to use sugar in my breads, as indicated in my French Country Bread. Most often, when I bake breads, I like to prepare a sponge, which is an initial step and an alternate proofing method. A sponge is prepared by incorporating all of the yeast and approximately ¼ cup of liquid into ½ cup flour from your total ingredients. Stir to mix, then cover and leave to rise, and within 45 minutes to 1 hour you will have an airy, spongy mass that indicates your yeast is alive and well. In addition, this first rising will improve the texture of your bread.

Temperature: Basic to working with yeast are correct liquid temperatures. When combining yeast with liquids, it is terribly important to understand that if the liquid is too hot, it will kill the yeast in as short a time as it would take to turn off a light bulb. To be very specific: Fresh yeast is stirred into liquid of approximately 80–90 degrees and granular yeast into water from 105 to 115 degrees. If you are uncertain about liquid temperature, err on the side of cool; this may perhaps slow down the rising of your bread, but slow rising is very often better.

Kneading: Today, with the sophisticated equipment available to many of us, kneading can be a simple task. If you really want to get your hands into it, kneading can be a very sensual experience. Kneading is an essential step in bread baking and is usually done by pressing into the dough with the heel of your hand, then folding it over and giving it quarter turns as you proceed. In this way, the yeast is evenly distributed and the dough is kneaded until its texture is elastic and satiny smooth.

Rising: After dough is kneaded, place it in a lightly greased bowl and turn to coat. Cover and let rise in a draft-free area. It is generally recommended that temperatures be moderately warm, or approximately 70 degrees. To test dough, lightly poke two fingers into it. If dough holds the indentation, it has risen sufficiently. This usually takes 1–1½ hours. The dough is punched down in the bowl by actually making a fist. (This is done to rid it of air bubbles and leaven gases.) At this point dough is shaped for final rising before baking.

Hint: Be certain oven is properly calibrated, because even the most perfect dough can be ruined in incorrect oven temperatures.

If ever "practice makes pefect," this is when. Bread baking, almost more than any other food, needs patience and persistence to develop that "feel." Once you get over the hurdle and are comfortable working with yeast, you will understand that beyond the kneading process, the actual baking of bread is a surprisingly simple revelation.

BREAD CRUMBS

No need to throw away leftover bread. It will provide the best bread crumbs you can obtain. There is almost always a time when we accumulate chunks and slices of French, Italian, or plain white bread. When they are hard but not moldy, make your own bread crumbs.

Toasted: Place the bread on a cookie sheet and bake in a preheated 375-degree oven 8–10 minutes until crisp and golden brown. Remove from oven and let cool. Break into smaller pieces if necessary and place in workbowl of food processor fitted with steel knife or in batches in a blender and grind with several on/off pulses or blend at high speed until you have a fine crumb.

Transfer to a clean, dry screw-top jar and store in a cool cupboard. Will keep up to several months.

Untoasted: Remove crusts, tear white bread into small pieces and place in workbowl of food processor fitted with steel knife or into blender and process with several on/off pulses or blend at high speed until you have a fine crumb.

Store in screw-top jar and refrigerate. The untoasted crumbs should be used within several days.

STRAWBERRY BREAD

A popular "receipt" from Elizabethan times.

2 cups flour
¾ cup sugar
1 teaspoon coarse (kosher)
    salt
1½ teaspoons baking
    powder
½ teaspoon baking soda
¼ cup unsalted butter,
    chilled
Grated rind of 1 orange
1 cup fresh orange juice or
    frozen orange juice,
    diluted ½ strength
2 eggs, lightly beaten

1 box fresh strawberries,
    washed and coarsely
    chopped
Confectioners' sugar or
    whipped cream
    (optional)

Have on Hand
9 × 5-inch loaf pan,
    buttered and well
    dusted with bread
    crumbs
Cake rack

Serves 8–10

Note: Do not use frozen berries, as they sink to the bottom of the batter and produce a wet bread.

Preheat oven to 350 degrees.

1. Sift together flour, sugar, salt, baking powder, and baking soda in mixing bowl or bowl of electric mixer.

2. Cut butter into flour mixture. With tips of fingers, 2 knives, a pastry blender, or flat paddle attachment of electric mixer, blend ingredients until texture of coarse meal.

3. Add orange rind, juice, and eggs to dry ingredients. Stir to mix just until all ingredients are combined thoroughly. With a large rubber spatula, fold in strawberries.

4. Pour batter into prepared pan and bake in preheated oven 1 hour and 10 minutes or until a cake tester plunged into the center comes out clean. Invert on a cake rack to cool completely.

5. Slice for serving. Serve warm with whipped cream or at room temperature simply dusted with confectioners' sugar.

To Prepare Ahead
Follow steps 1 through 4 up to one day ahead. Wrap in a tea towel and store in breadbox. Complete step 5 before serving.

PARTY BRIOCHE

When kneaded in the classic manner, brioche dough mixture is quite sticky and one's impulse is to add a lot of flour. It is better, therefore, to knead the dough in an automatic mixer with a dough hook or in a food processor fitted with steel knife. If these tools are not available, knead the dough by hand, using a slapping technique. That is, after the dough is stirred together, lift it up with a dough scraper and toss it back down with a thud on a lightly floured surface. This is actually fun to do and gets rid of frustrations more than any other kneading process I know of. So, have some fun and go make a brioche.

4–4½ cups all-purpose flour
¼ cup lukewarm water (80–90 degrees for fresh yeast *or* 105–115 degrees for dry)
½ ounce fresh yeast *or* 1 envelope dry
10 tablespoons unsalted butter
¼ cup sugar
1 teaspoon salt
½ cup milk, scalded

4 eggs at room temperature, beaten
1 tablespoon grated lemon peel

Have on Hand
6-cup brioche mold
Egg glaze: 1 white mixed with 1 tablespoon water
Pastry brush

Yields 1 large brioche

1. *Make a Sponge:* Place ½ cup of the flour in a small bowl and make a well. Pour in water and crumble or sprinkle in yeast. Stir with a fork or a chopstick to dissolve yeast, then draw in flour from inner wall and stir until a rough ball of dough is formed. Place bowl in a larger bowl, partially filled with warm water, cover with a tea towel, and let proof 30 minutes.

2. In a large mixing bowl, cream butter, sugar, and salt and set aside.

3. With a wooden spoon, stir milk into creamed mixture until it is tepid. Add the eggs, lemon peel, and sponge. Stir vigorously with a large wooden spoon 2 minutes. Stir in up to 3 cups of remaining flour to make a dough soft enough to handle.

4. *To Knead By Hand:* Turn dough out on a lightly floured board, then knead as follows. Lift dough from the board with the aid of a dough scraper. Brioche dough is sticky. Lift and drop it, turning it each time to coat surface ever so lightly with flour on board. Knead this way until dough is smooth and elastic, about 10 minutes.

In Automatic Mixer: Place dough in bowl of electric mixer with dough hook in place and knead at slowest speed about 7–8 minutes. If dough appears to be very sticky, add a bit more flour, about ⅓ cup gently shaking it in around the sides of the bowl. Continue mixing 2–3 minutes longer until dough clings to hook, cleans sides of bowl, and is smooth and elastic.

In Food Processor: Transfer dough to workbowl of food processor fitted with steel knife or dough hook. Run machine for 1 minute to knead.

5. Place dough in a clean, lightly oiled bowl, turning to coat on all sides. Cover with plastic wrap and place in a relatively cool 65–70-degree draft-free area. Let rise slowly until doubled in size, about 1½–2 hours or till dough remains indented when poked lightly with two fingers. Punch down in bowl, folding it over two or three times to reshape into a ball. Cover with plastic wrap and refrigerate overnight.

6. Next day, remove dough from refrigerator, punch down in bowl, and stir or fold down. Turn dough out onto a lightly floured board and knead into a ball. With a sharp knife, cut away a piece of dough about the size of a handball for topknot and set aside. Place larger ball of dough into a lightly buttered brioche mold and, with a dampened finger, make a deep indentation in center for topknot. Knead smaller piece of dough for a minute or two to expel the air. This will help to keep it firmly in place. Work it into a pear-shaped knob. Press point of knob firmly into indentation with round end sitting squarely on top of the dough. Be sure topknot is wedged in firmly enough or it may fall over while baking. With kitchen shears, snip in three places around knot so it keeps its separate shape. Cover lightly with plastic wrap and let rise almost to top of mold, about 1–1½ hours.

Preheat oven to 400 degrees.

7. Brush top of brioche with glaze and bake 25 minutes. Reduce oven temperature to 325 degrees and bake 20–25 minutes longer. If top is browning too quickly, cover loosely with a tent of foil. When it is golden brown and sounds hollow when you rap it with your knuckles, it is done. Transfer to a rack and cool several hours before cutting.

Note: For suggested use, see Chicken Marengo.

To Prepare Ahead

Follow steps 1 through 7 up to one day ahead, wrap in a clean kitchen towel, and store in a cool dry place. Or follow steps 1 through 7 up to one month ahead, wrap securely, and freeze.

FRENCH COUNTRY BREAD

The technique for doing this bread is rather basic. I first learned it at the hands of a Parisian friend. I adapted the sponge method of preparing the yeast, which I find gives the bread an extra degree of lightness and a very crusty exterior.

4½–4¾ cups all-purpose
    flour
Scant 2 cups lukewarm
    water (80–90 degrees
    for fresh yeast *or* 105–
    115 degrees for dry)
½ ounce fresh yeast *or* 1
    envelope dry
1½ teaspoons salt

Have on Hand
Dual French bread pan or
    14 × 17-inch cookie
    sheet
Egg glaze: 1 white mixed
    with 1 tablespoon
    water
Cornmeal

Yields 2 loaves

1. *Make a Sponge:* Place ½ cup of the flour in a small bowl and make a well. Pour in ¼ cup of the water and crumble or sprinkle in yeast. Stir with a fork or a chopstick to dissolve the yeast, then draw in flour from inner wall, stirring until a rough ball of dough is formed. Place this bowl in a larger bowl partially filled with warm water. Cover with a tea towel and let proof 30 minutes.

2. Place 4 cups of the flour in a large mixing bowl and sprinkle on salt. Make a deep well in center. Place sponge and remaining water in well, and with a large wooden spoon stir the flour mixture until you form a dough.

3. *To Knead By Hand:* Turn dough out on a lightly floured board, then knead as follows: With fingertips of one hand, lift mass of dough from the far edge and fold into center. With other hand, give dough a ¼ turn as you gently push into fold with heel of your other hand. Continue this lifting, turning, and folding motion, adding as little flour as necessary. As you continue to knead in this manner, you will find your own rhythm. Knead 10–15 minutes until dough is soft and pliable and no longer sticky.

In Automatic Mixer: Follow step 2 using bowl of electric mixer with dough hook in place. Beat at slowest speed about 8 minutes. Turn dough out on a lightly floured board and continue to knead by hand about 1 minute.

In Food Processor: Place 4 cups flour in workbowl of food processor fitted with steel knife or dough hook and sprinkle over the salt. Distribute sponge around center and pour on a tablespoon or two *less* of remaining water and process to mix about 1 minute. (This requires a large-capacity workbowl or processing dough in 2 batches.) Turn dough out on a lightly floured board and continue to knead by hand about 1 minute.

4. Place dough in a large, lightly oiled bowl, turning to coat on all sides. Cover dough with tea towel and let rise in a moderately cool but draft-free area of your kitchen. Allowing French bread dough to rise in a cool rather than a warm place results in a finer texture. Let rise slowly until doubled in size, about 1–1½ hours, or, when poked lightly with two fingers, dough holds its indentation.

5. Punch down in bowl, then fold dough over, kneading it several times in bowl to reshape it into a ball.

6. Transfer to a lightly floured work surface and divide in half. Shape each half into a long oval by rolling and stretching with your hands until it is approximately 14–16 inches long. Repeat with second half of dough and transfer to dual French bread pan or cookie sheet which has been sprinkled with cornmeal. Cover lightly with towel and allow to rise again in a draft-free area until doubled in size, about 45 minutes. Remove cover and, with a sharp knife or kitchen shears, cut 3 diagonal slashes across surface of each loaf.

Preheat oven to 450 degrees.

7. Just before baking, brush exposed surface of shaped breads with a brush dipped in glaze. Place in preheated oven and bake 25 minutes. Reduce oven temperature to 375 degrees and bake 10 minutes longer until breads are crusty and browned and sound hollow when you rap them with your knuckles. Turn off oven and allow breads to cool slightly in oven 5 minutes longer with door open. Remove and place on a rack to cool.

To Prepare Ahead

Follow steps 1 through 7 early in the day. Since there are no preservatives in this bread, use within a day of baking. Or follow steps 1 through 7 up to one month ahead. Bring to room temperature, wrap securely, and freeze.

PISSALADIÈRE 2

A pissaladière is a light herb-tomato French-style pizza.

1 package active dry yeast
  or 1 ounce fresh
½ cup plus 2 tablespoons
  warm water (105–115
  degrees for dry yeast,
  80–90 degrees for
  fresh)
2¼ cups all-purpose flour
1 teaspoon coarse (kosher)
  salt
2 teaspoons sugar
1 tablespoon vegetable oil

½ teaspoon coarse (kosher)
  salt
Freshly ground pepper
2 teaspoons fresh basil
  leaves *or* ½ teaspoon
  dried
2 teaspoons fresh oregano
  leaves *or* ½ teaspoon
  dried
1 tablespoon olive oil
¾ cup freshly grated
  Parmesan cheese

Topping
2 tablespoons unsalted butter
1 tablespoon vegetable oil
1 large Bermuda onion,
  thinly sliced
1–2 large garlic cloves,
  finely chopped
2 cups canned whole
  tomatoes, drained,
  seeded, and chopped
  (reserve about ½ cup
  of tomato juice)
2 teaspoons brown sugar

To Finish
1 tin (2 ounces) flat anchovy
  fillets, rinsed in cold
  water and dried on
  paper toweling
1 large green pepper, cored,
  seeded, and cut into
  julienne strips
½ cup pitted black olives,
  sliced in half

Have on Hand
15-inch-round pizza pan

Serves 8–10

1. *To Prepare Dough Make a Sponge First:* Crumble yeast into ¼ cup of the warm water and stir to mix. Place ½ cup of the flour in a mixing bowl and make a well. Pour in yeast mixture and with a fork draw in flour from inner wall to incorporate until you have a mass. Cover bowl and place in a larger bowl half filled with warm water. Allow to proof 30 minutes.

2. *Hand Method:* In a mixing bowl, combine remaining flour, salt, and sugar and make a well. Stir in the remaining warm water with a

large wooden spoon and add the sponge. Stir for another minute or two, incorporating the flour, then add oil and mix through. Knead dough on a lightly floured surface about 10 minutes until smooth and elastic. Place in a lightly oiled bowl, turning dough in bowl to lightly coat. Cover with a clean kitchen towel and let rise in a warm place until doubled— about 1 hour.

Food Processor Method: In workbowl of food processor fitted with steel knife, combine flour, salt, and sugar. Process with 2 quick on/off pulses to mix. Remove cover and add remaining warm water and sponge. Process with 3 quick on/off pulses. Add oil and let machine run about 1 minute until dough forms a ball and is smooth. Turn out onto a lightly floured surface and knead by hand briefly into a smooth round ball. Place in lightly oiled bowl, turning dough in bowl to lightly coat. Cover with a clean kitchen towel and let rise in a warm place until doubled— about 1 hour.

Preheat oven to 400 degrees.

3. In a skillet, melt butter with oil and cook onion slices until translucent but not brown. Place a sheet of wax paper on top of onions in pan. Cover pan and sweat onions over low heat 20 minutes, stirring occasionally. Remove from pan and set aside. Add garlic, tomatoes, seasonings, and herbs, and stir to mix. Simmer with cover ajar 25–30 minutes, stirring occasionally until the mixture is almost a purée. Test to adjust seasoning if necessary.

4. When dough has risen, punch down and place on a lightly floured work surface. Knead into a ball and with a floured rolling pin roll out into a large circle about ⅛ inch thick. Lightly oil pizza pan and place dough on it. It will be necessary to stretch dough out to the edge of the pan.

5. Brush on 1 tablespoon olive oil all over dough and scatter on half of the grated cheese, leaving about 1 inch of dough exposed all around. Distribute onions evenly over cheese, then spread tomato sauce over onions. Sprinkle on remaining cheese to cover.

6. Arrange anchovies and green pepper strips in a lattice-box pattern on top of tomatoes. Center an olive half in each box and brush olives lightly with a bit of oil. Bake in preheated oven about 25 minutes until crust is golden brown. Cut into wedges and serve hot.

To Prepare Ahead

Follow steps 1 through 6 up to one day ahead. Cool, wrap securely with foil, and refrigerate. Bring to room temperature and warm through in a 350-degree oven 15–20 minutes just before serving.

CASSEROLE HERB BREAD

This herb-flecked bread, made in a 2-quart soufflé dish, mushrooms over the rim of the dish when baked, and makes an admirable centerpiece.

1 cup half-and-half
1 teaspoon salt
2 tablespoons sugar
1 cup lukewarm water (80–90 degrees for fresh yeast *or* 105–115 degrees for dry)
1 ounce fresh yeast *or* 1 envelope dry
2 tablespoons chopped fresh basil leaves *or* 1 teaspoon dried
1 teaspoon snipped fresh thyme leaves *or* ¼ teaspoon dried

1 teaspoon snipped fresh rosemary leaves *or* ¼ teaspoon dried
2 tablespoons finely chopped Italian flat-leaf parsley
2 cloves garlic, finely chopped
4¼–4¾ cups all-purpose flour

Have on Hand
2-quart soufflé dish
Egg glaze: 1 yolk mixed with 1 tablespoon water

Yield 1 large bread

1. In a saucepan, combine half-and-half, salt, and sugar, and bring just to the edge of a boil. Remove from heat and stir to cool until mixture is lukewarm.

2. Pour water into a large mixing bowl, crumble or sprinkle in yeast, and stir to dissolve.

3. Prepare fresh herbs or crush dry basil, thyme, and rosemary in a mortar and pestle or rub with fingertips to release their flavor.

4. Add cooled milk mixture to dissolved yeast in mixing bowl, add parsley and herbs, and stir to mix.

5. Add flour gradually and with a large wooden spoon, stir vigorously around bowl to make a ball.

6. *To Knead By Hand:* Place dough on a lightly floured board and knead with a folding motion until smooth and elastic, about 10 minutes.

In Automatic Mixer: Stir dough in bowl of electric mixer with dough hook in place. Beat at slowest speed about 8 minutes. Turn dough out on a lightly floured surface and continue to knead by hand about 30 seconds longer.

In Food Processor: Transfer prepared dough to workbowl of a food processor fitted with steel knife or dough hook. Process to knead dough

1 minute. Turn dough out on a lightly floured surface and continue to knead by hand 30 seconds longer.

7. Put dough into a clean, lightly greased bowl, turning to coat dough on all sides. Cover with a tea towel and set in a moderately warm, 70–75 degree, draft-free area until doubled in size, about 1 hour. Punch batter down, knead in bowl for a minute or two and reshape into a ball. *Preheat oven to 400 degrees.*

8. Place in a lightly oiled soufflé dish, cover, and let rise 30–40 minutes more. Brush top of dough with egg glaze, then put in preheated oven and bake 20 minutes. Reduce heat to 375 degrees and bake 20 minutes longer. Remove from oven and soufflé dish. Transfer bread to a rack and let cool completely.

To Prepare Ahead
Follow steps 1 through 8 up to one day ahead, wrap in a clean kitchen towel, and store in a cool dry place. Or follow steps 1 through 8 up to one month ahead, wrap securely, and freeze.

FRENCH CROUTONS

Perfect accompaniment for pâtés, hot soups, and salads.

1 narrow loaf French bread about 15 inches long, sliced about ¼ inch thick	1–2 large cloves garlic, cut in half crosswise 5 tablespoons clarified butter*

Yield about 50 pieces

Preheat oven to 450 degrees.

1. Spread bread slices on a cookie sheet one layer deep. Dry in oven 8–10 minutes or until lightly browned on both sides.

2. Rub warm bread slices with cut surface of garlic halves.

3. Melt butter in a large skillet and sauté bread slices in batches just a few seconds to coat. Drain on a rack. Transfer to a cloth-lined basket for serving.

To Prepare Ahead
Follow steps 1 through 3 up to two days ahead. Store in a tightly closed tin or wrap in foil. Do not refrigerate.

HOT LEMON HERB BREAD

1 narrow loaf French bread
5–6 tablespoons unsalted
    butter
1 tablespoon fresh tarragon
    leaves *or* 1 teaspoon
    dried
1 tablespoon coarsely
    chopped fresh basil
    leaves *or* 1 teaspoon
    dried

2 teaspoons fresh thyme
    leaves *or* 1 teaspoon
    dried
1 large clove garlic, finely
    chopped
2 tablespoons fresh lemon
    juice

Serves 10–12

1. Place bread on a piece of aluminum foil large enough to cover it. Turn bread on its side for slicing. With a serrated bread knife, cut into thin, even slices but not through bottom crust.

2. In a small saucepan, melt butter and remove from heat. Add herbs, garlic, lemon juice, and salt, and stir to mix. Taste to adjust seasoning if necessary. With a teaspoon, spoon a little of herb mixture between bread slices, then, with back of spoon, spread to coat each slice. Bring up the two long sides of foil and join the two edges. Make neat folds to enclose foil over seasoned loaf. Tuck in ends. Can be made ahead to this point. Refrigerate until ready to use.

Preheat oven to 350 degrees.

3. Bring to room temperature, then heat through in preheated oven just before serving.

To Prepare Ahead

Follow steps 1 and 2 up to one day ahead and refrigerate.

11

ALL'S WELL THAT ENDS WELL

Lucky for me . . . as I was growing up, rich desserts were only prepared for special occasions and holidays. My parents' Mediterranean background kept the finish of the meal to stewed fruits, fresh applesauce, gelatin, rice, and chocolate puddings in small custard cups. I savored the chocolate pudding more than anything and was the lucky member of a family of five children to get the last spoonfuls from the saucepan . . . cherished moments from days gone by. How fortunate I was by today's standards!

When I married and served a roast chicken for the first dinner in my new apartment, my husband didn't understand when the meal ended right there. I shall never forget his expectant, wide-eyed, confused expression as he waited for the dessert course and then longingly asked, "Well, don't you even have a Lorna Doone?" When I plan a meal, I don't start with desserts, and when I order in a restaurant, I never look at the desserts first, contrary to the norm. And yet I enjoy a well-prepared dessert.

When I plan a special company dinner, my preferences run to light, creamy, and custardy desserts or a delicate meringue, such as my Apricot Meringue Torte. However, to balance a light entree, I will serve a rich, chocolaty dessert, such as the Viennese Nut Torte. I have noticed that a dinner party main course can be just mildly appealing, or draw quiet applause, but if the dessert is special, the whole meal is remembered as superb.

If dessert is your thing, have a wonderful dessert party. It's a fun way to entertain a large group of friends. You can put your personality into four or five desserts and make lots of people, including yourself, very happy. It's also a perfect opportunity to serve some of those special sweet wines, stored for the occasion.

COLD SOUFFLÉS

A cold soufflé is fun to make and dramatic to present. It can be completely made up to two or three days ahead and garnished, if desired, before serving. Cold soufflés are refreshing and light. Do a colorful trio of Chocolate, Lemon, and Raspberry, and invite your guests to take a little from each one. A spoonful of each on your dessert plate makes the soufflés go a long way.

When cold soufflés contain a gelatin and custard base they are also called *Bavarian creams*. Often, in a cold soufflé, the gelatin base is chilled about 15–20 minutes or until it rolls like an unbeaten egg white. Properly beaten egg whites and softly whipped cream are then carefully folded into the cold base and chilled until firm in a soufflé dish or mold. *To Heighten the Dramatic Presentation of a Cold Soufflé:* The volume achieved by adding properly beaten egg whites will increase the size of your soufflé mixture and necessitate the use of a collar around your soufflé dish. To prepare a soufflé dish with a collar: Cut a strip of parchment paper or aluminum foil long enough to circle and overlap the soufflé dish. Fold it in half lengthwise. Butter one side of paper, then wrap buttered side around dish (the butter will help initially to secure the paper in place where it overlaps). Encircle dish and paper with kitchen string. It's helpful to place the paper-collared soufflé dish on its side and secure the paper tightly with string, wrapping it just below the rim of the dish. When you place the dish upright, the collar should stand about 2–3 inches above the rim of the dish. A 3–3½-cup soufflé dish is ideal for cold soufflés. The larger the capacity of the soufflé dish, the less of the soufflé itself will come over the rim. If you already have a 4- or 5-cup soufflé dish and don't wish to invest in another, you can increase the height of the filling by piping out a row of whipped cream rosettes or swirls.

A WORD ON CUSTARDS

Milk and eggs in varying proportions are the two basic ingredients of any custard. There are two ways to prepare a custard. In one, yolks and milk are cooked together over gentle heat to a creamy consistency. The other type of custard combines eggs and milk, which are then baked or steamed together until firmly set as in a flan. The soft custard known as Crème Anglaise can be used as a sauce to top cakes such as Génoise and pound cake, poached or fresh fruit, or mousses and puddings. It can also be used as a base for ice cream or Bavarian creams.

Proportions for a soft custard are generally 2 egg yolks to 1 cup of milk. Additional egg yolks will make it richer for use as a custard sauce, while a little cornstarch or flour added to the basic custard will create a pastry cream.

Choice of proper utensils is essential to the success of a soft-custard preparation. A custard is best prepared in a double boiler, but with care it can be thickened over direct but gentle heat in a sturdy saucepan. Assemble all of your tools—a whisk for initial beating and a wooden spoon for stirring. And be sure always to scald the milk before adding it to the eggs.

Remember, a soft custard requires attention and must never be allowed to boil!

SEASONAL FRUITS IN SPUMANTE, UMBRIAN STYLE

Fresh fruits are happily becoming a popular ending to meals. Don't relegate them to outdoor summer luncheons or an occasional warm-weather barbecue. Fresh fruits are in season all year long.

6 cups freshly cut-up assorted fruits	1 bottle Spumante (Italian sparkling wine)

Serves 10–12

1. Combine ripe, juicy pears; sweet, tender peaches; and bright, moist cherries; or an assortment of fresh berries—or berries in combination with other summer fruits. Tangy winter grapefruits and dulcet navel oranges with apple wedges can be a wintertime variation. (I prefer not to use any type of melon as they exude too much liquid.)

2. Wash and dry all fruits eaten out of hand except blackberries and raspberries. Peel rind from citrus fruits; then cut into neat, even rounds. Cut peaches, plums, apples, pears, and nectarines, etc., into neat little

wedges, starting from the outer skin and working in toward the pit or core. Hull strawberries; then slice in half. Pit cherries if possible.

3. Whatever combination of fruits you are using, prepare a bowlful up to several hours before serving or very early in the day. Refrigerate, covered, but bring to room temperature up to 1 hour before serving.

4. In the meantime, chill a bottle of Spumante. Pour the bubbly liquid into the bowl of fruits and serve immediately from wide-mouthed champagne glasses or clear dessert bowls.

Your family and guests will thank you for this wonderful light finish.

To Prepare Ahead
Follow steps 1 through 3 up to one day ahead. Bring to room temperature before serving and complete step 4.

CREMA DI AMARETTI

10 egg yolks (freeze whites for meringues, soufflés, etc.)
½ cup sugar
⅓ cup cold water
1½ tablespoons unflavored gelatin (each envelope is 1 tablespoon)
½ cup Cognac or brandy
1½ cups heavy cream, softly whipped
5 packages Amaretti cookies (2 cookies in each package)

½ cup espresso (instant or freshly brewed)
½ cup heavy cream and fresh strawberries or candied violets for garnish

Have on Hand
2-quart loaf pan
Plastic wrap
Pastry bag with star tip

Serves 8–10

To Prepare Pan: Line loaf pan with a large enough piece of plastic wrap to leave approximately a 2–3-inch overhang all around after pressing into the corners of the pan. Set aside.

1. Combine yolks and sugar in a mixing bowl or bowl of electric mixer and beat 3–4 minutes until mixture is thick and pale in color and forms a ribbon when beater is lifted.

2. In the meantime, pour cold water into a 1-cup Pyrex glass measure, sprinkle on gelatin, and let stand several minutes until gelatin has absorbed liquid.

3. Bring Cognac just to the edge of a boil in a small saucepan. Remove from heat, then with a rubber spatula scrape all the gelatin into the hot liquid and stir until gelatin is thoroughly dissolved. Gradually pour liquid into egg-yolk mixture, whisking vigorously to incorporate thoroughly. Refrigerate 20–30 minutes until mixture has a consistency like the white of an egg. Be careful not to leave it in refrigerator too long or it will jell. Remove from refrigerator and whisk to soften and to remove any lumps.

4. In a cold bowl with cold beaters, whip heavy cream until beaters drawn across top of cream leave light traces. Gently fold whipped cream into yolk mixture and set aside.

5. Pour espresso into a small shallow dish. Place a strainer over a separate bowl. Dip Amaretti one by one into espresso, then transfer to strainer to drain. Do not allow cookies to soak or they will fall apart.

6. Arrange flavored Amaretti, rounded side down, in a single line centered along bottom of prepared mold. Spoon in half of soufflé mixture. Arrange remaining cookies in a single row and pour in balance of soufflé mixture. Bring up plastic wrap overhang to cover and refrigerate 5–6 hours or overnight. Can be done ahead to this point.

7. *To Serve:* Several hours before serving, unwrap plastic covering, place a serving platter over the pan to invert and unmold. Carefully pull off plastic wrap and discard. Firmly whip ½ cup additional heavy cream and put into pastry bag fitted with a star tip. Pipe rosettes of cream at each corner at base of mousse, connecting them with swirls of cream. Decorate rosettes with whole fresh strawberries or candied violets. Return to refrigerator until ready to serve. Serve with a bowl of additional strawberries if desired.

To Prepare Ahead
Follow steps 1 through 6 up to two days ahead and refrigerate. Complete step 7 up to several hours ahead.

FLAN
(Light and Creamy Caramel Custard)

Some years ago I was visiting my mother, who lives about an hour away.
I told her about a party I was giving the following week. She said, "Wait
a while longer. I will make you a flan to take home." "But, Mom," I
answered, "the party's next week!" "Don't worry," she said, "it will
keep." I waited.

1½ cups sugar
1 quart milk
6 whole eggs
2 teaspoons vanilla extract
Fresh strawberries for
    garnish (optional)

Have on Hand
6-cup ring mold or loaf pan
Bain-marie*

Serves 10–12

Note: Before preparing the caramel it is a good idea to warm your
mold by placing it in a larger pan of hot water. If the mold is cold, the
caramel will stiffen in place as soon as you pour it in and you will not
be able to coat the mold properly. Remember, too, that the caramel is
hot and when you pour it into the mold, the mold will instantly become
very hot; so wear mitts or gloves.

Preheat oven to 350 degrees.

1. Put 1 cup of the sugar in a small heavy saucepan, place over
moderate heat, and stir to dissolve. Simmer without stirring at first.
Sugar will begin to liquefy and then turn a light amber color. If crystals
form, brush down the sides of the pan with a pastry brush dipped in
cold water. Allow mixture to cook until it becomes a rich walnut color.
(Watch this procedure very carefully, as mixture can caramelize quickly,
then become very dark in just seconds and burn.) At the moment it is
ready, pour into warm mold with gloved hands, tipping it back and forth
to cover as much of the inside of mold as possible. Wait a few minutes
for pan to cool, then put it into the refrigerator for about 10 minutes to
firm up caramel. Remove from refrigerator and set aside. (Caramel
coating will be very hard and even cracked, but this doesn't matter.)

2. In a saucepan, bring milk to the edge of a boil. While milk is
heating, fill a large mixing bowl or skillet with ice cubes one layer deep.
Remove milk from heat and stir over ice to cool quickly. Set aside.

3. In a mixing bowl, beat eggs just until the yolks and whites combine,

then beat in remaining ½ cup sugar until dissolved. Add the cooled milk, then vanilla, and stir to mix.

4. Strain the custard into a mixing bowl and ladle into the mold. Place in a shallow baking pan and pour enough boiling water to come ⅔ of the way up sides of mold (bain-marie). Bake in preheated oven for one hour, or until a cake tester or a knife inserted in center of custard comes out clean. Surface of custard should shiver slightly and not be too hard. Remove mold from water bath and set aside to cool. Refrigerate in mold until ready to serve. Can be made ahead to this point.

5. *To Unmold:* Run a knife around the edge of custard to loosen it. Place a serving dish (with a rim to catch the sauce) over mold and invert quickly and decisively. Caramel sauce will run onto plate and around mold. Garnish with fresh strawberries if desired.

To Prepare Ahead
Follow steps 1 through 4 up to one week ahead. Cover and refrigerate. Complete step 5 up to several hours ahead and return to refrigerator until ready to serve.

GRAPEFRUIT SORBET

I love the tartness of grapefruit, and when served as a sherbet in the Tulip Cookie Cup and topped with a sweet Raspberry Sauce it is a perfect example of three simply done procedures combining to make a perfect whole.

4 cups water
1½ cups sugar, more or
   less, according to
   sweetness of grapefruit
About 1 teaspoon grated
   grapefruit rind
1 cup fresh grapefruit juice

1 cup grapefruit juice from
   frozen concentrate,
   diluted half strength
2 tablespoons vodka
Mint leaves for garnish
   (optional)

Serves 8–10

1. Combine water and sugar in a heavy saucepan and stir over high heat until sugar dissolves. Cook at a brisk simmer, adjusting heat as necessary, so that mixture does not boil over and the syrup lightly films a wooden spoon, about 15 minutes.

2. Add grapefruit rind, juices, and vodka. Pour into a stainless steel bowl, cover securely with foil, and freeze a minimum of 5–6 hours. When completely frozen, remove from freezer and break into chunks. Working in batches, transfer to workbowl of food processor fitted with steel knife or to a blender. Do not overload workbowl. Process or blend to purée mixture and return to the clean stainless steel bowl. Cover securely with foil and return to freezer for several hours or overnight.

3. Several hours before serving or up to 1 day ahead, purée mixture a second time and return to freezer. (This second processing will result in a lighter, creamier sherbet.)

4. *To Serve:* Scoop into Tulip Cookie Cups or spoon into wide-mouth champagne glasses and top with a spoonful of Raspberry Sauce. Garnish with mint leaves, if desired.

To Prepare Ahead
Follow steps 1 and 2 up to several weeks ahead. Follow step 3 up to one day ahead. Complete step 4 just before serving.

MOCHA POTS DE CRÈME

1⅔ cup light cream *or* 1 cup
   heavy cream plus ⅔
   cup milk
1½ ounces imported
   semisweet chocolate
2 tablespoons instant
   espresso
¼ cup boiling water
½ cup sugar
2 tablespoons cold water
1 teaspoon vanilla
5 egg yolks
1 whole egg

Garnish
½ cup heavy cream,
   whipped
Candied violets (optional)

Have on Hand
Set of 6 pots de crème cups
   with covers or
   individual ramekins
Fine strainer
Bain-marie*
Pastry bag with star tip

Serves 6

Preheat oven to 325 degrees.
1. Place cream in a small saucepan and bring just to the edge of a boil over low heat.

2. In the meantime, place chocolate squares on a cutting surface and chop coarsely. Set aside.

3. Place instant espresso into a 1-cup Pyrex glass measuring cup and pour in enough boiling water to reach the ¼-cup mark. Stir to dissolve and set aside.

4. Combine ¼ cup of the sugar and cold water in a heavy saucepan, stir to dissolve, then simmer over moderately high heat until mixture begins to caramelize. Watch this procedure carefully, as the sugar can be a light caramel color one moment and in an instant turn very dark and even burn. When mixture is a light caramel color, reduce heat to a bare simmer and gradually add scalded cream, whisking vigorously to a smooth sauce. Add chocolate, espresso, and remaining ¼ cup sugar, and stir to mix until thoroughly incorporated. Remove from heat and allow to cool for a few minutes, then stir in vanilla.

5. In the meantime, whisk the yolks and whole egg together in a mixing bowl. Slowly pour beaten egg into cream mixture, whisking constantly. Place a fine sieve over a wide-mouth pitcher (a 4-cup Pyrex glass measure is ideal) or a bowl and strain the custard. If using a pitcher, pour custard into the pots de crème cups or ramekins or use a ladle if custard is in a mixing bowl, then cover containers.

6. Place the covered pots de crème cups or ramekins in a shallow baking pan and pour enough hot water into pan to come halfway up sides of cups (bain-marie). If using ramekins, cover with foil so that moisture does not seep into custard. Place in preheated oven and bake 25–30 minutes. Custard should be soft and a bit creamy inside when cake tester or a very thin knife is inserted into center. If tester comes out clean, which is the usual standard for doneness, the custards may be heavy after they are chilled. Remove from water bath, then remove covers from cups and allow to cool. Replace covers and refrigerate for several hours or overnight.

7. *To Serve:* With a rubber spatula scrape whipped cream into a pastry bag fitted with a star tip. Pipe rosettes over top of each custard and top with candied violets if desired.

To Prepare Ahead
Follow steps 1 through 5 up to one day ahead. Refrigerate, covered. Complete step 6 up to several hours before serving and refrigerate until ready to serve.

APRICOT MERINGUE TORTE

I think this is my favorite dessert. It's adaptable to almost any meal, or simply to share with friends during a quiet visit.

Meringue
6 egg whites at room
   temperature
¼ teaspoon cream of tartar
½ teaspoon white vinegar
1 cup superfine sugar
1 teaspoon vanilla
1 cup finely ground almonds

Apricot Purée
4 ounces dried apricots,
   soaked overnight in
   water to cover
2 ½-inch-wide strips of
   lemon peel

½ cup water
½ cup sugar
2 tablespoons fresh lemon
   juice
¾ cup heavy cream,
   whipped

Confectioners' sugar for
   garnish

Have on Hand
2 9-inch round cake pans
Parchment paper

Serves 8

To Prepare Pans: Butter cake pans well and dust with flour. Line the bottom of each pan with a round disk of parchment.
Preheat oven to 375 degrees.

1. In a mixing bowl or bowl of electric mixer, beat egg whites at low speed until foamy. Add cream of tartar, adjust speed to medium high and continue to beat until soft peaks form. Add vinegar, beat just to mix, then very slowly beat in sugar, 1 tablespoon at a time. Continue beating for 1 minute until mixture is very stiff and shiny. With a large rubber spatula, fold in vanilla and almonds.

2. Divide meringue mixture into prepared pans. Reduce oven heat to 350 degrees and bake 35–40 minutes until just lightly colored and crisp to the touch. Turn oven off and allow meringues to dry in oven with door ajar for about 30 minutes. Remove from oven and cool. Gently invert meringue layers onto a cake rack, then carefully peel off paper and discard.

3. *Apricot Purée:* Place apricots and soaking liquid in a saucepan. Simmer gently over low heat with lemon peel 30–40 minutes until tender. Cool and transfer to a food processor or blender being certain to scrape out all contents of pan with rubber spatula and purée. Pour purée into a

small sieve-lined bowl and with a rubber spatula rub through to a very smooth purée.

4. Combine ½ cup water and sugar in a saucepan. Stir to dissolve sugar. Add lemon juice and bring to the edge of a boil. Reduce heat and simmer 15–20 minutes or until reduced to a thick syrup.

5. Fold ⅓ of apricot purée into whipped cream, then sandwich between meringue layers. Transfer to a doily-lined cake plate.

6. Dilute remaining apricot purée with lemon syrup and pour into a pretty glass serving dish. Can be made ahead to this point.

7. When ready to serve, dust top meringue layer with confectioners' sugar to cover completely. Serve with apricot sauce spooned over individual portions.

To Prepare Ahead
Follow steps 1 through 6 up to one day ahead. Refrigerate cake covered with a tent of plastic wrap and sauce in a suitable container. Complete step 7 just before serving.

COLD CHOCOLATE SOUFFLÉ

This cold chocolate soufflé has a mousselike texture where the gelatin is not apparent. The fun part of this recipe is that unlike a chocolate mousse, the soufflé will stand above the rim of the dish, with the addition of a collar.

3 ounces semisweet
    chocolate
½ cup confectioners' sugar
1 envelope unflavored
    gelatin
3 tablespoons cold water
1 cup milk
Pinch of salt
1 tablespoon vanilla extract

2 tablespoons Grand Marnier
2 cups heavy cream, softly
    whipped
Finely ground fresh coffee
    for garnish (optional)

Have on Hand
3–3½-cup soufflé dish
Parchment paper

Serves 8–10

1. Prepare a soufflé dish with a collar. (See Cold Raspberry Soufflé recipe.)

2. Melt chocolate in a heavy saucepan over very low heat, stirring occasionally, or place in a small heatproof dish and melt in a 250-degree oven 15 minutes. When mixture appears to be soft, stir to a smooth

cream. Remove from heat and, with a wooden spoon, stir confectioners' sugar into melted chocolate as well as possible. As you stir, lumpy coated particles of chocolate will develop but will dissolve later, with the addition of hot milk. Set aside.

3. Sprinkle gelatin over cold water and let stand until gelatin has absorbed liquid, about 3–5 minutes. Do not stir.

4. In another saucepan, scald milk until a film covers the surface; do not allow to boil. Pour hot milk into chocolate mixture and simmer over low heat about 3–4 minutes, stirring constantly to dissolve lumpy bits of chocolate. Remove from heat and stir in the softened gelatin to incorporate thoroughly. Add salt and vanilla extract and stir to mix. Transfer to a mixing bowl and let cool. Put into refrigerator and chill 20–30 minutes or until mixture just begins to jell around sides of bowl. Add Grand Marnier and whisk until light and airy.

5. With a rubber spatula, fold whipped cream into chocolate until thoroughly incorporated. Pour into prepared soufflé dish and chill several hours or overnight.

6. *To Serve:* Run a knife around the edge of the soufflé, then carefully peel back paper collar and discard. Garnish with a sprinkle of finely ground fresh coffee beans, if desired.

To Prepare Ahead
Follow steps 1 through 5 up to two days ahead. Place a tent of plastic wrap over collar and refrigerate. Complete step 6 up to several hours ahead. Refrigerate until just before serving.

PEAR SORBET

For pear fanciers—a sorbet of luscious perfection!

3 cups water
1 cup sugar
4–5 large pears (2–2¼ pounds), Comice or Bartlett
2 tablespoons fresh lemon juice

2 tablespoons pear liqueur or brandy
2 egg whites
Peppermint leaves and strips of lemon peel for garnish

Serves 6–8

1. Combine water and sugar in a saucepan and, with a wooden spoon, stir over low heat until sugar is dissolved. Bring to a boil and simmer briskly 10 minutes until a light syrup forms.

2. Peel pears and rub each one with lemon juice as you peel it to prevent discoloration. Core and halve pears, then remove any seeds that remain. Base halves on cutting board, slice, then cut into small dice. Add to sugar syrup and simmer, uncovered, until tender, about 10–15 minutes depending on ripeness.

3. Remove saucepan from heat, stir in pear liqueur, and stir to mix. Allow pears to cool in syrup.

4. Drain pears in a sieve over a bowl and reserve liquid. Place pears in workbowl of food processor fitted with knife blade or in blender and purée, scraping down sides with a rubber spatula as necessary. (This will take 1 or 2 minutes, to remove any lumps.) Add purée to liquid in bowl and stir to mix. Refrigerate about 1½ hours.

5. Remove pear purée from refrigerator. In a mixing bowl beat egg whites until firm but not dry peaks form, then stir into the pear mixture. Egg whites never completely incorporate into pear liquid but rather settle at surface like little white clouds. Transfer to 2 ice cube trays without dividers or stainless mixing bowl. Cover with foil and freeze several hours or overnight until firm.

6. Remove frozen pear mixture from freezer and break it up with a large kitchen spoon. Beat with electric beaters or transfer to workbowl of food processor fitted with steel knife and process until it becomes a thick purée. Return to bowl or ice trays, cover, and freeze a second time several hours or overnight. Several hours before serving, beat or process as above until mixture is creamy and smooth. (Freezing and puréeing mixture twice will assure maximum smoothness.) Return to freezer.

7. With an ice cream scooper, scoop balls of sorbet into chilled sherbet glasses or mound like a pyramid onto a chilled platter. Garnish with strips of lemon peel or peppermint leaves if desired.

To Prepare Ahead
Follow steps 1 through 5 up to several weeks ahead. Cover and freeze. Follow step 6 up to several hours ahead. Complete step 7 before serving.

GRAND MARNIER CUSTARD GRATINÉ

This custard preparation is similar to that of a Sabayon or a Zabaglione. Grand Marnier substitutes for the white wine or Marsala. It is particularly appealing when served warm over a combination of winter fruits. The fruits can be cooked or raw or a combination of both. They are placed in a baking dish and completely covered with the custard, then gratinéed.

6 egg yolks
6 tablespoons sugar
½ cup Grand Marnier
1 cup heavy cream
1 tablespoon confectioners'
    sugar

Fruits in Season
2–3 apples (McIntosh or
    Golden Delicious),
    peeled, cored, and cut
    up
2–3 tablespoons butter,
    grated lemon rind, 1
    teaspoon vanilla extract
    (for apples only)

About 1 cup of any one or
    combination of fruits,
    such as seedless
    grapes, strawberries,
    bananas, peaches, or
    apricots, etc.

Have on Hand
6- or 8-cup flameproof
    baking dish

Serves 6–8

1. Combine egg yolks and sugar in the top of a double boiler or in a mixing bowl that will later straddle a saucepan. With a wire whisk or electric mixer, beat mixture off heat until it is thick and pale in color and falls from the beaters in a slowly dissolving ribbon, about 6–8 minutes. Transfer mixture to top of double boiler, or, if using bowl, fit snugly in a saucepan partly filled with water that is heated to just below the boiling point. (Be sure water in saucepan does not touch the inserted bowl or top of double boiler.)

2. With a wooden spoon, gently stir eggs and sugar over moderate heat while gradually adding Grand Marnier, mixing steadily to incorporate. Continue to whisk until mixture increases to almost triple its volume and is thick and smooth. Never allow custard to boil even for a second or it will curdle. Remove from heat at once.

3. Transfer mixture to a crockery or glass bowl and stir a minute or

so to cool. Cover with foil and let stand for 1 hour until completely cool.

4. In the meantime, whip cream in a cold bowl with cold beaters until softly whipped or until beaters drawn across top leave light traces. Add confectioners' sugar and stir to mix through. When custard has completely cooled, fold in whipped cream.

5. If using apples, combine coarsely cut apples in a saucepan with butter, lemon rind, and vanilla extract. Cook over moderate heat, stirring frequently with a wooden spoon until sauce is thick enough to hold a mass in the spoon.

6. Spread applesauce in bottom of a buttered baking dish. Berries, grapes, or bananas should combine in their natural state; however, you might want to soften peaches, pears, or nectarines by quickly sautéing the sliced fruit in a little butter. (This is optional.) Distribute some additional fruits over top of applesauce. Spoon custard over fruits to cover them completely. Can be made ahead to this point.

Note: If made ahead and refrigerated, be sure to bring to room temperature before completing next step.

Preheat broiler to highest setting.

7. When ready to serve, adjust rack to about 6 inches under preheated broiler. Slide baking pan under broiler for just a few minutes to gratiné or color the top with streaks of amber. Watch carefully to prevent burning top of custard. Serve immediately.

To Prepare Ahead

Follow steps 1 through 5 up to one day ahead. Store separately in refrigerator, covered. Follow step 6 up to several hours ahead. Refrigerate, covered. Bring to room temperature and complete step 7 before serving.

COLD LEMON SOUFFLÉ

2 whole eggs
1 cup sugar
Pinch of salt
½ cup lemon juice
1½ tablespoons unflavored
    gelatin (each envelope
    is 1 tablespoon gelatin)
2–3 tablespoons grated
    lemon rind
½ cup egg whites

⅛ teaspoon cream of tartar
    or pinch of salt
1 cup heavy cream, softly
    whipped

Garnish
½ cup heavy cream,
    whipped firm
Julienne strips of lemon rind
Candied mimosa

Serves 8–10

1. Prepare a soufflé dish with a collar: Cut a strip of parchment paper or aluminum foil long enough to circle and overlap soufflé dish. Fold it in half lengthwise. Butter one side of paper, then wrap it around dish and fasten with kitchen string. Collar should stand about 2–3 inches above rim of dish. A 3–3½-cup high-sided soufflé dish will allow the custard to come up well over rim of the dish, which makes a dramatic presentation. Butter inside of dish.

2. Combine eggs, sugar, and salt in a mixing bowl or bowl of electric mixer and beat 3–4 minutes until mixture ribbons and is thick and pale in color.

3. In the meantime pour lemon juice into a 1-cup Pyrex glass measure, sprinkle on gelatin and let stand several minutes until gelatin has absorbed liquid.

4. Set the glass measure containing gelatin mixture in a pan of simmering water. The gelatin will slowly dissolve into a liquid state. At that point, remove it from heat but leave it sitting in the warm water.

5. Stir the lemon rind into egg-sugar mixture; then, with a rubber spatula, add all of dissolved gelatin. Whisk carefully to mix, making certain gelatin is distributed evenly through thick lemon mixture.

6. In bowl of electric mixer or in a mixing bowl, using slow or low speed, beat egg whites just until foamy. Add cream of tartar or salt. Increase speed to high and beat until whites are firm but not dry. (Silken peaks form when properly beaten.) Add ¼ of the beaten egg whites to lemon mixture and gently stir through to soften. Fold in remaining whites, working quickly but taking care not to deflate batter. Fold in just long enough to incorporate whites.

7. Fold cup of whipped cream into custard. Pour mixture into prepared soufflé dish and chill for several hours or overnight.

8. *To Serve:* Insert a kitchen knife between the soufflé and the collar. Carefully unroll paper collar away from sides of soufflé, then discard collar. Put the ½ cup whipped cream into a pastry bag fitted with a star tip. Pipe a ring of rosettes along edge of soufflé, leaving a 1-inch space between them. Insert a sprinkling of julienne lemon strips and candied mimosa between rosettes.

To Prepare Ahead
Follow steps 1 through 7 up to two days ahead and refrigerate covered with a tent of plastic wrap. Early in the day of serving, complete step 8 and refrigerate until ready to serve.

CRÈME ANGLAISE

A soft custard sauce to serve with fruits, puddings, or pound cake.

3 egg yolks
2–3 tablespoons
    confectioners' sugar
1 cup milk
1 2-inch piece vanilla bean
    split *or* ½ teaspoon
    vanilla extract (vanilla
    bean produces a much
    richer flavor)

Yield 1¼ cups

1. To facilitate custard preparation, use an electric hand mixer when beating egg yolks with sugar. Beat until mixture is pale yellow and slowly dissolving ribbons form when beater is lifted.

2. In the meantime, place milk in a saucepan. Scrape seeds from vanilla-bean pod into milk. Add vanilla bean and let stand 10 minutes to infuse the vanilla flavoring. Bring milk to the edge of a boil over moderate heat and remove bean with a slotted spoon. If using vanilla extract, do not add at this time.

3. Transfer egg mixture to a heavy saucepan or top of double boiler over simmering, not boiling, water. Gradually add scalded milk to yolk

mixture in a thin, steady stream, stirring constantly with a wooden spoon until sauce is thick enough to coat spoon. Custard should not run into path left when a finger is drawn across the spoon. Do not allow custard to boil at any time or it will break down and curdle. The moment it is done, remove from heat and stir for a minute or so to cool. If using vanilla extract, add at this point and stir to mix. Use as directed in recipe.

Note: A custard made in the top of a double boiler can take 10–15 minutes to reach the edge of a boil, while it can be made in a much shorter time in a professional-weight saucepan, such as tin-lined copper or enamel-over-iron.

To Prepare Ahead
Follow steps 1 through 3 up to one day ahead. Transfer to suitable container and cover surface of sauce with plastic wrap to prevent a skin from forming. Cover and refrigerate until needed.

SUGAR PLUM CAKE

Black Italian plums on market stands do signify the end of the plum season and, in fact, of summer. But the plums—so well suited to baking because of their meaty flesh—herald the time to make this delightful and simple plum cake.

7–8 dark Italian plums
2–3 tablespoons sugar
    (depending on
    sweetness of plums)
6 tablespoons unsalted butter
½ cup sugar
2 eggs
⅓ cup all-purpose flour
¼ cup cornstarch
¼ teaspoon salt
½ teaspoon baking powder
Grated rind of 1 whole
    lemon

1 teaspoon vanilla extract
Glaze or confectioners'
    sugar

Glaze
3 tablespoons apricot jam
1 tablespoon rum or orange
    liqueur

Have on Hand
8-inch round baking pan
    with removable bottom

Serves 8

Preheat oven to 375 degrees.

Generously butter baking pan, then dust with dry Bread Crumbs.

1. Rinse, halve, and pit plums and put into a mixing bowl. Sprinkle on sugar and toss gently to mix. Set aside.

2. Cut butter into another mixing bowl or bowl of electric mixer. Cream butter with sugar until light and fluffy. (If using electric mixer, use paddle attachment.) Add eggs and beat 2–3 minutes until smooth and thoroughly incorporated.

3. Sift flour, cornstarch, salt, and baking powder together and fold gently into egg mixture until thoroughly combined. Add grated rind and vanilla and stir to mix.

4. With the aid of a rubber spatula, spread batter, which will be fairly thick, into prepared pan. Place sugared plum halves round side up in one layer over surface of batter. Bake 25–30 minutes until top is golden brown and edges start to shrink from sides of pan. Cool 5–10 minutes.

5. To remove the cake from baking pan, loosen sides of cake by drawing an ordinary kitchen knife between cake and the sides of pan. Place a flat-top cylindrical object such as a coffee can on work surface and put the cake in its baking pan on top of the can. Bring the outer metal ring of pan down to the counter. Transfer the cake, attached to the metal bottom of cake pan from the top of the can to a cake plate. Glaze surface of cake or sprinkle with confectioners' sugar, as you wish, and serve.

How to remove bottom from removable bottom cake or quiche pan

6. *To Prepare Glaze:* Warm apricot jam in a small saucepan until softened. Add rum or liqueur and stir to mix. Spoon warm mixture over tops of plums, then spread with a spatula to glaze. I like to serve this warm with vanilla ice cream on the side.

To Prepare Ahead

Follow steps 1 through 5 up to several hours ahead. Can be served warm or at room temperature.

PEAR MOUSSE WITH CARAMEL SAUCE

A subtle and understated creamy mousse with the character of the nouvelle cuisine, fruity, light, and exquisitely presented.

4 ripe pears (about 2–2¼
   pounds) red Bartlett,
   Comice, or Anjou
2 tablespoons unsalted butter
2 tablespoons lemon juice
2 tablespoons water
1½ envelopes unflavored
   gelatin
⅓ cup sugar
2 tablespoons honey
Grated rind of ½ lemon
3 eggs, separated
2 tablespoons pear liqueur
⅛ teaspoon cream of tartar
   or pinch of salt

¾ cup heavy cream

Sauce and Garnish
½ cup sugar
1½ cups water
2 ripe pears—red Bartlett,
   Comice, or Anjou
½ cup heavy cream
   (pasteurized only, *not*
   ultra-pasteurized)
¼ cup slivered almonds,
   lightly toasted

Have on Hand
1½-quart charlotte mold

Serves 8

Note: Since the pears are cooked until tender, it is not absolutely necessary to wait until they are perfectly ripe.

Prepare Charlotte Mold: Lightly butter mold; line with a round disk of wax paper and butter paper.

1. Peel and core pears. Cut into large dice and place in a heavy saucepan with butter. Simmer with cover ajar, stirring occasionally, about 14–18 minutes or until fruit is tender.

2. While the pears are cooking, combine lemon juice and water in a small dish and sprinkle gelatin over liquid. Let stand until liquid is absorbed; do not stir.

3. Remove pears from heat and stir in sugar, honey, and grated lemon rind. To prevent egg yolks from setting, place them in a small bowl and stir in several tablespoons of warm fruit mixture. Return to saucepan and stir vigorously to combine. With a rubber spatula scrape softened gelatin into hot pear mixture and stir to mix until thoroughly dissolved.

4. Pour into workbowl of food processor fitted with steel knife or a blender and process for several seconds until mixture is a loose purée. Transfer to a mixing bowl. Add liqueur, stir to mix, and set aside.

5. In a mixing bowl or in bowl of electric mixer, beat egg whites until foamy, add cream of tartar or pinch of salt, and continue beating until mixture takes shape, and firm but not dry peaks form. Gently fold into pear purée.

6. Whip heavy cream in a cold bowl with cold beaters until beaters leave light traces when drawn across top of the cream. Fold into pear mixture until no whites show. Pour into prepared mold and refrigerate several hours or overnight. When ready to serve, insert a kitchen knife around edge of mousse to loosen sides. Invert a serving platter over top and unmold.

7. *Sauce and Garnish:* Combine sugar and water in a heavy saucepan and stir to dissolve. Bring to a boil over high heat, then reduce to a simmer.

8. In the meantime, peel, core, and cut pears into ½-inch slices. Add to syrup and toss gently to coat. Simmer 3–4 minutes until tender but not falling apart. With a slotted spoon, remove pear slices to a dish and set aside.

9. Continue to cook sugar syrup until it becomes a caramel color, being very careful not to let it burn. Quickly but cautiously add the ½ cup heavy cream (the moment the cream makes contact with the hot sugar syrup it will spatter, so stand back for a moment), then, with a wooden spoon, stir to mix to a smooth, creamy caramel. Remove from heat and allow sauce to cool.

10. *To Serve:* Unmold pear mousse into center of a large round serving dish and pour sauce around it. Arrange pear slices around rim of dish and sprinkle toasted almonds over mousse.

To Prepare Ahead

Follow steps 1 through 6 up to one day ahead; refrigerate in mold lightly covered with plastic wrap. Unmold up to several hours before serving and return to refrigerator until just before serving. Caramel sauce and pear garnish can be made early in the day. Cover pears and refrigerate; let sauce stand, covered, at room temperature. If desired, reheat sauce and serve warm.

POIRES NOIRES
Chocolate Pears in Raspberry Sauce

I teach this dessert in a basic technique course. There is simplicity in its preparation and a graceful elegance in its presentation.

6 cups water
1 cup sugar
Juice of 1 lemon
2 sticks cinnamon
4 whole cloves
6 firm, well-shaped pears
    with full stems attached
    (Bosc or Anjou)

Raspberry Sauce
1 10-ounce package frozen
    raspberries, thawed to
    room temperature,
    drained
Reduced pear-poaching
    liquid

1–2 teaspoons Grand
    Marnier

Chocolate Coating
5 ounces imported
    bittersweet chocolate
5 tablespoons unsalted butter

Tiny mint leaves or angelica
    for garnish (optional)

Have on Hand
Heatproof casserole or
    stainless saucepan
Cheesecloth or clean kitchen
    towel

Serves 6

1. Choose a large heatproof casserole or stainless saucepan in which pears can stand in one layer without falling over. Put in water and sugar and stir to dissolve. Bring to a boil over moderately high heat, add lemon juice, cinnamon, and cloves. Cover and cook at brisk simmer about 15 minutes until a light syrup forms.

2. With a vegetable peeler, peel pears, leaving stems intact. Cut a thin slice from the bottom of each pear and stand upright in the syrup. Drape a doubled square of cheesecloth or a clean kitchen towel over the pears like a tent to prevent them from darkening. Cover pan tightly and poach gently 15–20 minutes or until tender when tested with a toothpick. If pears are very ripe when you poach them, they may need only 10–12 minutes to cook tender. Let cool in liquid about 10 minutes.

3. Carefully remove pears with a slotted spoon to a rack set on top of a dinner plate and chill thoroughly in refrigerator. Place poaching liquid over medium heat and reduce about 12–14 minutes, until it starts to color and foam. Watch this procedure carefully, as the mixture can

burn. When mixture has caramelized, set aside. Do not allow syrup to stand more than 10 minutes or it will harden. If this happens, place over low heat to soften.

4. Purée raspberries in workbowl of food processor fitted with steel knife or in a blender and stir into the warm syrup until thoroughly blended. Strain sauce into a sieve-lined bowl, add Grand Marnier, and stir to mix. Set aside.

5. Break chocolate into small pieces and combine it with 5 tablespoons butter in a small heavy saucepan. Allow chocolate and butter to warm in pan over very low heat, then stir gently until chocolate melts and mixture is a smooth cream. Remove from heat and let cool to room temperature.

6. Dip each pear into the creamy chocolate mixture, spooning it up to the stem end to coat completely. Transfer pears one at a time to a cake rack over a dinner plate and allow excess chocolate to drip off. Continue until all pears are done. Refrigerate several hours until chocolate coating is hard, and place a tent of plastic wrap around pears to cover them. Can be done ahead to this point.

7. When ready to serve, spoon a pool of raspberry sauce onto six dessert plates (preferably white). Center pears in sauce. Place tiny mint leaves, or cut a small leaf shape from a strip of angelica and insert, at stem end of pear for decoration.

To Prepare Ahead
Follow steps 1 through 6 up to one day ahead and refrigerate. Place Raspberry Sauce in suitable container and refrigerate. Complete step 7 just before serving.

FROZEN PRALINE BOMBE

Praline paste lends its distinctive flavor to this ice cream dessert.

3 ounces hazelnuts
1 quart vanilla ice cream
2 ounces bittersweet
    chocolate
2 tablespoons water
1 cup heavy cream
4 ounces praline paste

For Garnish
½ cup heavy cream, firmly
    whipped
1–2 tablespoons chopped
    hazelnuts

Candied violets

Have on Hand
Chilled 1-quart ice cream
    mold or other metal
    mold (a metal mold
    helps dessert to set and
    makes it easier to
    unmold)
Flexible metal spatula

Serves 10–12

Preheat oven to 350 degrees.

1. Place hazelnuts on a cookie sheet and toast in oven about 10 minutes or until lightly colored. Transfer to a sieve-lined bowl and rub with a tea towel to remove skins as completley as possible. Pick out clean nuts and set aside. (Some of the nuts may still have a bit of skin clinging to them, but this doesn't matter.) Place nuts in workbowl of food processor fitted with steel knife or in batches into a blender and chop with several on/off pulses until they are finely ground. Set aside, reserving 1 or 2 tablespoons separately for garnish.

2. Let ice cream soften slightly in the refrigerator but only to the point where you can mix it with the other ingredients. Do not let it melt.

3. In the meantime, break up chocolate and place in a small heavy saucepan with the water and melt over very low heat or place chocolate and water in a small ovenproof bowl and melt in a 250-degree oven for about 15 minutes. With a wooden spoon stir to a smooth cream. Set aside to cool.

4. Whip the cup of heavy cream in a cold bowl with cold beaters until softly whipped or until the beaters leave light traces when drawn across the top of the cream. With a large rubber spatula, fold the cool chocolate into the softly whipped cream.

5. Praline paste is very thick (the texture is similar to that of peanut butter) and must be softened. With a flexible metal spatula, work praline

on a work counter until smooth and pliable. The procedure resembles the sculpting of clay.

6. With a large rubber spatula, fold praline paste into the softened ice cream, then fold in nuts and chocolate whipped cream until all ingredients are well distributed. Pour mixture into the chilled mold, cover with lid or foil and place in freezer for several hours or overnight.

7. *To Unmold:* Soak a towel in warm water and wring it dry. Remove cover from mold, then run an ordinary kitchen knife around the inside of the mold to loosen the edge, place a serving plate on top and invert. Wrap the warm towel over the metal mold for about 10 seconds to help frozen bombe release easily. If ice cream has not moved from mold, warm towel again and wrap it around sides of mold. Remove mold. Smooth any melted surface with the side of a knife and return to freezer until firm.

8. *To Garnish:* Pipe out a border of whipped cream rosettes around base of mold and garnish corners with a candied violet. Sprinkle reserved nuts over top of bombe.

To Prepare Ahead
Follow steps 1 through 6 up to a month ahead and freeze. Complete steps 7 and 8 up to several hours ahead and return to freezer. Transfer to refrigerator 10–15 minutes just before serving to facilitate slicing.

PRALINE POWDER

½ cup granulated sugar
2–3 tablespoons almonds or
    hazelnuts, skin
    removed

Have on Hand
Lightly oiled cookie sheet
Feather or pastry brush

Yields ½ cup

1. Place sugar in a small heavy saucepan and place over moderate heat. Simmer without stirring at first. Sugar will begin to liquefy and then turn a light amber color. If crystals form, brush down sides of pan with a feather or pastry brush dipped in cold water. When the color deepens to caramel, add nuts all at once, stir to mix, and remove from heat immediately. Saucepan will be very hot so be sure to grab the handle with a potholder or mitt and quickly pour caramel onto prepared cookie sheet. Allow to cool. Caramel will harden like a giant lollipop.

2. When completely cool and brittle, lift it off the sheet with a metal spatula. Break into pieces and place in workbowl of food processor fitted with steel knife or in batches in a blender and process or blend to a fine or coarse grain as desired. Transfer to an airtight container and store in refrigerator. Use as a topping over ice cream, cold soufflés, custards, and cakes. It will keep indefinitely.

COLD RASPBERRY SOUFFLÉ

⅓ cup orange juice made
    from frozen concentrate
    diluted half strength
1 envelope unflavored
    gelatin
2 packages (10 ounces each)
    frozen raspberries,
    thawed
1 cup sugar
1 tablespoon Kirsch or
    framboise (cherry or
    raspberry liqueur)

1½ cups heavy cream
3 egg whites
⅛ teaspoon cream of tartar
    or pinch of salt
½ cup heavy cream, fresh
    strawberries, and
    chopped pistachio nuts
    or praline powder for
    garnish

Serves 8–10

1. Prepare a soufflé dish with a collar (see Index). Butter the inside of the dish.

2. Pour orange juice into a 1-cup glass measure, sprinkle on gelatin and let stand several minutes until gelatin has absorbed liquid. Do not stir. Set aside.

3. Pour raspberries into a sieve-lined bowl, catching liquid. Allow raspberries to drain about 10 minutes or so. The juice in mixing bowl should measure about 1 cup. If necessary, add a little water to make 1 cup liquid.

4. Combine raspberry juice with sugar in a heavy saucepan over moderate heat and cook until liquid lightly films a wooden spoon, about 10–12 minutes. Add raspberries, reduce heat, and simmer about 10 minutes longer.

5. Remove saucepan from heat and, with a rubber spatula, scrape all the gelatin into the hot liquid and stir until gelatin is thoroughly dissolved.

Pour into a sieve-lined bowl and push hard with a wooden spoon to force purée through sieve and to remove all seeds. With a rubber spatula, scrape purée from under the sieve into mixing bowl. Place in refrigerator to cool about 10 minutes. When completely cool, stir in liqueur.

6. Whip the 1½ cups of heavy cream in a cold bowl with cold beaters until beaters leave light traces when drawn across the top of the cream. Fold into custard.

7. In bowl of electric mixer or in a mixing bowl, using slow or low speed, beat egg whites just until foamy. Add cream of tartar or salt. Increase speed to high and beat until whites are firm but not dry. (Silken peaks form when properly beaten.) Add ¼ of beaten egg whites to raspberry mixture and gently stir through to soften. Fold in the remaining whites, working quickly but taking care not to deflate batter. Fold just enough to incorporate whites. Pour into prepared soufflé dish and chill several hours or overnight until firm.

8. *To Serve:* Insert a kitchen knife between soufflé and collar. Carefully unroll paper collar away from sides of soufflé, then discard. Place 5 or 6 strawberries along perimeter of soufflé with a small space in between. Firmly whip about ½ cup additional cream and put into a pastry bag fitted with a star tip and pipe rosettes between strawberries. Sprinkle the cream and berries with chopped pistachios. Or place the soufflé over a large square of wax paper, scoop a handful of praline powder in one hand, then press it along sides of soufflé as you turn bowl with the other hand. Add a bit more praline over top if desired.

To Prepare Ahead
Follow steps 1 through 7 up to two or three days ahead. Cover with a tent of plastic wrap and refrigerate. Complete step 8 up to several hours ahead. Return to refrigerator until just before serving.

RASPBERRY SAUCE

1 package (10 ounces)
frozen raspberries,
thawed
¼ cup raspberry preserves

2–3 teaspoons confectioners'
sugar
1–2 tablespoons Kirsch

Yields ¾ cup

Drain raspberries in a sieve-lined bowl and set liquid aside. Combine raspberries and remaining ingredients in a food mill and purée into a clean bowl. Or place in workbowl of food processor fitted with steel knife or into a blender and purée. Strain purée through a sieve-lined bowl, pressing down hard with a wooden spoon to extract purée and eliminate seeds. If mixture is very thick, stir in some of reserved juice by droplets until desired consistency is reached.

To Prepare Ahead
Follow recipe up to one week ahead and refrigerate, covered, in a suitable container. Use as directed.

CHOCOLATE MOUSSE BASQUE

There are many paths to a chocolate mousse and I would probably love all of them. But my heart belongs to the very French, very chocolaty mousse learned at the source. To my Parisian friend Gracieuse, many thanks.

4 eggs
6 ounces imported
semisweet chocolate
2 tablespoons strong coffee
3 tablespoons unsalted butter
¼ teaspoon cream of tartar
3 tablespoons sugar
1 cup heavy cream

Garnish
½ cup heavy cream
Candied violets (optional)

Have on Hand
Pastry bag fitted with star tip

Serves 10–12

1. Separate eggs while cold. Place whites in a large mixing bowl; yolks in a small bowl. Eggs will come to room temperature more quickly

if you place the bowl containing them in a pan of warm water 15–20 minutes.

2. Break chocolate into small pieces and put into a heavy saucepan. Add coffee and melt over very low heat, stirring occasionally, or place in a small heatproof bowl and melt in a 250-degree oven 15 minutes. When mixture looks soft, stir to a smooth cream and remove from heat.

3. Add 1 tablespoon of butter at a time to warm chocolate mixture until well blended. Add egg yolks, one at a time, and stir until thoroughly incorporated. Set aside to cool.

4. In a mixing bowl, mix egg whites until foamy. Add cream of tartar, adjust speed to medium high, and continue to beat until soft peaks form. Very slowly beat in sugar, 1 tablespoon at a time. Continue beating 1 minute until mixture is very stiff and shiny. With a large rubber spatula, spoon about ¼ of the beaten egg whites into chocolate mixture and stir to soften. Carefully fold in remaining whites until thoroughly incorporated.

5. Whip cream in a cold bowl with cold beaters until the beaters drawn across the top of the cream leave light traces; then carefully fold into mousse. Transfer mixture to an attractive glass serving bowl or soufflé dish.

6. *To Garnish:* Whip ½ cup of heavy cream in a cold bowl with cold beaters until stiff. Spoon into a pastry bag fitted with star tip and pipe out a row of rosettes around the rim of the bowl. Top every other or every third rosette with a candied violet, if desired. Serve chilled.

To Prepare Ahead
Follow steps 1 through 5 up to two days ahead. Cover with tent of plastic wrap and refrigerate. Complete step 6 up to several hours ahead. Refrigerate until just before serving.

PINEAPPLE, PEAR, AND BANANA CRISP

4 ounces hazelnuts
1 ripe Hawaiian pineapple
2 ripe pears (Anjou or
　　Comice)
2 ripe bananas
¼ cup Kirsch
⅛ teaspoon freshly grated
　　nutmeg

Topping
1 stick (8 tablespoons)
　　unsalted butter
⅓ cup brown sugar
1 cup flour

Have on Hand
2-quart gratin baking dish

Preheat oven to 350 degrees. Adjust rack to upper third of oven.

1. *To Toast and Prepare Nuts:* Place hazelnuts on a cookie sheet and put in the oven to toast about 10 minutes or until lightly colored. Transfer to a sieve-lined bowl and rub with a tea towel to remove skins as well as possible. Pick out clean nuts and set aside. Continue to rub and work off the skin of the remaining nuts, discarding peels. (Some of the nuts will still have a bit of skin clinging to them, but it doesn't matter.) Put nuts back on the cookie sheet and return to oven, then toast 8–10 minutes longer until golden brown. Remove from oven, cool a bit, chop coarsely, and set aside.

2. *To Prepare Fruits:* To cut pineapple, run a knife between the fruit and inside wall to free the pulp; or use a pineapple corer; or cut away core with sharp knife. Cut ½-inch-wide slices lengthwise, then cut slices into 2-inch lengths. Place in a glass or ceramic bowl. Peel pears, remove core, then cut into ¼-inch lengthwise slices. Add to pineapple. Peel bananas, then cut into ½-inch slices and add to pears and pineapple. Sprinkle on Kirsch and nutmeg and toss gently with clean hands or with two large spoons to mix. Set aside.

3. *Topping:* Cut butter into sugar, add flour, and mix with a pastry blender or two forks until mixture is crumbly. Don't overmix; crumbs should be the size of small peas. Place on a cookie sheet and bake in preheated oven for a few minutes until crumbs are golden. Remove from oven.

4. Combine prepared fruits and hazelnuts and place in a lightly buttered gratin baking dish. Scatter topping evenly over fruit-and-nut mixture and bake in preheated oven for 50 minutes–1 hour until bubbly and light brown. Serve warm or at room temperature. Can be served with vanilla ice cream or softly whipped cream.

To Prepare Ahead

Follow steps 1 through 4 up to two days ahead. Refrigerate covered. Serve at room temperature or place in 300-degree oven and warm through just before serving.

POACHED PEARS WITH SABAYON SAUCE

6–8 nicely shaped pears for
  poaching (Bartlett or
  Anjou)
4 cups water
2 tablespoons lemon juice
2 cups white wine
½ cup sugar

1 recipe Sabayon Sauce

Garnish
1 tablespoon grated orange
  rind
¼ cup slivered almonds,
  toasted

Serves 6–8

1. Peel pears, being very careful to leave tapered ends intact and stems on. Slice off a small portion of the base so they will stand. Drop into a large bowl containing acidulated water (water plus 2 tablespoons lemon juice) to cover, to prevent discoloration.

2. In a large heavy saucepan, add wine and water and bring to a boil. Pan should be stainless or enameled iron and large enough to hold pears in a single layer. Add pears to liquid and place cheesecloth or a kitchen towel directly on pears to hold them down in liquid and prevent them from discoloring. Cook, covered, very gently 8–10 minutes, or until tender but firm.

3. Transfer pears to a rack over a dinner plate to drain and cool.

4. Meanwhile, add sugar to pear liquid and boil down to make a light syrup, or until syrup coats a spoon. This may take 20–25 minutes. Watch this procedure carefully or caramel could burn. Coat pears with syrup. As glaze falls into plate, spoon it back up and continue to coat pears.

5. *To Serve:* Pour Sabayon Sauce into a large glass serving dish with upturned edge. Stand pears in sauce. Spoon over any additional syrup that has dripped into the dish they were draining over. Top each pear with grated orange rind and toasted almonds. Chill until ready to serve.

To Prepare Ahead

Follow steps 1 through 4 up to two days ahead. Prepare sabayon sauce up to two days ahead. Refrigerate, covered, in separate containers. Complete step 5 up to several hours ahead.

AMERICAN HOTEL BREAD PUDDING

The American Hotel is a fetching 138-year-old building in Sag Harbor, a onetime whaling village on Long Island's South Fork. This is my version of the utterly satisfying bread pudding they serve in the hotel's dining room.

10–12 thin slices firm white
    bread
Unsalted butter
¼ cup golden raisins
¼ cup dark raisins
¼ cup diced citron
3 tablespoons dark rum
5 eggs
½ cup sugar

2 cans (5.33 ounces each)
    evaporated milk
1 teaspoon vanilla

Have on Hand
Lightly buttered 2-quart
    earthenware or Pyrex
    baking dish

Serves 8–10

1. Lightly butter one side of bread slices and toast in a toaster oven or under the broiler for a minute or so until golden.
Preheat oven to 375 degrees.

2. Soak raisins and citron in rum 5–10 minutes.

3. Whisk eggs and sugar together or beat in electric mixer until smooth. Add milk and vanilla and blend well.

4. Arrange half the slices of toasted bread, buttered side up, in the baking dish. Cover bread slices with half the rum-soaked fruits. Pour half the custard mixture slowly over this first layer. Repeat with second layer of bread, fruits, and custard. Bake in preheated oven 30–35 minutes or until a cake tester or knife inserted in the center of the pudding comes out clean. Cool and serve.

Variation: In summer I sometimes substitute half the dried fruit with fresh berries or sliced ripe peaches. Arrange one layer with fresh fruits and one with dried.

To Prepare Ahead
Follow steps 1 through 4 up to one day ahead. Refrigerate, covered with plastic wrap, until ready to serve.

SUGGESTED MENUS FOR ENTERTAINING

When extending a dinner invitation, most hosts and hostesses today will call their party "casual." This serves to put the guests immediately at ease and also to keep the hosts relaxed. Casual or not, most hosts seek "perfection" with their menus and still hope for the approval of their guests. The quality of the food and the effectiveness of accessories, serving pieces, and so forth, are all important parts. But, remember, people make the party.

Entertaining friends or being entertained by a friend is truly one of life's special pleasures. I prefer to be with a group of six to eight people, a convenient number to cook for. A dinner party should be remembered as something comfortable and enjoyable and not one where every dish was a tour-de-force and a whole repertoire of cooking was done for one meal.

When planning a menu I think of the entree first and then balance the foods around it. Select your ingredients according to what the market has to offer, the way the finest chefs do. When you plan your purchases this way, you will also save money.

One should stop to visualize how foods will look together on a plate. It is essential that taste, texture, and color come into play. For instance, chicken breast with a white sauce and cauliflower on the same plate is not only colorless but lacks contrasting texture. A little something fresh and green would add a sprightly touch.

In the following suggested menus I have chosen foods that are appropriate to the season and are generally available in the marketplace. These are foods that I have prepared for company—that people have enjoyed. Sometimes certain dishes will become part of you and family and friends will look forward to having you make that special dish again.

I do not believe in passing endless rounds of canapés and hors d'oeuvres before a sit-down dinner. If you love to do hors d'oeuvres, great—have a cocktail party. An apéritif or a glass of wine before dinner is fine while waiting for the guests to gather. The snacking should be minimal, however. Sometimes I will offer nothing more than a dish of nuts and raisins. Or I might choose to serve a first course around the cocktail table. It could be a pâté, a cold soup, a varied selection of appetizers such as Fennel Rings, Marinated Italian Yellow and Red Peppers with Baby Carrots and Onions, a piquant Wild Rice Salad, or a delicious Brussels Sprouts Vinaigrette. Keep it light at all times. Don't overshadow the work that has gone into the rest of the dinner.

Serve the courses unhurriedly, taking the time to enjoy your guests. Not only were the menu plans in this book designed to assemble foods artfully, but the "To Prepare Ahead" footnote at the end of each recipe will help you organize a detailed preparation schedule for a cooking countdown. This does not mean I've suggested it takes six minutes for this dish or eighteen minutes for that. It is simply an organized plan to provide some guidance in pulling it all together. The more familiar you become with a procedure the more quickly you will execute it. Keep the food simple, since an absentee hostess will make your guests feel ill at ease. And remember, "The bottom line is taste."

SUGGESTED MENUS FOR ENTERTAINING

Summer Breakfast for 4–6
Giuliano Bugialli's Frittata of Green Tomatoes
Blueberry Preserves
Strawberry Bread or Sugar Plum Cake

Luncheon Menus for 6–8
Caribbean Peach Soup
Shrimp with Mango and Rosemary
Vermicelli with Uncooked Tomato Sauce
Biscocho

Pâte Fromage
Poached Salmon Steaks with Mushroom Béarnaise
Julienne of Parsleyed Cucumber
Cold Chocolate Soufflé

Avgolemono
Baked Red Snapper from Salonika
Parsleyed Lemon Rice
Chocolate Mousse Basque

Do-ahead Brunch Buffet for 12

Torta de Salmone
Ratatouille aux Oeufs or Poached Eggs Provençal
Spinach Frittata
Tyrokopita
Pineapple, Pear, and Banana Crisp

A Summer Grill for 12

Mediterranean Eggplant Caviar
Gigot St. Tropez
Poulet au Bresse Grillé
Pommes Fondante
Fresh Vegetable Salad with Crème Fraîche Vinaigrette
Summer Berries in Lace Cookie Cups

A Summer Fish Cookout for 8

Chilled Strawberry-Rhubarb Soup
"Let's Grill a Fish"
Marinated Vegetables on the Grill
Génoise Blueberry Roll

Do-ahead Buffet Party for 12

Chicken and Broccoli Salad with Tarragon Cream Vinaigrette
Oriental Pasta Primavera or Cold Penne Salad abd Pumate
Cold Sliced Herb Veal Roast
Seasonal Fruits in Spumante, Umbrian Style

Dinner Menus for 4–6

Crustless Leek Quiche
French Roast Tarragon Chicken
Pommes de Provence
Poires Noires (Chocolate Pears) with Raspberry Sauce

Poached Striped Bass with Tomato Vinaigrette
Bretonne-Vegetable Garnish
Meringue Hazelnut Torte with Chocolate Butter Cream

Duck au Poivre Verte or Sautéed Duck Breasts and Legs in Red Wine and Cassis
Sauce
Château Potato Fans
Timbale of Lettuce Chiffonade or Purée of Parsnips and Carrots
American Hotel Bread Pudding

Salade des Champignons or Wild Rice Salad
Rack of Lamb Pérsille
Gratin Dauphinoise
Zucchini-Tomato Gratin
Mocha Pots de Crème and Madeleines

Dinner Menus for 6–8

Paglia e Fieno (Straw and Hay)
Herbed Veal Roast with Steamed Cauliflower Garnish
Green Bean, Chèvre, and Pignoli Nut Salad
Grapefruit Sorbet in Tulip Cookie Cups with Fresh Mint

Cuban Black Beans with Crème Fraîche, Cayenne, and Tomato
Chicken La Zaragozana
Endive and Grapefruit Saladwith Mustard Vinaigrette
Flan with Strawberry Garnish

Peppers and Zucchini—Mushrooms and Celery Italian Style—
Cannelini and Shrimp (Antipasti)
Pasta Vongole alla Veneziana
Pollo alla Giannino's and Escarole Sauté
Crema di Amaretti

Gougère
Salmon in Chive-Cream Sauce
Asparagus in Caper Vinaigrette
Chocolate Roulage

Pissaladière 1
Poached Veal with Crème Fraîche Sauce
Potato Galette
Endive, Watercress, and Beet Salad
Grand Marnier Custard Gratiné

Misty Fried Shrimp with Mustard-Fruit Sauce
Salade Mesclun
Escalopes de Veau Mornay
Steamed Green Beans or Broccoli
Cold Raspberry Soufflé

Stuffed Eggs Béchamel
Potage Crème d'Or
Chicken Viroflay
Savory Stuffed Mushrooms
Cherry Praline Torte

Poached Leeks Vinaigrette
Ris de Veau en Feuilleté
Truite Farci et Porto
Viennese Nut Torte

Coquille St. Jacques au Naturel
Grilled Tenderloin of Beef
Julienne of Carrot Bundles with Scallion Ties
Cauliflower Mousse Timbales
Apricot Meringue Torte

Holiday Buffet Parties for 10–12

Marinated Brussels Sprouts
Pear and Leek Soup
Roast Capon with Sautéed Fruits
Spiced Sweet Potato Pie
Fresh Buttered Broccoli or Green Beans
Tarte Tatin en Feuilleté

Crudité Basket with Crudité Dip
Skewered Sesame Shrimp on Noodle Nest with Pea Pods
Sauté of Beef Bourguignon with Fresh Croutons
Radicchio, Leek, and Chèvre Salad
Pear Mousse with Caramel Sauce

Taramasalata
Chicken Marengo in Party Brioche
Broccoli-Duxelle Loaf
Cauliflower with Mustard Mayonnaise
Cold Lemon Soufflé

Veal à la Suisse
Potato Galette with Vegetable Mirepoix
Buffet Tomatoes Mimosa
Pineapple Jelly Salad
Poached Pears with Sabayon Sauce

GLOSSARY OF TECHNIQUES AND KITCHEN INVENTORY

I have always maintained that there is no great mystery to cooking. The so-called secrets, all aspiring gourmets will be delighted to learn, are actually these: common sense, good judgment, and a few basic operations; together they are the sum total of good cooking. Keep in mind, some of the best dishes are simple ones carefully prepared from good, wholesome ingredients, rather than elaborate and complicated preparations.

Volumes have been written on the techniques of cooking. However, nothing can take the place of practical experience. My teaching kitchen is a veritable workshop of chop, dice, whisk, stir, cook, bake, and taste. If you take the time to become familiar with basic techniques, you will develop the confidence to use your imagination.

There are some additional requirements as well; a few tools of the trade and skill in their use and organization. Start with the finest and freshest ingredients and make sure to read the recipe through before you begin. Assemble the utensils and ingredients you need ahead of time and eliminate needless frustration.

A recipe will seem less forbidding if you look upon it as a lesson plan. Even the most complex and lengthy recipes are merely combinations of several elementary techniques. Here are some of the most frequently used fundamentals:

Blanching: Cooking quickly in boiling water to cover. Cooking time can be as brief as pouring boiling water over food such as mushrooms to whiten, or facilitate removal of skin; or as long as several minutes when parboiling vegetables to prepare them for cooking by some other means. The method is particularly useful when precooking vegetables for the Crudité Basket, Spaghetti Primavera, and Fresh Vegetable Salad, where crispness and vivid, bright colors are desired.

To Blanch a Vegetable: Bring 3–4 quarts salted water to a boil in a 5½-quart saucepan. The timetable below is a guide to cooking and should be adjusted according to the thickness and heaviness of your vegetable, or the way you cut it. Put the vegetable in the salted boiling water, reduce heat, and maintain a surface bubble at all times. Remove vegetable from cooking water with a strainer-skimmer and transfer to a colander to drain. Cool quickly to tepid with a fan or under a spray of cold water. Immediately transfer one layer deep to a clean kitchen towel to absorb excess moisture. The action from the time the vegetable is removed from the water to the kitchen towel must be very swift, as the vegetable continues to cook in its own heat.

Blanching Timetable:

Asparagus ⎫ Carrots ⎭	1½ minutes
Broccoli ⎫ Cauliflower ⎪ Green Beans ⎬ Pea Pods ⎭	30 seconds
Mushrooms	10 seconds

Boiling: Water boils at 212 degrees Fahrenheit (212° F.). Bubbles begin to form around the sides of the pot, then move rapidly to the center until the entire surface is agitated to a full rolling boil.

Boning a Chicken: First, sit the bird up on its tail and, with a sturdy sharp boning knife or medium-size paring knife, cut along each side of the backbone from neck to tail. Or cut out the backbone with a pair of sturdy kitchen shears. Always be careful not to veer away from the backbone. Now, starting at the neck and working down toward the tail section, insert the knife between bone and skin and keep the blade of the knife angled against the bones, gently scraping to loosen the skin and flesh. Turn the chicken around so the other side of the backbone is lined up with your cutting hand and repeat procedure, keeping in mind that you are working toward the breast bone from both sides. Always work as close to the bone as possible. If some of the flesh is cut into in the process, don't worry about it, since it can be tucked back together. The breast, however, should be left as whole as possible. As you work toward the breast, cut through both the wing and leg bone joints, but not through the skin. Keep them attached to the body of the chicken.

WINGS: To free wings, cut through the ball joint close to the neck, then angle your knife and scrape, scrape, scrape against the back rib bones toward the breast, separating the wings, flesh, and skin from the carcass.

THIGH: Remove the thighbone by severing it from the back, cutting through the joint. Scrape the flesh away from the backbone down toward the ball joint of the leg bone. With knife blade turned upward or with kitchen shears, cut through the joint to remove thighbone completely. Repeat with other thighbone.

BREAST: The breast area directly over the keel bone has a very thin layer of meat and so you must proceed very carefully not to tear the skin. With the knife angled against the breast bone, gently scrape away until you separate the meat and skin from the bone completely.

The completely boned chicken will butterfly open with the wings and legs attached. If skin has been slit in some areas, you can sew it up. If any flesh becomes detached, simply press it back in place. The gelatinous consistency of the raw chicken will allow it to stick easily. Proceed as directed in recipe.

Boning a chicken

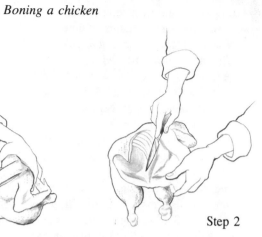

Step 1

Step 2

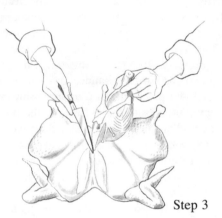

Step 3

Step 4

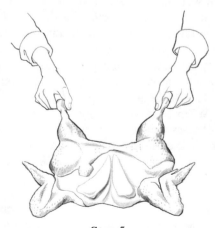

Step 5

Braising: Cooking in a tight-lidded pan by first sautéing in fat, then cooking slowly in a small amount of liquid. Used primarily with meats or vegetables, it is an effective technique which can be applied to most food substances. The moist-heat method of cooking over gentle heat is well suited to preparing less expensive cuts of beef and lamb, such as chuck, short ribs, shoulder, and shanks. Pork, which tends to be dry, and veal, a most delicate meat, are especially succulent when braised.

Broiling: Cooking by direct exposure to heat in an oven broiler or grill. Broiling is one of the simplest and quickest of culinary procedures and yet I find people are nevertheless bewildered and ask: "How hot should the broiler be?" and even, "Do I preheat the broiler pan?" Taking these questions and more into account, this simplest of procedures, called broiling, becomes more demanding. Yet the virtues are many. Foods can be cooked in minutes. Calorie counters can crisp and glaze without benefit of fat.

As a rule, the food is placed on a cold broiler or grid pan to prevent sticking. However, when broiling fish fillets, the grid pan is always greased and preheated. Fish cooks so quickly, especially in the case of fillets, that it is never turned. Both sides cook at the same time, from the broiler above and the preheated grid below. It is very important to build up heat for successful broiling. Preheat your broiler at the highest setting (550 F. for most household broiling temperatures) for 10–15 minutes.

Most meats cut 1 inch thick should be placed about 2 inches below the heating element. The distance is measured from the surface of the meat. If you are broiling double-thick lamb chops, however, or a butterflied leg of lamb, broil 4–5 inches below the source of heat or you will overchar the surface before the meat has a chance to cook through.

Slide the broiler pan out from the oven when ready to turn meat. Turn only once (except in the case of fish fillets), using a broad spatula or tongs. BROILING IN AN ELECTRIC OVEN: Turn on broiler to highest setting. To keep broiler unit working constantly, you must leave oven door ajar about 3 inches. Most doors will have built-in ability to stay ajar at that point. The thermostat in the oven will automatically shut off if the door remains closed, causing the temperature to drop below the broiling point. ROTISSERIE BROILING: Use only tender, even-sized cuts of meat or meats made tender by a marinade. Center meat on the spit for balance. If you are cooking fowl, truss the bird completely so wings and legs don't trail. CHARCOALING: When charcoal-broiling, keep a pan of water beside you as you cook. Fat from the meat will drip down onto the coals and it may be necessary to flick drops of water onto the coals to control bursts of flame that can develop. A helpful hint: Use an old-fashioned laundry sprinkler or save a household cleaner liquid dispenser to do the flicking.

Clarifying Butter: When you are going to sauté such delicate meats as veal scallopine or boneless chicken breasts, use clarified butter, the clear yellow liquid that results when butter is melted to separate out the milky deposits and can take more intense heat than regular butter without burning. The milky solids in regular butter will burn at a lower temperature than clarified butter. To clarify butter, cut ¼ pound (1 stick) unsalted butter into a small saucepan and warm over gentle heat until it melts. Tip the pan slightly and, with a large metal spoon, skim off and discard the foam that rises to the surface. Now pour off or strain the clear liquid, which is clarified butter, into a small jar or dish, leaving behind the milky deposit that settles at the bottom of the pan. Clarified butter can be kept refrigerated for weeks and even months. The foam and milky deposit may be used to enrich a sauce.

Cooking in a Bain-Marie: A bain-marie is a vessel holding hot water that heats the contents of another (immersed) vessel to the desired point. Set a filled container (bowl, soufflé dish, mold, saucepan, etc.) into a shallow pan of hot water and place in a preheated oven or on top of range, according to recipe directions. The flow of hot water used in this cooking method surrounds the dish and allows the food to cook evenly. Some of the dishes that would be cooked in a bain-marie include: custards; fish, meat, and vegetable mousses; and puddings. This method may also be used to keep foods warm.

Deglazing: This is a very useful technique for making a sauce from pan drippings by incorporating all the precious cooking juices and flavors into that sauce as part of its preparation. When you sauté any cut of meat, veal scallops, chicken breasts, and so forth, or when you brown a large roast, drippings are left in the bottom of the pan. Transfer the food to a warm serving platter, pour off and discard the fat, and simply add any liquid to the pan in which the food has cooked—stock, wine, lemon juice, brandy, vinegar, marinade, or even water. Stir up the drippings and juicy browned bits in the bottom of the pan over high or moderately high heat. The liquid is quickly brought to the boil, then reduced in quantity to intensify flavors. The sauce is spooned or strained to nap or lightly cover the cooked food.

To Fan or Cool Vegetables: I have learned from my good friend Elizabeth Andoh, author of *At Home with Japanese Cooking,* the very elegant trick of fanning vegetables the moment they are drained in a colander. "This," she says, "keeps your vegetables from becoming waterlogged." I think this is brilliant. If a fan isn't a kitchen staple around your house, reach for a kitchen towel, grab two ends, then flap it back and forth over the vegetables.

Frying: The art of frying includes pan frying, stir frying, and deep frying. These techniques can be employed with almost any edible food and yet they are all very different procedures. Pan frying is done in a shallow pan with about an inch of fat. Stir frying conjures up images of Chinese cooking, yet the Italians "stir-sauté" in just enough fat to coat the pan and may or may not need a small amount of liquid to complete the cooking. Deep frying means completely immersing smaller pieces of foods in very hot fat (about 375°). In this way the food is "seized" (as professional chefs would say).

A useful hint from my good friend Giuliano Bugialli: If a thermometer is not available when frying, a good way to test if your oil is hot enough, or about 375° F., is to insert the end of a wooden spoon in the hot fat. When fine bubbles form a bubbling circle around the handle, the oil is ready to cook your food. Many people love fried foods, but more and more shy away from them for reasons of diet. When care is taken to fry foods properly—in the right pans or deep fryers—and to heat oils to the correct temperatures (360°–375°), foods will not only be as free of fat as other methods of cooking, but will also be wholly digestible.

Measuring: Fingertips and palms of hand are no match for a nested set of measuring cups and spoons, but do consider the hand as a measuring device. Practice will have you knowing just what a ¼ or ½ or teaspoon of salt, sugar, herbs, etc. measures when pinched with fingertips or scooped into the palm of your hand.

Make a point of emptying measured spoonfuls of these ingredients into your hand before adding them to a dish. Look at the amount in your hand; it won't take long before you know what the approximate amount of a teaspoon or tablespoon looks like in your hand. To test yourself after several guesses in your hand, return the ingredient to the measuring spoon or cup to check your accuracy.

There are other useful ways to measure with the hand. I always pour enough water to come about 1 inch above the surface of rice before cooking it. To measure this inch, I rest the tip of my thumb over the rice in the pan and pour in enough water until it just reaches my thumb's first joint. Not only does using one's hands to measure speed up food preparation, but it adds significantly to one's sense of participation.

Melting Chocolate: You can melt chocolate in the top of a double boiler or in a small heavy saucepan over very low heat, stirring the chocolate gently with a clean, dry wooden spoon. If chocolate melts at too high a temperature or if the stirring spoon contains the slightest bit of moisture, it will cause the chocolate to tighten and become rough and lumpy.

A foolproof method is to melt chocolate in a low oven. Place the broken pieces of chocolate in a small heatproof saucepan or mixing bowl and put it into a preheated 250-degree oven for 15 minutes. The chocolate may appear not to have melted at all as you will still be able to see the outline of the chocolate pieces. Remove from oven, then stir the chocolate until it is a glossy and smooth cream.

Reduction: Boiling off some of the liquid of an ingredient, thereby thickening it. When deglazing, bring liquids up to a boil, then simmer briskly over moderately high heat to thicken and intensify flavors. The reduction process has taken on even more importance with the advent of the nouvelle cuisine, which de-emphasizes the addition of thickening agents, such as flour, cornstarch, etc.

Roasting: Like baking, roasting is done by dry heat. While the words roast and bake mean the same thing, we "roast" chickens and lamb, while we "bake" cakes and cookies. Roasting can be done in an open spit, on a rotisserie, or directly on an oven shelf. To roast on an oven shelf, the food should be placed in a shallow pan with sides no more than two inches high and just large enough to hold it. (High-sided pans tend to hold in steam and meat is then steamed instead of roasted.) Sometimes, in order to sear, or brown, the surface of the meat, roasting temperatures will be very high at the beginning of the cooking time (450°–500°), then are reduced to 325°– 350°. The intense heat seals in juices, but it can also cause shrinkage. As a result, I prefer to brown the meat in the roasting pan over heat first, if possible. The pan is then transferred to the oven and the meat basted as frequently as possible to prevent it from drying out.

Whenever I roast a chicken (Poulet Rôti au Vinaigre de Framboise), I prefer to brown it over heat before putting it into the oven. Put 2 tablespoons oil into a sturdy roasting pan and place over heat. When hot, put in the trussed bird and slowly brown it on all sides over moderately low heat, turning as necessary. This will take about fifteen minutes if done carefully. Be sure to adjust the heat so you do not scorch the skin, and continue with recipe as directed.

I prefer to season my roast before it goes into the oven so the seasonings permeate the meat and do not just remain on the surface. (I do not season the meat, however, before braising or sautéing—only as it browns.)

Roasting times are important and there are guides to be followed. Some of these are outdated today, since taste preferences are moving toward moister and rarer roasts. The cook should know the weight of a roast and have some idea of its cooking time. I have given updated roasting times in recipes where roasting is called for, but remember that these, too, are a guide. To be perfectly sure when meat reaches desired stage of doneness, rely on a good instant thermometer. This kind does not probe the meat the entire cooking time but is inserted toward the end of the cooking period for an instant reading. A professional chef will poke a finger into the meat. If it feels soft to somewhat mushy, it is undercooked. If it feels hard to the touch, it has overcooked. When the meat springs back gently, it should be at the perfect point of doneness. Some meats, such as a rib roast, beef tenderloin, or turkey, should stand 8–10 minutes before carving to allow surface juices to recede back into the meat making it easier to slice. Meats will continue to cook in their own heat while standing and this should be taken into account when timing roasts.

The best types of meat for roasting are the highest-quality grades you can find. Meat that is not liberally marbled with fat can toughen when cooked over high heat. Lesser cuts are better for braising and stewing.

Sautéing: The French word "sauter" means "to jump." To sauté is to cook quickly and brown food in a pan containing a small quantity of hot butter, oil, or other fat. Foods that can be cut into equal pieces, such as veal scallops, chicken breasts, small boneless steaks, and fish fillets, are ideal to sauté in a sturdy pan, which will allow even cooking. When cooking this way, do not brown heavily or crisply and do not allow the drippings that form in the bottom of the pan to burn. Never crowd the pan when cooking meats, or they will steam in their own juices. Most of the same principles apply when sautéing vegetables, except that you need not be as concerned with crowding the pan. You can stir-sauté vegetables in a skillet in exactly the same way as you would stir-fry in a wok.

Simmering and Poaching: Bring cooking liquid to the edge of a full boil, then carefully maintain a lazy surface bubble or a gentle simmer at all times: 202°–205° F. Do not leave the pan alone, since temperature changes constantly. If temperature increases too quickly, you may lose steam, which will cause liquid to evaporate. Watch the movement of the liquid and adjust heat accordingly.

When you put cold or room-temperature foods into simmering liquid, the water temperature will be lowered instantly. Adjust the heat until you can regulate it well enough to maintain a simmer.

Steaming: In a deep pan bring 2 inches of water to a vigorous boil over high heat. Place a rack in the pan, being certain it is elevated at least ½ inch above the water. Set the food either directly on the rack or in a heatproof shallow dish, which has been placed on the rack. Cover the pan with a lid, reduce heat to a simmer and steam the food, adding additional boiling water if necessary to maintain the proper level until food is cooked. Remove lid to let steam escape and then remove food.

Stewing: Cooking via moist heat. Similar to braising, except that stewing meats are usually cut into small, even pieces and are completely immersed in a circulating liquid. A gentle simmer is ideal for cooking a stew slowly. Less expensive cuts benefit from stewing, since streaks of connective tissue will dissolve in cooking and even give the gravy body and texture.

Trussing a Bird: The technique of securing the wings and legs close to the body of a bird so that it keeps its shape and cooks more evenly.

TO TRUSS WITH STRING: Cut a length of kitchen string approximately four feet long and set aside. Tuck the wing tips behind the second joint and push the legs back toward the body to expose the breast fully. Center the string under the tail and lift the two long ends around the drumstick tips and cross the string over the top. Now crisscross the string between the drumstick tips, bringing the ends under and around the tips and pulling the string taut.

Holding the two ends tightly, bring the string toward you along both sides of the body under the curve of the legs. This will secure the legs against the body and push up the breast at the same time. With your fingers, get a good grip on the string and flip the bird over, breast side down. As you turn the bird, bring the string tightly into the crevice of the wing tips and cross the ends over the back near the neck opening. (If there is a flap of neck skin, flatten it under the crossed string.) Tie the two ends into a secure knot.

After the bird is roasted, with kitchen shears or a knife simply snip the string at the knot. Tug gently at the string and it will come off easily.

TO TRUSS WITH NEEDLE AND STRING: Thread an 8- or 10-inch trussing needle with a long length of kitchen string. Push the chicken's legs back toward the body to expose the breast fully. Force the needle into the "ankle" end of the chicken leg to the right of the body (or the reverse side if you are lefthanded) and continue through the tail end across and through the opposite leg, leaving a 3–4-inch length of string dangling. Tuck wing tips firmly behind second joint.

Turn chicken breast side down and insert the needle through the wing section, the skin at the neck, and through the other wing. Turn breast side up, bring string down to drumstick tip where trussing began. As you work with the string, keep pushing legs back up toward the breast to plump the bird; then, pulling the strings taut, tie a knot at the base of the leg to secure it.

KITCHEN INVENTORY

As you discover the recipes that appeal to your cooking sensibilities, you will do well to acquire the utensils essential for your needs. While it is perfectly possible to cook a meal, and a good meal, in almost any kind of utensil, working with wisely selected implements will make the job easier. The purchase of quality equipment for your kitchen is an immediate investment that pays long-term dividends.

Knives: Several good-quality, sturdy knives are an essential investment. There was a time when a carbon steel knife was used by most professionals, as it was soft enough to sharpen easily. Carbon steel knives will oxidize and acidic substances, such as tomatoes, onions, or lemons, will become discolored and metallic-tasting and blacken the knife. When working with a carbon steel knife, be certain to wash and dry it immediately after use, or it will rust.

Today, most professionals will use high-carbon stainless, which has advantages over the carbon steel. They are stain-resistant and easily sharpened. The best-quality knives are hand-forged, and the blade is a solid one-piece construction which runs from the tip of the knife blade in through the handle. The fully extended tang, or metal running through the handle, is clearly visible and is held in place with rivets.

A good knife is an investment and should last a lifetime and then some. An 8- or 10-inch chef's knife can cost about forty or fifty dollars and a small paring knife will cost about twenty dollars. If you went out and purchased a moderately priced blouse, it might cost forty or fifty dollars. The blouse will last two seasons if you're lucky; the knife, used everyday, will last forever.

When purchasing a knife, hold it in your hand and feel for comfort, weight, and balance. A 3½- to 4-inch parer; a 6-inch slicer; an 8- or 10-inch chef's knife; and serrated bread and tomato knives should get you off to a good start.

Plan to use a large knife for a large job and a small one for a small job. A chef's knife is designed so that you can use it as a "rocker" for chopping vegetables, parsley, garlic, and so forth. It is also used to slice, to julienne, and to dice. A paring knife is useful for slicing small items and for paring and peeling.

Along with a basic purchase of knives, a 12-inch sharpening steel will help you keep the knife sharpened at home on a regular basis. "A regular basis" means a few strokes before and after using the knife. (A good knife should be sharpened professionally once a year.) In the meantime, at home, you just smooth and align the microscopic teeth along the edge of the blade. The more you use the sharpening steel, the longer the edge is going to last.

HOW TO USE SHARPENING STEEL: Hold knife in working hand with blade facing you and place blade at a 20-degree angle over the steel. Position the wide end of the knife blade at handle-end of steel. Draw the knife edge down along the top of the steel in a somewhat diagonal motion so that when motion is completed, the knife tip is drawn off the end of the steel. Repeat procedure, drawing opposite side of blade under the steel.

When working with a knife, think of it as an extension of your hands and let the knife do the work. You can't have too sharp a knife for food preparation as long as you handle it with knowledge and respect. You are more likely to have a cutting accident with a dull knife than with a sharp one, since you are apt to force down on the object to be cut, slipping and cutting yourself—not to mention wasting all that energy.

CARE OF KNIVES: Having made the investment in good knives, you will want to care for them. They should not be thrown carelessly in a drawer with other cutlery, as they can easily be nicked or even have their tips broken off. One can store them in a knife block or, lacking counter space, on a wall magnet near your work area. Never put your good knives in a dishwasher, as the extreme heat will dull the blade and may be harmful to the handles. Need I also caution you not to cut paper or open envelopes with your good knives or pry up jar lids and the like. Many a good knife has been ruined when it became a handy substitute for scissors, letter openers, and jar openers!

Pots and Pans: As any good cook knows, flimsy pots just can't stand up against heat. Even with constant stirring and temperature adjustment, it is almost impossible to avoid uneven cooking in thin, flimsy cooking equipment. The results are often sticking, burning, and hot spots.

Pots and pans should not be "matched sets." It is a mistake to invest in a large, expensive set all in the same materials. As the range of your cooking activities broadens, carefully purchase equipment little by little until skills and tastes are developed. Listed below are the materials I prefer to work with.

COPPER: The best of all cookware because it distributes heat so evenly and quickly. Copper is costly, however, and requires some care. (I love the look of my *used* copper pans as much as I do when they are highly polished.) As your purse allows, one or two pieces of copper should certainly be part of your cookware collection. If I could have only one copper pot, it would be a *sauteuse*. This remarkable slope-sided French saucepan is superb for anything that needs to be stirred, from a delicate sauce to a porridge. Of course, your pots don't have to be copper. What *is* important, though, is to get good utensils, and they will last forever.

ALUMINUM: Aluminum is the next best conductor of heat. One of my favorite cooking utensils is a Calphalon 12-inch black aluminum skillet. The heat distribution is so dependably even that I'm confident each time I use it. The special treatment of the metal prevents it from leaving a metallic taste when acidic foods like tomato, wine, lemon, etc., come into contact with it. In any event, a sturdy aluminum skillet is a must for your pan sautéing. The primary disadvantage is that aluminum discolors from certain foods.

ENAMEL OVER CAST IRON OR STAINLESS STEEL WITH ALUMINUM CORE: These are excellent materials to cook with. Various-sized saucepots with tight-fitting lids are extremely useful for braising and poaching meats, fish, vegetables; boiling water for pasta, rice, and beans; and simmering soups and stews. Different-sized skillets in these materials are also useful because, with few restrictions, they can go from stove top to oven to table.

Food Processor: In the seventies, the food processor was introduced to the home kitchen with revolutionary results. I have always been willing to spend unlimited hours to advance my cooking skills, but I have also welcomed any help I could get. I discovered that owning a food processor was like having another pair of hands in the kitchen. Although many cooks considered the machine to be a gadget (and perhaps some still do) my feelings for the processor have run high from the beginning. Once you have worked with a processor you will not understand how you ever did without one.

The food processor makes light, quick work of many culinary chores: chopping, slicing, and shredding all manner of vegetables: grating hard cheeses, making bread crumbs, puréeing soups; mixing pastry dough; and preparing your own fresh vinaigrettes, mayonnaise, and even a silken hollandaise. In addition, it will extend your range by simplifying formerly complicated and time-consuming procedures.

Essential Equipment for the Basic Kitchen

Two sturdy knives—1 parer and 1 8- or 10-inch chef's; high-carbon stainless is best.

A 12-inch skillet, preferably Calphalon or a fine-quality stainless with an aluminum core.

Several saucepans with lids of tin-lined copper, stainless steel with aluminum core, or pasta, and soups; and for small-quantity stock making.
> melting butter and chocolate; heating milk; blanching and boiling vegetables, pasta, and soups; and for small-quantity stock making.

One large 7–9-quart oval enamel-over-iron casserole for browning and braising meats, for stews and soups, and for poaching fruits, etc.

An 8–10-inch T-Fal, or other nonstick surface—perfect for omelets and frittatas.

An imported pepper mill with adjustments that determine variation of grind from fine to coarse.

A nutmeg grater for grinding and storing fresh nutmeg.

A flat wooden spatula to deglaze drippings in a pan.

Several sturdy wooden spoons for stirring.

A long-tined kitchen fork, metal spatula, kitchen tongs, large metal kitchen spoon, and slotted spoon.

A strainer-skimmer—a favorite tool of mine used when blanching and deep-frying. It has a wider surface than a slotted spoon and can lift out more food at one time.

Two flexible rubber spatulas, medium and large head, for folding airy mixtures and for scraping out bowls.

Portable electric hand mixer, indispensable tool for beating egg whites, mixing soft batters, custards, etc.

Medium-size stainless wire whisk with a good sturdy handle for many whipping procedures.

Sturdy flat wooden board or polyethylene surface for cutting and chopping. A plastic surface will damage your knife blades.

Sturdy medium-size stainless strainer with handle.

Colander for draining cooked foods. A colander can also be useful for flouring meats before cooking and even for transporting vegetables and herbs from your garden. This invaluable suggestion came from a student of mine.

One set of graduated metal measuring spoons, conforming to USDA standards.

One set of graduated metal measuring cups, conforming to USDA standards, to use for dry ingredients. Their flat tops enable you to level flour, sugar, etc.

Pyrex 1-cup measure with spout for measuring and pouring liquids.

Graduated set of metal, glass, or porcelain mixing bowls.

Vegetable peeler made of carbon, which will cut and retain its sharp edge forever. It must be washed and dried immediately after use to prevent rusting. Do not use a stainless steel parer, as they simply do not cut.

Kitchen shears, imported, in stainless that will cut through almost anything.

A ladle in stainless steel for ladling soups and sauces and for dispensing crêpe batters and the like; also for tasting and skimming.

Some Useful Additions

Food processor—for me it's standard kitchen equipment.

A kitchen scale, essential for the serious cook.

A food mill with 3 removable disks with tiny, medium, and large holes—a very useful tool to purée foods to a fine or medium texture without watering them down and to grate foods where a coarser texture is required. It also skins and seeds tomatoes in preparation for cooking sauces.

Automatic electric mixer for heavy-duty mixing procedures.

Spin-dry salad drier—even a small kitchen should have a make-room spot for this.

Cookie sheet—14 × 17 is a practical-size flat cookie sheet to own.

Jelly-roll pan—11 × 17 is not only useful for your roll cakes but is a handy "platter" to hold meats in one layer during preparation.

Chinois—a French conical mesh sieve, made with closely woven fine metal strands and used for straining stocks and sauces. When liquid passes through a chinois, the texture becomes much finer. To achieve a similar texture if a chinois is not available, line a large sieve with a double or triple layer of cheesecloth before using to strain liquids.

Batticarne—a metal meat pounder shaped like a disk attached to a post that fits comfortably in your hand.

Instant meat thermometer, to be perfectly sure of stage of doneness.

Convection oven. I am convinced the convection oven has a future. It is an electric oven that permits an air flow of dry equal heat to completely circulate around the food for even cooking. The hot wind blowing through the oven cooks the food more rapidly, keeps moisture in, means no turning or basting, and uses less energy.

INDEX